LIFE AND TIME OF AMANDA THOMAS

BILLY DEE BURNETT

Michael Terence
Publishing

First published in paperback by
Michael Terence Publishing in 2020
www.mtp.agency

ISBN 9781913289997

Contents

1: Ammi's Birthplace

For the sake of this story Amanda will be referred to as Ammi. Ammi was born back in the late twenties on the Island of Jamila in a little district name Danville in the Parish of St. Manor. Now Danville is a sleepy district where nothing much happen; but it's a wonderful place to live. Here everyone knows everyone and people say good morning and good evening; and the older folks are addressed as Sirs and Moms. Young people are taught to respect their elders and if they step out of line they would be chastised or reprimanded severely, and it's not unusual for an uncle to chastise his nephew in a fatherly manner, and his niece! She would be severely reprimanded with the approval of their parents. This is a closely-knit small community with four leading citizens; and even though there's no seat of Government here these men reigned over the district as though they were elected to do so, and the people honoured and respected them. The Government doesn't bother with these people; no; not at all; and that's the pattern all over the Island, Once every five years when members of Parliament need to be elected they come canvassing with music blearing and making big promises. However none of their promises ever been kept, no; once they're elected they'll never be seen here again until the next time when they need these people's votes. But for some reason or another the people are passionate about their politic; they would kill for it, in some parts of the Island it's unwise to make known you're your political flowering, to stay healthy you'll wise to keep it to yourself. But why they behave in likewise manner? It's hard to understand since they get no help from the Government or the party they're so passionate about.

But that is a burning shame though; because people here like in other districts are crying out and hoping from the Government to take an active part in their lives; but their hope is like pipe dream; these politicians are dishonest and unscrupulous people; they are not in the business of politic for the betterment of the people, no, they're in it for themselves; to feathered their own nest. But the people! They don't seem to consider the possibilities that they're just there to be used. So thanks to these men who tried to help these unfortunate people of the district; and they most certainly need do. They're mostly illiterate people; and their sibling will grow up just like their parent; in the same vein of ignorance. These men didn't set themselves up as rulers, no, they're God-fearing men who read their bible and believed there's a God; and there is goodness in everyone, they're not going to stand by and watch these people suffer, no; not if they can help it The main feature of the district is the church; and although not everyone is a Christian they do attend nevertheless.; and the children follow in their footsteps. It also wasn't unusual for a person as young as twelve years old and even younger to be baptised; and from that moment on he or she will be a follower of the church and their doctrine. However it hard to believed these youngsters understand the full implication of their action, what they're doing is following in the parent's footstep; totally oblivious of the whole situation. They would follow the church to meetings that were not always confined to the regular place of worship; but places outside of their comfort zone; like other districts far outside away from their own. Ammi's father; John Thomas was a regular visitor to the church but wasn't a confirm Christian; as one of the leading citizens he was an intelligent man who worked as an overseer on one of the sugar cane industry owned by Tate and Lyle; the biggest employer in the Island. He (John Thomas) would have a gang of men working under his control; and any new employees would have to get his approval before he or she could earn a dime. But he was a fair-minded man who would help the poor and worst off, these men and others would pay him lots of respect; the kind of respect a fine upstanding man deserved. Ammi's mother was once John's common-law wife; and even though he leaves he's to married her friend, Agnes; their relationship remained one of friendship. They never seem to be any animosity between them; Ammi would alternate between mother and mother-in-law as though she's got two blood mothers.

They lived within touching distance of each other and the relationship between them was a friendly one considering that John leave one to marry the other, that's how things are here; a married man living with his lawful wife could have another woman living next door and another one down the road; and everyone lived happy ever after, a kind of seraglio existence. This situation works amiably for everyone; the women know not to step out of line; well! You could say they've got no rights; and to prevent the wrath of their man they toed the line. But these two women Agnes and Mildred; well! They got along famously; almost as though they're the ones who created the system. When Ammi was five years old when she started primary school which was within walking distance of where she's living; so lunchtime she would come home for mom to prepare lunch and then walked back to school; a convenient arrangement. By this time John had two children with Agnes, Rupert and Maggie, and although they lived in separate houses Ammi and Maggie were very close. Ammi as a young child herself would be very protective of her little sister Maggie who was less than a year her junior, she loved to be with her little sister and wish they were living in the same house. She began to get the feeling that she should be living at her father's house with her sister and brother, she loved her mother like any good daughter should but she loved her father more; and from time to time she would put it to her mother that she would like to go and lived at her father's house. Of course Mildred wasn't averse to any such ideas, but with her first child Frank by another man is now nearly eighteen years old and hardly ever around; it wasn't an easy decision to make; to let go of her only daughter; and even though she's not going completely out of her sight, it's still hard for her to let her go. She probably knows that John would like the girl to come and live with him and his family; but out of compassion for her he wouldn't suggest it. Of course he could take her whenever he wants whether she agrees or not, well that's how things are done here; the men always have the final say. But now John had thought it would be a good idea for her to come live with him and his family, he thought about it for some time and discussed it with his wife Agnes who is in full agreement, however up till then he never mentioned anything about his intention to neither Ammi nor her mother, but to give the girl a better future it's wise for her to move in with her Sister and Brother.

He thought their relationship is far too important to do anything unsavoury that would cause disharmony with her and the family. Instead he's going do what any well-thinking father with discipline would have done; and as they were always on friendship terms he was going to sit down with her and discussed the situation, and that was with the approval of Agnes; not that he needs it; but he sees it as the right way to go. Well! Mildred a calm and placid woman still cares a lot for him; but she knows the rule; and even though she didn't want her daughter to leave her she realised it would be better in more ways than one for the girl to be living with her father and his family. Well! He's got a fair size house compare to her one bedroom one living room; and she'll be with her sister Maggie. Her mother-in-law Agnes always have a soft spot for her and was quite pleased to have her coming to live with them. So now the dye was cast and Ammi is coming to live with her father and family; and because of the close proximity of which they lived everyone will be seeing each other almost daily, it was the perfect arrangement. Ammi was now seven years old and been transferred to elementary school; this school is about four miles from home and there're no public transports; so children going to that school from here have to give themselves ample time to reach there for nine o'clock; but it's not stressful or difficult; these children are accustomed to walking long distances.

2: Ammi's School Days

Ammi was always a happy child and for someone so young she was showing sign of concern and affection for the poor and needy; those people around here who can't help themselves; and even at this tender age of about eight she would give help to anyone who needed it; this little do-gooder seem to see something good in everyone; she was about nine when she was nicknamed the little Miss Florence nightingale; after that famous lady. The name Florence nightingale is been talked about widely and her fate in the war; some people read about her; others heard about it, as a ten year old girl she would probably heard her elders talk of her; and she probably understands what she had done. So when she was daub with the name Florence Nightingale she didn't let it bothers her; in fact she was darn right proud to be referred to in the same breath as that famous lady. That was her nature though; and even though some thought she was a bit loopy or a little busy body to be helping people who didn't ask for her to; to her it didn't matter what anyone thinks or said; she just carried on doing what she thinks was right. However at school she wasn't doing too well at all; she couldn't learn; in a word she was a dunce, thick as two planks, her teachers realised from early that she's not going to be anything academically; they (the teachers) inform the parent of the situation. Meanwhile her younger sister had excelled beyond her grade; she skipped fifth class; she has excelled far beyond her age; unlike her thick Sister this girl is going places. Her parent was summed by the teacher to discuss her future, her father is desperate to hear some good news about her regarding her learning; but that's never going to happen. After several talks with the head Master he was put in the picture fully that it might be better served to find something else for her to do; something like learn some kind of a trade. But her father wasn't preparing to take her out of school just yet; he's going to keeps her there and hopes her learning would improve. We'll do our best for the girl said the head Master; that as much as we can do, that's all I'm asking head Master said John; and I thank you for your help and consider opinion. Then the head Master suggested that there's an evening class going; and it might be an idea to send her there after school; it might help in some way, it's one shilling and six pence per week he said. Without any consideration Mr. Thomas promptly agreed; anything to improve her knowledge and learning ability head Master I'm all for it he said. The two men agreed and shook hands on it, we'll do what we can for young Ammi Mr. Thomas; and I hope it work out favourable for the child said the head Master as John was about to walked through the door. I know you will head Master; and I thank you very much, and they parted company.

At home that evening he discusses with his wife Agnes and Ammi's; he outlines the situation and what the head Master proposed. But if he was expecting any encouraging words from Agnes it wasn't fort coming. She had noticed that Ammi was very much interested in clothes and needleworks; she would mend cut and patch her Brother and Sisters clothes and do it well; and she (Agnes) thought from then that she would do well in dressmaking. She lays it all out for John to understand; but he wasn't much interested to hear anything of that sort; his interest was in education and more education. Ammi is going to begins evening lessons come Monday; and when he was about to talk to Ammi about it he calls Maggie to join in the conversation; a kind of diplomatic move to let Ammi know how much advance in studies her sister was. But Ammi knew all along without her father reminding her; and she also knows she could never match up to her Sister's standard. The head master suggested that you should take evening lesion, how do you feel about that he asked, do I have to Dad she asked, well yes; it supposed to help you learn, don't you want to learn he asked; she didn't respond; instead she asked, when do I start Dad?. Well! You'll be starting from Monday; and remember I have to pay for this lesson; so don't let me down. The words do your best doesn't occur to John, no; he's demanding g success of the poor girl who just hasn't got it within her. I'm counting on you to do well he said; if Maggie can do it so can you. John! Don't you think that's unfair to say what you just said; why put so much pressure on the poor girl asked Agnes; there's an old saying; one cannot force water uphill, and I wish you would reconsider she said but he's not going to; he wants his favourite Daughter to go to college like his friend's daughter Jessy. I'll do my best dad; but what happens if I fail she asks. Well! You're not going to fail; if I thought you're going to fail I wouldn't be paying for you to go. But he was also doing his best to convince her that she's capable of learning, and it's good opportunity for you catch up with those children who're ahead of you he said. Maggie sat and listened but said nothing; she's been helping Ammi with her lesson without even her father knowing; she knows how thick her Sister is but got no say in the matter.

She commenced evening lessons; and a few months later; with the help of her younger sister it would appear as though she's making some kind of progress, but it wasn't so at all; Maggie was doing far too much for her at home and in the classroom her work hasn't changed at all from what it was before. However when the time comes for the chosen few to sit a test; a kind of local exam for that year; and if one was successful ones would move on to study for the coming year exam, the failures would remain and carry on studying; but only if the teacher thinks they're worth it. Ammi was given a pass to sit the exam; and that pleases her father emphatically, for now he's a proud man, well! If she's put forward to sit the exam for that year; then thing are looking up for the girl, he had thought she has turned the corner; Dad is a man now with spring in his steps. But unfortunately pump and pride would soon be gone from his attitude; three weeks after sitting the exam the result arrives, she has failed and fails badly. When John learns of her failure he was so disappointed he was near to tears; and for a time he has become very irritable and difficult. What did you expect asked Agnes, you know for yourself and the teacher told you to seek another profession for the girl; but no; you're too stubborn to heed their words. You're upset and disappointed because Ammi couldn't live up to your expectation; but the girl tried; she always tried; and you should give her some credit for that. But she's not the academic type; what you're hoping for is never going to happen, and I'll tell you this John; if you're going to forced her into doing too much; too much of what she can't do; she's going to end up hating you; then what will you do then?. Agnes was saying what she thinks needed to be said; she wants her husband to face reality and do what's right. Realising what Agnes was saying was true; he apologised to her for being so irritable and pig-headed; and acknowledge that what she was saying was the truth. We'll sit down together with her and talk about what she would prefer doing he said; we'll choose a good profession for her he said, John! What's wrong with you? there you go again; you can't choose a profession for her; that is so not what to do; we'll ask her; and I'll tell you now; she'll choose dressmaking. But John is not a pig-headed husband, no; when his wife speaks on matters of the family he listens; and in this instance he listened attentively.

The following evening after he came home from work, before they sat down for dinner he reminds Agnes of what they have to do after dinner; to sat with Ammi and find out what she would like as a profession. After they clear the table and the others withdrew; Ammi was called back to the dining room; now the discussion about her future began. What would you like to do as a profession when you leave school he asked, well! He's a bit tactful; he's not telling her of what the head master said; it's far better to take her out of school and find something else for her to learn; instead of trying to keep there until she's sixteen. I don't rightly know dad; I never really thinks about it, remembering what his wife told him he asked, well! How about dressmaking? Would you like to be a dressmaker? She paused for thought; I suppose I could be a dressmaker she said. Agnes interjects immediately, I'm sure you would make a good dressmaker, that's what you should consider, of course she's making a judgement from what she saw. you think so mom she asked, in her case mom doesn't necessary means mother, no; it means respect for the elderly, I certainly think so, I see what needlework you have done here; darning and patching for your Sisters and Brothers; oh yes; you'll be a good dressmaker alright. Well Agnes was laying it on thick to convinced her, she recognised her talent in that department, and even though her father would much prefer her to take up nursing because she's shown interest in caring for people; Agnes firmly believed that dressmaking should be her chosen profession. However Ammi had made up her mind; she's going to be a dressmaker even though her father wasn't too excited about it. So the discussion is settled; decision made; Ammi is going to learn dressmaking as soon as her father find a place for her. She's now gone thirteen years old and legible to be at school until she is sixteen; but it a futile exercise to keep her there; and now that her parents have decided a new direction for her future; she'll be leaving school as soon as they can find a dressmaking firm where she can learn the trade She'll remain in school until such time as her father can find her a placing; but she'll be taking no more evening lessons; it's just money down the drain.

3: The Search for A Dressmaker

In the town about four miles away there're dressmakers; but there're only two reputable ones; there're others but lesser in reputation. John will have do what he has no experience of doing; seek out these dressmakers and check to see if anyone of them is taking on apprentice. He's nervous about it; dealing with these city women he knows not what to expect; and would rather stay well clear of them, but he knows his family is depending on him for to get result. Saturday was a bright and sunny day; a day when everything looks good; the nightingale perch high up on mango tree; its singing sound so enchanting one could stand and listen for hours, John sets off on his errand; the old Hillman Minx is well polished so it glistens when coming out of the shadows. He'll have to pick his way through the potholes; but he's a good driver on a bright day like today it's a doddle. He reaches his destination; Browns town; he got out and have a good look around; there's no problem parking he could see; there're plenty of places now all he has to do is seek out the dressmakers. Even though it's a little town he has no idea where to look; so he thought the best thing to do is to ask someone, but he had to be very cautious of who he asks; this little town is full of unscrupulous people loitering around at all time ready to steal from people who lay themselves careless; so one had to be on their guard at all times. However John a big strong fellow; not a lot of people is going to take liberty with him, Browns town the Capital of the Parish is a busy little town; especially on a Saturday; and with people heading for the street market all day long, one sometime had to force their way through thick crowd. Now squeezing up against people is not a good idea; it gives the pickpockets the chance they want; one better off staying well clear of them. After John walks around for a while and couldn't find where he's looking for he asks the woman in the plod frock with a shopping basket, he explained to her who he's after but know not where to look. He was in luck; this woman seems to know where everything and everyone is. We're standing right outside one sir she said smiling, could be because John was standing right in front of the building and asking about it. This is Mrs. Marsden's dressmaking shop she said pointing; and she gives him full directions of where the others were. John thanks her and the woman went on her way. Now he has to go and try to do business with a woman; and he has some apprehension about it. But men like John are old fashioned;

still living in the past he believed a man shouldn't be doing business with a woman, no; a woman take orders; and an old adage; women places are in the home; and they shouldn't be sizing up to a man as their equal. But these are old fashion people; still living in the past; and they'll be that way till they die; but whether he likes it or not he'll have to put his outlandish idea on hold and deal with these women.

He crossed the road and went in; and as there wasn't anyone like a receptionist to talk to he walks straight up to the first person he sees, a young woman who's got what looks like a dress slings over her shoulder; it was obvious what she does; on a second observation she had a tape measure around her neck. Good day young lady he said in the most polite manner, and why not; even as an elderly man he's trying to make a good impression; some of these young women can be quite impudent. Good day Sir said; can I help you Sir? I hope so he said politely, I would like to speak with Mrs. Marsden if she's not too busy, I'll go and check for you Sir she said as she set off to find this Mrs. Marsden. It wasn't long before she returned with another woman whom he presumed was the person in question, when the young woman walk away to find Mrs. Marsden she didn't ask John for his name; so when the woman approaches him she just say hello, hello Mrs. Marsden he said with the assumption that she was the Mrs. Marsden, she was quick to acknowledge; should I know you Sir she asked inquiringly, no Mom; you wouldn't know me at all; but I know of you. John's comment seemed to bring a wry smile to her face; well what can I do for you Sir she asks looking all pleased with herself, my name's John, Mrs. Marsden; John Thomas; and I'm looking for someone to take on my daughter as an apprentices; she's very passionate about being a dressmaker; and I hope what I heard is correct that you do take on apprentice. He continues to be pleasant and polite; and even though he's an older person he endeavour to address her as Mom. Well one had to be polite when one is asking for something even though it might seem a little awkward. After he explained himself fully she then ask him in a polite manner; would you come this way Mr. Thomas? And they walk back the way she came to her office. Well it wasn't much of an office more like a small section of the small workshop. She took up some clothes that were on a wooden chair, sit down here Mr. Thomas and let's talk, she was very accommodating, John tells her about his daughter and what she would like to do, he make out a good case for her; But after a lengthy conversation Mrs. Marsden explains; I would like to take her on Mr. Thomas; but business is very slow at present; I'm not getting sufficient work to take on anyone right now; but when thing picks up again and it will; that the usual pattern; and if you didn't place her by then please come back and see me. John thank her for her time and get to his feet to walk away, but he was about to do so she ask him to wait, she open an exercise book and wrote something; she handed it to him and tells him where to go, it's a note from her to another dressmaker.

There's a dressmaker named Mrs. Hall; give him this note, Mr. Thomas she said handing him the note, she might be able to help you. She then gave him full directions of how to find her; and with that she wishes him good luck. Thank you very much Mrs. Marsden he said and then he left. At this time of year the sun's high in the sky and the evening are very long, John has got plenty of daylight hours to check out this Mr. Hall. But the woman he previously asked for direction did tell him about this other woman, now he's hoping he might be lucky the second time round. It was a short walk across town; he enters through the small door to the sound of calypso music, a young woman sees him looking as though he was lost and approached him, could I help you Sir she ask politely, I certainly hope so young lady he said pleasantly, I would like to speak with Mrs. Hall. Mrs. Hall Sir she asked surprisingly, John notice her reaction, yes! Mrs. Hall he said, I'll get her for you Sir she said promptly, she then paused, who should I say wants her Sir? Mr. Thomas; and tell her I was sent by Mrs. Marsden. The young woman seems a little surprised as she walks away, could it be by the mention the name Mrs. Marsden?. In a short while a woman emerges from behind a curtain accompanied by the young woman, she walks directly up to John. Mr. Thomas she enquires; yes mom; I'm Mr. Thomas he said with his hand outstretch to greet her. She accommodates him by reaching out and shakes his hand, I'm Mrs. Hall; I understand Mrs. Marsden sent you she inquires surprisingly, yes mom said John apprehensively. Now she looks as though her head is in a spin; John wasn't sure whether she was asking him or herself the question when she enquires, why would Henrietta sent me a man she asked, and a smile comes to her face, he didn't respond to that question; he's got no need to ask who's this Henrietta; she was Mrs. Marsden.

There were two small stools there; she asks John to take a seat while she went back from where she came, while she was away the young lady return and ask him if he was alright. I'm not sure young Miss; I might have upset Mrs. Hall by telling her Mrs. Marsden sent me, on no Sir, it's not you, there's a long-running feud between them and they haven't exchanged a single word for a long time now, don't worry yourself Sir the young said as she walks away. For John it was good to hear she wasn't upset because of anything he had said. She returns, what's the hell is that woman up to now she asks herself loudly, but John was very observant; he detect a hint timidity also, maybe she thinks I was the law John thought, so he acted swiftly, oh it's nothing to worry about Mrs. Hall; I'm just here to ask you if you're taking on any apprentices, you see I went and see Mrs. Marsden first and she's not taking on anyone at present so she suggested that you might, here's a note she gave me to give to you. Now she looks a little more than surprised as she reaches forward to takes the note, of course John have no idea what the note said; but when she reads it a big smile come across her face. As John looks at her he thought; this woman should smile more often; she's got the most beautiful smile. Well the decision was made there and then, I'm sorry Mr. Thomas for your wasted journey; but at this time I'm not taking on anyone,

With the sugar cane season over everything is slow to a Holt, but that's how it is here; the work is seasonal and so is the amount of work come our way, and now that the cane season is over no one have money to spend. But what she didn't know was that she's talking to the man who works in the sugar cane industry; he know too fully well of the situation. But before John leaves she told him of another dressmaker who might just be the person who can help, when she said it an old saying comes to mind; send the fool a little further. Is she sending him on a while goose chase? A question that comes to mind, but whether so or not he's will have to go where she's sending him. This other person lived on an estate just outside of town and she goes by the name of Mrs. Hollins; she might be taking on trainee, go see her Mr. Thomas. Thank you; I'll check her out he responds. She wishes him good luck but didn't give him a second offer if and when things pick up again.

Well it's getting late and John decided to give this one a miss today; but plans to check out this Mrs. Hollins another time; probably tomorrow. But then he recalled tomorrow is Sunday; he and his family will be going to Church. He sets off home feeling quite peckish; after all he been out all day, but he's not going to stop to buy anything to eat, no; he knows his dinner awaits him at home. But he's been wondering what was in the note he delivered to Mrs. Hall that bring a smile to her face, she was rather surprised when he gave it to her. He remembers what the young woman said; there's a secret war going on between these two businesswomen. Agnes probably more than Ammi is waiting anxiously for John to return; to hear if he is successful in his quest to finding a place for Ammi. He arrives when Ammi was setting the table; and it wasn't long before everyone take their places for dinner, but at the table John wasn't saying anything in regard to event today, he knows they are bursting to hear what happen; but he's just letting them stew a bit. Well! Are you going to tell us what happen or you going to keep it all to yourself ask Agnes sarcastically, John smile kind of mischievously, oh! I'm sorry; no one is taking on apprentice right now he said; and then he let them into the whole day's events. But there's another dressmaker I was told about; and I'm going to see her next weekend. But suddenly John taps his knife on the table and stops eating; this action he would never ever do. With a frightful stare on his face as though he has done something he shouldn't have. Tt's so unlike him to do something like that in front of the children, he hesitates, I didn't do the right thing he said, I went all the way and didn't do the right thing, he repeats. What didn't you do John Agnes ask with a worried look, by now the children were paying full attention, Ammi like her stepmother is getting concern about what her father didn't do. What's wrong dad she asked, please tell us she asked respectfully. He sat up straight in his chair, I'm sorry Ammi I let you down, and I let myself down too. I should have tell those dressmaker women that I'll pay for your training, how the Devil did I forgot to tell them that; if I did I'm sure one of them would have taken you on, oh my God; I'm so sorry; he was very apologetic to his family. But couldn't you go back and talk it over with them ask Agnes, I could; but I'm going to look a right idiot. There's sadness comes over him and he wouldn't eat anymore, this is a man who feels the hands of guilt whenever he feels he lets his family down. No! I'll have to go back he said, I won't let my pride get in the way of your future he said, next Saturday end I'll go back. But didn't you say there was another dressmaker you were told about asks Agnes sympathetically, well yes he said; and I think I'll go and see her first come Saturday; and then go and see the others if I'm not successful.

But young Maggie who's the clever one couldn't understand why her dad give them all such a fright; she puts it to him, Dad she said; did you know you give us all a fright; and it wasn't necessary, she's the only one who feels she can tell her Dad what's on her mind, she's the cheeky one. I'm sorry if I frighten you Mag; as he usually calls her, but you but you're a child and you wouldn't understand. There you go again Dad; because we're children you think we haven't got a brain to understand grownups talk, Agnes gave her one of those vicious stares to say watch your tongue young lady. I don't want to hear anything more from you Maggie she said with some authority, either eat or leave the table, well! That was the end of what Agnes calls her wantonness. Ammi is still going to school but only until her father can find her an apprenticeship, she would come home from school and assist her stepmother in whatever she was doing; and at times she would also go and see if her mother Mildred need anything doing She's not a young woman who likes to sit still, no, she must be doing something; a real little Miss busybody; some said she's very industrious; but her stepmother likes her just as much as her own children. Come Saturday John was supposed to go and see this Mrs. Hollins; but unfortunately something important crops up and he has to postpone it for another time, he was disappointed not able to go as he's anxious to get her started. By now Ammi has become a regular at church meetings, she was always a helper at Sunday school; but now she has taken it one step further and become a regular at these meetings, a move that pleases her father, well John himself is a regular at church and prayer meetings too; but he's not a committed Christian; at least not yet. But a God-fearing man nevertheless with strong Christian belief; and his children are brought up in likewise manner. On Sundays he and his five children must be in Sunday school. But Ammi been the oldest of the family and with her strong belief in the Lord; she's now a fully pledge Christian; and one day soon she'll be baptised. But Agnes was never a believer; well! She's not an atheist either; but she's not totally believed in their doctrine; and she occasionally go to church with her family. But her husband never forces to do what he does, how does one force another to believe in something they don't; leave her be he thought; one day she'll come around.

Sunday morning when Ammi was going to church with her sisters and brothers; there was a loud groan coming from a house they had to pass closely by on the narrow road, she knew the person who lived there. Well! Everyone here knows everyone, It's old Mrs. Brown; a nice old lady; she took ill after the death of her husband and became housebound ever since. Her only daughter after caring for her for some time just up one day leave; never to be seen or heard of again, she probably got tired of caring for her old mother. There was a distant family member seen occasionally look in on the poor dear; but it seem as though her visit was far and few between; and now if at all. At church Ammi was concern about Mrs. Brown; she knows the groan she heard was the poor woman in some sort of agony, she was anxious for church to be over for her to look in on her on the way back. She was still groaning when she returns, she tells her family to carries on home while she stops to see if there's anything she could do for her. The way the house situated one doesn't have to knock to enter; just push the door and walks in. Ammi was surprised to find her in the condition she was in, it was obvious no one had bothered to visit her for some time; and there's no way of telling the last time anyone come to see her, and right now she's in a bad way.

Of course there's no way she'll be able to see a medical Doctor , no; like most of the population here she can't afford the Doctor's fee, the only Doctor she could see without paying is one of the many bush Doctors here; and of course people died when they shouldn't because of silly superstition. Well Ammi does what she could for poor Mrs. Brown, she cleans her up and makes her comfortable. But there's nothing in the house for her to eat; so she went home and tell her parent and with the help of Agnes they fix dinner for she to return to her with. The poor dear was so weak she had to be hand-fed; she didn't even have enough strength to chew the food. However! From that time onward Ammi took it upon herself before and after school to care for her; something her parent wasn't too approved of; especially Agnes, she's almost like the people in this district; doesn't care too much about others; only her own family. But John was more sympathetic; he had no objection for her caring for Mrs. Brown; as long as it didn't get in the way of her schooling. But who else is going to care for the poor old dear; it obvious she was been abandon by her family; and everyone else for that matter. But there's nothing strange about that, here is every man for himself, family only take care of their own, many people died before their time through the lock of care, sympathy, and attention.

4: The Visit to Mrs. Hollins

The following Saturday as plan John sets off to see Mrs. Hollins, he's hoping for better fortune than he had with the other two dressmakers, her place of business wasn't hard to find, living on this big estate that runs along the highway adjacent to the town; it was difficult to miss, and the Manor was visible from quite a distant. Approaching the huge entrance there's large iron gate, John walks up to it and look for something like a bell; but there wasn't any, he looks to see if there was anyone about but there was no one either; so he looks around for something to rattles the iron girders; but there was nothing, the area is well kept with nothing lying around. So he walks back to his car and in the booth were bits and pieces drivers like him travels with in case of a breakdown. He picks up a straight bit of iron rod and went back to the gate; he discretely rattles the bars, and emerges from someway along the long hedge of privet was a man with a machete in his hand coming toward him, he looks a bit unsteady on his feet and menacing, John didn't wait for him to talk. Good morning young man he said, if he's conscious of what John said he must be flattered; because he looks nothing like a young man, but then again John doesn't know his name so he had was to call him something. Morning Sir he said in a rough manner and in the tongue the local dialect, his eyes are so red one could easily believe he couldn't see out of them, and the aroma of the canja carries by the cool morning breeze is so strong that if inhaled by one not accustom to it for any length of time would probably knock him out. I would like to see Mrs. Hollins said John, is she at home? Yes Sir; she's home, but I don't know if she's going to want to see you Sir he said, well could you go and tell her that Mr. Thomas would like to speak with her said John. The man looks a little reluctant but he moves away sluggishly walking up what is a long passageway toward the house some three to four hundred yards beyond. This is going to take some time he thought; the fellow was walking so slowly it will be ages before he gets there; so he went back to his car that is parked just outside the big gate and wait.

Well! It was so long he thought the man wasn't coming back at all, he begins to think he should rattle the iron bars again, but then suddenly out into the distance he could see him come walking back as slowly as he when he left, John got out and walks back to the gate looking at him coming towards still brandishing the machete. But it seems as though he speeds up a little, the effect of old ganja must be wearing off. Reaching the gate he seems a little friendlier, she said you must come up to the house Sir he said with a growl. Now in this Country more people lost their lives by machete than any other weapon, the machete is a working tool and everyone here owns one, and some people owns more than one, and it's more than likely that if and when two people got into a fight the machete will be used. There're quite a few disabilities all over the Island because of being maimed by this weapon. But John a big imposing figure; he's not disturbed by the sight of a man carrying a machete, no, during the cane season and after a man working tool is his machete and he's their overseer, however! When a man is under the influence of the ganja one had to weary of him carrying such a weapon. This stuff takes over their mines and that when they do things unintentionally. Untying a string from around his waist with keys on it he opens the gate and lets John through, thank you young man he said flatteringly and proceeded up the long passageway. He glances back to notice the man walking back toward where he emerged from at first. Approaching the house there was a young woman standing outside the front door, she looks like the maid and it turns out to be exactly so. Good morning he said as he approaches her, the young woman replies enthusiastically with a smile; good morning Sir; Madan will be with you shortly, please come in she said, he entered into what is the foyer. Beyond he could see a great hall, there were seats around where she leaves him but he didn't sit; he remains standing.

Not long after the door pushes open and a woman walks in, it was obvious who she is; this person was Mrs. Hollins She approaches him kind of cautiously, Mr. Thomas she asks in a questionable kind of way, yes mom I'm me. Thomas; extending his hand to greet her, she was quite accommodatable; she Shook his hand warmly. Do we have business Mr. Thomas she asked most kindly? Well! Yes and no mom; I'm come to see you regarding my daughter he said, your daughter Sir? Do I know her? Oh no! No Mom; you don't her at all; she would like to be a dressmaker; that's why I'm here. But before he utters another word she offers him to sit down, sit anywhere Mr. Thomas she said, they were still in the foyer. He took a seat on an upright chair and she takes a seat adjacent to him on a padded stool. Now then Mr. Thomas what is this all about she ask kind of friendly. Firstly John tells her he was told of her by Mrs. Hall and then went on to tell her he's looking for a dressmaker who would take on his daughter as an apprentice; and he was quite willing to pay for her training. Well! He's not going to make the same mistake as before, he should have told the two previous dressmakers he's willing to pay for his daughter training; nut he didn't; he completely forgot; this time he makes it quite clear he's willing to pay. But she was quick to respond; not about the training, no; about Mrs. Hall. You see Hannah? she asks as though she was suspicious of something, John replies, oh yes mom; I went and saw her last week, I went to her place of work for the same reason I'm here, she couldn't accommodate me so she recommended you might be the person who could take on an apprentice, so here I'm. But he was surprised and amaze at the next question, what do you think of her she asks inquisitively, John pretend dumb, who mom? Mrs. Hall; yes Mr. Thomas; Mrs. Hannah Hall, she sounded almost angry. The truth is Mrs. Hollins I don't think about her at all; I went to see her regarding my daughter future that's all, I hardly notice her, I have no judgement about her one way or another, he was straight forward and directly to the point.

She looks as though she suddenly thought she shouldn't have asked that question and wants to change the subject. How old is your daughter Mr. Thomas she ask, she just gone thirteen he replied; but shouldn't she been in school she asks, well yes; she's in school but she's not learning, then he went on to tell her why he wants her out of school. To keep her in school until she's sixteen is a waste of three whole years, in that time she could be learning something of her choice, something she's good at. He gets straight to the point, Mrs. Hollins! My daughter wants to be a dressmaker and I'm quite prepared to pay for her training if you would take her on. She crosses her legs on the padded chair before she responds. Well as you can imagine Mr. Thomas not many people buying dresses right now and to be honest I was never making dresses to make a living; no Sir; more of a pastime. But I could take her on she said, oh thank you, thank you very much he said appreciatively, she'll be awfully please to hear he said. But please bring her along for us to have a talk she said, oh sure; I'll do just that he said; sounding as though he has just won a fortune. When should I bring her along mom? Well you could bring her any day next week, how about Monday evening round about four o'clock she asks, oh that will be just fine mom he said. Well the sun was high in the sky and the day was really hot, their business is concluded and John rose to his feet. Well thank you again Mrs. Hollins; I'll see you again on Monday. But she wasn't ready to part company with him as yet, no; not just yet. Would you like a cold drink before you leave Mr. Thomas she ask respectfully, not wanting to appear unsociable or ungrateful he didn't hesitate, yes thank you he said; it's a very hot day. She acknowledges his comment. She got up and walks away and immediately there was a bell ringing, John suspects it was to alert the maid, she then walks back to John and invites him to come in the huge hall.

One couldn't help noticing the beautiful paintings on the wall and two huge chandeliers, take a seat Mr. Thomas she said, and they both sat. But John is asking himself; why she's so nice to him; they never met before; they're total strangers. John's a married man with five children but couldn't help but notice how beautiful this woman was, a beautiful mulita colour woman with shoulder-length wavy hair and stand about five feet seven inches tall and quite slim, this woman is got everything he thought, she would turn the head of any red-blooded man. The maid walks in with a salver with more than a cool drink; there were buns and cheese also, she was told to place it on a coffee table in the corner of the hall. They enjoyed the refreshment and she talks to him as though she knew him for years. He couldn't fully understand what was happening; but he's not going to do or say anything untoward that would jeopardise the chances of his daughter getting an apprenticeship. Then again he thought she could be one of those nice sociable women whom just like to be nice; and if that be the case he'll soon find out if they're to do business. He looks at his watch and it's nearly three-thirty; he been here since eleven o'clock and he really wants to leave. He finishes his refreshment and while he still sitting he comments, thank you for her hospitality mom he said, but now I must go; my family is expecting me back; and I'm already late. You're welcome she said looking at him amorously, at that point John got to his feet and start toward the door. Thanks again mom; and I'll see you on Monday, don't mention it she said as she got to her feet. While he was walking down the long passageway he glances back and he could see her still standing in the doorway looking straight in his direction. When he reaches the gate the man wasn't there to let him out; so he used his car key to tap on the Iron gate; and even though it didn't make much of a sound the man come walking from the same direction as before. He didn't utter a word; he just unlocks the gate and pulls it open for him (John) to walk through. As he was going through she was still waving from the front door in the distant, he waves back as he was going into his car. When he drove off he sighs a sigh of relief, he was extremely glad to get a place for his daughter as an apprentice; but he was also glad to get away; he wants time to consider his meeting with Mrs. Hollins and try to understand what took place today.

When he gets home he tells the family he might have secure a place for Ammi at this Mrs. Hollins; but she wanting to see her first, the family was happy to hear that even though it's not final. He doesn't sew for a living he told them, no; more of a hobby. But they weren't bothered; as long as she can teach Ammi dressmaking that's all they are concern about. Monday was another of that hot sunny day, John had to leave work a bit early as he has an appointment with Mrs. Hollins later that evening; and so is Ammi who leave school an hour before the break up time. By the time he got home Ammi was already home and ready to go. Well John didn't tarry; father and daughter loaded up and set off. On the way he reminded her to be civil when she meets this lady, I expect you to make a good impression he said, yes Dad; you know I will she said. Reaching the wide-open space before the gate John park at the spot he did before, he got out and proceed towards the big iron gate with Ammi behind him, she was aghast looking at the huge iron gate. This time John didn't have to rattle the iron girders the man was already standing there, he's the handyman; but here he's called a yard boy. As John and Ammi approaches the gate he promptly pulls it open. Well! Today he looks more sober but because he's obviously a hard ganja smoker his eyes are still very red. Thank you said John; but tell me; what your name? In a low growl looking at his feet he comments; my name is Roland Sir, well thank you Roland said John as they proceed up the long passageway towards the manor. Approaching the house John could see Mrs. Hollins standing at the door; she must have seen them coming up the passageway and awaiting them. There was no time for John to greet her; she beats him to it, good evening Mr. Thomas she said exuberantly as he approaches, he returned the compliment. This is Ammi she said looking at her with a very pleasant smile, Ammi with nothing much to say respond by saying good evening mom. She moves sideways of the door to welcome them in, come in, come in she said repeatedly; and they stopped into the foyer through to the big hall. Ammi had a glimpsed around; she marvelled at what she saw, she must have thought a person could get lost in here. Take a seat Mr. Thomas; and Ammi you sit over here; which is next to her, Ammi does as she was told.

Mrs. Hollins appears more anxious to be friendly; but John remains thoughtful of why he's here; he appreciates the welcome and all that but he wants to hear for definite if she's taking on his daughter. So you want to be a dressmaker she ask looking at Ammi, oh yes mom; that's what I wants to do she said; well I hope you know that there isn't much work available as of now; and the purchases of clothes is seasonal just like the work around here, sometime you earns a bit; other times you won't be earning anything at all. She was been truthful and directly to the point, trying to let Ammi be aware that the profession she has chosen might be a glamourous one but she's not going to get rich from it. But if you're sure that's what you really want I'll do my best to teach you, thank you mom; I'm sure I want to be; a dressmaker. Hearing that John sigh an inner relief, I thank you Mrs. Hollins for taking on my daughter; how much is it going to cost me? We'll talk about that some other times she said; let's have some refreshments. What you would like Ammi she asked hastily, but Ammi didn't accept anything at first, no; she asked her Dad if they're stopping. Again not wanting to appear unsociable he comment; Oh! I suppose we could stop for five minutes. Then I'll have some orange juice thank you Mom she said, and you Mr. Thomas; what would you like? I'll have orange juice too Mom thank you he said. She rings the bell and the maid enters, she tells her what to prepare for her guests; and off she went. While waiting for their refreshments Mrs. Hollins wants to know more about Ammi; she was making some kind of small talk; but what she's really after was a conversation with John; and the kind of conversation she wants with him was not about his daughter's future either. But with Ammi present whatever she's got in mind is not going to be said here and now. The maid return with whatever was ordered; she (Mrs. Hollins) told her to place the tray on the coffee table and she can go. After the maid had gone she got up and served her guest, they sipped and talk with most of the conversation coming from her, she just couldn't stop talking. But with business conclude John is anxious to leave once again; he appreciates the hospitality and was more than grateful to her for taking on Ammi; but he's got a wife to go home to. Then he thinks of this woman behaviour toward him considering they only just met, his feeling was she wanted to make a move on him romantically; but as a married man nothing must come in the way of his family, he holds them dearly. But then again he thought; she might be taking on his daughter because she want to have an affair with him, that wouldn't do at all, no sir he thought, and then again she might just have been a nice sociable person who just likes to talk.

However he'll find out later that his first assumption was the right one. He's ready to leave but they haven't agreed on a time when Ammi will commence her apprenticeship; so he asks, when you want Ammi to start mom? Well! She could start tomorrow, the sooner the better she said. John observed the anxiety in her attitude, well I would like her to finish the week at school and start the coming Monday if that's alright with you, oh yes she said; that should be alright, I'll look forward to seeing you on Monday Ammi. That's settle said John, next Monday it is; then he got to his feet along with Ammi, thank you very much Mrs. Hollins; you been very kind; but now we must go; and he walks towards the door with Ammi behind him. She follows closely after as they exit the door, it's good to meet you Ammi she comments, see you on Monday and don't be late now she said. Then Ammi remembers she wasn't given a time when she should be here, so she asked her father in a whisper, what time am I supposed to get here on Monday Dad? But Dad didn't know either. They were a few steps away from the front door and with she (Mrs. Hollins) standing there John stops turn and ask, what time she should be here Mrs. Hollins? But before she replies to John Question she calls and asks him to have a word, he suddenly gets a frightening thought; however he turns around and walks the few steps back leaving Ammi waiting for him. As he approaches her she comments, Mr. Thomas! If we're to do business we can try and be a little more formal; don't you think? It's kind of awkward we keep referring to each other as Mr. and Mrs. I would like you to call Florence; my entire friends do she said. Thinking to himself he thought of what she had just said; "all of her friends do" but we just met for the second time and suddenly she's implying that we're friends? He had an uncomfortable thought where this might be leading and he didn't like it; no Sir; not one bit.

Well! John himself is a handsome fellow; over six feet tall and not too black; he cut a fine figure; a man most women would find attractive. But he's married with children and wishes to keep it that way, he would prefer if temptation wasn't put in his way. But I don't know if I could do that Mrs. Hollins; we only just met he said facetiously, not wanting her to feel as though he didn't think much of her. She looks at him with an amorous smile; and with those beautiful glossy brown eyes squinting she responded; come on now Mr. Thomas; I told you what I would like you to call me; tell me what you would like me to call you she asked most lovingly. This constant informality is something we should put aside she said, and I have a feeling… but before she could complete the sentence John interrupts, and you can call me John Florence he said; she smiles broadly, a regular name John she said and it sounds much more friendly, that makes me feel so much better, she said. Ok John; have a good evening, and ['ll see you nine o'clock on Monday Ammi, she spoken a bit loud as Ammi was a little distant away, ok Florence; she'll be on time he said as he walks away. Approaching the gate Roland was already there waiting for him, he appears much more friendly, holding a spade in his hands it appears as though he was doing some digging along the high garden hedge. He promptly opened the gate and held it to one side for them to exit, thank you Roland said John as he walked through with Ammi in front of him, but Roland didn't said anything he just closed the gate behind them. As he glances back he could Florence still standing at the door and waving goodbye, he waves back too; but Ammi just went straight in the car. It was a pleasant drive home and with the sober thought that he has accomplished what he set out to do, it leave him feeling a bit chuff with himself. But for him; whatever the implication behind Florence actions he's not too concern as of now; all he's concern about is for his daughter to get into training to be a dressmaker; and if there're some difficulties along the way he'll have to deals with it accordingly.

However! What John doesn't know is the history of the lady of the manor, but how could he? He only just met her, this woman who lives alone on a big estate with a gardener and a maid; she's a well qualify dressmaker but never ever work at it as a source of income. It's obvious she doesn't need to; this woman is obviously quite wealthy. But why is she living alone in this enormous house? She's still very much in her prime; about thirty-four years old and of mixed race, a beautiful elegant woman who could have the pick of any man around here. Well! It could be she doesn't find the local men around here appealing. She was married when she was in her early twenties and her husband Mark a white man and grandson of a wealthy slave owner. He inherited half the estate but let it go to pot; he died nearly five years ago by falling from his horse. This man was a hard drinker; his lifestyle was one of carefree; on this day it rains heavily; and after a bout of heavy drinking; he was returning home riding his horse across the estate. He lost control of his mount when he tried to jump a very high obstacle, his fall was a bad one; his death was instantaneous. When the dust had settled over his death things were never the same again; for her suddenly her life was over, she considered that the bad blood between Mark and his family because of her was the main cause of his death, they never forgave him for marrying her. Mark was like an outcast; his father gave him his share of the estate as his inheritance but had nothing to do with him after, and now that he's gone she also knows that his family will not recognise her as a part of their family. This beautiful woman never had any children; and that's a crying shame; she would make a wonderful mother; and that be the cast she's completely alone. She withdrew herself from the public; this beautiful mulita colour woman has become a recluse; people it seems don't interest her anymore; without her beloved Mark she's a lost soul.

But this big house must have seen some actions; good times with Entertainments of wealthy people; some of whom were slavers, these affluent people who used the natives as a kick about are noted for living it up. But if she had friends or close acquaintances they're not around anymore, so probably that's why she has become a loner and never ventured out. This lady was living off her husband popularity; the people weren't here for her, they weren't her friends at all, no; they were all her husband's; and now that he's dead they totally ignored and abandon her; she's now become an outcast. However that's not an unusual situation; if one wasn't white even a beautiful mix race woman like Florence they would have little or no regards for her, this woman would be one who is regarded as good company; the tops; on the strength of her white husband, but now that he's dead in their estimation she's back to be a nobody. But having her own principles she might decide she's not going to force herself on them; they that abandon her; so she decide s to keep herself to herself and be a recluse. This is a beautiful attractive woman that would turn the head of any red-blooded man; she's alone because she's chosen to be alone, some people on the parting of their love ones i.e. Husbands or wives will go into mourning for long periods; and in some cases they even take it with them to their grave. Mrs. Hollins is from the working class of ordinary people; she deserted them when she was married into a rich white family; and now that her husband is dead she might be finding it difficult to link up with those people she once knew; or; on the other hand she's ashamed to do so. However! It could be a case of once out of the gutter not wanting to return to the gutter again. But now that fate has it that she met up with this Mr. Thomas it appears she fell for him in a big way, she knows it but he only suspects it, woman like Mrs. Hollins only waiting for the right man to come along to fall in love; and it appears she's got no qualms whether he's married or not.

The family is well please for Ammi; but how is she' going to get there when she starts come next Monday? Well! It's a touch too far to walk and her father can't drive her there and then go to work after, no; it would be too much a hustle, so he decided to buy her a bicycle. So before the week was out he manages to get her a second-hand ladies wheel, one of those bicycles without a crossbar, a one-person only bicycle; and that's the only preparation she needs, she's now fully equipped and ready for Monday. The days leading up to Monday were an ordinary one; nothing changes or happened in the days before, Ammi will be finishing her last days at school; something she's looking forward to. Come Sunday the family will dress in their Sunday best for church; this's the usual procedure. But before that Ammi will carry out her usual task to care for poor terminally ill Mrs. Brown, she'll continue to do her best for her; but how long; her condition is not looking encouraging. Agnes like most of the people here haven't got too much sympathy for the down and out but she's making an exception of this Mrs. Brown, when she prepares breakfast or dinner for her family she usually provides some for Ammi to take for her. She had to feed her too; she's got no strength in her hands, she would then see to it that she's clean and comfortable before leaving her to joins up with her folks for church. But Mrs. Brown is not the only one she's caring for, she would always visit Mr. Wilson who lives on the edge of the narrow road, he's got no family; according to her father Mr. Wilson turned up in the district a few years ago looking for work; but no one knows where he's from But a nice and placid man is MR. Wilson; and even though he's not a Christian he would visit church from time to time. He's not an old man but because of hard work and bad care he looks ancient, over a year ago he nearly drowned in the dry river and from that time he never recovered enough to work again he becomes house ridden; and without someone to cares for him his condition worsen. Ammi would see to him whenever she can; but he's really weak and always in pain, the story here in Danville like many other districts in the country is a pitiful one, the country has a Government but only in name, once the election is over whoever gets the nomination never return to checks on the plight of the people who put them in office, and the people? Well they don't seem too bothered, once they're strong and able to carry out their work is every man for himself, their sick neighbours are never their concern. They have no mercy or sympathy for the sick and helpless, in a little district like this people die and no one knows for days. Those who live on their own whenever they get to old age they're quite vulnerable; and the fact that they got no money to pays to see a trained Doctor their only chance they have is to trust the bush Doctor. But these people are quacks; they help sent more people to their death than needlessly be, but as the old saying goes; a drowning man catches after straws.

But this one young woman the little busybody takes it upon herself to be the Good Samaritan and cares for these sick people whenever she can; her step-mother is not too comfortable with the idea even though she sent food for her (Mrs. Brown). She argues that a young teenager shouldn't be putting herself about to care for sick people, there're older people here and in the church should be doing just that. She criticized them for calling themselves Christians and doing nothing to help these sick people. But her father is not averse to what she's doing even though he would much rather she didn't, he Understood what his wife Agnes is saying but if what Ammi is doing gives her fulfilment, "a word commonly used in the church" he's not going to stop her. But he promises Agnes he would raise the matter in church come Sunday with the Pastor, but you shouldn't have to confront him with situation like this argues Agnes; he should be the one to notice what is happening and take interest, what kind of a Pastor doesn't do that she ask, is he walking around with his eyes closed? He knows the situation here regarding those who're sick and he never at any time visit them. He's a Pastor and a leader, he's supposed to be a Christian and a man of God but he's done nothing that his bible tells him to she said quite angry. What do you mean he supposed to be a Christian John asked with concern; don't you think he's good Christian? Good Christian mumbled Agnes; if he was he would be concern about these poor unfortunate people. However John wasn't too pleased about the criticism of his Pastor even though he recognises what she was saying is true. He knows he's got to do something; so comes Sunday after service he'll have an audience with the Pastor regarding the matter, that he promised his wife.

5: Ammi Commences Training

Monday was overcast and there's a chance of some rain. Ammi is preparing to leave out for what will be her first day with Mrs. Hollins, she needs no instructions from her parents about behaviour; she's going fourteen years old and a God-fearing young woman who knows how to conduct herself, nevertheless her father would remind her of it. She sets off on her bicycle; she's hardly been off it since her father bought it, it's just over four miles journey but she gives herself ample time to get there, her journey will take her past her old school but by then the school will be in class. Arriving at the manor she approaches the huge iron gate but no one was there for her to gain entry, she begins to think how to get someone attention, there's no bell but by using her initiative like her father she uses her bicycle pump to gently rattles the gate and wait. Minutes later she could see Roland coming down the long passageway but he's in no hurry. Reaching the gate he puts the key in the lock without even a word of good morning, he swings the gate open for her to enter. Thank you she said as she walks through, but he took no notice, it was clear he was under the influence; he was more than a little unsteady on his feet; and the smell of the ganja coming from him is so strong she doesn't want to tarry. Well even as a young person she knows the smell of the stuff; its general used by people here; some used it as a form of medicinal purpose; they would boil it and used it as herbal tea. She leans her bicycle against the wooden pole that is provided for that purpose and horridly gets away fast from the smell of the ganja, she then commences walking in a bit of haste towards the house. Reaching the front door she doesn't know what time it is but she knows she's not late, she rings the bell and almost immediately the maid opens the huge wooden door. Good morning she said enthusiastically, come on in she said holding the door to one side. Good morning said Ammi as she enters, but the maid didn't let she tarry in the foyer, no, she takes her straight through the great hall into what looks like a workshop, take a seat she said; madam will be down shortly. Thank you said Ammi; but what's your name? My name's Mary Miss; well thanks again Mary said Ammi, she (Mary) then walks away but leaving the door ajar.

Now that she's alone she got up and have a little look around, she was scrutinising the foot machine when Mrs. Hollins walks in. Good morning Ammi she said smiling pleasantly, have you ever used one of those before she asks, no Mom; but I've seen it before she said, but Mrs. Hollins didn't continue about the machine or anything else; she asks Ammi to come and have breakfast with her; and she gladly accepts. Entering the dining hall Ammi notice the table was set for two as though she was expecting a guest, could that be for me she asks herself quietly, and as it turns out it was for her; she was the other person. Sits over there Ammi she said; we're having acke and salt fish; I hope you like it, Ammi thought that's a funny thing to asks; everyone here eats acke and salt fish, oh yes Mom she said; I eat acke and salt fish. But they're much more on the table; including a beautifully ripe avocado cuts in pegs; and hard dough bread; and even though she's not hungry what's on the table is quite appetising. There was a strong aroma of mint tea coming from the tea urn; one of the Favour breakfast drink here. While she was pouring the tea she's waiting for Mrs. Hollins to ask or talk about something; she's got a feeling she wants to, and she didn't have to wait for long. I think you're going to like it here Ammi she said, I always wanted to train a young person, I don't get plenty of work and I don't really want to; I give most of the work I get to Mrs. Hall; but it would be good to passes on what I know to someone who wants to make a living from it. So tell me Ammi; have you done any sewing before? Not much Mom; I only patch and darn clothes for my sister and brothers, well that's a start she said; getting accustomed to using needles and thread is part and parcel of learning. Then she went on to ask Ammi about her family and her father, but Ammi was coy with her answers; she's only approaching fourteen but she's a sensible girl and she's not going to discuss her family in details; not even with this rich woman.

After breakfast they retire to what is the workshop; and there she shown her a couple of old catalogues, have a look through a few of those she said; see if you find then interested. Ammi was fascinated with the catalogues; she had never seen one before; and looking at the dresses she was overcome with the fascination. However they didn't do much in regards of making dresses today, no, Mrs. Hollins wants to do more talking than working, she took her (Ammi) out into the back garden where there's a fish pond, and there they spent time looking at the beautiful fishes. Round about one o'clock lunch was provided for two; the maid is a very good cook; she cook the most delightfully tasting curry mutton accompany with rice and peas cook in coconut milk. She's nearly over eaten, she could eat some more when she put her knife and fork together, madam had wine with her curry but Ammi only had soft drinks, well she never had wine before and she wouldn't like the taste of it anyway. After breakfast they spent the rest of the day sitting in the big hall looking at more Magazines, and even though she didn't do anything in regards to dressmaking she's enjoying the time they're spending together. Mrs. Hollins is a very nice and kind person and she believes they're going get along famously. At the end of the day Mrs. Hollings action was as though she didn't want her to go home; she would talk and talk about everything and anything. When she (Ammi) was about to leave she (Mrs. Hollings) walks her to the gate, ride carefully now she said; and see you in the morning, I will thank you Mom said Ammi; and off she went. Back home she reports the day's event to her family, she tells them that she could eat some more but she didn't want to appear gluttonous. Her father was quite pleased that she's with someone to whom she feels comfortable.

6: The Attraction

Things were to take a romantic turn, as time progresses Ammi was doing quite well but Mrs. Hollins was pining after her father, she begins to send notes after notes to him that she would like to discuss certain matters with him. However John believes that there's nothing important left for them to talk about; so with all the notes that his daughter brings to him he resist going. He believes she's got this romance notion on her mind, and so he didn't reply to any of her notes, nevertheless the notes keep coming. However even though John spurns her advances she didn't behave anyway different in regard to his daughter, no; not Mrs. Hollins, she was more attentive to her and treats her more like a Sister, is as though she was lonesome and Ammi come along to fill the void. There're times when she would like Ammi to sleep over, but that's never going to happen, she's not even going to ask her father if she could; no; she politely declined, this young woman couldn't sleep away from her family. But Mrs. Hollins is waiting no longer to overstep the mark, like any love-smitten woman who was been spurn by a man she would steps up their action; and that's precisely what this woman does. On Wednesday evening as Ammi is about to leave she call her for a talk, well it wasn't much of a chat, no, as John wasn't responding to her notes she has decided to change tactics, she's now decided to give her a message to give to her father, but of course it wasn't a message in details, no, she couldn't do that, just a few words to say tell Mr. Thomas it's rather urgent that she speaks with him. Ammi thinks nothing of it; she memorised what her friends and tutor tell her. She's accompanying Ammi to the gate; something she done quite often now; and halfway down the long passageway she pauses, Ammi she said, tell your dad if he can't come and see me I'll have to come and see him, tell him we have business to discuss. Of course in all her action she trying not to let Ammi suspect she's got feeling for her Dad; the notes she's sending is all about business. But she's deluded; if she believes this thirteen-year-old didn't catch on to her caper she's so mistaken. But Ammi believes in her Dad; he's not going to allow himself to drag into an affair with her, well that's her thought. As she was exiting the gate Mrs. Hollins was waving goodbye, don't forget now Ammi to tell your dad she said loudly, no mom I won't she said. However she's got no intention of giving her father any such message, if it means she has to tell a little white lied to her (Mrs. Hollins); then she'll do so and later pray to the good Lord for forgiveness.

On return to work the following day Mrs. Hollins was up and about, breakfast is not yet quite ready; it's now been accustom that breakfast is prepared for them both, so Ammi tend not to eat anything before she leaves home. She went straight into the workshop and start working on the material she's been on now for over a week, well it lasted longer than usual but she's in no rush, for wanting to turn out a good job she tries to be meticulous as possible. It's about an hour since she arrived when Mrs. Hollins walks in with flowers for the big hall, good morning Ammi she said chirpily, put that away it's time for breakfast she said as she proceeds to the big hall with her basket of flowers. Ammi puts her stuff away and went to wash her hands and then went to the dining room. Breakfast is on the table but she's alone there, she takes a seat at the table but she's not going to start eating before Mrs. Hollins come. Minutes later she walks in humming a song; something she does constantly nowadays, she sits and makes herself comfortable. Did you give your Dad my message she asks, she's obviously expecting a positive answer. Ammi hands were in her lap below the table; she crosses her fingers before she replies, oh yes mom; I told him, what did her say she ask, he will be coming Mom but he didn't say when. She makes a sighing groan, I'm going to swing for that father of yours she said flippantly with a smile. There was no more said about the matter; they have a healthy breakfast; calloo and salt fish followed by fresh orange juice. After breakfast they withdraw to the workshop and even though she's nearly three times her student age the two women seem to manage a hearty conversation. One thing though; for Ammi who is usually a placid non-conversational person; since she's coming here her talking skill has improved no ends; thanks to Mrs. Hollins.

October is a rainy month; it rains every day; not usually heavy but it never stops; is like the monsoon in India, and then comes the floods; all over the Island many rivers overflow their banks, and people got washed away along with their livestock. During that month there's a half-moon and the evening closed in pretty quickly; and the night is frightfully dark. On this day Ammi was told to stays home as it continues to rain non-stop; but she insists on going to work, the weather got worse with the rain pours more heavily. It's now about four o'clock and as the weather worsens; John thinks of Ammi coming home, if she leaves to come home at the usual time she'll be coming home in heavy rain and pitch darkness; and there's a flat bridge she has to cross; and in weather like this it usually flooded and the bridge become treacherous to cross; and to ride a bicycle across it would suicidal. Now John is hoping she's got the good sense not to attempt it and stay put, however he's not going leave anything to chance; he's going to drive and pick her up. After consulting with his wife; he got in his car and sets off while it's still raining. Frank wanted to come along but he thought if the worst happen one man should be with the family; and he didn't want to risk this eleven-year-old son. No son; not this time he said, well Frank was disappointed; regardless of the weather he loves the car ride like any young boy would. The journey will take longer than usual because of the weather and with the visibility down to a few yards there's no chance of avoiding some of the potholes, so driving was down to a crawl. Reaching the gate he knows Roland won't be there, not in this weather, if he got out of his car to rattles the gate he'd get soaking wet in minutes, so he drives closer to the gate and blows his horn hoping someone at the manor would be alerted, and he was in luck. Even though visibility wasn't good he could see Roland coming down the passageway; he's got what looks like a piece of zinc over his head and walking very quickly. John was still sitting in his car when he reaches the gate; he recognised John and immediately opens the gate. There was nothing in the car for him to put over his head, he'll be soaking wet by the time he gets to the house; but without a choice he gets out and slam the car door behind him; and saying hello to Roland he hurries through the gate and continues as quickly as he can towards the house; but by the time he got there he as expected he was soaking wet.

At the front door there are eaves which are purposely built for weather like this, one could stand at the door without getting further drench. He rang the bell and it wasn't long before the maid comes to open the door, good evening Sir she said, oh Sir you're soaking wet, come in Sir, he steps in trying to avoid the furniture, I'll go and tell madam you're here Sir, and she leaves hurriedly. He was still in the foyer when almost instantly Mrs. Hollins emerges into the big hall; she was most surprised to see him, in this weather she must have thought; who would want to come out in this weather? She must be feeling right chuff thinking that he's the cause for him been here; and with twinkles in her eyes she exclaims, oh John why didn't you tell me you were coming? And in this weather, you're soaking wet, she must be thinking the message she sent by Ammi has done the trick. But of course John knows nothing of any message; he's not even thinking of all the notes she has sent him, no; all he's concern about now is to get himself and his daughter home safe. I didn't come because of your message Mrs. Hollins; I'm here to collect Ammi; I couldn't trust her to come home alone in this weather. The sparkles have gone from eyes and a look of disappointment cast a shadow over her face. So you didn't come because of the message I sent you; but at least you could have the decency to reply to at least one the notes she said angrily, but John respond in the calmest and gentlemanly manner, Mrs. Hollins he said; but she interrupted, I see we're back to the formality even though we have agreed to be informal with our names. But John was somewhat tactful, now look Florence; I'm not here for and argument, no; I'm here just to collect my daughter; but since I'm here now you can tell me why do you want to see me?. Well she was mad but somewhat pleased to responsd. She delays with her answers, however deep down John was angry with her; he knows what she's pushing for; and she's pushing hard. She wants a relationship between them; and if she continues it's going to be almost impossible in the long run for him to resist her advances, and then again he doesn't want to say or do anything to offends her that would jeopardise the future of his daughter's training, he's in a catch twenty-two situation; he was damned if he do and damned if he don't.

But John was back to the informality just to please her, Florence! Are you going to tell me what's the urgency regarding the notes he asks knowing he's never going to get a straight answer. I can't tell you while you're standing there all wet she said; let me get you something dry to change into she said, oh no, no thank you; I must collect Ammi and go because this weather is not letting up, I'll have to stay wet until I get home. Well even though she didn't tell John why she wants to see him she's feeling somewhat better; he even reverts to calling her Florence; and she's pleased about that. Ammi was going to sleep over tonight she said, I wouldn't allow her to cycle home in this weather, oh! That's very considerate of you Florence; had I think of that I probably wouldn't have bothered to come to collect he said. Well I like your daughter John; I like her very much and I would never put her in danger by sending her home on a night like this when the weather is so atrocious. After hearing what she said John becomes much more at ease with her; his fear of endangering his daughter future is put to rest. Well I thank you very much for looking out for Ammi he said, but she puts him straight, I'm surprised you might have thought otherwise she said, while she's here she's under my protection; did you think I wouldn't protect her? Oh no! He said, I wasn't thinking that at all, it's just that I'm a father and it's my duty to look out for my children, their unfriendly chat has now become a conversation; and a friendly one.

Ammi was aware of her father's presence even though she was a long way back in the workshop, she could hear his voice, and however she's not going to intrude. Here in this country children must be seen and not heard, an old heathen attitude handed down through the ages from their fore-parents; and even though Ammi is a big young woman approaching her fourteen birthday she maintains the old discipline. Well I must go home and get out of these wet clothes he said, Flo could you get Ammi for me? Hearing him call her Flo she smiles most delightfully; she must have thought this is the beginning of the friendship she craved. I wouldn't want you to catch your death of cold; so you better hurry home and get out of those wet clothes she said while she remains standing there, well unless you get Ammi for me and quickly I might still catch my death of cold he said flippantly. This time she breaks into a little laugh, ok! If I must she said, she then hurries off to fetch her. Ammi was already ready to go from the moment she heard her father's voice, get your things together Ammi your father is here to collect you she said. I'm ready Mom; I heard his voice she said, come along then; he's soaking wet and need to go now, she got up and makes her way out. Thanks for coming for me Dad she said; I wasn't planning on coming home tonight, he responds; but he wasn't going to said anything like; I didn't want you to sleep away from home, no; all he said we must go now. They say good night to Florence and about to leave, but it was still teeming down and Florence didn't want them to be waiting at the gate for Roland to open it, wait there she said; let get Roland to open the gate, she rings the bell and the maid appears, go tell Roland to go and open the gate she said, they remained there until Roland open the gate. As they were about to depart she (Florence) asked them to wait, again she summons the maid, she said something to her in a whisper, she hurried away and quickly returns with a parasol, here you're Ammi she said, you might need to use it tomorrow again. Thank you mom; I'll bring it back in the morning.

They bid good night and hurry down the long passageway while Florence stood in the doorway and watches them leave. John was quite appreciative of her gesture and the interest she has taken in his daughter; whatever the motives. It was difficult getting home; just as John thought; the flat bridge flooded but it wasn't bad enough to prevent him driving across; however he had done so with caution. But no one riding a bicycle would be able to cross over, tomorrow will be different proposition; if the rain continues and there's a good chance it will; the whole area will be flooded; the bridge will be of no use at all. She apologised to her father for not heede4d his warning this morning when he told her she shouldn't leave home, and if the weather is as foul tomorrow I won't be leaving home Dad she said. When they got home Agnes has supper ready for them. Well supper here is basically dinner; people don't bother with supper; and dinner could be at any time after five o'clock. while they were eating the conversation was about the weather, you should stay home tomorrow with the other Ammi said Agnes, the rain is not going cease, but that suggestion by Agnes was only a guess; however it's the usual pattern for the month of October; so her guess is most likely to be correct. But Ammi gets to like what she's doing; and not only she likes the idea of making dresses; but she also likes the company of Florence; she doesn't want to miss a day if she doesn't have to. Ok Mom! I'll keep watch on the weather; if it doesn't stop raining then I'll stay home. Well it was a safe bet the bad weather would continue, in the morning it was raining even more heavily but now there's a strong wind, Ammi didn't bother to get out of bed and her sisters and brother stay home from school too. But John! Well he can't afford such luxury; he will have to go to work regardless of the weather; there will be men waiting idly for him.

For the rest of the week it rains with high wind occasionally; that in some places trees were brought down, but nobody here is complaining, well! They're accustomed to this kind of weather this time of year, however! Sometimes the month of October gets angry and causes severe damage. The following few days the rain become intermittent; the wind ceases and water recedes, but it will take weeks before life is back to normality. The kids are back to school and Ammi once again is back out doing what she likes best; learning to make dress. But then a strange development happens. After John has rejected Florence advances later he begins to have dreams about her and couldn't get her out of his head. But as long as she didn't send any more notes he's not going to turn up at her house for any reasons, but that was a futile thought, no sooner the following month the notes begin to come again. At first Ammi plans not to deliver any of the notes to her father; but if she didn't she would have to continue lying to Florence if she questioned her about it; and she abhors telling lies, however her father spears her that sinful action. He couldn't holds out any longer; he plans to go and see her but not when Ammi is there, so the only time she's not is during the weekends; so the plan is to pay her a surprise visit come Saturday. It was approaching the yuletide season and everyone was building up preparing for the Christmas. That Saturday was a gorgeous day; this time of the year leading up to Christmas the weather was usually cool, the light wind blowing gently among the trees, the sun is high in the sky; just this gentle breeze gliding over your skin, one of those days when it feels good to be alive.

It was about eleven o'clock when John sets off to see Florence; he has to drive through the busy little shopping town with more rum bars than grocery shops locate. There was an accident and the main road was block; and everything grinds to a halt. Then suddenly he was spotted by his alcoholic brother-in-law, John still sitting in his car and for how long he was there was anybody's guess, There're no other roads leading away from this one main road; one just have to sit and wait, he's now an easy target for his brother-in-law, he can't avoid him; he wished he could. At the best of times he can be overbearing, but with a few drinks he's a pompous induvial. He's one of those brother-in-law's who can't take no for an answer, he's going to want John to go for a drink with him even though he knew John doesn't do that sort of thing anymore, and of course John has no intention of going back to the rum bar, he gave up been a rummy long time ago, those days are long behind him. Derick (the brother-in-law) makes a beeline through the traffic for him, he didn't wait to be invited in; he opens the passenger door and hops in, he appears sober, he hasn't started drinking yet. Hi John; where are you off to now? No! Don't tell me; you're coming to have a drink with me he said, oh come on now Derick; you know I don't drink anymore said John, well come and sit with me for a while, oh no; I can't; I must be somewhere in a hurry; and even if I wasn't I wouldn't be sitting with you. Spoil sport he said; and I hate drinking on my own, where's your drinking partner Raymond John asked, not coming out today? Oh He'll soon be here. Anyway! Where's this place you're going in a hurry he asks, you usually be at home this time reading your bible, well since you know so much about me why bother asking me to have a drink with you said John, I was only joking man. Anyway a little drink is not going to harm you, your bible said you can have a little drink but don't get drunk. John looked at him curiously; knowing this man never open the holy book in all his life; he asked him; did you read that in the bible? No; but I heard it someplace; of course you would say John sarcastically. But John couldn't see the funny side of it; all on his mind was to get away; and by now the road was nearly clear and he really wants to go. Come on now Derick; out you get; I must go now, and don't get drunk today, a pointless comment; the man hardly ever sober. Well since you won't tell me where you're off to John; have a good day; and if you can't be cautious be careful he said, I will said John with a wry smile, and you be careful too, he went on his way.

It's just gone one thirty when he reaches Mrs. Hollins house, he's wondering what she's going to think of him turning up at her home unexpected, he did that once before but for different reason, why am I doing this he again thought to himself, but of course he already knew; she's got to him and now he's got the hopes for her, he's going into a sinful situation with his two eyes wide open. Approaching the gate he could see Roland on a step ladder cutting the hedge of one corner of the privet, he alerts him and waits, he wasn't in a hurry to climb off the ladder; maybe he was under the influence again. Morning Sir he said in his broken English even though it's long past morning. Good evening Roland said John as he walks through and away up the long passageway. But Florence spotted him coming and went to the front door long before he got there, she was obviously delighted to see him; she was waving to him while he was still coming. As he approaches her he greets her with a good evening Florence, maybe she was expecting him to said Flo, she would much rather that. Good evening John; what do I owe the pleasure she asked beaming with delight. Well I was in the neighbourhood and I thought to myself; John old boy; why don't you pay this wonderful lady Florence a visit? So here I am. Well to her it didn't matter one iota where he's coming from or how he got there; all that matters is he's there. Well that's considerate of you John she said, what should I do now kiss your foot bottom she asks facetiously, oh no! You don't have to do that now; at least not right away he said mischievously. Anyway now that I see you I will leave now he said, a bit of a tactful comment just to see her response, you'll do nothing of the sort she said; come on in, and she moves to one side of the door to let him enter. She's not the woman to stand on ceremony; she asks him into the living room, he had a glance around while they make small talk. They were still standing, oh! I'm sorry John; I forget my manners; have a seat, John make himself comfortable while looking at the huge chandelier, well he seen it all before but he still has a look. what would you like to drink John she asks, it was approaching three o'clock and the heat seem to just suddenly erupts, he's feeling really hot and that's no lie, I'll have lemonade and ice if you have any he ask, I might she said, she then rings the bell to alerts the maid, no sooner the maid walks in, you rang madam she ask obediently, Yes Mary, would you prepare some lemonade with ice for Mr. Thomas and orange juice for me, certainly Mom she said as she turns and went away. From then on the conversation was much more than friendly; it was romantic, however John would like to know why she was alone in this big house, then again he thought there must be a husband or a man somewhere in her life. There's a picture in the big hall to that regards, but if that be the case then why's she alone? From he's coming here there's never a man in sight. However! If the man in her life was the one shown in the portrait on the wall he could be the grandson of some dead slave owners; and he might be away in England as they usually do, that could be the reason for her to be alone. These rich white men usually from tome to time went away for months on end and even some time for years and not in any hurry to return, and some never bother to return at all. There're many people like Florence living on estates here that fit the bill, however he's not presuming Florence was any of those; is just his curiosity getting the better of him, but if he keeps his powder dry one day soon he'll hear the Florence life story. He didn't have to wait until tomorrow that evening they enjoyed each other's company and she tells him all about her husband Mark who died nearly five years ago, his father went back to England long ago and leave the estate to him, but he really couldn't manage it properly so he sold half of it to a Mr. Wallace.

Well she wasn't cagy with the truth; is as though she was waiting to bear her soul to someone about her husband's death and the relation she had with his family. His father came to the funeral but no other relatives, on his return to England he wrote me a letter; and his closing sentence was; you won't see me again; have a good life and goodbye. Well whether he's alive or dead I have no way of knowing; he never write again and the one letter he wrote is got no returning address. Then what about your own blood family or friends John ask, where are they? I never see anyone from I been coming here, and you won't she said; I didn't really have any friends; while I was married there were lots of people usually come here; we usually entertain quite a lot, but they weren't really my friends; they were Mark's. I've got a friend; Beryl; but she and her husband move to the city about a few years after Mark's death; and I haven't seen or heard from them ever since, and before you ask me where's my mother and father; my mother is dead and my father! My mother never talks about him. It was like a confession; it's as though she was yearning for someone to come along for her to get the weight lifted off her shoulder. But John instinct tell him that maybe just maybe Mark's family didn't approve of the marriage, a mulita colour woman; the daughter of a slave marrying into a white upper-class family; they're bound to be severe opposition and hostility; and that could lead to the young couple been disbanded from the family. They were so relaxed that John seemed to forget where he was, he glances at his watch and see what the time was, he quickly jumps to his feet in surprise, oh my God; Florence look at the time he exclaims, it was approaching midnight and he never been away from home this late for many a year, the family will be concern about him. But Florence very understood about his plight; she hurriedly fetches his shoes and helps him get ready. It was a moonlit night she didn't call for Roland to open the gate, no, she drags on her shoes and walk him to the gate and lets him out, he didn't tarry; he gets in his car; waved goodbye and speeds away. It was a beautiful night and he was almost alone on the road, driving mostly slowly to avoid the potholes he's got time to thinks up an alibi to tell hers indoors, he doesn't have to; but he thinks it's the right thing to do, he knows he's gone against Principles regarding this Mr. Hollins; but whatever it takes his family must never know of his little indiscretion.

When he walks through the door Agnes was still up waiting for him, well! When your man stays out late beyond the time he usually does; a good woman wouldn't go to sleep until he's home, but she didn't give him a second look she just continues with her knitting. He asked calmly; knitting this time of the night Aggie; as he usually calls her, I'm just… and she pauses, did the car break down again she asks not looking at him, on the way home he couldn't think of a credible excuse but the question Agnes asked has just put an idea in his head. Oh no! it wasn't the car, I was in the square when I met up with Mr. Baily and …Agnes interrupts, who's Mr. Baily? Of course he never discusses anything or anyone about his work with her so she knows nothing of the personnel who her husband answers to. Oh! Mr. Baily is my boss and he's going away for one month so he asked me to have a drink with him, but you don't drink anymore she said, or did you start drinking again? Certainly not; I just went along and had a couple of juices while he and the Brutus drink their liquor, but we had a good chat, she just gives a painful groan. Well did she believe him? He takes it that she does, but whether she does or she doesn't he's not in any trouble, here the man is king, a wife never walks out on a husband regardless of the issue, unless he wants her out, divorce is not a function operates here. In any case; her query was not to checks upon him coming from another woman's home, not at all, her in door's wouldn't dare ask any such question, a man could have two or three women living side by side with his wife knowing all about them, a kind of seraglio arrangement. But John is not that kind of man anymore; he loves his wife and family far too much, he would like to be straight and decent with his family; and even though he steps out of line this one time he's got no intention of having a lasting affair with Mrs. Hollins.

But the one dilemma he faces with at present; his visit to Florence must remain a cloak and dagger operation, Ammi must not in any way even suspect of their encounter. But the man is naive; the fourteen is innocent; she never had a boyfriend and by all accounts seems not intent on having one, but she's aware of her utterer's intention toward her father, so whatever he thinks she more than one step ahead of him. Well! He might think he's a man of the world but his thinking is falling short, the notes that kept coming to him is been carried by his daughter; didn't he thinks she would be sensible enough to suspect there's a motive behind all these notes, and even though Ammi has never seen him visit her during the days of the notes she (Ammi) she had a suspicion he visited her (Florence) when wasn't there. But whatever she knows or suspect it's going to remains a secret, as a teenager she wouldn't have the audacity or nerves to say anything to her father regarding his behaviour; and she's certainly wouldn't dare mention anything to her step-mother about it, she probably wouldn't Believe her but reprimand her for mentioning it. All she could do was hope that the affair will run its course pretty quick and her father breaks it off. After about three months John had enough of the cloak and dagger situation and wants to finish it, his visits to her were becoming far and few between and she didn't like it, no she didn't like it one little bit. Now she's becoming anxious and even jealous when she didn't get the visits she was expecting; and once again she begins to used Ammi as the postman for her notes, but little does she knows that her notes weren't been delivered, Ammi was doing whatever she can to shield her father without causing friction between she and her tutor.

But John's conscience was playing havoc with his mind, he knows he got into this relationship because of lust and the persistence of Mrs. Hollins, but then again it was extremely difficult to resist the advances of this temptress, any red-blooded man would have fallen for her, but as all good things have to come to an end and he wanted to this to come to an end and quickly. Suddenly the guilt was piling up on him, more often than usual he reads his bible for comfort and answers. He tells himself that at his age he shouldn't be involved in this sort of caper, hiding around corner like the days when he was a young irresponsible man, he built up a respectable reputation within the community for himself and his family and that mustn't be destroyed, and most important he mustn't lost the respect of his family. On Friday when Ammi was about to leave Florence was getting overwrought; she's thinking up ways how to get her man to come to her, she asks Ammi in a coy manner; is your father ill Ammi? oh no mom; but he's got an awful lots of work to do; I would like to talk to him about certain matters she said, give him this note and tell him I'm waiting for an answer; she handed Ammi the note in a sealed envelope, Ammi thought to herself; this's not a note; it's a letter. But at this point Florence doesn't seem to care whether Ammi knows about their relations; she wants to see him and she wants to see him bad; and with desperation she seems to lose all sense of discretion, she doesn't give a damn about endangering the man and his family. This time Ammi gives her father the envelope but didn't say anything more, now John is getting very irritated, her persistence in using Ammi as a messenger was out of order and has got to stop; but how? he knows he's got to face her; he must; now he's regretted he had ever started this thing; and even though he's not a Christian he's been praying to the good Lord for forgiveness and to help him gets out of this thing. Now he knows what he's got to do, face up to his responsibility like a man, he suspects it won't be pleasant; but it's time he faces the music and put a stop to this thing, he's not going to try, no; he's going to put an end to it. However he's not going to go in with all guns blazing, no; he'll treat her with the respect he always gives and try to reason with her and hope she'll see that this can't continue.

7: The Confession

On this warm Sunday evening when the church was having one of their prayer meetings away from the church; these are regular occurrences; on occasions they would target one of the local districts for their evangelistic meetings and most time these meetings are well supported, this's where they found new souls. It would be announced in church like the week before and even though there're no posters or any kind of media to spread the good news the words would travel just as fast; and soon the entire districts and around would know of it. This Sunday evening was a beautiful one, the evenings are long and warm; one of those evening when it's prime for a stroll, and with Christmas approaching the cool December breeze makes it feels even more pleasant. Tonight they could have a big crowd for their outdoor meeting and that means a lot of souls could be saved. Tonight's meeting is out of their district about three miles away; and John and Ammi will be going, he's not usually going with them to these meetings but tonight he feels the compulsion to go. Now these Pentecostal meeting can most time be fiery and quite loud, and with the clapping and shouting hallelujah amen when the spirit takes control; it can be a noisy affair. Some of these Preachers can be quite persuasive; if he's one of those they call hellfire preacher; he'll be preaching and pointing his fingers; one can be forgiven for feeling guilty; thinking he's preaching about them. At times people came away thinking that he was talking about them. Tonight John was feeling guilty about his affair with Florence; right now he's a troubled man; he needs to be freed of his burden, tonight he wants to confess his sins and ask the good Lord forgiveness, he's been doing so in secret; but tonight he'll do so tonight kneeling at the altar. Standing there listening to the sermon the tears are running from his eyes as though he's got no control over it, well the preacher must have hits on his case and his guilt getting the better of him.

At this time there's an alter calls; this is when those who think they committed a sin or sins like John; they would kneel at the altar and confesses and ask the good Lord for forgiveness. Needless to say even some of those who are Christian will be at the altar too confessing to something they might think they've done wrong, regular occurrences. With the many others who are delivering their supplications; so was John.

Of course in what would seem like confusion; no one probable hearing or try to hear what the others are confessing to, everyone is doing their own thing. At this point the spirit usually takes control; and then things seem to get out of control, the shout of hallelujah praised the Lord, the speaking in lounges to which no one understood; is a part of the ritual. But John is sincere in his confession; he asks the good Lord to help him ends this affair with little or no fuss; and without his family ever be wised about it. His action pleases Ammi no ends, and although he's not a baptised Christian, "at least not yet" tonight she believed he has become a converted Christian. She's been sending up her own prayers to the good Lord on his behalf all along; and now she believes her prayers had been answered. He was always a regular churchgoer; but tonight he's got religion; tonight he fully accepts the Lord and become one of the brethren's. From now hence he'll be referred to as Brother Thomas; that is to say you're one of us now; and the next step for him to take is to be baptised, but that will come later.

When Ammi went to her place of work on Monday she takes delight in tells Mrs. Hollins that her father has turned to Christianity, in a frightful way she asks, from when? Well! Ammi tells her what her father never told her; he was always a churchgoer mom but wasn't a Christian, but last night he confesses his sins and now he's has given his heart to the Lord; and soon he'll be baptised. That bit of news is not what Florence wants to hear, How could he become a Christian so sudden she asks suspiciously, oh no Miss Florence; it's not sudden; he was always Christian minded but he never confesses his sins and make the commitment; but last night he confessed and the Lord will forgive him for any wrongdoing she said. She was trying to tell her in a tactful way that she knows of their sinful carrying on. Now she (Florence) tries to hide her disappointment; but it was obvious to even a fourteen-year-old that she was bitterly angry. But even though she's hearing it from Ammi and probably believes that she (Ammi) wouldn't lie to her; nevertheless she wants to hear it from the horse's mouth, John himself. There was no more talking about the matter; they carry on as usual; but Mrs. Hollins action was somewhat subdued, she had become somewhat quiet and at time miserable since he stopped coming. But today after hearing what Ammi said; she! Well she's not so much miserable, no; more like very calm. But today Ammi is feeling different from all other days; she's hilariously happy even though her boss and friend Mrs. Hollins is not feeling too good, but she tries not to show her delight. This young woman is a Christian-minded and honest person and even though she behaves ignorant to the situation she was always conscious to the fact that one day her family is going to find out and will point the fingers at her. They would accuse of treachery; being there every day she must have known about it and she keeps quiet about it, something to that effect; and they would be right. Her relationship with the family wouldn't be the same again; and she would be certainly being cast out of the family foul. This family take exception to anyone who sides against the family, and as far as she is concerned; if that would be the case and was abandoned by her family; she might as well be dead. Hearing what Ammi told her it to seem to take some time to register or she didn't give it much credence, suddenly she exclaims, so he became a Christian? She said sounding like some condemned person. But Ammi didn't respond, it was clear that she was broken-hearted even though she hasn't heard it from John himself as yet, and until she hears it from him she's going continued waiting for him to come to her.

Well! the news has cast a dark cloud over her; Florence has lost her mojo, days after her eating has become less; she's not enjoying her food at all; and Ammi was becoming concern; she's not saying anything about their romance; but she's hoping her father would come and have it out with her so she doesn't keep hanging on. But her friendship for Ammi has never relented, in a way Ammi hate to see her so unhappy; but she knows the relationship between them was an unhealthy one; and one that could possibly cause the breaks up of her family if it was to be known; and of course she herself would be compromised. She doesn't to see her father in a relationship with anyone other than her step-mother. This teenager is got a lot of thinking to do and she's been trying to do it the only way she knows how, she has been praying to the good Lord day and night. She's been caught between the Devil and the deep blue sea and only the good Lord can help her. She has developed a liking for her tutor; but her love and loyalty is with her family. It's nearly two weeks now since she heard the news about John becoming a Christian and he hasn't come to tell her so, she was getting angrier by the day. She begins once again to send him notes, but she was only building pie in the sky; he was planning to come and see her but never in a romantic manner. This time Ammi delivers all the notes to her father, she was confident he was never going to return to that life again; and since his confession he's been testifying at meetings, which means he's now a fully-fledged believer in the doctrines of the church. Now John knows what he's got to do; but he wishes he didn't have to do it, sooner rather than later he has to face Florence to settle the matter, and if she makes a scene he just has to face up to it. For all the time he delayed in seeing her it send his nerves jangling; he begins to think that maybe; just maybe she would try to understand and not make a scene. Of course that wouldn't do his reputation any good; and what would it do his family.

Well! He gives it plenty of thought; he must go and sees her and quickly, he mustn't delay or leave anything to chance. So he gives Ammi a return note; it reads, dear Florence; I must apologise for my ill-manners and lack of concern for others; please forgive me; and if it's alright with you I would like to come and see you on Saturday round about midday, you needn't reply; if you're in agreement with my preposition, yours truly John. On receiving the note that Wednesday morning there was a sign of relief spread all over her face; and when she read it she wasn't too disappointed even though it didn't mention anything that should give her hope like; "love John" or "xxx" nothing to indicates they were still lovers; but she was still holding to her dreams that the romance was still on. However with all that her suspicion was telling her he's got another woman; and she must see him and soon to have it out with him.

8: The Confrontation

Saturday was a miserable day, it begins to rain from around midnight; not a good day to leave home; and he wouldn't about to leaving today if there wasn't an urgent situation, and if he did his family might be wondering as to why he's going out in this awful weather even though he drives. But no one is going to question him about it; neither does he have to justify himself to anyone for going out. He looks at his watch and the time was approaching one o'clock; it later than he thought; he had promise Florence in his note that he would be there about midday. He walks horribly in the rain to get to his car; as usual when it rains heavily the potholes, some as deep as a craters, are full of water and that makes driving a little more treacherous. It takes him longer than usual to get there partly because driving was down to a crawl, he reaches the manor and although he didn't expect to see Roland anywhere near the gate; but there he was walking away from it; it appears he was just coming in; he was soaking wet. John alerts him by calling his name, on seen John he turn back and open the gate, good evening Sir he said in his usual growling manner as he pulls the gate ajar. Good evening Roland said John as he walks through and hurried up the long passageway, standing at the patio he is away from the rain; he brushes himself down before ringing the bell. Mary opens the door with her usual zest and smile; she stands on one side as she holds the door open. Good evening Sir; come in Sir she said, he steps in trying to avoid anything that would get wet from his wellies. She closed the door behind him, I'll get madam for you Sir she said as she walks away, usually he would proceed to the living room without been told to do so; but on this occasion, no; he remains standing in the big hall. There was a footstep on the concrete floor coming from the dining room section of the house; "he knows it's Florence" he was standing in a position facing the door that she would see him as she's coming through; he wants to see the expression on her face when she first sees him. As she emerges through the door he could see the look on her face as she glares at him, the expression was enough to tell the story. Oh! You manage to come to see me now, do you? she asked angrily and looking at him with a fierce stare, and good evening to you too Florence he said sarcastically trying to be light-hearted, but she's in no mode for funny talk; she wants an explanation. Are you going to stand there she asks, you never used to, no he said; but now I'm all wet. He was still standing there in his wellies, then why don't you take off your wellies she asks in an unfriendly manner. He took it off without replying then walks by her to the living room; but he didn't sit down, he was too wet She walks in behind him but she didn't sit either, she stood in front of him almost touching him. Now John was beginning to feel a little uncomfortable, he could see that she was extremely angry, this six-foot plus well-built man standing in front of a woman about five foot seven; and even though he tries to hide his nervousness he's shaking inside. He's hoping that when he tells her his intention she's not going to make a scene. Why didn't you respond to my notes John she asks furiously, I sent you quite a few she said, he was long to answer, well! The last time I drove away from here I felt rather bad, what do you mean you felt rather bad she asked anxiously, did you catch something from me? Did I give you the claps? Now you been childish said John; you know that's not what I mean, then what the hell do you mean she asked furiously. I was feeling a sense of guilt he said, let's take a step back and look at what we're doing he said calmly, I'm a much older man than you; I'm nearly fifty and you are a much younger woman; he paused, how old are you he asked; or that's an impertinent question. You never concern about my age before; why now? So you can use it as an excuse for whatever your reason she said. Well let me guest; I say you're about thirty-something, she interrupt, I see what you're getting at; you're trying to make me feels guilty about something; but what John? Are you trying to tell me something? If so let's have it; she was thinking about what Ammi told her. But it won't wash she said, what's the hell is age got to do with anything she asks, well don't you see; I fell in love with you because I couldn't help myself, your charm and beauty overwhelms me, any red-blooded man would have fallen for you. But in as much as I still love you and it hard not; I have my family to consider, so you see Florence it's with extreme difficulty and regret that we must end this affair. She calmed down somewhat with no reply for a while. Any red-blooded man indeed! I didn't fell in love with any red-blooded Dick, Tom or Harry; I fell in love with you; you John Thomas she said seriously.

But John line of argument seem to be gradually having the desired effect; So you say age doesn't matter; that could be true in some cases; like if I wasn't married; but I love and respect you far too much to be hiding around corners with you, no, that's not right, that's not right at all. You! A woman of your stature and beauty should be seen with a younger man; someone who you can be seen out with and make you happy. A beautiful woman like you shouldn't be hiding yourself away locked up in a big house waiting to see a married man, no; that's not right at all; you should be out in the public with your own man and a man of your age he said. Well I must say after I haven't seen or heard from you for over a month and here you are; turns up here with some kind of sermon to make me feel guilty of falling in love with you, come here talking about age and younger men, you find another woman; why don't you just tell me so. Don't be ridiculous he said, not because I fell for you it doesn't mean I go around chasing women, I'm a married man and I do have my principles. Well don't to tell me anything about age; I didn't tell you but my late Husband was older than you and we were happy, so stop trying to make me feels guilty for loving you she said with some venom. Well I certainly didn't come here to make you feel guilty of anything; all I'm trying to do in my clumsy manner is to let see that what we're doing is wrong and you could do so much better than a married man like me. Oh John! Stop trying to put yourself down; it's doesn't become you she said. She takes a deep breath and rose to her feet pushing back her long wavy hear to the back of her head, your sermon makes me peckish she said calmly; I'm ordering something to eat for the both of us, but with John didn't want to say anything to ruin the uneasy calm and caused an affray; and even though he would like to leave now he's going to eat with her. But Florence is not an unreasonable person; she understands the situation and reluctantly she knows what John was saying was right; and even though she loves him still she knows she must let him go.

They didn't have to wait; the dinner was already and on the table, Mary have already see to it, she then walks in and knocks the door, come in Mary said Florence, she pushes the door open, dinner is on the table Mom said Mary, thank you Mary she said. But before she asks John to come along he was up on his feet and ready to go, acting as calm and normal as he could; he's trying his best to keep the situation calm and civil. They make their way to the dining room, they usually sat side by side to eat; but this time they sat on the opposite side of the table. But John enjoyed the dinner; he usually does; this Mary is a very good cook. But for Florence she seems not to enjoy it very much; however this will probably be the last time they will be having dinner together. Although John feels a little more secure; he was still somewhat apprehensive that if he says the wrong thing; something she didn't want to hear she might blow her top, he also feels he has said what he came to say and even though he's not sure what she's thinking he would like to leave now. But he's not going to insist on leaving; not just yet; that might aggravate the situation. The rain begins to teem down again so he tries to relax. Why don't you be honest with me John she asked calmly; You found a new woman, now you been silly he said, I thought we pass that point of conversation, I should have told you from the offset, I've got converted and now I'm a Christian, I've given my heart to the Lord. Of course she heard it already from Ammi but she wants to hear it from him. Then why didn't you reply to any one of my notes and said so she asked, I didn't want to tell you in a note, no; I wanted to tell you face to face. How considerate of you John; do you think telling me face to face makes it any easier for me she asked calmly. But these people have great respect for the church and hold a kind of reverence for anyone who has become a Christian, she knows deep down that John wouldn't be telling lies and using the name of the Lord.

She paused for thought, but why John? And why so sudden she asked, But John looks at her in amazement; I can't believe you ask such nonsensical question; I'm not even going to try to answer that; you're just been childish, oh! So I'm a child now am I she ask, you know what I mean he said but it seems she was taking little digs at him maybe to try and catches him out. Well let me tell you; I was always a churchgoer; I told you so Remember? Only I wasn't a practicing Christian, I never confessed my sins until a few weeks ago he said. So you take your heart away from me and give it to your God she said flippantly, John looks at her in a frightful manner, you don't joke about God in an idle manner; it blasphemous, it'll do you good you remember that, he's the all-mighty one who sees and hear everything, amen hallelujah she said facetiously. But he wasn't amused; such comments make him uncomfortable, in his world the name of God is to be feared and only to be used in reverend. All I'm saying if I know you are seeing another woman I would fight for you; but God! I can't fight him she said, what sinful in saying that she asked, and I'm saying be careful how you used the name of the Lord our God, and anyway you know I'm seen another woman he said and then he pauses, she looks at him as though she wants to hurt him, You're seeing another woman she ask furiously, John look at her and have a little laugh, the joke is on you now he said, are you forgetting my wife? Very funny she said sarcastically. It seems as though John prayers were answered, he prays to the Lord for a favourable outcome of his situation and it seems as though he has achieved exactly that. The rough ride he had anticipated didn't materialize; even though he suspects that Florence isn't Finish with him as yet. It's time for him to leave, he feels he had explained his position sufficiently enough and trust that this will be last time he will be discussing this situation with her.

The rain has ceased and the birds are out, when Florence opens the window the nightingales perch high up in the trees actively singing their song. That usually the case after a heavy shower; the birds come out in numbers and they are quite chirpy, a beautiful sight to behold if you're a bird watcher. John looks at his watch, gosh! Isn't time flies he said, it's a shame we weren't having fun she said flippantly, but John didn't respond, it was approaching five o'clock, so I'm not going to see you anymore I take it she ask, but before he answers he thinks about it, he feels he's in a good place with her to be frank and to give her some furtherly advice. Why don't you come to our church? It always good to come to church he said, but I don't know anyone there she said, really Florence? What about Ammi and me. Anyway you don't have to know the people at the church for you to go there, you're not going there to know people even though in the long run you'll know everyone, and you're going there to worship the Lord. She smiles broadly; and that pleases John, are you going to start preaching again John she asks while still smiling, no he said; but I hope that I'll see you at church tomorrow. Not tomorrow; but I'll surprise you one of these days she said. But there's one thing I want to ask you about, what's that she ask in a hurry, take it easy he said, "he's now feeling rather relax" it's nothing to be frightened about. Then what is it she asks anxiously, well! Do you think Ammi knows about us he asks in a humble manner, come on now John; Ammi is a big girl and she's not stupid, she knows alright; but because of her respect for you and me; she'll go on pretending she doesn't know. So what you must do is say nothing just go on doing what she does pretend you don't know she knows; that's what I do, and you should do the same she said, so you're giving me advice now he said with a smile. But seriously; I think you're right; I'll go on pretending, and what will the Lord think about you doing that sinful thing she asked facetiously, there you go again with the jokes he said, you're are been blasphemous, I'm going; it's not safe around here anymore he said. But of course he wasn't kidding; people her are fearful of using the name of the Lord in vain, they were brought up that way. Now John is ready to make a move, he dusts himself down and reaches for his car key, she knows he must go, he's here the best part of the day.

They walk to the front door but she didn't open it, so when I'm going to see you again she asked kind of respectfully, he looks at her with sorrowful eyes as to say I regret to have to do this, whenever you come to church; and I'm looking forward to seeing you there. She opens the door and as John was going through, he turns and asks her, oh! By the way; have you ever been to church at any time? I've been to church alright; but it was a long time ago she said, like when you got married asked John, some people that's the only time they set foot inside of a church; when they got married and when they died. Well! I've been to the Presbyterian church once or twice; but I'm not a member, you're not a bad person Florence; you should remember that; in fact you're one of the very best of people I ever had the pleasure to have met. Listen! Church is the very best place for anyone to be; and I look forward to seeing you there.

He then begins walking toward the gate, Roland was already there awaiting him, thank you Roland he said ask he walks through towards his car. He then waved goodbye to Florence who was still standing at the door; and even though it was quite a distance away he could see her waving frantically. As he drove off he breathes a sigh of relief; this what he considers a whirlwind romance is now over thank be to God; and he hopes Florence will find someone soon who will make her happy, she deserves it. A beautiful woman like her shouldn't be on her own living in that big old house; it's not healthy he thought. The drive home was much more relaxing than the one coming to see Florence; he was in no rush and had time to think of the situation he was in, before tonight he wasn't sure of what to say to his family if the situation was to be known. He thanks the good Lord it's over and apart from Ammi the rest of the families are none the wiser. Indoors he's feeling rather good with himself, he made his peace with God, he made peace with Florence and he's now at peace with himself, tomorrow at church he'll pray for Florence to find peace and happiness in her life.

At the dinner table he wasn't too hungry, he pretends to have wind in his stomach and of course no one take much of a notice, except Ammi who suspect her father was at Florence's during his absence, and of course with her mum is the word, but according to his religion he's got a lot a praying to do; all these little white lies added up. Sunday the family will be off to church as usual and Ammi will tend to poor Mrs. Brown and Mr. Wilson as usual, her church Sisters who promise to help; after a few visits they stop caring. After her father's confession at prayer meeting Ammi believes her father went and see Florence to make peace with her, if he's sincere about following the Lord he has to confront her and tell her the romance is over and she suspects when he came home late on Saturday that's where he was. Now she (Ammi) anxious to get to work to notice if there are any changes in Mrs. Hollins attitude. Arriving a little later than usual she parks her bicycle and start walking in a hurry toward the house when she spotted Florence in the garden, she loves to be in the garden among the beautiful flowers; but Ammi didn't expect to see her out so early, "it's not quite ten o'clock as yet". Good morning Miss Florence said Ammi in a loud voice as she was a little way beyond, she pushes aside the tall sunflower and holding on it she yells, good morning Ammi; go ahead; I'll be in shortly she said. The front door was open when Ammi got there and Mary was about with her duster, good morning Miss Ammi said Mary, well even though she (Ammi) is only a teenager and the maid is a grown woman she will always address her with respect, good morning Mary she said as she continues to the workroom. Minutes later Florence walks in, right! Come on; let's have breakfast she said cheerfully, Ammi got up but didn't follow immediately behind her; she was packing away some clothing. The meal is already on the table as usual but Florence is not going to start without her, perhaps that's why she was out in the garden as Ammi was a bit late. Ammi walks in and they settle down to eat, how was your weekend dear she asks, Ammi had a sneaky peek at her without raises her head, she never calls her dear before. Oh! Just the same as usual Mom, but she was more upbeat than when they parted company last week. Ammi would like to ask her if everything is alright; but she wouldn't dare, it wouldn't be respectful; but it was good to her so chirpy; almost back to her old self again. Back in the workshop later that day Ammi was a little curious when Florence begins to ask her about the church, she couldn't understand why until sometime later. Are you considering coming to church Mom asked Ammi, I might she said, your father said I'm a pagan, did he really said that Mom she asked wanting to hear some more. No! But he said I should come to church and give my heart to the Lord, Ammi had a thought; her father had settled the situation with her and it seems as though everything is alright. That would be wonderful Miss Florence; please come; the people are friendly there; and I'm sure you'll like coming to church once you get started. Just like your Dad; you're trying to convert me she said with a cheeky smile. But one day I'll visit; I do believe that there's a God, amen to that said Ammi. But Florence would like to belong to a family; and she thinks she has found one; the Thomas's. Now that their romance is a thing of the past; she now realised that all that John said was the truth; and since neither she nor him holds any animosity; she feels she could be part of his family. In fact she completely and utterly come to her senses and thank him for putting her straight, now she would like to attach herself to his family; and she does just that. She latches on to Thomas and becomes an adopted part of the family. John was a bit apprehensive at first; thinking she might have had anterior motives, but as time lapsed and she proves there're no other motives than wanting a family to belong to the Thomas welcome her with open arms. Ammi and her tutor are getting on famously as usual; Ammi is the Sister she has never had. Their friendship grew stronger and the older woman treats her like a little Sister. Her father's little indiscretion that was a stumbling block is well and truly bury, he now treats Florence like a Daughter and she loves it. The secret of that unholy alliance rest between the three people; and with God's help it will remains with them to the grave.

9: The Good Samaritans

The week is going pretty well as far as the family is concerned; but then Thursday was a miserable day, the sun was low in the sky and the day was murderously hot, there was no breeze at all just a still hot day. On her way home about one and half miles from her home she could hear a groaning sound coming from the direction directly adjacent to the right over the bank where there was a big cluster of bamboo tree, she slows down to have a good listen while making sure her bicycle doesn't fall into one of the potholes. The groaning gets louder and louder as she gets closer, it was clear someone was in agony. She scaled the low bank to have a good look; she could see someone through the cloister of bamboo but couldn't see who the person was. She had to plot her route through the thick cluster and try to enter from the other side. When she got to the person it was Mr. Perry; a local man not living too far from where he was lying, he seems badly hurt. But with a closer observation Ammi could see he was bleeding and lying in a heap of blood, she didn't panic, no; she kneels over him to ask him what happened, Mr. Perry, Mr. Perry she kept calling repeatedly but he couldn't respond, all he seems able to do is groan. With no formal medical training she wasn't sure what to do, but she notices his cloths were ripped all over and with a closer look there were gore marks all over his body where the bleeding was coming from. She then has a thought as to how he came by them, he was gored by a bull. Well here in these parts it's not unusual for someone to be attacked by a bull and can even be killed, looking at the marks on him she thinks that is the case. Close by there was a meadow; she could see some cows there, she knows there must be a bull there too; sometimes there're more than one, and at times the bull broke loose out of their flimsy wired fences. Mr. Perry was wearing an almost red shirt; a target for the bulls, she knows this fierce animal will attack anything or anyone wearing red clothes. Now she becomes fearful for herself even though she wasn't wearing anything red, what if the bull returns to finish the job she thought; she would be in danger too.

But poor Mr. Perry needs help and fast; and she's unable to help; so she thinks of the only thing she can do; is to go and get someone who could help. She makes him as comfortable as she could and leave him with the hope that the bull won't return, she then sets off in the direction of her home. About half of mile on she saw a cart coming towards her, she knows who it was instantly, it was Mr. Barker; the only person who's owns mules cart in the district. The cart was empty; it could be he either just finished a job or going to start one, she stops him and tells him of Mr. Perry's accident. He didn't hesitate; he turns his cart around and makes for where Mr. Perry was lying. He was still lying in the same position Ammi left him, since there's nothing they could for him there they didn't tarry, she helps Mr. Barker gets him on the cart to take him home. On the journey home he was in more pain than when he was lying on the ground. Well! The cart is of iron band; and on this bad road Mr. Barker can't avoid all of the potholes; and every time the wheels falls into one of these holes the poor man groan in agony even more. He tries to guide the mules through this labyrinth of potholes; but he's not going to avoid them all. The five minutes journey take much longer as he had to drive very slowly, however they manage to get him home and get him in his bed dripping with blood. They can't take him to conventional Doctor; like most of the locals here he can't afford to, they rely on the bush Doctor; needless to say most of these people who seek out the bush Doctors died or suffering long term sickness. Well what else can these people do? As the old saying goes; a drowning man catches after straws. They are doing the best they can for poor Mr. Perry, Mr. Barker gets a basin of water to try and clean him up while Ammi went to get madam Bell; one of the local bush Doctor. She's not living too far from Mr. Perry; and It wasn't long before Ammi return with Madam Bell, by then Mr. Barker done a good job cleans him up; but he couldn't stop the flow of blood, the poor man was groaning in agony.

Madam Bell taken over, she knew him like she knew everyone in the district. She looks at him and gently slapping him all over, she then reaches into her bag and takes out a small vial; she then holds his head up and give him a sniff from the vial, she then laid him back down. Meanwhile she was doing that she was mumbling something, she then grabs her bag and in a crusty voice she comments; I soon come back she said in the native pathway lingo. She was away for some time; Mr. Barker said she was cooking up bushes. She returns with a large paper bag looking as though she was in a hurry, she told them to stand back away from the bed. As they did she takes up a position sitting on the bed, and then she begins to rub him all over with stuff from the brown paper bag, the stench was quite vile; but they endure it. They hope that whatever she's doing would ease Mr. Perry's pain; but It didn't; the poor man is in severe agony. Well needless to say whatever madam Bell had done with her bushes doesn't seem to be working; if anything Mr. Perry is in more pain, and when she was leaving she whispered something in his ears, Mr. Barker looked at her with disdain as she was going through the door, he doesn't like people like her, he thinks they're a waste of time and probably help some people to an early grave. But for some people she is the only help they can get whenever they fell ill; and moreover some believed in her method.

It was now approaching nine o'clock and Ammi hasn't reached home yet; she knows her parent will be concern about her and might even come looking for her. She hates to leave Mr. Perry alone and in pain but there's nothing more neither she nor Mr. Barker could do, Mr. Barker said he'll stop with him a while longer but Ammi must go. It's a beautiful moonlight night; one can see for miles around with the naked eyes, she sets off home and she'll be there in no time. But her father won't be pleased at all she's coming home this late; and he wants to know why, well! Like any good parent would. In the presence of her stepmother she told them what had happen, but you should come home first said her father, I couldn't dad she said calmly; how could I leave this poor hurt man and do nothing, I just couldn't dad; I just couldn't. But He wasn't too hard on her, he knows it's a good thing she had done; and when she tells him that she must look in on him in the morning on her way to work he offers to go with her to see what he can do. In the morning when they got to him there was no change in his condition, the swellings had drawn down a bit but he was still in pain. This man who is got no family and no one to relies on is at the crossroad of his life and without the help of Ammi and Mr. Barker he would probably have died already. However without proper medical treatment he will certainly die anyway. These are poor people who have got nothing except their small plot of cultivations and a few lives stocks; mostly pigs and goat; a few of them owned cows; Tate and Lile own most of the cows here but they are working animals. These people! Their little small plot provided them with a living, not much; but a living nevertheless. The ones whose small form produced a good crop they would take it to the market come Saturday. But this is only seasonal; and whatever little money they make from the sale of their produce is not sufficient to have any put aside for rainy day, it's a hand to mouth existence. But they have become accustomed to their way of life; learning to be satisfied with very little; the cause for some to died needlessly; their lock of finance put them out of the reach of a proper Doctor whenever they were taken ill.

Ammi and her father did whatever they could for Mr. Perry before they leave, they don't hold out much hope for him though. But Ammi will visit him mornings and evenings to see that he gets something to eat and whatever else she can do. She gets to her place of work late that morning and of course Mr. Hollins doesn't appreciate her arriving late, but Ammi describe the whole incident to her; the purpose for her lateness. why do you take these people burden upon yourself she asked, why do you believe you should help everyone; you're only a teenager and got your own young life to prepare for, take it from someone who is older and got your interest at heart. Don't go thinking you should help every Dick tom or Harry who fell ill, Sometime one must put themselves first she said. I know what you're saying is right mom but I just couldn't walk away leaving the poor man groaning in agony, if I didn't he would probably be dead by now. Ammi tells her that she and her father look in on him this morning and she'll look in on him again in the evening when she's going home. They have breakfast and carried on as usual; Mrs. Hollins was out among the orange trees; she was in graphing a branch; one of the things she does usually. But at lunch she surprises Ammi, she offers to come along with her to see what help she can give to Mr. Perry, the big softy Ammi thought, after the way she talked tough you never thought she would want to help. Are you sure Miss Florence asks Ammi, yes! I'm quite sure Ammi, I'm not cold-hearted as you might be thinking she said, but Ammi didn't think she was cold-hearted at all; she just didn't count on her doing anything like tending to sick people. Have you ever cared for any sick person Mom she asked, well no; but maybe there's something that I can do to help. Ammi is pleased to have her along, are you going to drive Mom? But before she answers Ammi thought to herself; what a silly question; even though the car is there she'd never seen her drive it; in fact she never seen her driver any vehicle at all. Oh no! she replies; that car hasn't been moved for a long time, maybe it can't even start, I'm riding my bicycle. But Ammi had a thought; I wonder if she's coming because she heard my Dad was there this morning; and thinks he will be there in the evening, but whatever the reason she's got no way of knowing.

The evening was nice and sunny, this time of year the sun takes a long time to set and the evening becomes stretched, it's four o'clock and they set off to see Mr. Perry, it's about a three minutes ride that will take longer. When they got there Mr. Perry was just as she left him this morning, in pain and groaning, he must be hungry; but she doesn't think the food matters to him right now; he's in too much agony. Between them both they change his clothing; then Ammi cooks up something for him to eat. But he's not eating much and whatever little he swallows come right back up again. right now there's nothing more they can do, But for Ammi it's the first time she sees the human side of Mrs. Hollins, it looks as though she wants to grieve for Mr. Perry, she really feels sorry for the poor man. It's getting late and they have to leave; and once they're gone he's on his own, the bush Doctor never returns to see if her portion did worked. He can't move or help himself in any way, he'll probably die during the night, Ammi. Leaving the scene Florence was visibly shaken by what she had seen, probably in her kind of life she had never witnessed injuries like those sustained by Mr. Perry. She must leave now before it gets dark; here at this time of year the night gets really dark; and she's got the furthest to go. See you in the morning Ammi she said; and they parted company. After Ammi look in on Mr. Perry one last time she sets off home, and when she tells her father about Mr. Hollins' action he was most surprised. I didn't think she had it within her; that goes to show he said; goes to show what Dad? That there's good in everyone, Ammi thinks of something else but said nothing. How was he when you leave him he asked, there's no change in his condition Dad, he probably won't live to see the morning, I'm so sorry for that poor man she said.

The following morning her father didn't come along; on the way to work she pops in to check on Mr. Perry, well! He's still alive but there's little change in his condition, she did what she could but the man was in great pain. However she must leave; she was late again when she got to the manor; but this time Mrs. Hollins is not going to ask why she's late. Did you see that poor man this morning she asked, yes Mom; I did; but he's just the same, if anything he seems a little weaker; I think that because he can't keep food down, that poor man she exclaims. But ever since Ammi told her of Mr. Perry misfortune she seems to feel a deep sense of sympathy for him, yesterday when she saw him she was near to tears; that poor man she kept saying. Aound about three-thirty that afternoon Florence who was out in the garden walks in the workroom, she was carrying some beautiful flowers in the flowers basket, she adores flowers. Ammi she said; I'm going do something for that poor sick man, it seems she couldn't remember his name, that poor man need to see a Doctor; and I'm going to him one. Ammi thought to herself; I should be a mind reader, I know something was bothering her. Really Miss Florence she asked; that would be a really good thing to do Mom, yes I will she said. How about you and me go and see the Doctor Tomorrow; you don't mind do you? Oh no Mom I love to, said Ammi, ok! That settles; we'll go first thing in the morning. Back at home Ammi tells her father about what

Florence was going to do; he was surprised about her first action when she went along to see Mr. Perry, but he even more surprise now to learn she's going to pays for his medical treatment, he had to admit he had by far underestimated this person, she has gone way up very highly in his admiration; one day I'll congratulate her for what she's doing he thought. The weather they're having now is somewhat unsettled, the rain is not heavy; only light intermittent showers; and although our winter never brings snowfalls; at times some people have to put on something warm; the usual pattern leading up to Christmas. That morning about ten o'clock Ammi and Florence sets= off to see the Doctor; it's within walking distance but a long walk, on the way Florence tells Ammi she hasn't been to town for a very long time; and she hopes the Doctor'ssurgery is at the same place she remembers. For Ammi this is the first time she will be going into the town, she's almost excited to be going.

Florence goes directly to where she once knew; the surgery should be over there she said, and at first glance there was a sign displaying Doctor surgery. She entered the surgery with Ammi behind her, as she walks in the receptionist recognised her, hello Mrs. Hollins she exclaimed, it's good to see you Mom, but it seems Florence couldn't recall her or remember her name, hello! How are you she said, I'm fine Mom; you're here to see the Doctor, Mom? Yes; I would like to see the Doctor urgently, she said. But there was no need to suggest urgently, there was only one other person waiting. Sure Mrs. Hollins; take a seat Mom and I'll go see the Doctor for you she said, oh! And tell him we're not here for treatment, yes mom; I'll tell him that. After a few minutes the receptionist return, they were sitting in the far corner of the waiting area, she walks over to them, the Doctor will see you shortly Mrs. Hollins she said very humbly, thank you said Mrs. Hollins; and the receptionist turns and walks back. But Florence makes no effort to find out her name; but it is obvious that this receptionist knew her very well; probably from the time when her husband was alive. They thought they would have to wait until the Doctor had seen the one waiting patient, but after about five minutes of waiting the receptionist walks over to them again, the Doctor will see you now Mom, she said. They approach the door and knock, come in Florence said the Doctor, she walked in; hello Florence said the Doctor who couldn't wait to greets her it seems. It's clear these two knew each other well; well enough to be on a first name basis. How are you Florence; long time no see, how are you Robert she said almost as though she doesn't care. How are you keeping these days Florence he asked facetiously, don't answer that he said; I can see you're keeping just fine. Well thank you Robert; you don't look too bad yourself she said pleasantly; and yes; I'm feeling quite fine she said. Then who's this young lady; A patient he asked, oh no! I'm sorry; pardon my manners Ammi, Robert! This is Ammi; the young woman who is trying to cares for everyone who is sick; the Good Samaritan you might say she said kind of sarcastically; and a very close friend of mine she said. Hi Ammi; good to meet you; so you're the do-gooder he asked; I hope he doesn't think I'm doing him out of patients by trying to help them she thought. I thought we should help the helpless if we can Doctor she replies; it was a good answer; of which Florence didn't think Ammi had within her. Well! Well done to you young lady; it refreshing to see someone as young as you hold such thought, thank you Doctor she said. But it seems this Doctor is a bit of a live wire too; and it appears he knew the Hollins family very well. Do you realise Florence that the last time I saw you were at Mark's funeral? How long is that now he asked, nearly five years she said, well, well, he repeats; and you never feel sick until now, well! I'm sorry to disappoint you Doctor but no, no I'm still not sick she said; neither does Ammi, we're here for someone else.

But the Doctor was in high spirit; maybe just for seeing Florence, so why are you here Florence; you have not just come to look at my ugly mug he said flippantly, Florence couldn't help but laugh, no Bob; but it's good to see you anyway; you always make me laugh she said. What we come about Bob; we would like you to visit a sick man who is moulded by a bull and he's in a bad way, it would be good if you could see him sometime today she said humbly. I don't know if I can today but let me checks, he then presses a button on the wall behind him; and in walks the receptionist. You rang Doc? Yes Helen; would you bring in the appointment book please, sure Doc, and she turns and walks back, a minute or so later she returns with the book. Here you are Doc she said; you want me to leave it with you? Yes Helen; give it here and you can go. Looking through the appointment book take a few minutes, Florence! I can do you for three-thirty today, would that do you? Sure Bob; that will be fine she said, but we'll have to come along with you to show you where she said, that's fine; but where should I meet you he asked. Well since you have to pass my house would you mind to call for us there? Oh sure; if you're still at the manor I'll call for you there about five o'clock, are you still at the manor he asked sarcastically, Florence looked at him and shook her head; same old Bob; always with the jokes. Yes Bob I'm still at the manor; and five o'clock will be just fine, we'll be waiting for you. It's so good to see you though Florence; and you're looking very well too; he must have forgotten he said that before; well thank you again Bob, Mark is dead but I'm very much still alive, of course you're Florence, of course you are, right! I'll see you later, he got to his feet to say goodbye. But as they were going through the door she turns and asks him; how is Doreen these days? Say hello to her for me she said. Well Florence I would love to but we're not together anymore, oh! Said Florence surprisingly, what happen she asked, well! She said she have found a better man; so she ran off with him he said with a smile, as though he didn't care, and for the first time Florence seem appear in sympathy with him. Oh Robert! I'm so sorry to hear she said ruefully, oh don't be; I'm not. But you two were so good together, well things are not always what they seem, he said; Florence you should know that he said as though he knew Florence used to suffer some kind of indignation behind the scene. Well! From their conversation he seems to know something about the Hollins history. With his stethoscope around his neck he got up and walk towards Florence, anyway that part of my life episode is now well and truly behind me, I'm a new man he said gleefully. He didn't prolong the conversation; with patients waiting he needed to get on with his work, any way Florence my dear you have a good day now; I'll see you later and you too Ammi he said.

Strolling home and enjoying the evening breeze Florence tell Ammi about the Doctor, he was our family Doctor and a good friend to Mark. There was never a dull moment when he's around, a free spirit we always said he was, but I never thought he and Doreen would separate, he seems a nice man though Mom said Ammi, I suppose he is she said. But Ammi hasn't got much to say on the matter other than those few words, she just listens while Florence tells talks about the Doctor and when her husband was alive. But what young woman approaching her fifteenth birthday would have to say about any such matters; but Florence feels she could talks to her about most anything, if she needs someone to gossip to Ammi is not that person; what she do good is listen; she won't be responding; and she's got nothing to gossip about. She continues about the Doctor, he's like a comedian; always makes us laugh, but we never keep in touch after the death of Mark. Well the truth is; after the death of my husband all the people who used to visit suddenly stop, including the Doctor, they weren't coming for my sake, no; they were Mark's people. But whether so or not the way the receptionist and the Doctor respond to her, they still hold some sort of respect for her Ammi thought. However one could see the old colonial way of life in action once again, the one person waiting before they got there to see the doctor was overlooked in preference to Mrs. Hollins, and that's how it is in the colony; and you don't have to be rich either, no; just very brown or mulitta colour; you'll always get preferential treatment. Back at the manor Florence tells the maid to inform Roland to look out for the Doctor, she won't want him to tarry when he comes calling for them. But the Doctor arrives sooner than she had expected, while she and Ammi were carrying on business as usual the maid comes to tell her the Doctor is here and he's coming up the pathway, it seems the Doctor wants to have a look at the place he usually visited or probably seeing Florence and knowing Mark is dead he might have something else in mind. Florence got up to meet him, he was still coming up the long pathway, and she stood by the door waiting for him. I thought I surprise you Florence he said as he approaches, it's a surprise alright; you haven't walked these paths for nearly five years, come in she said as she widens the door path.

As he steps in from the foyer into the big hall he begins to gaze around, nothing has changed since I been here last he said, I Remember getting drunk at the funeral reception and Doreen went home without me remember? Oh yes she said; So she did, but I also remember you were quite drunk and obnoxious, upset most of the guess; and after all Bob; it was my husband funeral reception, yes! I know; I was out of order; but I was drunk. So you were Bob; but you get yourself intoxicated; not anyone, well go on; tell me off he said, but in those days I couldn't resist the bottle. Tell me Bob she asked, at that moment what if someone wanted medical attention; would you attempt tending to them? He didn't respond; except reprimand himself, it looks bad doesn't it, he asked, yes Bob; quite bad she said. As a Doctor one should always keep a clear head, thank be to God I don't touch the stuff anymore, oh good, I'm pleased for you Bob she said. Well you must tell me what you been doing with yourself these days he said, It's hard to believe my surgery is within walking distance of here and from the death of Mark it's the first time I walk back in this house, there's got to be an explanation he said. Oh yes, there's an explanation alright, I never thought I could go on living without Mark so I became a recluse, I haven't been out of this house for over three years; thanks to Mary who do everything for me; without her I don't know how I would manage She paused and look at the clock on the wall, shouldn't we be going now? Oh yes; we better get moving he said. But where's your little friend he ask, she looks at him sorrowfully, Bob, she's not my little friend; she's Ammi; and she and her family is the best thing ever happen to me since the death of my husband, please remember that Bob she said with some venom. She didn't appreciate the term little friend, he was taken aback by the way in which she reprimanded him. Oh I'm so sorry Flo he said; you know me;

always with the jokes; let's make a move he said trying to end that line of conversation.

Florence went and get Ammi, hello again Ammi said the Doctor as she walks into the hall, hello Doctor she said, then Florence ask the Doctor if Ammi bicycle can hold in his gar booth, he was very cooperative, I'm sure it can my dear he said. Then they set off toward the car; the Doctor fitted the bicycle into the booth, and they set off on their way. While driving the Doctor is curious to know why she's paying for this man to be treated, is this person a family member he asks, to be honest I never met him before until yesterday, Ammi found him injured by the roadside; he's been gored by a bull; and Ammi been Ammi she's been taking care of him ever since. But I went with her yesterday and to see the poor man in so much pain I couldn't forgive myself if I didn't do something to help him. The Doctor seems amazed, I must say Florence I didn't think you have that kind human sympathy in you, that's really decent of you. But Florence will have none of it, oh no! This young lady is the one with the human kindness, she's not only caring for this poor man but she talking care of others too, and without pay I might add, she is to be commended. Well who ask you to nurse these people Ammi ask the Doctor, no one Sir; but I know these people very well she said, then what about the older people in the district; why can't they help he ask. Bob you don't understand said Florence; in a district like these is every man for himself, people knows you when you're on your feet; not when you're sick and need help, that's why it's good to have a family. I think I beginning to understand now said the Doctor, but for one so young to take on such responsibilities; that can't be right somehow. I blame her parents though; for allowing her to take such responsibilities. Have you ever consider been a nurse career Ammi he ask, no Doctor she said, it seems to me that's profession you should consider and I think you and your parent should give it some thought he said, and if you were to consider it as a profession I could lay the groundwork for you he said. Thank you Doc, but I'm a dressmaker; and I never considered being a nurse, but the Doctor suddenly seems to take an interest in her; he would like to have a talk with her parent regarding her been a nurse, but will he? Only time will tell. They reach their destination, the state of the place doesn't surprise the Doctor at all; he's been call to places like this from time to time. He examines Mr. Perry and then gives him an injection, he then calls the two women aside for consultation. He makes it clear he can't do much more for him; he's too badly beaten up inside. The injection is to ease the pain and he'll leave some pills and medicine to give to him, but he warns them his condition is only going to get worse. What are you saying Bob; he's going to die? asked Florence. Well I'm sorry to say; but yes; I'm too late to do any good. When should I give him the medication Doc. asks Ammi, she's a right little Miss Florence nightingale isn't she Flo. Asked the Doctor, she most certainly is she said. Then he wrote on a sheet of paper the dosage and gives it to Ammi. He's about to leave, will it take you long to get home from here Ammi he ask, he was thinking probable he should take her home; oh no Doctor she said; just a few minutes; I'll home long before you sir, well you try and get home she said, don't stay too long here; there's nothing more you can do. I won't Doc; as soon as I get my things together I'll be off. Then I suppose I'll be taking you back Florence he asked, yes thank you Bob; if you think you can manage; well as you can see the car is full but I'll try squeezes you in he said facetiously smiling broadly, I think you're in the wrong profession Bob she said. Good night Ammi he said, remember what I said, good night Doc, and thank you. See you in the morning Ammi said Florence; and don't stop here too long now, no Mom; I won't be. Ok Bob! I'm ready if you are she said, I'm ready he said, she had a quick chat with Ammi from the comfort of the car front seat, the Doctor then drove away.

It's nearly eight o'clock but the evening is reasonable bright, Ammi will stay with the patient for a while and gives him his last dose of medicine. However she won't wait until it gets dark before she leaves; she won't want a telling off from her father. So she makes him as comfortable as possible then leave, she'll look in on him again in the morning. When she gets home she tells her father that Florence has taken the Doctor to see Mr. Perry, but his condition remains critical, the Doctor hasn't given him much hope; he's too badly beaten up inside. Once again John was surprised of the interest Florence has taken in this man, he begins to looks at her in a different light; this woman is really a good person he thought, and she's got a heart of gold. But Agnes is not too happy that Ammi should be shouldering such burden at her young shoulder. She once before told John he should speak to the Pastor about getting his followers to do what Ammi is doing, he should be the one setting the example and not leaving it up to a teenager. The man should be ashamed of himself she said; calling himself a Pastor. It's written in his bible that they should help the weak and needy; how could he not tell his followers to do what the good book said, these people needed help and they turn a blind eye, she was most critical of them. I promise to talk to the Pastor and I will come Sunday said John, I don't want to be critical John; but you said you would last time and you didn't, did you forget? Yes, unfortunately; but come

Sunday I sure will, take my word he said. Thursday morning when Ammi look in on Mr. Perry she couldn't see any changes in his condition; he wasn't groaning as much as before but there was a strange look about him. However she give him his medication and then feed him something to eat, but he's not keeping it down; he'll be bringing it back up and there'll be no one there to clean him up, he'll be alone until Ammi return later that evening. Back at her place of work Florence wants to know how the patient, there is little or no changes in his condition Mom, if anything he seems to be getting worse. Well we've done whatever we can for him let's hope he pull through she said.

She was wondering to herself how much Miss Florence pays the Doctor to treat Mr. Perry; but she certainly not going to ask. Sunday was one of those pleasant days and a busy time in the Thomas's household; after breakfast the family is busy getting dress for church, but Ammi have already up and away to see Mr. Perry and Mr. Wilson, and return in time to visit Mrs. Brown; she'll take breakfast for her and see to her needs before leaving for church. But Mrs. Brown is not looking too good either; who will survive longer she or Mr. Perry; only time will tell. These people need regular more care and attention of which Ammi can't give them, they're just barely alive. At church John has done what he said he would; he raised the matter with the Pastor before church commences, he (pastor) was in full agreement with him about the matter, today this will be the theme of his sermon. He tells his brethren they should be more aware of what's happening around them, in this little district where everyone knows everyone they do know when anyone is sick; and they should try to help them when they can't help themselves, you should make it your duty to help those who can't help themselves he told them. We're Christians and as such those are the things we should do; it right in the sight of God. We should always be mindful of the Ten Commandments; and one the commandment said to help those who can't help themselves. So we're going to start from today brethren's; we're going to do what's right in the sight of God. He then calls Ammi to the rostrum; and with she standing next to him he tells his congregation what Sister Ammi has been doing, she's a shining light in this little community he said. Let look at ourselves Sisters and Brothers; Sister Ammi is a teenager and taken up such responsibility; and here we are; Christians and adults and we turn a blind eye. It that mean we don't care about the needs of these sick people? I don't think so; we just didn't notice. But from now on we're going to pay full attention and help in every way we can; right Sisters and Brothers? And there was a loud amen of agreement from the Brethren's. Then he turns to Ammi; tell us what you been doing sister Ammi he asked, then she outline to the congregation what been happening with the people she's been looking after, and there're others she said; but I can't reach them. Did you hear that Sisters and Brothers; she's far too young to be shouldering such burden, we shouldn't be feeling good within ourselves today; no; in fact we should be a shame. But now we're going to do something about it, we're going to arrange between ourselves how to go about helping, they all agreed. That very Sunday the Brethren's have put a plan in place, they'll visit all the people who're ill. But how long will they carry it through; only time can tell, most of these Brethren's are not really sincere Christian, no; they just like the idea.

After church that Sunday evening Florence was having dinner with the Thomas; something she do quite often now a day; of course John is now like a father figure to her, their love affair is a thing of the pass. During dinner John has a brainwave, he told the family that he thinks he should bring the situation here to the attention of the local Member-of-parliament, they should be made aware of the situation here regarding these sick people. During the election they canvassing for our votes but now they have completely forgotten about us, that cannot be right, what do you think about me going to see the Minister Aggie he asked But Agnes is not too keen about it; party politics is a dangerous business to get mixed up in she said. What she was getting at is, if people know the party you vote for or affiliate to it can cause conflict and sometimes leads to something more sinister. In some case, there is confrontation between party supporters; which in many cases people got badly injure or even lost their lives. But I'm not going to see him to talk party Politics said John; I'm going to talk him about these sick people, Yes! said Agnes; But people see you coming out of his office they are not going to think you're on a mission of mercy, no; they're going to believe what they want to believe; you're one of his supporter. Nonsense said John; his responsibility is to everyone regardless of their politics. But Agnes wasn't satisfied, what do you think about that Florence she asked, I think John is right Agnes, he supposed to deals with everyone regardless of their political belief she said, she wasn't too agreeable with Florence response, well I hope what you intend to do won't put this family in any danger she said. But John put his intention on hold for a while. In the meantime the Brethren's are do as promised; tend the sick. But as Agnes thought; their efforts were short live, after a few weeks they complain of too much to do; and it wasn't long before their efforts come to an end. They've been castigated by their Pastor who told them they should be ashamed of themselves, but there's little he can do to; he can't force them to do what they don't want to do. However he wouldn't to cities them too much, no; he doesn't want to lose their attendance, no preacher wants to see his congregation dwindled. So this hypocritical man who calls himself a Pastor lay the matter to rest; his Brethren's will never hear anything more about the thing they should be doing; at least not in the same way as he did before. They are just like the rest of the non-church goers here; they only take care of themselves, and Ammi was left to continue her solo effort.

10: The Visit

John has decided to start a kind of crusade; ignoring the warning of his wife he's going to see the Government minister, he never been to see a government Minister before; he had no reason to, but come Saturday accompanied by his daughter he's going see him regarding the plight of the sick people in the district. But they won't be alone, no; Florence has decided to go along with them, an offer that John was very thankful for. He has no idea as to where the Minister office location except he knows it's in town, and it shouldn't hard to find. The plan is to get there before midday; but he has to collect Florence on the way, so they will leave a little earlier than they would like. Agnes tells them to be careful; she still doesn't like the idea of them going one little bit; nevertheless she wishes them good luck. There's no need to plan any strategy; they will simply tell the Minister the way the situation is in the district and how these sick people are suffering; and hope that their complaint won't fall on deft ears. It was around eleven o'clock on Saturday when they set off to collect Florence, she was ready and waiting. When John got there the gate was open so he drove right in; and so Ammi went to get her while he waits in the car. It wasn't long before they come walking down the long passageway with the maid behind them, maybe Roland is not about and she's coming to closed the gate. Good morning Sir said Mary as she approaches, good morning Mary he said; she stood waiting to close the gate behind them. They set off, do you know where about is the Minister's office John ask Florence, well no! But I thought you would, no I don't John; I don't think I ever met the man; my husband probably would have known him. Well I know of him; but I can't remember his name; and I should; I was at one of his meetings when a couple of hagglers want to break up his meeting; I had was to intervene he said. What did you John; beat them up asked Florence flippantly; don't be silly; I just quietly asked them to stop; and they did. Anyway his office shouldn't be too hard to find he's a public servant; he should have a large sign up somewhere saying so he said.

The town is a small one but it's very busy, He parks his car and make sure all doors are lock, any chance these pickpockets have they'll break into your car, they then headed out in search of the Minister's office. But it wasn't hard to find; there was a sizable sign saying

Government office, they make for it. Entering the office there was a young woman sitting at a desk reading the Gleaner newspaper, they presumed she was some kind of a receptionist; they look around and there were five people waiting. John approaches the desk, good morning young lady he said, good morning Sir; can I help you Sir she ask, we would like to speak with the Minister he said pointing to his two companions. You can Sir but there're all those people before you, oh! We can wait he said. What's your name Sir she asks, Mr. Thomas, John Thomas he said, ok Mr. Thomas take a seat, he walks back to join the women. What are we doing John Florence ask, we're waiting so let's make ourselves comfortable; all those people are before us he said. He takes a seat next to Ammi on the long beach; it's going to be a long wait it seems he said. But Florence was to get a sudden surprise which changes everything, one of her husband one-time friend walks in, she was surprised to see her as much as Florence was to see her. Flo! Flo Hollins she exclaims in a loud voice, good heavens; fancy running into you here, where on earth have you been hiding she asked gleefully. But it seems Florence wasn't as pleased to see her; surprised! Yes; but please! No. It appears she wishes she didn't have to talk to her. Hiding Carron? Why do you think I'm hiding; if I'm hiding I'm at the same place you left me the last time she said she said with hostility. I think the last time I saw you were at Mark's funeral, oh! It's a long time ago Flo she said, and you never consider to visit the house again said Florence, oh! So much had happened since Flo; you know how it is she said, no Carron; I don't know how it is; why don't you tell me. But whatever it is Carron didn't seem be prepared to discuss it, at least not in front of two other people. Anyway it's so good to see you Flo; I always think about you, you're here to see Donald I take it she asked. Who the bloody hell is Donald asked Florence, John looks at her curiously as to say there's no reason to swear, realising what she just said; she apologised; not to Carron, no; to John and Ammi, I'm so sorry John she said with her hands over her mouth. Donald Faster she said; your Member of Parliament; don't you know him she asks, no! I heard of him but never met him. So how are you keeping these days Flo; you're looking very well; and aren't you going to introduce me to your friends? Flo thought the cheek of the woman; she only just notices the people sitting with me. They're not my friends; they're my family; is there anything else you want to know?. John thought; whatever happens between these two women it's not healthy for them to meet; Florence seems to be holding anger for this person.

John observed Florence was getting rumpled so he interrupts, so Carron you live here in town he ask; of course Carron doesn't know his name; Florence didn't introduce them; all she said they were her family. No, I only come to see Donald; I live in Merryville; you know Merryville Mr.; she paused waiting for a name; Mr. Thomas; oh! And this is my daughter Ammi. Hello Ammi she said with her hand outstretched to greet her; I'm Carron, good to meet you Mom said Ammi. I heard of Merryville said John; but never been there, is it far from here? Not too far; about half an hour drive. Well it's good to meet you Mr. Thomas she said, Flo dear I would love to talk longer but time is of the essence, good to see you too Carron said Florence without any sincerity, she's glad to see the back of her. She then talks with the receptionist who then got up and went directly to the office, presumably to tell Donald Carron is here, she returns promptly; minutes later a client emerges from the office, it seems Donald hurriedly concluded business with him to accommodate Carron. This Carron is a white woman; she's no doubt amongst the elites here, in these Islands what white people want white people get. You can go in now Miss Carron said the receptionist, but whatever business they have it never takes long, she was back out shortly. Flo dear; I must dash and I must come and see you one day soon. Are you still living at the manor she ask, Florence hesitates and gives her grievous glare; she probably was thinking of something horrible to say to her. Oh yes! But I'm thinking of moving soon she said, that comment was more of an insult but Carron doesn't know it. But where would you go dear? Are you thinking of selling up? But Florence had enough of Carron, Have a good day Carron she said; I must talk with the receptionist; and she got up and walk toward the desk. Well Carron seems to take the hint; she said goodbye to John and Ammi and leaves. As she went through the door Florence walks back, that woman gets me so mad I could throttle her, she's a dirty hypocrite; I don't want to be anywhere near her if I can help it she said. I can see you're angry and only you know why said John; but don't let it gets to you. I'll try not to John; but from the mere fact she come talking to me just make me mad, anyway calm down now; she's gone he said. Of all the time they knew each other John never seem her so angry; there must be something rather bad that Carron has done within the once family that gets Florence so mad; he thought.

It seems as though Carron tells the Minister that her old friend Mrs. Hollins is waiting to see him, the receptionist approaches them; Mrs. Hollins the Minister will see you now Mom she said, when they got up to go John have a look to see the people who were there first. They didn't seem happy that they were there long before Florence and friends and they got seen to before them, however John thought it's a good job Florence come along; otherwise they would have a long wait. The door was left open for them to enter; the Minister must have thought she was alone. As they approach the door, he calls; come in Mrs. Hollins; come in he said repeatedly, they all entered; and it was obvious he didn't expect anyone else other than Florence; oh he exclaims looking somewhat surprised. Good afternoon Minister she said, however it was approaching two o'clock, good evening Mrs. Hollins; I thought you were alone, oh no she said; they're my family, he's Mr. Thomas and his daughter Ammi. Good afternoon John and hello Ammi he said; please take a seat; Mrs. Hollins you sit here; he pulls up a chair close to his desk for her. Now they're all seated his attention was focus directly on Florence. You don't remember me Mrs. Hollins do you he ask, should I minister? Not especially; but I been to Mark's funeral and I was also at the reception, a nice and a good man Mark he said, I think so Minister and I'm glad you think so too. He's been talking mostly to Florence but his eyes catch something about John. Have we met Mr. Thomas he asks, not formally, no; but I been to your meeting once or twice when you were canvassing in the district. Which district is that Sir he asked curiously, Danville; just over four miles from here, but he keeps looking at him; tell me Sir; what's your first name; John he said, then the Minister stood up and walk from behind his desk towards John, I know who you are now he said, you're the man who saved me from what could be an awkward situation and I never see you again to thank you. But why didn't you say Sir when you walked in, well Minister I couldn't very well walk into your office and said; you remember Minister; I was the man who saved you from a moulding, no Sir, that would sound as though I was bragging. Anyway people shouldn't stand back and allow the hooligans to take over, well Sir let me shake you by the hand and thank you; thank you very much. Now Mrs. Hollins what can I do for you? Well it's about some sick and needy people in the district; they're dying prematurely because of lack of attention and proper medical treatment. But firstly let me ask you Minister have ever been back to Danville from the time you won the election? That sort of a question he wasn't expecting and one he would rather not ask. But of course only someone like Florence would ask such a question; someone with influence.

That question is to let me look bad he said; and I deserve it, no Mrs. Hollins I haven't been back there; and I know it's a shame; but I'm glad you bring to my attention whatever going on there so please; enlighten me. Well Ammi could tell you more than I can; but maybe I can explain it better, the people there are dying; dying because of lack of medical attention, your government had given up on them; they're old before their time; you can't help that but you certainly could help the ones that are sick to gets care and attention. Ammi has just turned fifteen and training to be a dressmaker; and she took it upon herself to caring for those people; and no one asks her to; and without pay I might add. The Minister looks a little bemused; and you Mr. Thomas; that is how you see it too he asks. John takes a deep breath; Mrs. Hollins say how it is and there're lots more, one thing about these people even though they're living on the bread line you'll never hear them complain, no Sir; they're too proud to do that. But that doesn't mean they don't need help; they most certainly do he said. You've painted a dreadful picture said Mr. Thomas, and I know I shouldn't but I'm amazed and totally ashamed, but what has been brought to my attention today will most certainly be reported to my government; and you can rest assured that something will be done. What I can't tell you is how soon, but Sir; let me tell you; I'm going to push hard; very hard Sir to get things moving. Thank you for your assurance Minister; but I'm a doubtful person; and no disrespect; but until I see something been done I'm not going to hold my breath. Can't say I blame you Sir said the Minister, but I'm going to give this matter total priority, yes Sir; something will be done. Well the Minister appear sincere with his promise; but like his predecessors; when they get into office they totally forget the promises they made and the people who put them there, so there's nothing new in that regards. But tell me Minister; have you ever consider visiting your constituencies to see how the people live asked Florence, Mrs. Hollins! I dreaded to answer your question; it's only going let me feel more ashamed, but I'll say this, it's good that people like you bring such matter to my attention so that I can report it to my Government, there should be more people like you doing the same. He paused with a little smile, So you're the Good Samaritan young lady he asked looking at Ammi, yes Sir she said selfishly. But why do you care so much for these people; did they ask you to? No Sir; I just thought they need help Sir she said, well Young lady! You should be commended; I wish there were more young people like you here in this country of ours.

After hearing the history about the district and it's residences the Minister was rather sympathetic to their cause, well Sir he said looking at John; it's good thing the three of you have done, without information like what you've told me I have no knowledge of what goes on in districts like yours, and we who are in Government shouldn't allow situation to gets as bad. We should have representative there to tell us, and I'm sorry if it seems as though once in office we abandon the electorate, but your Government is going through a difficult time at present; and I know that shouldn't be an excuse for not knowing what you're telling me; but that's how things are at present. Nevertheless what you have brought to my attention will never get ignore; something must be done and quick, and starting from now with your help; together we'll help those people. He sounds like he was giving a lecture; or trying to remove any criticism from himself, nevertheless what he was saying was true. Well how can we help Minister ask Florence, Ammi has done what she can and is still doing it; we're just here to tell what she's doing and it can't go on. Right now Mrs. Hollins! I don't know; but I'll think on it, but there's something the people of the district can help me with, like report anything they think need government attention, just as you have done, but let me think on that he said. But Florence is not completely satisfied, If it's information you requires about the sick Minister then Ammi will tell you all you need to know she said, that would be helpful, come on now young Ammi; fills me in he said cheerfully while opening a huge note pad; and he recorded Ammi's report. It seems to me that you would make a wonderful nurse Ammi; is that the profession you're considering he ask, oh no! Said John; she will soon be a qualified dressmaker; she's been trained by Mrs. Hollins here, and a darn good one she's going to be to Florence interject. The Minister makes a sighing grunt; he seems to think like the Doctor she's in the wrong business. So you like to makes dresses young lady ask the minister, yes Sir; I like it very much she said, but wouldn't you rather be a nurse? You're taking care of sick people that is a part of nursing too he said, she has made her choice Minister; and as Mrs. Hollins said; she's going to be good at it said John. Well if ever you have a change of mind Ammi and want to go into nursing please don't hesitate come and see me; I might able to pull a string or two for you, thank you Minister said John we'll keep your offer in mind.

However this's what I would like you to do for me Mr. Thomas, I going to jump the gun on this occasion; I'm not going to wait until I converse with my Government; the picture you paint seem fat to grave to delay. I'm considering sending carers to take over from young Ammi; can't say how many as yet. But first I would like to send a representative to see you about the details, and you folks can tell him all he needs to know so he can set up a workforce, you think you could do that Mr. Thomas he asks. Well Sir that question should be put to Ammi; she the one who knows everything. Then how about it Ammi? Could you tell this gentleman all he needs to know? I certainly can Minister, anything to ease the suffering of those poor people. Good! That's settled, should we say around about Saturday next about midday then Mr. Thomas? "Well the Minister chooses Saturday as he knows that's when most people will be at home". Saturday is good said John, but what's the name of your representative he asks, his name's David Dunn; a pleasant fellow like me he said flippantly, well! He was feeling kind of self-assured, but unfortunately for him the visiting party didn't see the funny side of his little comedy. Their business concluded and they are about to leave, but the Minister all through their conversation he having a sneaky peek at Florence, it was obvious there was an attraction. So Mrs. Hollins! I never see you at any of my meetings during canvassing; I do hope I have your support, why Minister? Are you having another election so soon she asks sarcastically? Oh no! He said smiles; a badly put question; I'm sorry, what I meant and I shouldn't be asking you; but do you support my party. "But the Minister fancies her but he hasn't got a good chat-up line; right now he's making a fool of himself". Well why you ask; since you know you shouldn't ask Florence, I'm sorry Mrs. Hollins to be going around the houses; what I want to ask is; could I see you again. But before she answers she glances back to see if John and Ammi was still standing there at the door; but they had walked away and now in the waiting area. John realised that the Minister wants to talk to Florence alone so they gave them space. She looks backs at him, maybe she said; but I've to think about it. Oh good! I look forward to see he said; but where? You can call at my house but only on Saturdays she said, Well he didn't ask why on Saturday only; he seems quite happy to accept any condition as long as he can see her, she bid goodbye and leave. However it's not a one-way street; she wasn't averse to his advances.

But John had a strong feeling that this Politician would be attracted to Florence; of course he would; any red-blooded man would. He also thought this politician Mr. faster is not a bad looking fellow and probably could be the man for her. A bit on the fairer side of black but a man of standing and a good stature, if he could pull Florence and it leads to marriage he would land on his feet; and would stand him in good stead for his political career, and it seems she's not averse to his advances either. John was ready it seems to give the Politician a hand if he was after romance with Florence; and if he read the cards right that's what he's after. Florence joins the others outside, why did you walk away she asks John; that wasn't nice at all, oh come on now, what would we be doing standing there, the Minister wanted a private conversation with you not with me and Ammi. Anyway I could be wrong; but I think he's a nice fellow, what's that got to do with anything she asked, well I see the way he looked at you; or are you going to tell me you didn't notice? I did notice; but so what? So that's why I walk away; I think he's a nice fellow. Well you can have him them she said facetiously, don't talk so silly said John; I mean he could be good for you, so you're matchmaking now are you John? No; I'm only saying, he strikes me as a nice well-meaning fellow. In other words; what you're saying John I should talk to him; did I say that he asked kind of suggestively. Well Florence didn't tell him that she had agreed for the Minister to call on her; she withholds that bit of information.

But Florence will listen to any directive from John; she now sees him now as a father figure, and the coming months ahead will be a turning point in her life. There was an air of hush on the way home and it was only a short drive to Florence home, she would like John and Ammi to stop for dinner but they decline, but it doesn't matter; tomorrow however after church she'll be having dinner with them. When they got home Agnes wanted to know of their encounter with the minister; did anyone see you going in or leaving his office she asked; still weary of the dancer to her family if anyone thinks her husband and family support the Minister's party. Well yes! There were plenty of people about and everyone sees us he said sarcastically, Agnes he said you're painting these people blacker than they are, you're too judgemental about them and don't forget we're living here too. But Agnes wasn't painting a too bleaker picture at all; no; she was just been cautious. "The conversation continues" But taking everything in account John was pleased with their day's work; he only hoped that this Minister is a man of his words.

11: The Minister's Envoy

Nothing strange new or untoward happened in the past few weeks, life continues as normal, until one bright Saturday evening John was studding his bible, Agnes was doing dinner and the children; well the children were about. The big bulldog Brutus begins barking, he likes blood, his master John is a part-time butcher, he didn't do it himself he only supervised it. But Brutus wasn't going anywhere; he was on his leash; but Beany the little one runs to the gate barking, it's a sign of someone entering the yard. John sitting on the long family bench outside the back of the house went to see who. There was no build gate just two hedges of privet either side of the entrance to the yard, there was a man standing there; it seem he's afraid to enter because of the dogs. But the little fellow minty never stop barking; however he's harmless; all he does is to alert big vicious Brutus. Hello! The man shouts, Mr. Thomas he asked, yes! I'm Mr. Thomas; and you; who might you be John ask, I'm Mr. Dunn Sir, Dave Dunn; and I'm a representative of the Minister Mr. Faster. He send me to talk with you Sir; I hope it's convenient, oh no; not at all; come on in; I've been expecting you from last week he said, sorry Sir; I was away. They walk toward the house, minty cease barking but Brutus sees a new person and began to keep bark. But one command from his master and he quiet, don't worry Mr. Dunn you're safe, I'm not a dog lover I must tell you Mr. Thomas; I'm quite nervous around them, well you're quite safe here; don't you worry said John. As it was a warm evening John took him to the back of the house where they would be comfortable sitting on the family bench in the shade. There was none of the children in sight except for Ammi who was doing her usual patching and darning for the local. The men make themselves comfortable, So what can I do for you Mr. Dunn? Well Sir! The Minister told me of events here and about the job your daughter has taken upon herself to do, and I must tell you Sir I was most in awe of what the Minister told me she's doing. Opening his briefcase; her name is… he pauses looking at his notes, Ammi said John, forgive me Sir; I'm terrible on manes, but a wonderful young woman; is she here Sir; I would like to meet her; yes; she's about somewhere he said. Then I would like to talk with her Sir if you don't mind, would that be possible sir? I don't see why not said John, oh good! Then let me tell you what the Minister wants me and you to arrange.

We've got two nurses lines up to take over from your daughter and if she would; we would like her to introduce these nurses to the patients and scrutinised their work, we will get someone to do it in the long run. This measure is only for a month for the good of the patients; they might not react too well to strangers; but Ammi could introduce as a friend. And a good idea is that said John; but she can only do that in the evening said John; that's when she finishes sewing; that I was told Sir; and that would be alright if she could do it for the month. John thinks it over, he thought it's not a bad idea; but Ammi is the one to decide if she can do it. Well let's get Ammi and hear what she thinks of the idea said John, would you like something cool to drink Mr. Dunn? He asked as he was about to leaves, yes thank you; anything cool he said, he then went to ask Agnes to provide some refreshments. Ammi was in the house doing her needlework as usual, she knew her father had a visitor but didn't try to find out whom. Come on out here Ammi; there's someone here to see you he said, to see me Dad she ask surprisingly, yes! To see you; come along, they went back to join Mr. Bunn. As they were approaching he suspects that this is the young woman in question, this is Ammi I presume he said raised to his feet with his hand extended to greets her, how are you young lady he asks, I'm fine Sir she said, at the same time Agnes Arrives with drinks. She was introduced to the government man, hello Mrs. Thomas he said exuberantly, and thanks for the drinks Mom, oh don't mention it; you're welcome, and she returns to her chores. Now then young Ammi; we have a proposition for you; you remember your meeting with Mr. Faster; the Government man? Yes Sir, well! He would like you to help him out for one month. Well you're going to stop caring for your patients; there're two carers who are going to take over from you; but we would like you to introduce them to the patients and supervise them for one month; could you do that Ammi? Yes Sir I could; but I only could do so in the evening, yes Ammi; I know; your father told me, but that would be alright; you'll just make sure the carers are caring for these people properly. Then I suppose that would be alright Sir she said.

But the big surprise is yet to come, we're not going to let you work for nothing though Ammi like you been doing he said, no; not anymore, you'll receive one month's pay for overseeing the carers; and it doesn't end there either; and this is what the Minister told me to do. See to it that young Ammi gets twenty five pounds, he reaches into his briefcase and brings out an envelope; he handed it to her. This Government is beholding to you for what you have done Ammi, on behalf of the Government thank you. Her father stands tall when he heard all that praise heaps on his daughter. But financial compensation was the last thing on their mind or expected; and to receive twenty-five pounds; that amount of money is like a windfall. Well thank you and thank the Minister for us said John, it's good to know that the Minister thinks the job that Ammi had done need rewarding, we thank him very much. But the Minister was doing this thing to also let him looks good in the eyes of both John and Florence, he wants them to think of him as a good man; that will help to boost his chances with Florence. Then when will the carers be taking over ask John, we would like them to come here and see Ammi first, we would like her to take them and introduce them to the patients; just to assure them; could you do that Ammi? Yes Sir I can; just let me know when they're coming. He open his ledger and looks through it, how about Monday morning say about nine o'clock; would that be good for you Ammi he ask, "her father looks at her as though he's got an objection, but only to observes his daughter's reaction. It can't do Monday Sir; I have to go training and Miss Florence is expecting me, but I could take Tuesday off. Well Tuesday it is then at nine o'clock said Mr. Dunn, they'll be here promptly. Business is concluded and Mr. Dunn is about to leave, he walks down to the kitchen which is separate from the house to say goodbye to Mrs. Thomas. Goodbye Mom he said extending his hand for a shake, wiping her hands on her apron before extending; good to meet you Mr... she paused; she wasn't told his name when she brought him drinks, Dunn Mom; Dave Dunn, good to meet you Mom; and thanks again for the drink, think nothing of it young man, you have a good evening now; and forgive my smelly hands she said, oh that's alright Mom; I'm not bothered, and off he went.

At dinner John tells the family of his and Ammi encounter with the Government man, "oh the term Government man is a term the locals used for someone from the government even though they might know his name". When he told them about the money Ammi received Maggie become sort of red eyes; she wanted to do some caring work too. But John puts her right, Ammi didn't do what she did to be paid; she was helping those who couldn't help themselves; and because no one else here couldn't be bothered. But fortunately for her the Minister think highly of the service she has provided he decided to reward her for it. You get your mind away from that and concentrate on your education, Sorry dad; I knew but I was just thinking of the money. But what are we going do with all that money she asked, this money belonging to Ammi and we're not going to do anything with it; it will be going to the bank as soon as I have time to take it there. But Ammi being Ammi comments, the money belongs to the family Dad not just me, Agnes looks at her in admiration but says nothing.

Life in these part is habitual; nothing changes from day to day, in the morning the ones with their small farms will heads out to their cultivation and there they will spend the entire day working. Tomorrow and every day after they will do the same all over again, but Sunday is a day of rest; and even though they're not all Christians they would all observe the Sabbath. They would down tools and rest, and even the ones who cannot read and most of them are; but they would tell you that commandment, honour the seventh day and keep it holy, of course they heard it from somewhere. Monday Ammi informs Florence about the Government man visit and the arrangement they made; and she would like to take the rest of the week off. Florence wasn't too happy about it but she knows it's for a good purpose. Ok Ammi; but don't work yourself into the ground, I know you're young and energetic but try not to overdo it, no Mom I won't. Tuesday morning as promise the two carers turn up at the Thomas's home to call on Ammi, she's ready and waiting, they introduced themselves and without delay they set off to their tasks. On the way Ammi fill them in with the situation, some of these patients alive but only just she told them; she is hoping that these carers will do so much better than she was doing; after all they're full-time carers. The day went well; Ammi let it be known to them that these two nice people will be caring for them from now on, everyone was reasonably pleased except poor old Mr. Wilson; he didn't want any new people caring for him; one of those miserable old folks who doesn't appreciate changes. I won't have them touching me he said, why can't you do it Miss Ammi, you see that one; I don't like her; she's the devil he said pointing to the brown carer. Well his head is not always in the right place whispered Ammi to the carer; and at times he can be quite cantankerous and would lash out too, but it's all intentional. But Ammi calms him down; I'm not leaving you yet Mr. Wilson she said. But the carers are very good at what they do; they handle all the antagonism from patients like Mr. Wilson and Ferris in a humane manner. Ferris a young man but look very old; he arrived in the district like many others without a family, he's been known by no other name except Farris; and whether that's his Christian or Sir name no one knows. He was fallen from a tree and broke both legs; people have it to say he was stealing coconuts. The week is over and Ammi writes a good report about the carers, she tells her father these carers are good workers but she doesn't believe poor Mr. Perry is going to last much longer, he can't keep anything down; food or water and he's very weak. Well you've done your best said Agnes; and when men on earth have done their best angels in heaven can do no better, a quote from the good book. Monday Ammi will be back with Florence; and in the evening after work she'll look in on the carers to oversee their work. But she's satisfied with their work, and if they continue in the same vein; at the end of the month she'll put in a very good report about them.

On Friday evening when Ammi turns up the carers were at Mr. Perry's home; they were standing outside; but the look on their face speaks a thousand word, Ammi knew the worst had happened. The carers told her that Mr. Perry had passed away some two hours ago, of course she wasn't surprised; it wasn't unexpected; and it's probably a relief; the poor man was suffering terribly. Ammi went in to look at him, he almost has a smile on his face; and the carers clean him up and he looks presentable, she told her father when she went home that poor Mr. Perry was looking peaceful. But her father had time to reflect on this man illness, he was aggrieved; it's a crying shame that people like him had to die prematurely he said. This man probably could have lived if he had proper medical treatment from the offset, but up till the people here are forgotten by their Government, and this situation is not related to our district alone, no; it's indicative to what's happening all over the Country. What do we do now Dad asked Ammi; he's got no one to take charge of his funeral, well! You'll make out a report to the Government man; it's should be his job o deals with it. But Ammi appeared concerned, she wasn't quite satisfied or sure that the Government man would deal with the situation, her father notices her concern. Speaking fatherly like Ammi he said; don't worry; you've done whatever you can; there's nothing more you can do; Mr. Parry will get buried, she acknowledged her father's words. He'll get buried alright; and you don't have to have money to get buried here, no; it's almost as though the people of the district look forward to people dying, they love a funeral. The locals will give him a good burial of their own; they'll build a coffin and bury him on his plot of land, that's how it is here without Government intervention. Well Ammi time is up; her one-month supervision of the carers is over; now she must make out her report to the Government man. He was satisfied with the report he received; and he paid her for her service and wished her all the best for the future in her dressmaking profession.

12: The Visitor

Around about three-thirty one Wednesday evening the Government man, Mr. Faster wants an audience with Mrs. Hollins, he was told he can visit but only on Saturdays; but it seems his anxiety to woo her gets the better of him. He turns up at the gate but no one was there, he did the only thing he can to alert someone attention, he rattles the iron bars, he then wait a while before Roland appears. He needs no introduction; Roland knew who he is, I would like to speak with Mrs. Hollins said the Minister, oh yes Sir said Roland respectfully; I'll go and tell her Sir, he hurries off but without opens the gate. But she wasn't surprised to hear the Government man come to see her, in fact she was more like pleased. She tells him to show the Minister in; Roland went back and did just that. The Minister walks kind of hastily along the long passageway, it's not strange to him; he walked it once or twice before when he was invited to function before the death of her husband. The maid would normally open the door to a visitor; but she chose to do it herself, she was waiting for him at the door. Good evening Mrs. Hollins he said kind of doubtfully; good evening Minister she replies, what brings you here? Well Mrs. Hollins you did say I could call on you; so here I am, yes! But I did say on a Saturday, but now you're here what can I do for you? Well as one of my most important constituent I would like to know more about you, more about me Minister; but you don't know anything at all about me she said in a rough tone as though the question was impertinent. quite right he said; that was wrongly put; what I should have said I really fancy you and that's why I'm here, she smiles ruefully as to say; you're a politician and not a bad looking fellow; but it seems you know nothing about women. Well he's short on tact and obviously hasn't got a chat-up line, the man wants this woman and it seems to be that he's in a hurry. But she fancies him too but obviously he doesn't know, but she was holding her cards close to her chess and playing the hard to get game. Well he got as far as the big hall and they chatted for some time; but unlike her previous encounter with John she didn't ask him to stay for refreshments, in fact their conversation was brief. It's good to see you Minister but I have Ammi waiting on me, but please call again. Even though he would like to stay longer; those few last words from Mrs. Hollins were music to his ears. She holds the door ajar and they parted company in good spirit, he would call on her a few times after but his advances weren't getting him anywhere, she clearly likes him but whatever she's holding out for only she knows.

But it wasn't him alone after the hands of Mrs. Hollins; the Doctor was pursuing her also, as a onetime friend of the family he could visit almost any time, but what he doesn't know yet is that Florence likes him as a friend and nothing more. However when the Minister got wind of the Doctor's visits so he becomes more anxious even to the point of jealousy. Now this Doctor is a handsome man stands about six foot plus tall, he's more of white than black, his bloodline shows he's mostly of white than black; his hair is the only evidence to show he's of mixed race. Florence likes him not only because he's a very pleasant character but he always makes her laugh, there's no romantic interest there at all. As time lapsed she was seeing more of the Minister and he's been invited to dinner once or twice during the weekend, and young Ammi would have dined with them too before she went home, but never on a Sunday, that day is reserved for dinner with the Thomas. Well that's the way she wanted it; at least for now; and he's in full agreement. But the Minister always leaves in good respectable time; he wanted to make a good lasting impression while biding his time, and with Ammi present he wanted show a good example. Well after a couple of months the Minister decided to step things up in his courtship, he wants this woman and he wants her bad, so he decided to ask her to marry him. Well it's a few months since they've been seeing each other even though they haven't been seen out together, in fact they've never even kissed. It was a rainy Saturday and she was alone, the Minister turns up with a plan, he intends to ask her for her hand in marriage. But when he pops the question she turns him down, but she told him she would think about it. However he wasn't too disappointed, he takes hope from the fact that she'll think it over. But he'll ask her again in a couple of weeks; however the answer was just the same. He begins to wonder if the Doctor was in the way, however as a Member of Parliament he must maintain standard, he couldn't afford to allow his jealousy to get the better of him, in as much as he's in love this woman he must not allow himself to be less than a Parliamentary figure.

But he had another idea; he knew that Florence respected and thought highly of Thomas's; she considers them her family; so that's where he's going to seek help and advice. One Saturday evening the Thomas gets a surprise visitor, during his usual chore around the house that evening Minty began barking; of course no one pays any attention; Minty barks at anything, but when Brutus begins growling they must take notice. John looks towards the gate and he could see a tall figure standing close to the privet in the shadow, he recognised the person instantly; it was the government Minister Mr. Faster. Surprised to see him John sets out to greets him, good evening Mr. Thomas he shouts as John approaches, good evening Minister he said in a welcoming tone; what brings you here he asked, I come to see you Sir but your dog's kept me standing here, you mean little Minty here? The dog was standing beside his master; oh his yap is more dangerous than his bite, come on in, he repeats. walking back to the house he stops to admire the beautiful flowers in Agnes garden, I love flowers he said, may I pick a posy Sir he asks, oh sure said John; I don't think the wife would mind. But the woman he's wooing has got the most beautiful flower garden; so his reaction to the flowers could be something of a diplomatic exercise. He picks a flower and begins to smell it, well he's got nowhere to put it; he's not wearing a jacket; the weather is too warm for that; it's a shirt sleeve weather. John takes him to the family bench under the eave; there's shade there and it much cooler than inside the house; he usual place for visitors. Agnes was at her usual place; in the kitchen seeing to dinner; she sees the person walks in with her husband but as usual it's none of her business, so she carries on with her chores. So how can I help you Minister ask John now that they're seated, well Sir I'm after advice among other thing and I thought I should come to you, but what can I advise you on Minister ask John, please don't think I'm a fool Sir but it's about Mrs. Hollins, what about Florence, is anything wrong he asked hastily; showing real concern. Oh no; nothing bad happens Mr. Thomas, oh no; she's fine, you see Sir we been seeing each other for some time now; and Mr. Thomas I love her; yes Sir; I love very much; and I would like to marry her; but when I asked her to she kept turning me down. Oh! She said she'll think about it but it's a few times now; and frankly Sir I'm not quite sure where I stand with her. However John already knew they had been having dinner together; Ammi told him; and he's hoping for all concern that they will be a couple. So why are you telling me Minister John asked curiously; he's wondering if Florence told him anything about their affair, at this point a lot of bad thought come rushing through his head. Please God let it not be what I'm thinking he thought. Well Sir I know she thinks highly of you and your family; and I wonder if you could advise me what to do. Well! His heart was racing away with anxiety; but after The Minister comment it was back to normal.

But John knew he loves her from the day they met at his office and would like to help him if he can. I think I know what you want me to do Minister; you want me to put in a good word for you don't you, he asked kind of sympathetically. Well Sir I seem I'll need all the help I can get; and your help would be most appreciated.; John smiles wryly as though he's been relieved of something; at the same time he's feeling rather chuffed that the Minister needed his help to fix his love life. But rest assure Sir I do love her he said most sincerely; but did you tell her that Min… he pauses, you don't mind me call you Donald do you he asked, oh no Sir please do, I was going to tell you to drop the Minister. Well Donald did you tell her what you're telling me? Yes Sir I did; but not in so many words, not in so many words? What's that supposed to mean Donald, I ask her to marry me Sir, but did you tell her how much you love her? His response was slow in coming; to the point that John almost reprimanding him like a father. Good heavens man; to woo a woman you must first tell her how much you love her; and kept telling her; you don't propose marriage first. But every time I proposed she said she'll think about it Sir he said, but of course she said that said John; because she doesn't know if you love her; and if you've never said it how the devil is going to know. But John knew what Donald didn't know, she loves him and she's ready for a relationship, he's only got to play his cards right. Then what would you have me do Sir he asked, go tell the lady you love her and keep telling her, I wouldn't encourage her to marry you though, no; it's not my place to do so; and to be honest I wouldn't even try, if she marries you it's because she wants to; not because of any advice from me, but you could put in a good word for me couldn't you Sir?

But John thought as a politician this man lacks the way to handle a woman, now listen Donald, there's an old saying when it comes to relationship, it's a woman prerogative to say no, but there's also another saying, if at first you don't succeed try, try and try again. However Mr. Politician this is a new role for me; but if Florence asks my advice I'll try my best to help, I don't know but I'll try to give some fatherly advice; I don't think it's my place to do more than that. I thank you very much Sir, I can't ask any more of you he said. Now then Donald; what the other things you want to see me about, well Sir! I was hoping I could talk to Ammi about the carers, she puts in her final report to Mr. Dunn and he to me; and even though I see her at Mrs. Hollins what I want to ask her I wouldn't ask her there, so I thought coming here I would her ask her. John begins to wonder what he's on about; she finished with the carers nearly two weeks ago. John looks around for her, I can see why not he said; let me see if I can find her. But she was nowhere to be seen, sorry Donald she's not about, no matter; it was just a thought he said. Well are you going to tell me what this is all about asked John; after all I'm her father. Well Sir it about her doing month supervision for us until we get someone to replace her. That I wouldn't be able to tell you; but I will ask Ammi and you can check with me again, thank you Sir; I'll do just that. Well it's approaching sunset and they been talking for nearly two and a half hours, John gives him all the advice he can and he's about to leave. Well thank you Mr. Thomas I'll work on your advice and keep on trying, but I would like to come and see you again Sir if it's even for a talk, you can call on me anytime Donald; I would like that very much, then that I'll do Sir he said. He stood up about to walk away, say hello to your good lady for me Sir, I hope I'll meet her the next time I'm here he said, and you might have time to share dinner with us said John. If that's an invitation Sir I'll hold you to it he said, John then walk with him to the gate and say goodbye.

The following Saturday John had reason to go to town; there he bumps into Mr. Faster, good day Mr. Thomas he said gleefully; are you out shopping Sir?, good day Donald, you could say that said John; but not your everyday shopping, I need a suit made so I'm on my way to the Tailor. You know I could do with a new suit myself but I haven't the time to go to the tailor he said. During their short talk John remember he did promise to invite him to dinner sometime in the future so he asks him Oh! Would you like to have dinner with me and my family tomorrow Donald? He didn't give it a second thought, I certainly would Sir; what time is dinner he ask, oh! The usual time; about three o'clock said John; oh! And by the way Florence will be there too, I thought I put you on your guard. Thank for telling me sir and for inviting me Sir and for inviting me to your home, I'll be there prompt, they shook hands and parted company. But the Minister had a thought; since his conversation with John last Saturday he hasn't got the time for courting, and thinking of what John told him he thought this could be the perfect time and place and opportunity to pop the question; over dinner in full glare of the family what better place he thought. It would be romantic too and will prove to her of his love, well those are his thought.

Sunday was another of that windy day, this time of year leading up to Christmas the cool breeze generally whips up a little strong, not cold but if you're wearing a hat hold on to it. The family went to church and back, now Agnes is in the kitchen with the help of Ammi preparing dinner, they're expecting a special guest today for dinner. However Florence is oblivious to this arrangement; John is keeping her in the dark. The Minister was a little early, Florence was sitting on the family bench all unconcern; when she sees him she was very surprised. Hello Flo he said as he was accustomed to call her, Donald! What the devil are you doing here she asked kind of angrily, Oh! You didn't know? I 'm invited to dinner he said. Don't tell me; John invites you; how did you guess he asked; doing his best to hide his nervousness. But Florence is not too critical of him been there, after all she does like him but she does not tell him, at least not yet. John comes out to join them; they were standing near the flowers patch. Why didn't you tell you invites Donald to dinner John she asked, well if I tell you I forget I wouldn't be true, I thought I give you a pleasant surprise he said. Are you sure that the only reason John she asked; are you sure there isn't an ulterior motive; like matchmaking for instance? I'm not answering that on the grounds that I might incriminate myself he said, there was a funny side to this conversation and they finish in good humour. Now dinner is ready and everyone including the children gathers round for dinner, the dinner conversation was all about the children, Maggie's good school report continues on the up and even though Ammi is now ab almost qualify dressmaker John would much rather his favourite daughter be in education. But he's quite proud of Maggie too; she's one of best brains around here he said, she most certainly will enter one of the best colleges around; and hopefully go on to university. What university would you like to enter Maggie asked the minister, I'm not sure Sir, I'm leaving my option open, the Minister could talk about university; he's one of the graduates. I could recommend the Collard University; that's the one I attend; and look at me; I didn't turn out too badly he said smiling. Florence looked at him and smiles broadly; John looked at her and smiles too, he seems to like her reaction to Donald little joke. You take your time Maggie, take your time and think it over when the time comes, it's important that you make the right choice he said. Thank you Sir, I aim to do just that. But all the time during this conversation Donald was biding his time to ask the all-important question, and of course no one else knows or suspects the Minister devious intention.

But he's not going to do so with the children at the table, no; he knows that wouldn't be right; and once dinner is over then the children will leave the table, he's waiting for that moment. The drinks are been served, including cane liquor, a much tasty liquor direct from the cane plant; and John's own homemade mixture of eggs, milk stout and condense milk with orange peels, that's his own homemade tonic he brewed most Friday evening. Today he chose to do it for his special guest, and the children look forward to it too. You've got to invite me again to dinner again Mr. Thomas, I just love your homemade brew, glad you like it Donald and you can come to dinner anytime, Florence gave him the look to say; I know what you're up to. The children had their drink and asked to leave the table, thank for your advice about university Mr. Faster said Maggie, I'll try to remember it, oh! Your welcome Maggie he said, Ammi asked to be excused and leave also. Now with four adults at the table the Minister thinks the time is right to pop his question, but he's not going down on one knee, no; that's not the ways here. During conversations John was talking about baptism; but Agnes who is not exactly a believer wants to talk about something else, at the moment the two people were talking at the same time when Donald calls out in a loud voice, Flo! Will you marry me, and then there was a frightful hush of absolute silence. Florence sitting on the opposite side of the table look at him in frightful amazement, the surprised on her face was plain to see, she had no knowledge he would dare to ask her here. But with her surprise she didn't seem angry; and with John and Aggie looking at her she asked; they're too are waiting for her response. What did you say she asked looking at him amorously almost with a wry smile. Will you marry me Mrs. Hollins he asked kind of humble, there was no immediate response, then gradually there was a beautiful smile spread across her face. She looks at John and the smile gets broader, did you put him up to this she asks, who me? Oh no! I do no such thing, but what a wonderful way to propose he said. Remembering that he told her he thinks the Minister is a good man, she knows he wants her to have a relationship with him, and been she hangs on his every word, she's going to accept his proposal. Ok minister; I heard you the first time; but ask me again she said, without any ring of engagement he stretches across the table and held her hands and gazing into her eyes, Mrs. Hollins! Will you marry me? She pauses as though to taunts him, then she utters the words he's been dying to hear, yes Minister; I will marry you. Agnes was the first to congratulate them follow by John, I know you're going to make a wonderful couple said Agnes. Wait said John, I have some more of that cane liquor, and he pours four glasses, to the future Mr. Faster and Mrs. Faster, I know you'll make a lovely couple, let's drink to your future; cheers, and they all touch glasses.

We'll start to plan this wedding soon he (John) said; and they all raised their glasses again and drink to it. But Florence has a question, when are we going to start planning this wedding John? And there was a moment of laughter, well she said; you arranged it; now you plan it, did I said that he asked, you didn't have to; I know it's all you're handy work. Agnes looks at him; John! Did you do this; John looks at Donald, will you tell them it was all your idea Donald before they stung me up, ladies I must tell you; it was all my idea; don't you think I'm capable by myself of asking someone to marry me? No said the women; and everyone burst into laughter. There was a good feeling around the place, and the Minister was feeling rather chuff with himself that his plans come together, and John! Well he was feeling good too; to see Florence get herself a man was a load off his mind. I feel like making a speech said Donald, well don't let us stop you said John. He stood up and begins to talk, most of what he said is about Florence; he promises to be the best husband and make to her happy. Now Florence seems to be in the mood to make plans, she got up and walk to the door, she calls in a loud voice, Ammi, Ammi where are you, she wasn't far away; only in the house. You want me Miss Florence she asked looking through the window, would you come here please, and she went back to her seat. Ammi walked in, she gets hold of her hands, Ammi dear; how would you like to be my bride's maid? Looking most surprised she asked, are you going to get marry Mom? Yes Ammi; I'm going to marry that man over there she said humorously, and they all laugh. Well congratulation Mom, but I never bee a bride maid before Mom, don't worry; there's nothing to it; and I'll show you how. Then of course Mom; I love to be your bride's maid. The evening was going with a bang and Ammi took a seat at the table, Florence is feeling elated, this person who was so obnoxious to her now fiancée is now so happy she can hardly contain herself, not long after she says yes she's been making plans for her wedding; and of course she's relying on John and the family to be at the heard of everything. But whatever her plans the Minister is not too bothered, he wants to get married to her and he's not bothered how or where it happens, as long as it happens quickly.

But with glees in her eye she wants to start the preparation right away, she's looking to John to tell her what to do, Agnes herself was eager to get the ball rolling, I can bake the cake she said, I bake a few in my time without any complaint. Oh that would be wonderful Agnes she said, and the talking went on until the Minister who just sat back observing look at his watch, good heavens; look at the time he said, it was approaching midnight. Mr. Thomas he said still sitting down, I'm in your debt Sir; and I thank you and Mrs. Thomas for a wonderful and eventful evening, but I'm afraid I must go now, there's lots for me to do tomorrow. What about I ask Florence; aren't you taking me home? Or you want me to cycle home this time of night? Oh no darling, would I do that? She smiles; it appears she likes the sound of the word "darling". Well I don't know; the way you're saying good night is as though you're leaving me, oh no; I was waiting for you to say your own goodbye. Agnes sat listening to them, this is going to be a healthy relationship, you're not married yet and you've have your first quarrel, you think so Mrs. Thomas asked Donald, I was only kidding, that's not a quarrel; just a little disagreement she said. Then again; I thought you were stopping here he said, well maybe I should; but you can drop me home can't you, she asked; she now really wants to be alone with him. John stood up, you two are not married yet and you're behaving like a wife and husband, Donald! You're welcome here anytime, he stretches his hand to say good night, good night Mrs. Thomas, and good night Ammi he said as he emerges from the dining room. Florence bid good night and as they were about to depart Florence calls to Ammi; I'll see you in the morning Ammi, yes Mom she said, they'll have a lot to talk about tomorrow, and that was the end of an eventful evening.

13: Wedding Plans

The courting is over and wedding plans are in full swing, it's not exactly a whirlwind romance but it wasn't a long one either, at this moment not only Donald is anxious to tie the know but Florence herself can't wait for the big day. She seems to find her soul mate, a man she can call her own after the since the death of her husband. Now they want to set a date but like everything else Florence will talk to John about a suitable time, he's her father figure. On Sunday Donald joins his future bride at the Thomas for dinner, he's becoming a regular visitor there, but they're not only there to eat, no, this evening they're there to set the date. Well they chose a date which suited Donald and everyone else; it's on Saturday the fourteenth of November; and from now on wedding arrangements will be in full operation. Florence and Ammi will make the dresses for them both, a bridal gown and a bridesmaid dress, while Donald will use the same tailor who made John's suite to make one for himself. During the conversation that evening John has a brain wave; he comes up with an idea which he hopes they will agreed to, I just have an idea he said, what's that Mr. Thomas asks Donald. Well! It's just an idea you understand; you don't have to agree, of course. He had no knowledge of Donald's denomination or if he subscribed to any of the churches here. Florence is a regular at his Pentecostal church now but she's started out life going to a Presbyterian church, so he was a little coy with his idea. It's probably a silly idea anyway he said, well tell us what it is John said Florence; don't keep us in suspension. Well! Would you consider announce your bond in our church? I know it would be the first time that anything like this would have happened there; but it would be good for the church reputation to have the Member of Parliament announce his coming marriage there. Quickly Florence responded, what a brilliant idea, why didn't I think of that, what do you think Donald? she asked, would you mind? Not at all, John thinks it a good idea and so do I, did you hear that Agnes, asks Florence, because John says it's a good idea he thinks it's a good idea too, who are you marrying Donald? John or me, and then there was laughter. But it was all happy talk coming from her, she was only letting off steam; she was more than pleased that Donald finds John's idea a good one. Right that's settles it then said John, but when should we make the announcement asked Florence, how about next Sunday; but of course you both will have to go see the Pastor in advance. But he doesn't know me Mr. Thomas said Donald, comes on man; you're a politician; and anyway he knows your future bride said John; and he's certainly not going to say no. It will be a huge surprise to the brethren's and the district to have a Member of Parliament come to our church and to announce his wedding there; and it will be an even greater honour when you get married there. So when should we see the Pastor Mr. Thomas ask Donald, how about Friday evening, I'll mention it to him after church tomorrow that you both would like to speak with him and for what purpose. He will say yes; so you'll see him round about three o'clock on Friday, is that suitable to you Donald he asks, oh yes, for sure Mr. Thomas, and how about you Florence? You'll be ok with that? Sure Dad, whatever you say Dad there was another moment of hilarity. Then Florence clears her throat, there's one thing not talk about she said, what's that ask Donald, who is going to walks me down the aisle? They look at each other, that shouldn't be a problem said Agnes, your father will she said and they laugh some more, is that alright with you John; to walks me down the aisle? Well do I a choice he ask, no said the women, Donald put his hands to his face laughing quietly. Well I'll tell you, nothing would give me more pleasure he said; I love to walk you down the aisle Mrs. Faster, John! I'm not married yet. Then what about the reception ask Donald, where's that going to be? good heavens Donald I didn't know you care, said Florence, you do consider something, John looks at her as to say; don't overdo it. I have an idea about the venue for the reception she said, oh! Where do you have in mind asked John, at the manor where else; outdoor in the yard hoping; it doesn't rain of course. Oh that would be beautiful said Agnes, but I suppose you would have to dress up the surrounding, you could help do that Agnes ask Florence, I don't think I would be good at that Florence she said, don't worry said Donald I've got the right person for that sort of a job, he was thinking of his Sister who none of these people knows. She leaves the area some time ago to live in the Capital on account of a bad relationship with her mother, she (the mother) have no wish to see her again though; but she's his only Sister and they always keep in touch.

Who is this person you got in mind Don; her new name for him, oh! You don't know her and he pauses with a mischievous smile, maybe to see Florence reaction. Well the man is got a sense of humour too she glares at him, well! Not in anger; but in wonderment. Who's she Don she asked again kind of anxiously, I hope is not any of your one-time woman, none of them is going to do anything for my wedding. But she's not any of my one time women he said calmly, she's my Sister, everyone has a laugh except for Florence, and the joke was on her. That said; what about your father and mother Don ask John, what will they be doing at the wedding, oh, my father is dead nearly ten years now; and my mother? Well she hardly leaves the house at all since father's death, but I was thinking, I would like to take her to meet your family Sir, if I'm not too presumptuous. Oh no! I wouldn't mind at all, would you mind Agnes he asked, Oh no, it wouldn't mind at all, and then we must arrange a dinner said John. Ok Mrs. Thomas I'll speak to her about it, she would love to meet you and your family, and Florence hasn't met her as yet either he said; and I think that would be good for them to meet here. The evening business is concluded; everything moving on nicely; and the invitations will soon be sent out. When this news gets out the locals will be looking forward to it as though they were invited, and they would be thinking that the Prime Minister will be there along with other Members of Parliament; after all it's one of theirs getting marry. But they're in for a big disappointment, on Florence's wish this will be a strictly low key and private affair; most of the invitees will be her newly found church brethren's. However this function wills not only attend by the invitees, no, the locals will turn up in their numbers also, they don't need an invitation; they'll dress up as though they were invited only to be a spectator, It's a way of life here so the bride and groom won't be bothered. Things are moving on nicely; they went and see the Pastor regarding their wedding band, well he was surprised when John told him to expect them. But he was even more surprise when the Member-of-Parliament and his future bribe to talk with him about it, he's so chuff he would marry them today. There wasn't too much for them to discuss; John has already laid the groundwork; they'll be at church this coming Sunday to announce their wedding band.

However the local got wind of it and there was a packed Church that Sunday, even those who haven't been to Church for years turns up at Church that Day. Well! There's a v.i.p. going to be there; be it may a Politician who some of them doesn't support. Preparation is in full swing and everyone doing their bit, but two days before the wedding there were some discrepancies between Donald's sister Muriel and some of the church people. She has done a great job decorating the court; but it seems she wants to be in command of the more of the arrangements, she's not satisfied with what she's told to do, she now believed she should be the one arranging her Brother's wedding, but these church people would have none of it. Well this Muriel who is said to be some kind of manager for two singers, she's a strong-headed woman; she probably feels she's got the credential and the right to manage this whole affair; therefore she should be in control of proceedings. But when Florence got wind of it by the church sisters she was mighty angry, now she's got to tell this future sister-in-law where to get off, she won't want to have an argument with her but if she interfere beyond what she's asked to do and if she continue upsetting her (Florence) friends; then she will have to be content with doing nothing. Well Florence was considering having a word with Donald, but decided against it, this is a job for myself she thought, so she took her to one side and put her straight in no uncertain term. Now listen she said, this's not your brother wedding, no, this is our wedding and you don't have any what so ever in the way I want thing done, you can stay or you can leave, and thanks for the job you've done to the court; but now your job is finished you're not to interfere in anything else. She didn't have much too said for herself, well I think I could do a better job she said in a low voice, I don't want to hear it said Florence most angrily, don't interfere; in fact you not needed here anymore, she was most direct. I won't stay where I'm not wanted she said, she then walked slowly away. Her warning works a treat without the need to involve her brother. From that moment she (Muriel) was a changed person, now she wants to make friends with the church sisters, and even though they had reservations about her they still made her welcome, well they're Christian and not supposed to bear malice, if they do then they're not be adhering to one of the ten commandments.

14: Wedding day

The big day has arrives; and Pastor Green will be having a packed church today, and there will be a huge crowd outside looking in, well today is a special day; a member of parliament is getting married in their district at their church, as for as they're concern it's the biggest thing that ever happened in their District. There were cheers and whistles when the groom arrives; but there was an even bigger cheer when the bribe arrives with John and Ammi, the rest of the family are already there along with Donald's mother Dorothy who sits alongside Agnes, she herself is a Pentecostal church goer but since the death of her husband she hasn't been. It was a beautiful ceremony apart from Pastor Green stretches it somewhat a little too long, that's the way of these Pastors; when they got a huge crowd they seem to want to show off their preaching ability. It's the custom here when the bride is walking down the aisle the guests cheer, and when John walked Florence down the crowd cheer enthusiastically, the family was well proud. Emerging from the church there were lots well-wishes from the crowd outside, they put their political beliefs aside for today and there were shouts of good luck Minister. This is the district he nearly got lynched at one of his political meeting way back when, but today he probably forgot that ever happen. It nearly four miles drive back to the manor and the locals will gather outside there too to cheer the bride and groom when they arrive. The day was dry but a little breezy and cold; a bit unusual for this time of year leading up to Christmas. It normally would be a shirt sleeve day; but today even the non-invitees are dressed in suites, most it's the only one they got. it's now about four o'clock and reception is in full swing, John is a good speaker and he gave a wonderful speech mostly about Florence; and he went on to praise her husband, I didn't think he was the kind of person he is until I went to his office, he pauses, my daughter Ammi and the then Mrs. Hollins went to see him regarding the sick in our District, and the interest this man took to help those sick people had made a great impression on me; and folks; you know me; I'm not easily surprised he said with a big grin, and they cheer. From that time I began to learn a little more about him, Florence! I've think you have found a good man who will make you happy, and he raised his glass, let's drink to their future happiness he said, and they all raised their glasses and cheer. But he was probably thinking of Ammi during his speech, she and only she knew of the romance between he and Florence; and here he is esteemed her in every department, he's got a lot of praying to do. Florence beckons to the Master of ceremonies, he comes by and bends over by her, she whispers something in his ear then he walks back. We'll now call on the bridesmaid to say something he said, well the poor girl was most surprised, she's not one for too much talking, never mind giving a speech; she never had anything much to say and here she is called upon to talk at a wedding. Come on Ammi said Florence with encouragement, her father and stepmother were most nervous too, what will the poor girl said? They wish she was never asked to speak. But Ammi got up, good luck Mr. faster and Miss Florence, I hope you'll be very happy, cheers she said with nothing in her hands like a glass; but the guests laugh and cheer; she sits back down again. Of course she's like her church brethren, they don't drink anything alcoholic; the only thing they would be drinking would be soda, lemonade or ginger beer.

But the loudest cheer was reserved for the bride; talking about her life she commented; I had become a recluse after the death of my husband, Mark, I almost gave up on life. My maid? I don't know what I would do without her, thank you Mary, who was sitting amongst the guests. Until one day John came and asked me to teach his daughter Ammi to be a dressmaker, and from that day my life began again. They are my adopted family now; and I'm so lucky the day they walked into my life; and because them, I met my husband. I owe them an enormous debt of gratitude; and she raised her glass not to herself and her husband, no; but to the Thomas, and they cheer. There were quite a few speakers and one of the last to speaks was Donald long-time friend Winston, they been bosom buddies for as long as they can remember. He stood up with a class of the hard stuff in hand and a smile on his face, well now! Where do I start he ask, from the top says Donald, there will I start my friend. He then went on to tell the guests about their wild days, be careful now Winston said the groom, no; go on, tell us, shout the guests. But joke aside folks he said, I love every moment of our time together, this man is a real friend and I'm so please for him today; he finds this wonderful lady to make his life complete. But! He said looking at him with mischievous intent, but you know folks there were times when he got me worried, I was beginning to think he was ... and Donald looks at him, Winston! Watch it now he said, and everyone laughs, and laugh. Really though folks this man is a wonderful human bring; and I'm sure he's going to be a wonderful husband. So without further ado; let's raise our glasses to a wonderful couple and wish them good luck, long life and happiness, and they all cheer. The evening is running late and the master of ceremony ties up proceedings, there won't be any music but the guests will be in their own little groups all over the estate. But outside in the street the celebration will be in full swing, most of these people are rummies, the white rum will be flowing and before the night is out there'll be an awful lot of intoxicated people about. It's not customary here for newlyweds to get away on honeymoon, and for these newlyweds that will be the case. But come Sunday they will be in church to sanctify their marriage. In years to come Mr. faster the politician and his bride will become a favourite here in Danville, he served the people well and the link between him and the Thomas's has strengthened his position.

15: Ammi's Mother Taken Ill

One Saturday when Ammi visit her Mother Mildred; she wasn't out and about in her little cultivation; and she was nowhere to be seen. It was nearly midday; she had no reason to think anything untoward. She calls entering the front door; and still there was no answer, she looks straight ahead and there she was in bed. It's unusual to find her in bed this time of day; immediately she fears the worse. What are you doing in bed this time of day Mom she asked; But she didn't respond, she advances to her while still calling, but still there was no answer. So she removed the covers to find the bed was soaking wet. She was in a state of shock fright now; she shook her; Mom, mom she calls, but it appears she was unconscious. Not knowing how to deals with such situation she raced away to get her father; he'll know what to do, he's only a few minutes away, she need not explain to him the whole situation; they was on his way back; well he didn't bother to drive even if he wanted to; where Mildred lives cars won't be able to go there; however it's only around the corner, so he grabs his son bicycle and quickly they were there. Well he's an old hand at a situation like this, he manages to get her back to consciousness; but Ammi begins to blame herself for not noticing all along that her mother wasn't well. It appears as though she's been ill for some time but never told anyone, she blames herself for tending other people and not noticing that her mother was carrying an illness. Her father calmed her; how could anyone tell if she hides her illness; don't worry he said; we'll care for her. From now she'll devote herself to caring for her mother; and with the help of her family she'll get the best care possible. But as there was no improvement in her condition over the past week Ammi thought she should move back in with her where she'll be there for her day and night, and her father agrees. But a few days after she returns Mildred condition worsen and there was a real concern that unless she gets medical treatment she's only going to get worse. Ammi decided to talk to her father about taking some money from the bank to pays for her mother medical treatment; of course she knew her father would be in agreement, they decided immediately to take her to Doctor Robert. Mildred was to be taken to the Doctor on Wednesday morning; but unfortunately there was a problem; John's car has broken down. They now have a problem; his great friend the Minister was close by he could borrow his car; but he's some four miles away; and they can't delay her been treated for another day. So John decided to put his pride aside and go see his neighbour Mr. Milton Walker for the use of his Hillman Minx. These two men knew each other for as long as they can remember; their land runs parallel to each other and their children go to the same school; but they never talk for years. There's not a lot of love for this man in the district; and not because he had done anything bad but he's a proud man who feels he's better than everyone else. His wife passed away some time ago and he lives alone with his one son Eugene, his first son was drowned in the dry river that runs between their land; and for that incident he blames the families whose children his son was bathing with, in fact he blamed the entire District.

That Wednesday about eleven o'clock John went to see Milton, he didn't walk across his land to his house, no, he approaches from the main road, young Eugene was sitting on the veranda, a very nice young man about the same age as his daughter Maggie. Hello young man; how are you, I'm fine Sir, is your father home he asks, oh yes Sir he replies politely, he's around the back I think; I'll get him for you Sir. But his father heard John voice and leave what he was doing, hello John he said heartily, I heard your voice from the back, I was picking a couple of breadfruits, so I can see said John, as he was holding the two breadfruits he picks. Then how are you Milton John asked, are you well? Oh! Fair as can be John, fair as can be he said repeatedly. Now the formalities are over John wanted to tell him the purpose of his visit, but Milton wants to talk some more; is as though he was dying for a visit from his closest neighbour, he couldn't stop talking, He seem to want to talk about every topic under the sun. But John was in a hurry and wanted to tell him the purpose of his visit, Milton! Couldn't get a word in adware he asked, but John words fall on deaf ears. You're a decent man John; I always know that; and we should be talking like the decent human being we are, we surely should, said John; but you decided to blame everyone for your son's death Milton, I know; and I was wrong John; I know it now and I'm sorry he said. But I was in a bad place after the death of my dear wife and I couldn't come to terms with anything or anyone. When John heard that he feels real sympathy for him, I understand that and it must be difficult for you to lost two members of your family in such short time said John. But we're men and we should act that way, even though I know when it comes to the loss of love ones it takes time to get over. Thank you for those kind words John and you're right; men should be men and stand up to such consequence.

However Milton I'm in a bit of a hurry, I would like to stop and talk but I have a bit of a situation, I need a favour, I would like to hires your car? Mildred must get to the Doctor in a hurry and my car is out of commission. Why didn't you say John he asked, I tried Milton but you didn't give me a chance, of course you can have the car John; and you don't have to hire it, just put gasoline in it if needed, let me get the key. He calls to Eugene, go fetch the car key, meanwhile they walk towards the vehicle that was parked in the yard. Eugene returns and John is given the key, no rush John I'm not going anywhere, just get that sick woman to Doctor. Thank you Milton; thank you very much, I'll be back as soon as I can; and he drove away. They get to the Doctor John and Ammi, of course the Doctor knew Ammi and heard so much about John. At the Doctor's there were no patients waiting to be seen and they didn't have to wait, the receptionist alert the Doctor who tells her to get them in immediately. As they walk in he remembers Ammi, and you must be Mr. Thomas he said, we meet at last; I heard so much about you, all good things I hope Doctor, oh yes Sir; all good things he said while looking at the patient. How long is she been like this, he asks, we don't know Doc. It seems she's been ill for some time but she didn't tell anyone said John. The Doctor keeps examining her, whatever he diagnosed he didn't say but he prescribed some medication and gives her an injection. Give her a dosage three times a day and make sure she eats something, if she's not eating bring her back to see me. But before they leave the Doctor asks Ammi if she told her father what he said, John looks at Ammi; what was that you should have told me he asked. Well Dad! The Doctor thinks I should be a nurse; and what did you said he asked, the Doctor respond, she said she's a dressmaker; and Mrs. Hollins has made a good case for her. Well thank you Doctor for your interest; but she has chosen her profession; and as you said she's doing nicely. Well the Doctor didn't pursue that conversation any longer; he realised her father wanted her to be in her chosen profession. There was a short conversation between John and the Doctor before they leave; bye Ammi said the Doctor as they were leaving. They get her home and prop her up in bed, she (Ammi) will be with her always to keep a watch on her as the Doctor said. She would like to get in touch with her brother Frank but no one knows of his whereabouts, as her Mother's first child by another man he left home when he was a teenager, never to be seen again. She would like to see him now that their mother is ill but she's not holding her breath. Here in this island that's a common occurrence for a youngster to up and leave home, they almost never return.

On Thursday after work John returns Milton's car, thanks very much Milton he said; I appreciate it, don't mention it John; I was happy to help. Have you got time for some cool lemonade drink? Oh sure, why not said John, they settle down and begin talking. John! He said; we should be a shame of ourselves, we have lived in this district as long as anyone and we never really get to know each other. We the senior citizens should be setting an example for our children and the people of the district; and before you tell me John, yes I know I'm the culprit here, what you said to me yesterday keep ringing in my ears, I hope the people of this little district can forgive me. Of course they can Milton; and they will; and don't be so hard on yourself, you used to be a church-going man with your family; you have lost two of them and I know it's hard to bear; but remember that life goes on regardless of any difficulties. You have to try and put it all behind you and move on; you still have Eugen; he growing up to be a fine young man and he is depending on you. You're a wise man John Thomas; I hang on every word you said; I will begin to go to church again with my boy. The evening was running late and John is about to return home, he thanked Milton again for the use of his car, but Milton who hasn't got anyone to talk to for some time enjoyed the chat and would love to talk some more. John he said why not walk this way home and I'll walk with you to the bottom of the line, what he was saying was; John should walk across his section of the land to get home, it was a good quarter of a mile walk but John didn't mind, in fact he's well pleased that he had this conversation with his neighbour; and the only regrets is that it takes an emergency for them to break the ice.

Come Sunday the family set off to church, Florence was in attendance but her husband was away on Government business, she reminds John that when Donald returns the families will have dinner at her mother-in-law's home. But also in church too was Milton and his son, John went and sat next to him, he whispers in his ears while shaking his hand; it's good to see you Milton, the two men sat together all through the service, well John wants him to feel welcome and for him to come again. After the service the Pastor makes his way to join them. Mr. Walker! It's good to see you and you too Eugene, it's a long time since we haven't seen this young man at Sunday school he said looking at him, are you're going to start coming again? Yes Pastor he said. He'll be coming from now on said Milton with tears in his eyes, well everyone so nice to him and his boy he's feeling a sense of remorse, but it seems he'll be back in the fowl again thanks to John; and John will be there to encourage him. Ammi who wasn't in church that Sunday report to her Dad that her mother is not looking too good, she's can't keep anything down and she's quite weak; she's cause for concern. When John went to see her he's got the feeling she won't be much long with them. But he remembers what the Doctor said, if she's not keeping anything down, they should take her back to him immediately, but with his car still out of commission and we didn't want to bother Milton again for his car, he was thinking of any alternatives when Ammi tells him, Dad! I will ride my bicycle to go and fetch the Doctor. When John returns home and tell Agnes the situation; Florence who just arrived there offers to go with Ammi, it doesn't take two people to fetch one Doctor said John, no! But we can ride together there and I can stop off home said Florence, it agreed and they set off without delay.

Arriving at the Doctor's surgery Florence didn't hesitate; she talks to the receptionist who went in to tell the Doctor; she returns to tell her (Florence) the Doctor won't be long. Well whatever the Doctor was doing it seems he cut it short to deal with them; well he knows why they were there and he's going to leave with them right away. He put the bicycle in the car boot and they set off to Danville. The Doctor is not a quick driver and it wouldn't pay to drive fast here anyway; one slip and you're in a pothole and that could be the end of your axle. They return with the Doctor some two and half hours later, on examined the patient he looks at John and shook his head, of course he knows what that means, he gave her an injection and then talk to John and Ammi together. I'm afraid there's nothing more I can do he said; it's all up to your mother now he said. But even though the Doctor led Ammi to believe that there's a chance; he and John know she's dying and it could be a matter of days. What's going on asked Florence who wasn't told anything, oh1 I'll fill you in on the way back said the Doctor. But even though neither the Doctor nor her father tells her the whole truth Ammi knows her mother was dying. When the Doctor was gone she said to her father; Dad! I know she hasn't got long to go, why you say that he asked; Dad come on, I'm not a child anymore, I see the doctor shakes his head to you and I know what that means. I'm so sorry dear he said; we were just trying to keep you from been too hurt, I know Dad; but if the Doctor can't help her she's obviously going to die, John sighs with a groan, he has nothing to say to daughter to give her comfort and he's hurting badly for her. But he learns one lesson today; his daughter has grown up; she's not a little girl anymore. Well less than two days later Mildred condition has become critical, there's nothing more they can do; they just have to wait for the inevitable. That same night the family hold a vigil at her home, they think she won't last out the night; and they were right, by four o'clock that morning she was gone. Well it was a sad time all round, the family was now in mourning, especially Ammi, she was shaken up badly for the loss of the real Mother. But now the family have to prepare for the nights ahead, it will be at least nine days before they bury their dead; sometimes even longer. But for those nights the people will come from all around to sing all through those nights till the big hours of the morning. They'll cook through the night and of course the white rum will be flowing, a tradition handed down to them by their slavery fore-parents. But Ammi had a thought, she can't stand to have her mother lying around day after day, no; she wants a quick burial, she puts it to her father and he agrees. Of course it was a disappointment to the local not to carry on with the traditions, but these young people are gradually breaking away from what they see as a pointless exercise. Here a funeral is supposed to be a solemn occasion; but the way in which they would turn out in their Sunday best it's could be term as some kind of celebration. There will plenty to eat and drinks, some of the food would be given by the locals; and the drinks will be of all descriptions including rum punch which is stronger than the real thing. But even though the Thomas's try to move with the times; to satisfied the locals some of the old tradition they had to adhere to. She was buried on her small plot of land behind the house; and with Pastor Green take charge of the ceremony she's got what they expect; a good burial. Well Ammi will miss her mother; but she's got her family behind her; they'll grieve with her and console her; and make sure they get her through the best they can. The coming days the Thomas will receive visits from members of their church; they come to hold prayer meetings at the house to help the family get over their loss; and that will probably go on for days; until they feel the family has got over their grief. Well the Fasters were never far away; they too will do what they can to help the family through their time of grieving.

16: The Exodus

It's now the early fifties and the rush is on to travel abroad; and people are going to America on what is known as farm worker's ticket, they are going there to cut sugar cane, the same as they do here in the Island; except over there in America it's a dangerous job. The American's have to burn the sugar cane fields to rid them of dangerous snakes before it can be work in. But these men from the Island are super tough guys; they are capable of stand up to extreme condition. It was said that these men have gone to work to help pays off some of the debts the British owed the American. But whether there's any truth in that the men don't bother one iota, they have gone to earn more money than they can ever earn at home. Every year the Government would give a certain amount of tickets to the one or two leading citizens of their District; and they would give it to who they think was the best person to travel to America; and there's always a stampede for those tickets; underhand tactics were used to get a ticket; even blackmail; to get one of these tickets is a sure thing that your life will improve. But these men will go away on a five years contract after which they'll be sent back home. But most of them done themselves proud; when they returned home they could afford to buy themselves land and build themselves nice houses. But the bigger rush to travel was to come; the British Government wants people from the commonwealth to come to work in England. When the courter was open up the whole country become restless; everyone wants to go to England. The first shipment of immigrants sailed in the late forties; and from then on the only thing the Islanders talked about was going to the mother country. It was a wide-open courter; anyone who could afford the fare; boat or the plane was leaving for England. Those who couldn't get their hands on hard cash were now selling up their entire position to accumulate the fair, some would sell their homes; it means they got nothing left, and in the event of things didn't work out favourable for them in England they have nothing to return to.

But it seems that eventuality doesn't bother them; the desire to go to this country, England, is greater than the desire for them to remain here. Young and old as long as they can rustle up seventy-five pounds they'll be on the plane or ship to England. Ammi's two older first cousins Daphne and Hillary are already there; and now she wants to travel too, she's gone nineteen and feels she's old enough to take care of herself. But she's going to have a difficult time convincing her father that she can take care of herself; to live over five thousand miles across the ocean away from her family is not something he wants for his daughter, no; like all his children he wants her here. But she's not going to talk to him about it now, no; she will discuss it with her mother-in-law to find out what she thinks about it. She has already talked it over with Florence and it was with reluctance; but she agreed with her. Well she (Florence) knows that although she's (Ammi) a fully qualify dressmaker now the chance of earning a proper living here is pretty slim. A young person especially one with a qualification shouldn't waste their time here; they should take their chances elsewhere; and if that means going away from home to England then so be it. When she confronts her mother-in-law with the preposition she too was in agreement, but you know your father is not going to allow you to go said Agnes, I'm hoping you could talk to him Mom she said, yes! But that's all I can do is talk; you know how stubborn your father is. But the chance of her father agrees to send her away is absolutely zilch; he's going to tell her she's not old enough, well here you're not regarded as an adult until you're twenty-one; and some close-knit families never want their siblings to leave home at any price, and this family is one of the same.

At this time Ammi is restless; she's not doing much in the form of work; what she was told by Florence keep ringing in her ears, you're not going to make a decent living from been a dressmaker here. Right now the most sewing she's doing is patching and darning for the locals and her family; nothing to show for all the years she has done training. She begins to have regrets she didn't take up the offer of being a nurse; probable by now she would be into a job. But for Ammi the horse had bolted; she chose her path as far as a profession is concerned; and as the saying goes; you make your bed now lies on it. Sunday at dinner Ammi had expected Agnes to speak to her father about her desire, but she didn't; and she (Ammi) didn't either, later sometime after dinner when Ammi ask her mother- in-law why she didn't speak to her father, she told her it wasn't the right time. Why not Mom she asked, well! At this moment he's fighting with a problem; he's been told to lay off some of his workers come the end of the week and he doesn't like to do it. You know your father; he hates to know that these men now working; they can't earn a living doing nothing he'll be thinking; that is been bothering him greatly; and I don't want to give him anything more to worry about. But give it time; you don't have to be in a hurry she said; oh poor Dad; he wants to help everyone she said. Well! You're no different said Agnes, there's an old saying; the chip never fall far from the block, what's that means Mom she asks, never mind; when you're older you'll find out for yourself. The following Saturday the Thomas was having dinner at Dorothy's; the mother of Mr. Faster; this arrangement was in the pipeline before her son got married. The families did meet at the wedding but only for a fleeting introduction, Dorothy is a very warm and nice person; she has become withdrawn since the death of her husband, she's not exactly old but her appearance suggest otherwise. She adores children and shows interest in the Thomas's youngsters, of course her only daughter Muriel rebel and leave home some years ago. At the wedding they never even change a word until she (Muriel) leave for the Capital immediately after the wedding. Like any good parent she grievde the absent of her only daughter; but what can she do? That daughter chose to rebel; a situation which any well-thinking parent wouldn't and couldn't tolerate, the daughter up and leaving home. Of course her only son the Member-of-Parliament hasn't got time to spend with her, he's busy in his position as a minister; and now it seems her only friend her neighbour is not too well and is not leaving home either; for Dorothy loneliness sets in.

At dinner the families got on famously and Donald is hoping his mother has found a friend in Agnes, the dinner is still in progress but Florence is already inviting everyone back to here's the coming Saturday. John was about to say something but Florence interact quickly; oh! It's not at my place it will be at the Thomas she said; well! Whatever John was about to say he didn't bother. Donald looks at her curiously, you're inviting us to the Thomas's home for dinner? Of course she said, does Agnes have anything to say about it he asked, I can invite people there she said. Agnes was quick to intervene; now then Donald! You marry her but there's no reason why she can't invite your mother to our home, and as she said; we're having dinner at the Thomas's on Saturday. Dorothy burst into a laugh but no one else, why are you laughing mother asked Donald; Don she said; I'm old but my brain still function; didn't you heard what Aggie said, then the penny drops; and every start laughing. So we're having dinner at the Thomas's right Aggie comment John; that was to let them know that he knows what the joke was all about. Florence is fully indoctrinated into the Thomas's family; and even though she had already told her husband so; and knowing that the family welcome her with open arms; she wanted to show her claim to the family by making such statement. Since everyone is relaxed and the conversation rages on Agnes thought now is the right time to break the question about Ammi ambition to travel to England, it's not a secret so there's no qualm talking about it in front of their friends. But she didn't go directly into asking, no, she begins to talk about the young people leaving this country to go abroad because of the lack of opportunity; and the Government isn't doing anything to keep them here. Well after hearing her mother - In – law comments Ammi wait for her to ask her father. But she could wait no longer; and I would like to go to England too dad; I can't stay here anymore. I would like to go where I can get a proper start in life she said, her father heard but didn't respond. Did you hear me Dad? I heard you, but did someone tell you to say that he asks. Florence was quick to intervene, John! Ammi is approaching twenty-two; and you might not notice but she's a big young lady now; and a sensible one too; sensible enough to make a statement like that without anyone having to tell her to.

But John doesn't want to hear any such conversation about his daughter wanting to leave home, no; he's the old fashion type; he believes all his children should remain here, married and give him grandchildren; and he could watch them grown up. That may be so he said, but she's far too young to be on her own, but I won't be on my own Dad; Daphne and Hillary are already there; don't you remember them Dad? Of course I remember them, but they're older than you; and I don't forget why Bradly (his brother) sent Daphne away either he said. Nevertheless! You will give it some thought John won't you ask Florence, I'll think about it he said unhappily. Donald what do you think? Do you think I'm living in the dark ages; refuse to let go of my children? No; I don't think so at all Sir, I haven't got children; but if I did I would probably think the same. Then Agnes speaks; look around you John; everyone is leaving here; why do you think they're leaving? Well I'll tell you, because there's no future here for them, and there's no certainty that they'll make a better living abroad; but they're willing to take a chance said Aggie, and life is all about taking chances interact Florence looking at her husband. Why you looking at me he asked, well I'm taking a chance on you don't i? There's a smile come to Dorothy's face, of course you are dear, it's always a chance with these men she said, but Mom you're supposed be on my side said Donald kind of serious, yes! I'm on your side son; but you're a man aren't you; and they all looked at him before bursting into laughter. Of course Florence was only trying to make a light-hearted conversation; and she succeeded. But seriously though John you'll think about it; Ammi need a future and she's not going to get it here. But John had enough of this going to England conversation and wanted to hear no more of it. I said I would and I will;

let hear no more about my daughter leaving home; let's eat he said. But Agnes notice hr husband was getting little bit irritable; she wanted to turn the conversation to something else. However Mrs. Faster senior wasn't quite finish, no; wants to know from her son what the Government is doing to keep people from immigrating to another country. There was a hush; but the Government are doing absolutely nothing, and they know it, over the years they done nothing for the people of this country, and it difficult to see them start now. But with the presence of their politician friend they're certainly not going to criticise his party, even though they're the ones in Government.

But he did talk about what the Government is hoping to create in the form of work; but only in certain fields. However it's only a plan on the drawing board he said, you hear that Ammi? Things could change in the future said John. Don't be so naïve John said Agnes; you can't sit back and wait on what may or may not happen; no disrespect to you Donald; but consecutive governments make promises but never carries them out; why should we think this one is going do any better?. No offense taken Mrs. Thomas; and you're totally right; as a Minister we would like to do things for our constituents; but there's no money to do anything. I can fully understand why people are leaving in droves; it's not all about the fascination of knowing the mother country, no Sir, people want a good life; and right now they're not going to get it here; and believe or not I speak about it in the house. Well suddenly Ammi finds herself with another ally; and even though the politician wasn't talking on her behalf, her father must have thought he was. But what the Minister said must surely be ringing in her father ears, her hopes rise; she feels now he'll give it some serious thought. Well dinner was over; but before they said their goodbyes; Florence had a thought, she wants them to have dinner at her place instead of the Thomas's; well why asked Agnes, I thought that was settled, well my mother-in-law here hasn't seen anything of the manor; and you Agnes and her could have a wander around the place, I would like that said Dorothy; how about you Agnes she asked, well since you put it that way; how can I refuse, ok! That settled, we'll meet again at the manor next Saturday evening she said. An eventful evening comes to an end; Thomas was confronted with a decision to make concerning his daughter leaving home; he'll probably try to talk her out of it, and why not; if you're a parent with a loving family no way would you want that family to be broken up.

The week has started in its usual manner; since Florence got married Ammi has spent most of her days at home with near nothing to do. That's not the nature of this young woman, no; she would like to be busy doing something; anything. Since she passed out as a qualified dressmaker some two years ago she's only made three dresses to order; apart from the occasional darning and patching for the locals, she stands idle. So from time to time she would return to the sick to see if she could help in any way even though the carers are taking care of them adequately. Saturday was one of those beautiful, the sun is high up in the sky and the cool breeze blow gently amongst the trees; it feels heavenly on the skin, today the Thomas is to have dinner at the manor; it's approaching three o'clock and Agnes is ready and waiting, she's in anxious to meet up with Dorothy again. Now they're ready to go; but young Rupert is already gone; he took off on his bicycle as the car is fully laden, he'll probably be there before them. But it's good to see the two senior women hit it off so well, their first two meetings they get along like house on fire, and that pleases the Member of Parliament. He's been concern about his mother isolation since the death of his father; he's happy to see her meet someone to whom she can have a good rapport; and possible trump up a good friendship. Arriving at the manor John drives straight in; well! The Faster's are in residence and on a beautiful day like today, the gate is left open. Now with the weather is as beautiful as the surroundings, the youngsters will have an awful lot of land to explore if they wish. But two days before this union Ammi met with Florence to raise the matter of going to England at dinner again; with the hope that this time her father will make a decision on the matter. Since the last time the matter was raised he promised to give it some thought; but he said nothing since regarding, Ammi knows he's stalling for time and hoping that she'll have a change of mind. But Florence knows that too; she promises Ammi she'll raise the matter at some point during dinner. While dinner is been prepare Agnes and Dorothy went upstairs, well these two golden oldies have things to talk about; things that could enhance their friendship, the others were doing their own things. Some two hours later the maid went and tells Florence that the table is set. She was about to ask the maid to fetch Agnes and Dorothy but she went herself instead. What are you two ringing each other ears about, she asked, putting the world to rights I suppose. We're just catching up said Dorothy, well you can catch up some more later, but now dinner is served, so come along now you two.

Dinner is going with a swing, the conversation was about everything and everything until Florence raises the question about immigration a conversation John rather not have. But as of now he's going to hear plenty about it; to the point where he ends up making a decision, an agreeable decision to send his daughter to England. Well as a family man he hates to disappoint his family and always tries to do the best for them, however he wasn't ready to concede yet; but this time he was tactfully ambushed by his own family to make a decision there and then. But even though he reluctant agreed; he's not going to be in any hurry to book the fare, no; he'll still stalls for time; as much time possible to keep his favourite child home as long as he can. But John is a wise man, as much as he would like to; he knows he can't keep her ties down at home forever, one day the bird will fly the nest, the time has come for her fly. But from now on even though he never travel anywhere; the conversation with Ammi is how to behave abroad. But Agnes would like to finish the job; she knows the girl is anxious to travel and would like John to agree a date now; if he doesn't do that now he might use it as an excuse to stall for time. So what date are you thinking about Ammi she asked, when would you like to travel? After the Christmas mom, sometime in January she said. What do you think about that John ask Agnes, don't think I don't know what you three are trying to do; trying to badger into decided here and now, I agree; and not because of your three underhand tactics; but I agree because of circumstances and the way things are here now; and without any light at the end of the tunnel sending her abroad probable is the best thing to do. So there; you three can come clean now, I suspect this was plan beforehand isn't it? he asked. I don't know what you're talking about John said Florence, do you know what he's talking about Agnes? No idea, no idea at all she said. Donald looks at John smiling broadly, now that I think about it John you're right, this was a plan they hatched up to gang up on you, I marry a devious woman. but his mother enter this particular conversation for the first time, well if you men think that you're the only one who can be smart you can think again, right ladies? she asks. Right said the other two, the children look on with nothing to say.

But it was all light-hearted and it went down well with the dinner, the date was set for Sunday the fifteen of January for Ammi's departure. Dinner is over and the children are out exploring, Agnes and Dorothy decided to take a walk along the estate. Agnes is a strong active woman nearly fifty and Mrs. Faster senior is an older person in her early sixties but looks much older. They set off in no particular direction on the vast estate; and with the warm evening sun and the gentle breeze they stroll casually along the footpath that takes them to the fish pond, Ammi and Florence spent plenty a lazy day there; they stop to enjoy some large tropical fish before moving on deep into the estate; probable in the future they'll be spending more time by the fish pool. This friendship is good for

Dorothy; she's now found someone to whom she can confide in and Agnes is a good listener. After some time the trees begin to cast long shadows and is time to leisurely stroll back. The time is about seven o'clock and they settle down for supper, that's the usual time for supper here in the tropics; probably because people don't retire to bed early. Did you have a good stroll ladies ask Donald, oh yes thank you said Agnes; we sit by the pond and enjoyed the beautiful fishes. Well the next time you two are going for a walk I'm coming along to hear what you talk about said Donald, he can see that his mother and Agnes have hit it off. The evening has drawn to a closed; and as all good things must come to an end said John; it time for us to go. The children were already sitting in the car; but not Ammi; she was in the workroom, Agnes calls, come along Ammi; we're leaving, she was out prompt. But Dorothy wanted to hug them before they leave, so John beckoned them to come inside, she embraced them all with delight. You must take the children to see me Agnes anytime at all she said, I would love to spoil them; I certainly would Dorothy; but only when I can find the time, and John can take us. You have to make time for yourself Agnes, all work and no play makes Jack a dull boy she said, Florence begins to laugh looking at Agnes; she comments sarcastically; I thought your name was Agnes; now I know it's Jack, and the family laugh, and laugh. This arrangement of family gathering seems as though it's going to be a permanent fixture for time to come. The Faster walk the Thomas to the gate to see them off, it was the end of a happy eventful evening of which Agnes and Dorothy seal their friendship. It was a quiet drive home; little or no talking at all; it seems everyone must have been tired. But Ammi is feeling much better now than when she left home earlier, she's now has her date set to travel to England, and now she can start making plans.

17: The Baptism

This little church is the centre point of the district; they usually, from time to time, go out looking for souls to save, they do that by holding evangelistic meetings in various places; like the night when John was converted. Then whenever they gather enough souls sometime later they would be baptised; and there could be several of those who would be baptised at any one time. This is an event the locals look forward to; well! They haven't got much to celebrate about; they're not the creative type to think up anything; they just carry on as though they're waiting for something. They're melancholy about everything; they're like the people that time forgot; and when an event like a baptism comes along they'll treat it as though it's an exciting event. John is one of those who will be baptised; he's been converted not quite a year ago; and after his soul confession that night he has become one of the brethren and began to testify. This procedure is after one gives their heart and soul to the Lord and become a Christian, he can now testify and tell the world he's sanctified and now he's clean. But somewhere along the way he changed his mind, after some time of following the religion he had become disillusioned and slid back, that is to say he stopped following the Church and the religion he once followed; he even stopped going to church. His wife Aggie has become concerned; and even though she's not an avid believer in their religion; she's concern he might return to his old ways. But sometime later he had a rethink of his position and realised he should be back amongst the fold; not only as a churchgoer but as a fully committed Christian. Well he was feeling guilty about his pass action, and when he thinks he was in trouble i.e. the Mrs. Hollins affair; he pray to the good Lord for help and deliverance and he manages to get out of that situation without his family been affected. So after some long deliberation he decided to visit one of the evangelistic meetings. One Friday night when there was a meeting away from the Church; he decided to go along. There was an alter call; the usual occurrence to get souls; and John went along and re-confessed his sins. Well! He'd done it before and Ammi thought he was sincere; will he hold fast to his conviction this time and be the Christian person he would like to be. Now Brother Thomas is to be baptised along with four other brethren. The baptism is set for late

November; however on that day it rains so heavily there's no chance of the event taken place, now they have to re-think their position.

The Baptism pool in the middle of a river bed; and this river isn't called the dry river for nothing; it's quite deceptive; and people have drowned in it. You could be standing in a dry river bed one moment and the next there's a mountain of water coming down on you. What this means it may be dry here in Danville but when it's raining in the Parish beyond it brings the water come flooding down below. However all plans were laid and preparation got on the way, but it's always a chancy business if the pool is to be used for any such purpose. However a new date was set for the event, the news gets as usual and a good crowd is expected; the pool will be clean and monitor constantly to avoid any vandalism. When it not was used for an event like this; the local used for bathing and washing. But now the Pastor will purify the pool with prayer; then they'll keep watch on it so that no one uses it for any purpose. Everything is calm the weather is looking favourable here; they're now hoping it doesn't rain in the Parish beyond. All of the brethren who are to be baptised are ready and prepared, the locals and people from beyond are ready and prepared, this is one of the big events they're looking forward to. They'll dressed in their Sunday best, usually it's the only one they've got, after this it will be put away never to be worn again until one such occasion comes around again. It's Sunday morning and a good crowd is expected; today is baptism day; but the sky is blackened; it looks a certainly to rain; and it did, around about ten o'clock, there was a cloud burst; and rain and rain. Well the river didn't overflow its banks but it was a rushing stream that could wash a man away, and again they were forced to put the proceedings on hold. So is back to the drawing board for these Christians; they'll have to plan another date and hope and pray it doesn't rain again. Well the news bulletins not usually broadcast the weather forecast; well it did; but not even those who've got a radio listen to it. There are times here when the weather behaves like a monsoon; but that's around the October month; nevertheless there can be some heavy showers also in the months leading up to Christmas. Well they're not going wait around waiting, no; these brethren's are anxious to take the plunge, so the Pastor set another date; it's for Sunday the twelve of December, right in the yuletide preparation. The news will go out again to the district and beyond; and it's all by word of mouth. The dry river recedes as quickly as it arrives; it's the usual pattern it's a rushing stream now but in a couple of days it will run dry. They'll go through the whole procedure all over again by cleaning the pool and bless it, now for the next three days they'll keep around the clock vigil.

Thing are looking favourable; the weather for the past few days is dry and hot, and they're hoping and praying it continues right through Sunday.

The crowd is expected to be huge, and when there's a special person like John Thomas taking the plunge it creates an extra interest. But there even a bigger interest when the news gets around that sister Ammi is to be baptised too, the entire district will come out to watch. Well here she's a bit of a celebrity; the young woman they daubed Florence Nightingale because of her ceaseless work with the sick and helpless will draw the crowd. The riverbank will be pack on the day, people will come early to get a vantage point, and some will bring their own seats. Ammi had been an active member of the church; she's been that way from her early days; and even though the Pastor wanted her to be baptised from she was about twelve; and of course she wanted to; but it didn't happen, not because of her father, no, but because of her mother - in- law. She always holds the opinion that it's wrong to baptise young children into a religion and having them to go along to these meeting and testify like the adults to something they're not guilty of. She (Agnes) manages to overrule her husband all this time even though he wasn't pushing extra hard. But now she (Ammi) approaching twenty-two years old, and with the knowledge she'll be leaving for England in a few weeks; she has decided the time is right for her to be baptised, her father is well please of the idea. Well! He holds the notion that being a Christian will hold her in good stead; especially now that she'll be away in England; there she'll need her Christian faith to help her through. The scene is set ready for the big day; there'll be lots of supplication that the weather remains dry through the day. Early that morning the brethren's would go along and decorates the river banks, it will be a beautiful sight to behold. It's Sunday morning and it's a beautiful day, there's no sign of rain; it seems the brethren's supplication have been answered, and there's an air of anticipation in the atmosphere, something spiritual and holy is about to happen. The people starting to take up their position, the early comers are looking for vantage points closest to the pool, and those with seating arrangements were the first to arrive, they'll make themselves comfortable as best they can; there's no telling how long this event will go on for. These brethren's are noted for very lengthy meeting and on this special occasion it might go on for a very long time, so they come prepared for the inevitable. The time is now and there's a blessing at the church before they set off on the short walk less than a quarter of mile to the pool. There'll be an orderly procession with the participants wearing their long white gown and a bible in their hands, screened by the brethren's they'll be singing and playing of tumbrels as they go along; and shouts of hallelujah praise the Lord as they march towards their destination.

Approaching the scene the crowd claps and cheer, the Participants will be shown to the special seating that is provided for them. Now the Pastor will conduct a service before they're taken to the water, the meeting is in full swing with the audience getting involved. This meeting is now a highly charged atmosphere, Pastor Green is in great form he aroused his Brethren's to a crescendo. Some get the Holy Spirit and begin to speak in tongues, a language which no one supposed understand except the Lord; and some will be weeping. After some time in the heat of things they're ready to enter the pool, there two of the strongest men and a woman took their position in the water along with the Pasto, these three people will dip the participants under backwards when the Pastor said these words, I Baptism you in the name of the father the sun and the holy ghost. Then there'll be cheers for everyone as it happens. But some of these people are here for their own gratification; not only to cheer the Brethren's. They're here waiting to see how the participants react when they're held under the water for that few second; possible to satisfy their own curiosity; strange behaviour at what supposed to be a holy affair. But the loudest cheer was reserved for sister Ammi, well done sister Ammi and God bless you sister Ammi; were shout coming from crowd. But of course what they're not aware of is that this could be her last action within the community before she leaves for England. Emerging from the pool in their white soaking wet gown the crowd continued their rapturous applause; then they would make their way to change behind the makeshift tent provided. The service would continue while they're away; and usually some new souls would be saved too. These newly converts will kneel at the alter and confessed their sins; and from then on they'll be avid followers, then one day the time will come for them to be baptised. The brethren's return in dry clothing to more rapturous applause; and there're people wanting to shake their hands. Especially sister Ammi; she's been treated as though she's got special powers, they're here especially for her. It's now running late and proceedings are coming to an end; it's time to make their way back to the church. But this event is not over; only over at the pool; prayer meeting will continue back at the church and there's no telling what time they'll wind up proceedings. But on this joyous occasion there was a disappointment for one person; Florence; she was unable to attend to see her one-time lover and now her adopted father been baptised. Unfortunately she was taken ill days before and couldn't leave home.

Well! Ammi was concerned when she wasn't at the Baptism; and so was John; so come Monday after breakfast Ammi will go to visit her, but her condition was something not too serious, however Ammi will probably stop over with her for a day or so. She'll tells her all about the event, but she's going to wants to know John's reacts when they dip him under; and she'll tell her; no different from the rest of us Mom; This baptism has been talked about and will be for days to come, not only for the people who had been baptised; but to have father and daughter been baptised on the same day at the same time it's a talking point. However there was a bigger talking point; only this time based on miraculous suspicion. Later that evening after the ceremony; almost immediately after the brethren's entered the church it begins to rain; and it rains so heavily that this dry river has now become a torrent. It washes away trees and carries away everything in its path includes lives stock. The people suspicion rages, some said it's a miracle, others? Well they thought the good Lord was angry. Of course one could see how it could appear to be a miracle; and it probably is, but these people are believers in their God, be it may that not all of them are sincere in their action. Nevertheless they're believers; and to them anything like this would be construed as a miracle. From now hence they will treat this pool as some sort of holy ground; now they'll probably build a monument along that edge of the river bank as a shrine. Outsiders might call it superstition; or the people are loopy, but here in Danville and around; the people believed in their bible and the bible talks about miracles; so who's to say what happened here isn't a miracle, it's best to leave them to their belief.

18: The Yuletide Season

Christmas is approaching and people are busy decorating their surroundings, there's no electricity here but that doesn't bother the locals, it's a case of what one never had one never miss but they'll use other forms of decoration to decorates their surroundings. Their little houses are surrounded by trees, and they'll use a mixture of white lime to whiten the trunks of the trees; they would also erect small stones structures and do the same, and in the moonlight it shines out beautifully. Of course there're balloons and streamers to decorate the houses, well in their somewhat primitive way they're using whatever at their disposal; and using it in the most beautiful and constructive manner. They can be more creative than that too, there are some beautiful carvings here; then some crafty unscrupulous white man from abroad would come by and pay them a pittance for their work as there's no one here to appreciate their graft. There'll be more to eat and drink at this time of the year than any other times; the people are not flush with money to spend in the shops they would give as present produce from their plantation. And there'll be an awful lot of baking of Christmas cakes to buns; that the favourite treats here. But there's a prestigious competition too, the best baked spice bun will be the highlight they look forward to. This's a serious competition; it carries a cash prize of twenty pounds this year; the most it has ever been; that's the amount of cash very few people here earned in a year, and with everyone want to collect; the competition is not always fair. There'll be plenty of underhanded methods; competitors have to guard their entries to avoid sabotage, some of the methods they used were darn right dirty. Now firewood is an extremely important commodity here; without wood one doesn't eat cook food, but to gather up this firewood one has to go to the hills and beyond; and since there's no great forest here and with everyone doing the same the firewood had become very scarce. The oven is heated up by the very same and without it there'll be no baking either; and with this scarcity of firewood some contestants will try everything to ruins the chances of the oppositions. There're times when contestants would wait until late night when everyone is asleep; they would sneak in and remove all the wood or vandalised the oven. Now there's a good chance that competitor won't be able to enter the competition that year.

For some! It doesn't matter how they win; this prize money could set them up for a very long time.

To make things noisy there're firecrackers and the big blast from cribs through the night, and of course all through the silly season there'll be an awful lot of people under the influence on the only main street. Well not many people here are beer drinkers, no; they prefer the hard stuff; the white rum, they take pleasure in trying to out drinking their colleagues; one is almost famous here when you can hold your liquor. For the Thomas's and the Faster's this will be a busy time too, Florence is planning a celebration at the manor for family and a few friends, and the Thomas! Well they'll be doing what everyone else's is doing; keeping up the tradition. Ammi probable will get a few dresses to make, it's the sugar cane season and the ones who work on the farm will have a few bob to spend. But she'll be doing her usual Good Samaritan work to; she'll be visiting the poor and needy to help them through these busy times; and even though they now have the carers looking after them, she's helping to make sure they have a good Christmas. The big day is getting closer and the activities in this little part of the Island are building up to a crescendo, there is lots of goodwill here now; which is not always the case. But people will be People; sometime one has to take them as one finds them; but Christmas brings out the best in them. It's Christmas Eve and this is one of the most important day in the calendar, tonight is watch night; no one sleeps. The church which is the centre of everything holy will be in progress until very late; and with most of the district will be going there; the Pastor will be a long time on his rostrum. But meanwhile in all the hustles and bustles Ammi had to remain mindful of her main objective; her plans to go to England, it's less than a month away, she'll never stop thinking that very soon she'll be leaving her beloved family for the unknown; and this will be her last Christmas here with them, it saddens her plenty. But what's the alternative? is to remains here and hope for the best. But she knows hope doesn't bring success if the opportunity doesn't present itself for one to gravitate, at church on a night like tonight they'll praying for her, for the good Lord to watch over her during her travels on her quest abroad.

The pastor would make it a point to gets her to the rostrum to stand next to him; a way of using her as an example to the other. We're losing our dear sister Ammi he said; take a good look at her; soon she'll be gone; the one person in our midst with a kind heart and the attitude to help others, sisters and brothers we should bow at the feet of our dear Sister Ammi. Well the Pastor wanted them to feel guilty; they backslide on the offer they made to help care for the sick and helpless. How is it she can be kind-hearted sisters and brothers and rest of us are so unkind even to the ones who need our help. Thanks to her and her father (Brother Thomas) along with Mrs. Faster those that are sick are now cared for. Sisters and Brothers there's a lesson here to be learnt and unless we learn that lesson and take it on board we certainly cannot call ourselves Christians. The Fasters were in church too; and the Pastor makes it an issue to thank the Minister for helping the people of his district. It's never been done before by any of your predecessors Sir he said, from the bottom of our hearts; and I'm speaking for everyone here; we thank you. But Mr. faster been the politician he couldn't pass up the opportunity to lay down markers for the future, so he takes to the rostrum, he thank them again for the contribution they made towards his wedding; and of course he went on to made promises. Well what else would a politician do given the chance?. He speaks of Mr. Thomas in high esteem, this gentleman shows me the error of my ways amongst other things; and now I'm a happily married man; thank you sir. Well! Tonight supposed to be a night of celebration about Christmas; and nothing must get in the way of that, the night is young and Pastor Green must have his pound of flesh, wouldn't it be a grand idea if the ones who can would share Christmas with your neighbour or someone whom have less than you he asked, and then there was silence; there was no response; Christians or none Christians; on this day they like their solitude with only their family. Well Sisters and Brothers I leave you with your own conscience, and always remember this, the good Lord is watching down on you always. He now hopes they'll go home with his words ringing in their ears; and some of them might comply with his suggestion. They'll be going home in the big hours of the morning, some won't bother to sleep; they'll be putting the finishing touch to their Christmas preparation.

Christmas day has arrived; the surroundings are quiet, there's a hush here it's almost eerie, something wonderful has happened; it's Christmas day; and everyone even the non-believers; and there aren't many of them here, they'll reside to their homes like everyone else. This silence will be observed until the sun goes down, then the District will be woken up, friends will be visiting friends and fire rockets and cribs (the big one) will be going off all over the district; the celebration is now well and truly started. From now on the twelve days of Christmas will be more like a month; well most got nothing to do nowhere to go; so they continue celebrating. Today is Boxing Day; for some it's competition day; today someone not only going be rich but also going to be famous. Today the winner; he or she; will be the toast of the district for one whole year. There'll be whispers as to whom the public think got the best bake; but there'll be no betting, no; it's not taboo, but some will be doing good business in the meantime selling all kind of goodies. But the contestants will do well to kept watch on their entry; even at this late stage their goods can be sabotage. The judges arrive and take their places ready to go; however if any of the competitors have any objection towards any of the judges he or she can have that judge removed from the panel, and there were objections. They want these two particular judges removed and replaced by sister Ammi and Mr. Wilson, there're rumours that they have vested interest in one of the competitor. There was a bit of unpleasantness regarding these two judges; and somewhat a surprise as they're supposed to be Christians. The panel withdrew to consider the situation; while outside they want to know if this rumour was true, they're somewhat ashamed that that one or two of theirs has brought their prestigious competition into disrepute. Well they might not able to found the culprits guilty; but they most certainly have to leave the panel, and of course their replacements should be trustworthy, respectable citizens. Sister Ammi who's like an angel here is been revered in the district and beyond, Mr. Walker who is one of the more affluent citizen of the district has found his place again amongst the people he once withdrew from, thanks to his neighbour Mr. Thomas. The judges return with the announcement of the withdrawal of these two judges, there was cheers of relieves. But there was an almighty cheer when their replacements were announced; Sister Ammi and Mr. Walker; and even though they had asked for the two people in question, there were shouts of God bless you sister Ammi and other collections of praises. They were welcome on the panel with rapturous applause. In all the years of this competition this's the first time a judge or judges have been replaced, the prize money was pittance then; but now the prize money is twenty pounds; a big enough prize to tempt someone or some people into foul play. But they put a heavy load on sister Ammi young shoulder, irregardless of who's on the panel they see sister Ammi as the trustworthy one, the one to cast an honest eye over the proceedings.

The long delay is over and the competition begins, the entries all laid out on the table; but these entries have got no name visible, no, the names are in disguise. The aroma of buns are everywhere; and quite pleasant too, the judges will cast their weary eyes over the baking's; they're looking for that certain texture, they'll smell and cut a little bit to taste, and when all that is done they'll withdraw to make their decision. Outside there're lots of activities; the traders will be doing business and of course there're lots of speculations of who's the possible winner. They are anxiously waiting in anticipation of who'll be called the winner. Someone is going to be rich today; and the waiting is unbearable. But there're entertainments going on too, youngsters take to podium to do their recitations; and Government man Mr. Dunn who takes pleasure in his storytelling gave them a rendition of one of his mission when he was a fisherman; and it always makes good listening. They got singers too; these people love to sing; and there're plenty of them. There should be cheering when the judges emerged; but there was an uneasy hush, maybe there nerves jangling. The judges have an announcement, Mr. Walker who wasn't on the panel was asked be his friend Mr. Thomas beforehand if he would like to be an additional judge to the panel, oh yes he said; I would be honoured. He's doing that as a gesture to let him (Mr. Walker) feel welcome back into the fold. Mr. Thomas who was the head judge stood up, attention, attention; we have got an announcement, the crowd hold their breath; they thought he's about to announce the winner. He could see the look of anticipation on their face, you 've got to wait a little longer folks he said, but as he delayed the announcement the restless crowd shouts; come on, come on. Ladies and gentlemen he said, after many years of judging this competition I've decided to stand down, and the crowd shouts; no, no, no and why. But his influence here is stronger than any other in the district. So he calmed them down, folks! I'm not walking away, no; I'll still be a judge, but now we've got a new judge; and they wonder in silence, they're waiting in anticipation that this new head judge will be sister Ammi, but no; it can't be her; she'll be gone soon; and this appointment supposed to be a long term affair, so they're in for a disappointment but not too much of a disappointed. When the announcement was made that the new judge was Mr. Walker they cheer and whistle. I know you would approve said Mr. Thomas; he's missing from amongst f far too long; let's give him a rousing welcome, and they cheer.

Mr. Walker stood up, good people of Danville; is everyone had a good Christmas? Yes they shout, oh good he said; I'm so please, thank you for your kindness and for giving me this chance to be back amongst you' and thanks to my good friend Mr. Thomas for making me your head judge. I could go on but I know you're waiting anxiously to hear who the winner is, and they shout; yes, yes; tell us quick, patience folks; good things are worth waiting for he said, but not too long some shout, the crowd is now in high spirit anxious to hear the winner. Firstly I must tell you that all the entries were wonderfully tasty; you all have done a wonderfully good job; and I wish everyone a very happy and prosperous new year, and I hope we all will be here next year to do it all over again. I wish everyone the very best of luck; but there can be only one winner; and I hope it will receive in the good spirit; the kind of spirit we always show. But they're in for another big surprise; there'll be two runners up for the first time; of which they welcome. Here we go he said, at this point one could hear a pin drops. In third place; he paused; Mrs. Jenkins, and they cheer, come along Mrs. Jenkins; she was given an envelope with cash; but of course she doesn't know how much. In second place; Mr. Miller, and there were shout of boos from a section of the crowd. Well! He's not liked very well; he's one of those unpleasant fellows. And Now Ladies and gentleman I know you'll be please when I tell you that we have a tie; and the crowd shout; a tie; how could it be a tie; they weren't too happy about that, but the panel have their reason for doing so. Let hear it some shouting; but he paused for a while; probable just to keep them in suspense. Then he calls Ammi to stand next to him; handing her two envelopes with the prize money. Ladies and gentlemen here are your winners; and the crowd waited in in suspense as they've never had a tie before. The winners are; he paused; Millicent Grey and Mrs. Barker; there was an eerie hush for a while; then he repeats their name; and there was muted cheer. Would you come forward please; they walk forward; give them some cheers said Ammi nervously; well she's not used to all these eyes on her. However those few little words bring out an almighty cheer from the crowd for young Ammi. But some behave as though were disappointed regarding the dead-heat; but that was a deliberate ploy by the judges to share the prize money amongst them. Then suddenly there were rapturous applause and whistles; is as though they just come to their senses and realised who are the winners are; but it was Ammi and her father taking a bow and thanking them for making this competition possible. Head judge Mr. Walker ties up proceedings; he thanked everyone for coming; and thanked the participants for their good work and contributions, and God will we'll see you all here again next year, and they cheer. But that was a good move by the panel to splits up the loot; they knew there's a great deal of unrest amongst some of the people regarding the amount of cash. It was never so when the total cash prize was five pounds; and that is not healthy in this small community, so they did what they thought was best; split up the loot; with the prize split four ways; the winners get eight pounds each. The winners will be congratulated by most; not only for their win but from today they'll be honourable citizen, that distinction will be bestowed on them for one year of the year; an enviable position. The proceedings are over but the jollies continue long into the evening, and the Christmas celebrations? Well that will continue for some time yet.

But the winners of the competition have come together and decided to give their local community a treat, they have decided to spend a little of the prize money a hold a shindig, well! They're still in the grips of Christmas and the merriment continues; so these two winners think they should in a way share their winnings; and what better way to do so than have a party that they're paying for. It will be announced in church on Sunday and the words will get around as usual. Well Mrs. Barker and Miss Miller were in church to hear Pastor Green make the announcement, the Pastor talks about honesty and kindness and sharing; like these two people are doing. Then they were called to the rostrum to take a bow, and the congregation cheer. What's a shindig here? Well! These bush people can celebrate too when they get the chance, they ached for the chance to dress up in their one pair of Sunday best and show off, as this like the baptism will give them that chance. The children will be there too; and even the aged as long as they can walk will attending, a free for all. There'll be fun games of all sorts for both children and grownups alike; and the food? Well! With people bringing in their own home cooking; and there's plenty of that; there'll be plenty to eat, and of course the old run punch will be flowing in plenty. But not for everyone of course, some including the Christian, are teetotal. However! One or two of these Christians will hide and take a sneaky sup of the real thing, and as long as no one sees them; well! They get away with it; they're not thinking that the good Lord is looking down on them. At the end of the celebration there'll be lots of drunken bodies about; but it doesn't matter; wherever they fall they could lie there and sleep it off. But here it's not unusual; anytime during the week one could find someone lying by the roadside stone drunk,

But during the celebrations tragedy was to strike, the unexpected happened, it suddenly begins to rain. It was about six o'clock and there was an unusually warm breeze for this time of year. The sky was blue without a cloud in the sky; it suddenly got very warm; the suited people removed their jackets and perspiration pours. Then suddenly it was overcast; and it got darker and darker, the revellers are becoming concerned; it's time to go home and fast. Some were on their way when what could be described as a cloudburst, the heavens open and the rain just pours and pours. As people run for covers; taking shelter in the church; they couldn't believe what they're experiencing, never before had they experienced rainfall so heavily. The party come to an abrupt end; all that some of them are wondering about now; is how they are going to get home; these are those who live on the other side of the dry river. The chances are they'll be held up in the Church probable for a few days until the dry river recedes. In the meantime they'll get help for whatever they need from the locals. When the rain ceases some four hours later some of those who held up in the church are now returning home, these are those who live on this side of the river. Others will probably hole up in the Church until tomorrow and hoping the water would recede. Others will probably try to get over the amount of rum punch they drank, one thing for sure; they would do it again tomorrow if the money people would lay on. Sometime during the morning there's a rumour going around that someone has been found dead, as the news gets around and wouldn't take long, not in a little district like Danville, and when it was known for sure; the dead person was one of Christians, a Mr. Johnson; a man in his forties looks about seventy, it seems as though he's been getting at the rum punch sneakily. He obviously had too much of the stuff; how did he manage to get to where he's been found dead? That's the question on everyone lips. Well when it rains heavily here the water table (the path along the roadside) sometimes runs like a river, not enough to drown anyone or wash away thing other than tin cans. But if one was to lie face down in it and become unable to move one could be drowned, and that's how Brother Johnson was found, and innuendoes begin. Like the speculation when the rain fell after the baptism; it's the same now. It's a sign from God some said, he's a Christian he shouldn't be drinking the rum punch, others suggest that the party shouldn't be taking place in the churchyard with rum punch and other hard drink flowing. Remember the darkness? What darkness one asked; I never see any darkness, and everyone was putting their own spins on the matter.

The Pastor! Well whatever his thought he kept it to himself, but he knows that as long they believe that a miracle took place; and it's a sign from the God; showing them the folly of their ways; that belief will bring them flocking to the church; a clever move; or probable a sneaky move. The death of Mr. Johnson has put a damper on everything, for the rest of Christmas everything will be below keyed; the family will be thinking about the funeral. In Pastor Green sermon that Sunday he reminded his flock and others that they shouldn't forget that in the midst of elation there can be death, we witness it with our own eyes this week he said. He's getting at them and he's getting through to them, these people are fearful of the almighty; as one should; even the ones who are not regular at Church. A man could come at you with a machete and you probably run away; because you have no means to defend yourself, but there's more than a good chance if you confront him with the words of God before he assaults you he might spear you and walks away; such is the power of the Lord he reaches. But bear in mind that most of the people here are illiterate, they've never been to school so what they believe is what they have been told; and some will hold steadfast to it. This story will be told for generations to come, about the day when the clear sky suddenly turns black and the heavens open; and there was six months rain in a couple of hours; and brother Johnson Drown on the street. But who's to say the way that they interpret it isn't so, it happened; every word of it; but why it happened no one can tell for sure. Mr. Johnson was buried some four days later with the full attendance of the district; and because he was found dead on the only main road in the district; that spot will be marked. However because of their superstitious beliefs, they'll try to avoid that area of the road at all cost.

The Christmas celebration is somewhat dampened but it won't be for long, the advent of the New Year will raise their spirits once more. Most will be going to church to welcome in the New Year; others will be at the rum bars, and the chances are they'll be drunk long before midnight, not knowing when the New Year arrives. The ones who are sober probably are going by friends and neighbours to wish them a happy New Year and to carry on celebrating. However the good times must come to an end and even though some of them will go on celebrating long after the twelve days of Christmas; the good times will gradually fade away until everything is back to normality. On reflection this was the first Christmas they experienced joy and tragedy at the same time, in the Pastor sermon the following Sunday he reminded his brethren's to watch and pray and be faithful to the Lord and to yourselves, be not like brother Johnson who wasn't true to himself, one cannot fool the Lord by pretending that one is a Christian, no, the Lord sees and knows everything; one cannot hide himself from the Lord he preaches. Let us and learn a lesson from the death of Brother Johnson he said, you can't cheat God. Well! He was laying down the scripture to them in no uncertain way. On this day there're a whole lot of souls saved, the confessions were plentiful, some in fear because of what happened to brother Johnson, others probably feel it's time for them to give their heart to the Lord, Pastor Green's flock is getting bigger by the day.

19: The Preparation

Ammi is now busy making plans for her travels, there're quite a few loose ends to tidies up, but she hasn't got a lot of packing to do; with only one suitcase and some of what she's carrying will be things for her two cousins. But with less than two weeks to go she'll have plenty of time to spear. First the family have a dinner appointment at Mrs. Faster senior, she's giving this dinner in behalf of Ammi, and for a woman living on her own she also welcome the company of the Thomas entire family; and of course Florence and her husband will also be present. Saturday was overcast but dry; maybe it will rain later. About three o'clock the Thomas's set off for their appointment. but Rupert is gone ahead riding his bicycle and he'll probably be there before the others who drive, and he did, when John arrives Rupert was having something to drink, well Mrs. Faster senior loves the children; she behaves like a grandmother and love to spoil them. No sooner Florence arrived with her husband, she and her mother-in-law get on very well; and that caused the two families to have what seem to be a harmonious relationship. Well Mrs. Faster senior don't have to prepare dinner, no, Florence took her maid Mary along to do the cooking, she has to start from scratch; but no one is hungry; and it seems they'd rather talk than eat right now; and with Dorothy and Agnes have the world to put right food is the last thing on their mind. Of course Donald is back in his childhood home; since he leaves home to take up politic he hasn't returned as often as he would like, but now that the two families have formed a union he'll be certainly visiting more often. It's a good time for the families; whenever they meet there is never a dull moment, the children will be playing games, and as they can't go exploring like at the manor; they'll be playing their favourite game; snakes and ladders. But Rupert is a sore loser, this is his favourite indoors game; but that doesn't mean he's very good at it; his sister Maggie is so much a better player. Whenever he was beaten by her he usually throws a tantrum, and his father often warned him, if you cannot stand losing you shouldn't play the game; he usually sieged the game until he's calmed down. For Ammi! She'll be doing what Ammi likes doing; even away from her own home she'll be reading her bible, she doesn't go anywhere without it. in every home even those who cannot read there'll be a bible, the good old king James version comes in huge volumes and it usually takes pride of place in the home. Florence would often pick up the good book too; ever since she and John had ended their romance and he somehow managed to convinced her to visit his church; she's been a regular ever since; and some time with her husband too, she'll probably one day soon confess her sins and be baptised.

The time is now approaching four o'clock and dinner is about to be served, Mary has everything ready waiting for the dinner guests. Dinner is ready Miss Florence she said approaches her sitting in the swing in the yard, thank you Mary she said, go and tell Mrs. Faster, soon they all gather at the dining table. The conversation rages but mostly about England, a few people are returning home; they can't stand the cold said Dorothy, how did you know that Dorothy asked Florence, I read it in the Gleaner she said. Well that's the whole story; not everyone is going to like it said Donald. But I'll bet there're plenty more staying than those who are returning, and before long I believe those who are staying will no doubt come to make it their home and probably come to like it. But whatever they written in the Gleaner doesn't deterred the people from selling up to go said Florence, only yesterday paper there was an article about discrimination, this man wrote to his family about when he went into a shop to buy something, minding his own business; when this white man look at him and said, nigger why don't you go back home; but he wouldn't be drawn into an argument with the white man; then he came in his face and repeated, nigger! I'm talking to you; go back to where you came from. I'm sorry Mom; I know you wouldn't approve; but my temper gets the better of me and I punched him in the mouth. The article went on to say he was arrested for causing an affray, but was released the following day, the police officer just let me out and tell him; you're free to go, and Mom; I was so glad to get out of there I just hurried home. I read that article too said Donald and I must say I agree on one thing, if I was planning to travel to that country I would probably be having a second thought. On that same page another article talks about them (the white people) calling black people monkey, but also in the same article that man told his mom he's won't be coming home just yet until he gets what he went there for, and the conversation continues. It was the kind of conversation that John wants Ammi to hear; in the hope that it might deter her and help her changes her mind even at this late stage. But as far as that young man letter to his mother is concern it doesn't bother Ammi one bit; this young woman is a tough cuckoo; only her father thinks she's a soft twenty-year-old.

What do you think about that young man's letter to his mom Ammi asked John, but Florence was quick to come to Ammi's; come on John; it's only person's account of the situation, look around; the people who're leaving not exactly running back, and that young man also told his mom he's not coming back until he gets what he went there for, something good must be there for him to say that. Florence knows that John would pull all the punches to prevents Ammi from going to England, there's an old saying; if one wants to make good of himself his nose has to run said Agnes, hard work never killed anyone. But we're not talking about hard work Aggie said John, it's about living in a foreign land amongst people who don't like you; and you can't exactly pack up whatever you got and return home. Dad! I know you don't want me to go; partly because you think I'm incapable to look after myself; and I appreciate that Dad; but I know I can look after myself; so you just have to trust me said Ammi. I seem to remember we had this conversation once before and all was agreed said Florence, I haven't got any children of my own but I'm old enough to know that as a parent you can't hold onto your children forever; one day you'll have to let them go. Thank you Florence said John; I know that comment was made for my benefit, you're right; but it doesn't mean I shouldn't worry; and she's not leaving home to go to another parish in the Parish, no, she's leaving for another country some five thousand miles away; and if anything should go wrong, God forbid; I can't jump in my car to go and help her. A day might come when she wants to get married; I would love to be there to walks her down the aisle, like I did you Florence, but it's so far away I wouldn't be able to attend. Imagine I'm here as a father knowing that some strange man walking my daughter down the aisle, for me it's not a good feeling he said. It happens all the time though John said Dorothy; we as parents can't always be there; so as you said; some strangers will have to do the honours. But I fully understand your thinking John she said, a good parent will worry all the time about their children; it's the right thing to do. However Dorothy could be reflecting on her relationship with her only daughter Muriel; whatever took place between them at no time did she ever mention her name; she must be grieving; probably that's why she gravitates towards the Thomas's children; she's no doubt hoping that Donald will give her grandchildren soon. So remind me again when you're leaving Ammi asks Dorothy, on the sixteen mom said Ammi, that's just over a week said Dorothy in a kind of surprising manner, well young lady you're going to be missed around here she said. Florence glares at her husband with a gentle shake of the head as to say; don't make any more comments like the one you just made; she knows it will make John even sadder. If the politician had intended to say anything further; after that glare from his wife he withholds his thought. Dinner is over; and for afters? Well the locals don't do dessert; but Mary places some lovely Julie mangoes on the table, the mangoes are from the manor; the ground is laden with all kinds of fruits.

The evening has brightened up from its gloomy condition earlier, however it's running late and when John glances at his watch; we better make ready to go he said, he's thinking of returning home to make plans for church in the morning, Rupert who went outside to checks on his wheels return to say goodbye; he's leaving before the others as usual. Ride carefully now Rupert said Dorothy, she'll miss them when they are gone, as an elderly person on her own for most of the time; having company is a welcome relief; she comes alive when she's with the Thomas's and her son love it. Now it's time for John and his family to leave, they greet each other out in the yard before they loaded up and take off, Donald and Florence will stay a little longer before they themselves leave. But it's wonderful how out of what are considered dire situations come the making of two families, it was only when the three people went to see the Minister on behalf of the sick people in their district that the beginning of what is now the union of the two families; one could say it's a match made in heaven. But they'll have one more dinner at the Thomas before she departs. That Sunday evening Ammi pays a visit to her mother's grave; it was overcast but wasn't too dark; she was buried under the mongo tree and they built a seat there; she sat there for hours; some time with members of her family and reminiscence about her life with her, in a few days she'll be gone but she knows that her family Will take good care of the grave, but she'll come again before she leaves for England.

20: The Last Days

Ammi would pay one last visit to the people she usually cares for; she couldn't leave without saying goodbye; and she'll be saddened to do so, but Ammi been Ammi it got to be done. Old Mr. Wilson was upset when she told him she was leaving tomorrow; she couldn't very well tell him that she'll back soon; that would be a blatant lie; and a good Christian doesn't do that. So she done the next best thing, she sat with him until he calms down and gives him a hug and then leave. The others were more understanding; Mrs. salmon who lost a leg and barely hops around on a single makeshift crouch, a woman in her thirties but the sickness take its toll on her; she looks ancient, God bless you Miss Ammi she said, I hope I'll see you again, I hope so too Mrs. salmon she said, I really hope so too, even though she knows it highly unlikely. This will be the last time she'll see these poor unfortunate people, she knows she'll never see them again; and how long will they be around for? God only knows. But the carers are doing their best for them; but for some, the regular help came for too late. Unfortunately their time will soon be up. There's nothing more physical left for her to do; just enjoys her surrounding; she might never see it again. She'll visit the old water hole she usually fetched water from, the cosy spot under the black mango tree. Sometimes she and her sister Maggie usually sat there to talk nonsense, and that's what they'll do today; only instead of gossiping, they'll be talking about what she'll be hoping for in England. When you're settled I'm coming to join you said Maggie; I'm going to ask Dad to send me, Ammi laugh! You know he'll never do that; he wants you to finish you're education and get some kind of office job. I overheard a conversation he had with Miss Florence and Mass Donald the day we were at the manor and… She paused as Maggie butted in, and you were eavesdropping; Ammi how you could you? she asks, I did nothing of the sort said Ammi; and don't you go thinking that I'm listening into other people conversation. I was walking by the window when I heard; I'm not deaf you know, sorry said Maggie; I know you wouldn't; I don't know what came over me. Somehow young Maggie feels ashamed of accusing her Sister of listening into other people's conversations. Anyway what did you hear she ask. What! Exclaimed Ammi out loud; after your accused me of eves dropping into Dad's conversation you now want to know what they were talking about? Maggie laugh, talk about been hypocritical said

Ammi. Alright! I'll tell you anyway, you know you want to said Maggie, You can't keep a secret from me; you're just dying to tell me; so go ahead and tell me. Well Dad was telling them he would like you to be a teacher; and Miss Florence was agreeing with him, that's it? That's all there is asked Maggie; Maggie sigh, and you call that a secret? Well I never she comment.

But as far as Maggie's comment is concern about Ammi cannot keep a secret; she's so wrong; only she knew the secret between those two; her Dad and Florence, and that secret she'll take with her grave. So he would like you to be a teacher? What do you think about it Maggie? I never give it a thought; the truth of the matter is; I don't really know what I want to do; as least not yet; and with everyone is leaving this place; it will soon be like a ghost town; and with you gone I'll be alone. Maggie! Don't be so dramatical; is not like you, Rupert and Annie are still here; don't day? Annie is a little girl and Rupert is a boy; I can't talk to him about things I talk to you about. Rupert! He's got no time for me; he's got no time for anyone, he does things and gets away with it, Dad is not saying anything, yes I know said Ammi; Dad spoils him rotten, he'll get a job with Dad working on the estate. Anyway you'll be alright Maggi; I'm sure if things not working out as it should Dad will consider sending you away to England. But you have to try your best to achieve the best in school; he's counting on you; and you're doing very well now; try to continue to do so and make him proud, yes mother she said sarcastically; I'll do my best, Ammi slap her gentle over the head; and they laugh. So don't go spoils it because of your consideration of going abroad, that wouldn't be wise said Ammi, I wouldn't do that, why do you think I would? Dad would be throwing his money away, I'll do my best and if my best isn't good enough then I'll think of something else. It was a healthy conversation between two sisters; but Maggie is not done yet. Over the years these two sisters hardly ever talk about boys; even though from time to time Maggie sneaks away to talk with Eugene, her parent knows nothing about it of course; if old man Thomas ever gets wind of it he would go mental. Well people here are old fashion, types of parents like Mr. Thomas don't like to see their daughter talking to young men, and probably they're thinking that a young woman should wait until she's more mature or even old. Are you going to get married when you go to England? Well give me a chance; let me get there first; I don't know what I'll do or find when I get there; and who said I will find a man whom I'll marry? So what are you saying; you're not thinking about looking for a man over there? Christian does look for men too you know, Maggie! I don't know what came over you; why are you so eager for me to find a man? Are you trying to tell me something about you and Eugene asked Ammi? if that be the case you better not let Dad finds out. Don't be silly; nothing is going said Maggie; we just meet and talk, really asked Ammi, if that mango tree at the line could talk it would tell a whole lot of things, isn't that where you and meet generally? But how did you know? I know; and your secret is safe with me.

At this point Maggie saddens, and close to tears, honestly Ammi; we only hold hands and nothing more; and I'm sorry; I should told you him. Well never mind me; is what Dad is going to say if he ever found out, as a matter of fact I think you should tell him, what! She exclaims loudly; He would kill me; you know that. Well! You asked me about marriage; if he loves you and the feeling is neutral then you can get marry. Really Ammi? How could you say that; Dad would never agree for me to get marry; not until I'm old; and anyway I don't want to get marry; I'm far too young. Ammi thinks about it; then you have a problem dear Sister; what if you got pregnant; then your whole life is over and Dad will probable kill you then, they both laugh out loud, I told you we only hold hands; we never even kiss. But how long that will go for before it leads to something else asked Ammi; and how long he will be patience for? Listen! I never at any time tell you what to do; but right now I'm going to tell what I think you should do. Either tell Dad you're talking to this boy, after all he and Mr. Walker are good friends now; he might see things a little different, or stop seeing him completely. Put your feelings aside and tell him you can't see him anymore; you must not let Dad found out for himself. Ok big Sister; I take what you said on board; and you know what; I'll stop seeing Eugene, I didn't really love him anyway; he was just convenient to talk to. Ammi laughed; convenient Maggie; I never heard convenient been for a conversation. But seriously though Sis; don't you hope to get married one day asked Maggie, I never give it a thought said Ammi; it never crosses my mind, Maggie laugh out loud, why you laugh ask Ammi, I never thought I would live to see the day my sister tell a lie, what are you saying ask Ammi with a sad expression, what lies have I told you? Ok! Then What about Harry? he's always fixing your bicycle; he fancies you rotten and… she paused as Ammi interrupts, well that's his business; and if what you said is true; I never gives him any reason for him to felt the way. Anyway if I'm looking a boyfriend… Maggie interrupts, I know; you wouldn't be looking at Harry. But who knows what the future holds for them, one day probably they will get married, as of now it's the furthest thing t from their mind, at least Ammi's mind.

It's now about five o'clock; they been sitting with her for the past three hours, They set off back home with Maggie and have a decision to make, Ammi last words to her, I don't want to be in England and hearing dad throws you out of the house or worst. She also told her to talk to her mother about it, Miss Agnes usually sees things differently from Dad; you know that she said. But what would Agnes be saying about this delicate situation, she'll probably be taking the side of her husband, after all is her daughter's future in question here. Maggie wasn't too nervous to talk to her mother about it though; nevertheless she wanted her sister with her when she approaches her mother. It about eight o'clock and their Dad isn't home yet; a good time to talk to their mother. Mom! Could I talk to you? of course dear; what about? She hesitates, well it concerns a boy mom, a boy? What about him? Well I've been talking to him mom, what do you mean you been talking to a boy she asked, and then suddenly she has a thought; except it's the wrong one. Well! She was thinking her daughter was pregnant. Oh my God she exclaimed, are you pregnant she asks with eyes pulping and her hands on her head, oh my God she exclaim again and again. But mom I said I'm talking to the boy; I didn't say I slept with him mom, why did you think that mom, she begins to cry. But before this encounter gets out of hand Ammi ventures in, Miss Aggie! All Maggie is saying she's talking to this boy and nothing else; she's telling you because she likes him and would like to go on seeing him. Did you know of this Ammi she asked, well I saw them together once or twice miss Aggie but that's all, and they only hold hands, how can you be so sure she asks, she said so miss Aggie and I believes her. So you think I was pregnant mom she said smiling; well she's the bold one of the family, she usually said whatever comes to her head. If you think it's a laughing matter just you wait until your father to hear about it she said, but that's why I'm talking to you about it mom; so that you can talk to him for me, what would I be saying to him; your daughter want your consent to have a boyfriend, he'll probably kill me for asking, no! I won't talk to him about it, and you shouldn't be thinking about boyfriend; you should be concentrating on your studies; you're far too young. Mom! I'm nearly twenty; and you think you're old enough now do you? Your father has invested lots of money on you to make him proud; if you want to get him mad then you tell him. Ammi was listening attentively but without anything to say, she's in agreement with her stepmother but she's not talking against her sister either. But she doesn't want to go away leaving her father and her sister at war, she knows how strong-headed Maggie can be; but she's hoping that this time she doesn't take the high road.

Agnes was still in a shock; she doesn't even remember to ask who this boy is; and bear in mind there are only a few upstanding young men in the district. Well as she didn't ask Maggie didn't bother to tell her. So what are your intentions now madam she asked, are you going to tell your father? No mom; I'm not; I won't talk to Eugene again. Well she didn't mean to mention his name either; it just pops out, Eugene? Yes Mom; Eugene Walker she asks, yes mom, so when the both of you meet she ask, well we go to the same school mom remember? Agnes makes a sighing grunt, I do hope you're not going to bring shame on this family. Mom! What are you thinking about, I told you before and I'll tell you again; we only hold hands; I'm never going to get pregnant holding his hands, Ammi smile looking away, not wanting her stepmother to see her, you want to watch your mouth Madam; I don't like what's coming out of it, I don't want to hear any more; go find something to do, when your father comes in you can have it out with him. But after hearing her mother's anger and her fear of her father; she has decided there and then to break off their friendship without her father knowing anything about it. Ok mom, I won't talk to him again, we won't hold hands again; so please don't tell Dad Mom, and if he ever found out and then gets to know that I knew about it and keep it from him; then what; oh no! You must tell him or I will. Well the fearless one suddenly gets the jitters, she's afraid to face her Dad and tell him she been holding hands with a boy; even though the boy is his friend son. Please mom! Don't let me do it, I said I won't talk to him again and I will. Ammi intervene, she knows her sister is in deep trouble if their Dad ever hears of it, Please Miss Aggie; can't this be a secret between the three of us? She promises not to talk to Eugene again so Dad doesn't have to know. The car drives in the yard, John is home, please Mom said Maggie; you want to see me kill? I'm begging you Mom. Keep quiet said Agnes; talk about something else while I think. Is anybody home he calls out, there was no one about he could see; the three women are in the kitchen. Down here John shouts Agnes, as he makes his way to the kitchen Ammi calls out, hi Dad; but Maggie said nothing, she's trembling with fear; wondering if her mother is going to tell her Dad. Maggie! You're here too in the kitchen; what a surprise he said fatherly like; but Maggie didn't respond, well! Unlike Ammi avoid the kitchen like the plague, He didn't tarry with them; no; he's got to go work on his book, generally before Friday he has to total up the amount of hours his men work then hand his book into the accountant.

Dinner will be ready soon John so don't go anywhere said Agnes, he walks away to the dining room; that's where he'll do his work. I'm sticking my neck out here for you said Agnes; we'll speak no more about it, you're a young woman and growing up fast; maybe too fast, and I know whichever boy you talk to won't be good enough for your Dad. So what are you going to do? You're going to give yourself time; time to finish your studies and probably get a job, you'll be old enough then to stand up to your father when you find someone you love. Thank you Mom, oh thank you Mom she said hugging her, let me tell you; you're my daughter and I love you, but I'm keeping this secret not because of you but because of your father, yes Mom, I know; but thank you just the same. Alright! Now go set the table, I thank you too Miss Aggie said Ammi; I don't know what would happen if Dad hear about it, he would probably take it out on me too, Maggie she set off to the dining room leaving her mother and Ammi. So since we're on the subject; have you ever consider having a boyfriend Ammi asked Agnes; after all you're going away to live and work on your own, your father won't be there to have a say on who you choose. I really never give it a thought Miss Aggie; not while I'm here, I was far too busy; and anyway there isn't a boy here I would choose for a boyfriend, but I suppose one day I might find a boyfriend. Well you will get married one day too; I know you will, but make sure he loves you more than you love him, a decent young lady should get marry a virgin; the man would have more respect for you, Ammi smiles wryly. Did you marry a virgin Miss Aggir? That's not a question you ask a woman with five children she said; and in truth I wouldn't tell you; what I'm telling you is what the right thing to do is. She was thinking of saying something like; so I can take it that you weren't a virgin when you got marry Miss Aggie; but she thought that would be too presumptuous, she had a sneaky giggle behind her back. Well your father was my second love, my first died in an accident, but look! All I'm trying to tell you is to be careful and be on your guard when men come after you; and they will, and they'll tell that they love when they're only after one thing. I know Miss Aggie; I see the way they behave around here; many girls' lives are ruined; they end up with babies without any fathers. But I'll be careful Miss Aggie; don't worry, we'll be counting on you she said. Now the lesson in love and relationship is over; Ammi load up and take the food to the dining room, Rupert is out and about so there'll be six for dinner. At the table three people shared a secret; Maggie keep giving her Mom the odd look, she's still on tenterhooks; she can't be sure her mother won't decide to raise the matter with her Dad, but Agnes looked at her and tell her to settle down and eat her dinner.

It's approaching seven o'clock and they were still having dinner when Minty began barking; but no one moves, it could be someone passing by; he usually barks at most everyone who goes past by the gate and would stop barking only when the passers-by have gone out of sight. But he kept barking and alert Brutus; and he began barking too; which means someone is about to enter through the yard. John got up to have a look, it was his half-brother Denis Bradly, he came to say goodbye to Ammi even though she's got two full days left, he brings something for her to take for his daughter Daphne in England too. John told minty to be quiet, Come on in Denis he said, is that dog in chain he asks referring to Brutus the big dog, don't be a wimp man come on said John, he walks in, we're having dinner; Agnes could fix you a place if you want, if it's not too much bother said Denis, I heard that Denis said Agnes, don't talk daft man; come and sit down. But before he sits down he greets the girls, are you all set to go Ammi he asked, Yes uncle Denis; but the waiting is a little depressing, maybe you're anxious to leave us he said; I'm don't rightly know what I'm feeling Uncle Denis; all I know it saddens me to be leaving. But I'm looking forward to see Daphne and Hillary again, I'm sure you are; three young women together; I imagine it will be fun. Agnes set him a plate and served him, so what do you want? Denis asks John, my niece is going away and you are my brother; do I need more reason to come here? Oh yes there's another reason though, oh! What's that ask John, to eat at your table he said, very funny, said John. Then why don't you come more often ask Agnes, you got no woman cooking for you; there's always be a place here for you. He can't, a gambler got no time for himself said John, and the dice game is always on his mind. You remember what Mom always said to you John ask, I'm sure you're going to tell me said Denis, yes, I'm going to tell you alright; because she's gone to her grave the poor dear thinking about you. You'll die a pauper because of your gambling she always said, that was over ten years ago and you've still never given it up. Well I tried you know; you don't know how much I tried; but it's difficult to give up he said. John if Denis choke on his food it'll be your fault said Agnes, let him have his dinner in peace, that's what he does always Aggie; give me grief said Denis. Everyone can't be the same brother; and you weren't always a Christian, were you? No! if I remember you were no saint he said. But I see the light and I changed my bad ways said John, praise be to God he said; you could do the same too. Ammi hearing all that; she knows what her uncle Denis was saying about her father was true because she knows some of his pass secrets, but she also knows he has put all that behind him now.

Well it's getting late and Denis is ready to leave, well Ammi if I don't see you again before you leave, have a good flight and tell Daphne I'm fine. Thanks Uncle Denis and I will tell her said Ammi. He stood up, thank for dinner Agnes he said; I'll come again on Sunday for dinner, don't just said it said Agnes; come and have dinner, he won't be coming said John; he'll be throwing dice and clapping his fingers, never mind my brother Agnes; I'll be here for dinner come Saturday and to say goodbye to Ammi, well see that you do, said John; we'll be expecting you. It's ten o'clock and the night is pitch dark, John holds the gas lamp so that he could see as far as the gate, that's where he leaves his bicycle, they say goodbye and off he went. Well another interesting day is over; and there'll be no washing up of plates tonight; it's too late, that will be done in the morning. The girls say good night and leave their parent; they're not in any hurry to retire. But Maggie won't be dropping off to sleep in a hurry; she'll be wondering what if her mother tells her father about their conversation that afternoon. But Aggie didn't say she wouldn't and she didn't say she would either; so all she can do is hope and pray. While at the table John got a thought, you know Agnes I should ask Denis if he's saving the money Daphne is sending him, you know I have a bad feeling about that, knowing Denis all that money is gone in his gambling. You should ask him said Agnes; he's not going to like; but it would be a disaster if that girl sending money to him to put away and he's squandering it, yes John; you must ask him she said. I think I have a better idea he said, then he paused; as a matter of fact I think I have a brilliant idea, well are you going to keep it to yourself said Agnes as John dolly over his idea. I won't ask him at all, no, I'll write a letter for Ammi to take to Daphne; and I'll put it all in there, don't send any money for your father to save for you, there's a chance he might be gambling it away. But you don't know that for sure said Agnes; you only assume that might be the case, you know what Aggie; now I think about it I'm sure he hasn't got any of that money saved. I know my brother and Daphne must be told, and as a matter of fact I think I'll ask him too, he's my brother and if can embarrass him enough for him to see the folly of his ways; then it wouldn't matter if he gets angry; and It would all worth it. After thinking that poor girl might be wasting her time in England because the few pounds she sent home for savings is frittered away by her father; Agnes has agrees with John in his approach to the situation.

But John won't wait until Saturday when Denis comes by for dinner as he has promise to, no; he's going to pay him a visit after work tomorrow. He's self-employed like many of the people here, meaning they are cultivators on a very small farm and most of their days are spent there, at time they even sleep there, It's a chance when John calls on him he might be there; and if he's not John would know where to find him. That evening after work John calls at his home; but he wasn't there; so he set off to his farm. He drives as far as he can in the narrow bush road then parks the car. It's quite a long walk through a narrow pathway, after about three or so minutes he arrives at the farm. He calls out for Denis several times while looking around; but there was no sign of him. He's thinking of a few places he might be; so he sets off to the most likely place he might find him. Then there was a rustling and a sound like someone groans coming from the overgrowth of runner beans, he moves toward the plantation and he could see a bicycle lying in the hedge. He recognised it; it belongs to Denis, he suddenly gets a bad feeling, but he didn't have to look hard; he could see Denis lying among the runner beans. Denis, Denis he calls; but he didn't respond, getting hold of him he raised his head and with a quick glance he could see he's bleeding from the left eye and his face is badly swollen, it appears he's been badly beaten. But John didn't panic; no; all he's thinking is how to get him to his car so he can get him to the Doctor. Well! John is a big build of a man but it's going to be hard to carry a not too small man that distant, and with no one in sight to help he do the next best thing. It's going to hurt like hell but he'll have to bear it, he puts him on the bicycle with him (John) shouldering the weight, and he pushes the bicycle through the narrow footpath to the car, it was hard and to hear him groaning didn't make it any easier. It was quite late; and the Doctor probably stops working by now, nevertheless John guts him in the car and set off to Browns Town. It's over a six-mile drive; but even with bright headlights in this pitch dark night he won't be hurrying; he has to pick his way through the potholes. He was in luck; Doctor Roberts is still in his surgery; from the street he could see movement in the building, he parks his car but didn't try to carry him in, no, he went in to talk to the Doctor first. Of course these two knew of each other through their mutual friend Florence, now Mrs. Faster. Whatever John said to him they didn't tarry; quickly the two men emerge from the building to the car, they carefully took him (Denis) from the car and into the surgery. After the Doctor examines him he tells John the bad news, he has lost an eye, John says the Doctor; and he's badly beaten. But John wasn't surprised; he could see the condition the eye was in when he first found him. How did he come by such injury asked the Doctor? No idea he said, I got angry with him last night so I decided to go and see him this evening, he wasn't at his home so I went to the farm only to find him lying there, and he could be in a worse condition John if you didn't find him when you did said the Doctor. Do you think you'll find out who the beater was, John? I don't know Doc. but I'll ask around. However! With his influence in the community John will almost certainly find out who's the culprit.

After the Doctor administered his medication he helped John get him back to the car, they shook hands and parted company. But Denis is not going to his place of abode, no, he's going home with John. Arriving at his home he called for Rupert, he needed help to take him inside. Rupert comes out; and when he sees his uncle all bandaged up he was shocked. What happens to him Dad he asks looking all startled, I don't know; I found him beaten up, but by whom dad? I don't know that either; I don't yet; but I'll find out. Poor Uncle Denis; is he going to alright Dad, but John had enough of the question, come help me get him inside, he's going into your room that's alright Dad; and they get him into bed. You can sleep with your little sister, poor Uncle Denis he repeats, go on; you go to bed now said John. Meanwhile Agnes and the others in bed unaware of Denis's predicament, John tiptoe into bed; he didn't want to wake up anyone. However Agnes awake as he enters into bed is there anything wrong John she asks, well the way he tiptoed into bed make her suspicious. Well yes and no he said, Agnes with sleep in her eyes asked; what do you mean, he didn't want to alarm her so casually said; I bring Denis home; he's in Rupert's room. Agnes becomes more wide awake, why? Is there something wrong she asked, Now they both sat up in bed, he's in bad trouble Aggie, what do you mean she ask with anxiety, and then John tell her the whole story. I'll go and take a look at him she said, he's resting now; look in on him in the morning said John. Oh my God, what would have happened if you didn't go looking for him? she asked. He probably would have died, well he's not out of the woods yet; and he lost an eye too. He lost an eye? asked Agnes in amazement; oh my God; poor Denis; what are you going to do John? Well I can't give him back the eye but I can find out who done it. Let's hope he looking better in the morning, they chatted until they fall asleep. Early that morning Agnes went to his room, he was sitting up in bed; but Agnes was shocked to see him with his head bandaged up. Denis she calls softly while pulling up the one chair in the room to his bedroom, good morning Agnes he said in a faint voice, Denis, what are you doing to yourself; how are you feeling? Very bad my eye is killing me he said, but Agnes cannot take a look at it; it's in bandages. Not knowing what to do she call John who was just getting dress, he might go to work today; and then again he might not depending on Denis condition. He puts on his housecoat and goes to see. How are you feeling? he asks, my eye, he said in a whisper, he went back to the room to fetch the pain killer the Doctor gave him, here he said, open your mouth, and he swallows, it will take a while to work I should imagine he said. You should lie back, Agnes shakes up the pillows and put them together so as to raised his head and lays him back, I'll go and make you some breakfast; you must be hungry.

However they didn't tell him he's lost the eye, no; they didn't want to worry him anymore; he'll find out for himself. Ammi whose room is in the back heard the talking but as she got no reason to budge she was still lying down, but when she went to the kitchen and her step-mother was there doing breakfast, somebody was up early this morning Miss Aggie; what happened? She was straight to the point, it's your Uncle Denis; he's been beaten up badly, and he lost an eye but he doesn't know it yet. She heard the first but she repeats it again, he lost an eye Mom? Oh my Good Lord; poor Uncle Denis, So where's he now she asked, he's in Rupert's room, oh my God she said as she leaves to see him. She enters the room quietly but observing him at the same time lying in the bed, he has no idea who's in the room. Uncle Denis how are you feeling she ask standing over him, he mumbles something but she didn't hear, are you in pain? Yes he said in a whisper, the pain killer is slow to work or it doesn't work at all. Agnes walks in with breakfast but someone has to feeds him, Ammi is trying to but it's difficult; he can hardly chew, you should make him some porridge Miss Aggie; he can't chew; yes; I should have done that in the first place said Agnes, I'll go and do that now. She leaves again for the kitchen while Ammi tries to feed him some cocoa tea. By now John has left for work; with the two women looking after him he's in good hands. At work John is having talks with his workmen, some of these men are the people he (Denis) gambled with and John holds the belief that the beating he took is caused from gambling; and if that is the case then someone must know something. But for today no one he talks to know anything. He also believes the culprit won't want to hang around; it won't sit comfortably with most of these men knowing that John's brother has been beating up. Well! They are loyal to him; and you don't beat up John Thomas's brother and get away lightly, certainly not, they're more than likely to take revenge.

Friday morning the sun was up and the sky was blue, the breeze was gentle and warm, it was a great morning, the women change the plaster on Denis' eye, it's in a bad way and probably has to visit the Doctor again, but his pain has receded. There was a commotion when John got to work, no one was working, and the men were waiting for him. People were whispering and talking amongst themselves, his right-hand man approaches him with the news, early this morning Fred was found dead lying in a trench he said. What the story ask John, how did he die? It seems as though he was beaten to death Sir, well who was he fighting with he ask, no one knows Sir said the man, ok men said John; gather round. The men were about seventeen strong, now then; I would like to know how it is that Fred is dead and who was he fighting with? But to a man no one knows. But he suspects right away that this could be revenge killing; none of these men knew anything? The conspiracy was plain to be seen. Ok men; go on back to work; I'll have to notify the police. But crimes here whether its murder or otherwise; the police is as useless as a dumbbell. But John knows it's a revenge killing and he'll never know the culprit or culprits, and as for his brother indoors this is a concern; his death had been avenged; except he doesn't know and probable never will. It was Saturday morning before the police turn up, after their investigation they visit John at his home, not to interrogate him but to inform him of their findings; which is nothing. But they would like to talk to his men on Monday when they gather at work. Of course John agrees; but says nothing of his brother's predicament. Right now John is got more pressing matters on his mind; his daughter leaving for England tomorrow, today is the last day the family is got together; they'll want to spend the evening together with the faster's.

Today is the last day Ammi has to reflect, the family will have their last dinner together with the Faster, and there'll be sad faces and even tears the dinner table today. Well! It's not exactly a good time for the family; With Denis serious beating and God only knows whether he'll survive; and Ammi going away to England the situation is bad news all round. However they have to carry on; Agnes is seeing to dinner; this could be one of her special ones; she's preparing chicken; one of their own homegrown produce; it's not often people here have chicken for dinner; and if they did it will be on a Sunday. As the Fasters arrive Dorothy calls for Agnes; down here Dorothy; I'm in the kitchen she said; and she makes her way there. But Donald wants to know how Denis is doing, he's not acquainted with him (Denis); but he knows he's the brother of John so he make it his business to visit him while he's there. Denis was still in bed and still in bandages and will be for some time, and his pain has eased somewhat with the help of the pain killer tablets. The two men never met before but Denis knew him, not because he's the Member of Parliament and canvasses here many a times; but because he got married in their district and everyone was there. Hello Denis; how are you feeling he enquires, with his left eye lost and the one good eye partially closed he can hardly see anything or anyone, I'm alright he said in a low voice, Donald was standing close to the bed but he didn't ask him about his eye. I hope you're not in too much pain Denis he enquires, not too much he said almost in a whisper. But who am I talking to he enquires, it's your Member of Parliament Donald Faster, I heard of your accident from your brother so I come to see how you are, thank you very much he said a little louder. But Donald doesn't want to over-tax him with any more questions and talks, he can see that he's a very ill man, he'd better leave him alone and allow him to get some rest. Well I must go now Denis; but I hope you'll feel better soon; he slowly raised his hand in acknowledgement to him as he walks away. But the Member of Parliament has just told a big white lie; he didn't come specifically to see him, no, while he's here with his wife and mother he'll kill two birds with one stone, as the saying goes.

He went back to join the others; but John isn't here; he'll come later. However Donald can't stay; as a Government man he's got pressing matter; he won't be staying for dinner. Ammi he said; I must go; I'm sorry I can't stay for dinner, but I wish you all the best and hope you'll have a nice flight tomorrow; thank you very much Sir she said. He greets with a hug and gives her an envelope; it's her going away present, and without knowing what's in it she thanks him anyway. He bid goodbye, but as he about to leave Florence calls out, see you tomorrow love and don't stay up too late; she'll be sleeping at the Thomas's tonight to accompany them to the airport. He walks back and embraced her; bye mom he said; see you when I see you; she waves to him as he leaves, of course John will take her home later. It's approaching four o'clock and Agnes and Dorothy are sitting under the ackee tree, these two always have a lot to gossip about, whenever they meet time stood still. Meanwhile Florence and Ammi accompany by Maggie are busy putting the finishing touch to any packing Ammi have left to do. About seven o'clock Ammi expect a visit from some of her church sister, they're coming to hold one last prayer meeting with her, but that will come after dinner. The dinner is already cooked from earlier and is sitting on the coal fire to keep warm, but they're not going to set the table until John comes home. He's away to sort out some matters but it seems to be taking him longer than it should. Rupert arrives; he went straight to his mother who was still with Mrs. Faster senior under the ackee tree. I'm starving mom he whispers in her ear, she smiles, dinner will be ready as soon as your father gets home she said. I wonder what's keeping him she enquires, she then tells him to tell Ammi to set the table, He started to walk away, on second thought she said leave Ammi alone;

tell Florence to do the table for me, yes mom he said as he dashes way. The two women got up and went to the kitchen and prepare dinner together, Dorothy finds this sort of thing rewarding; since the death of her husband she's got no one to cook for and even though she's just giving Agnes a helping hand it feels so good.

While they were chatting and doing the dinner John drives in; he could see the women from where he was but he didn't make his way to them, no, he went into the room to see his brother. He already makes plans for the Doctor to come and see him on Monday. He tiptoe into the room, and in a whisper he calls, Denis, Denis, but there was no answer, he suddenly had a bad thought, he walked by the bed and put his hands on him, he takes a deep breath and sigh, he's only sleeping. But he notice he was perspiring heavily, he mopped his brow gently so not to wake him, it's time for him to have another dosage he thought; but he's not going to wake him, he walks away. By now dinner is on the table and they're awaiting him. Good evening ladies; has everyone had a good day? Yes thank you John said Dorothy, how was your day? Oh! So, so, nothing especially happens he said Did Denis eat anything Aggie, he asks. He took a little porridge; I know that's not enough but he can't chew anything at all; it hurts when he tries. Whatever happens there's nothing much more we can do until Monday when the Doctor comes to see him. Where's Donald he ask as he realised he wasn't there, oh! He has some work to attend to and he couldn't stay said Florence, so you got us to yourself said Dorothy; all three ladies; I hope you're please she asked; oh no! I'm having all you three ladies by myself; no thank you; that wouldn't be wise. What would I be doing with three women he asked, did you hear that ladies asked Dorothy, should we let him eat with us? What do you think Agnes ask Florence, well! Maybe just because he's hungry said Aggie, alright, alright, he said; I can see you all are going to gang up on me, ladies! I apologised; I would love to eat with you lovely ladies he said. Ok! Take a chair Mr. Thomas; you can share our table said Dorothy, thank you very much madam; don't mind if I do he said. Then he sat down and mumbles something, what's that you said John asked Agnes, oh! Nothing; I was just talking to myself and thinking of Donald, I'm going to have a quiet word with that man he said. About what John asked Florence; Oh! A personal matter he said, oh! What could be more personal than talking about three women ask Agnes, did you know dinner tastes better when you talk and eat ask John, and you want to change the subject comment Dorothy, but it was all light-hearted and the family moved on to another topic.

It's nearly six o'clock and dinner is over; they're now waiting for the church sisters and Pastor Green is coming along; he cancels his appointment to be there, he must pray one last time with sister Ammi. The Pastor was the first one to arrive and not long after the brethren's come along, Dorothy never attended one of these evangelistic meetings but she was not averse to being there, she's takes the notion that if it's good for her friends, the Thomas's, then it good for her too. But Agnes herself never attends any of these meetings; even though her husband and stepdaughter are Christian and always be at there, and for Florence! Well! She's has become well indoctrinate in the religion. The meeting commence and the Pastor begins his sermon, this meeting usually goes on for some time; but tonight it will be short. They're making allowance for Ammi to get a good night sleep in preparation for her flight tomorrow. After the meeting there were a lot of good wills and handshakes, there were a few tearful eyes too, this sister will be well missed when she's gone. Well even at the tender age of twenty she was the pillow of the community, she showed them what they should be doing; like she has done. She shows them how to be good to others and care for the sick and helpless, and when they default in their promise she bears no animosity against them. Well the Pastor said his peace to Ammi and is now gone, the sisters are gradually drifting away, soon they all will be gone and the families will be alone once more. But John has to take Dorothy home, I never been out this late since the passing away of my husband said Dorothy. That's not true said Florence, what about my wedding; you were still up and about when everyone was gone that's true she said; I completely forgot that; I'm making it a hobbit now it seems. You like it really said Florence, I didn't say I hate it, good company and good conversation; why wouldn't one wants to stay up. John call Rupert to accompanied him taking her home, coming Dad, just let me get my bumpers on, a new style of footwear it's light like plimsoll but more like shoes, he's out and ready to go.

Dorothy has one last quick one to one with Agnes then embrace Ammi and wish her good luck; and her last words were, you'll write to me Ammi; won't you? I sure will Mom said Ammi, and that was their last words, they loaded up and leave. Ammi is not going to waste any time; she's going straight to bed, she's carrying a secret fear; a kind of phobia, she never fly before; other than what she heard from others she never even been close to an aero-plane, she probably won't be getting much sleep tonight thinking about it. Get some sleep now Ammi; I'll wake you early in the morning said Florence in a whisper, she doesn't want to disturb Denis. Soon all is quiet in the household but Agnes won't fall asleep until John returns; there're things she wants to talk to him about before in the morning. When John returns he looks in on Denis, neither he nor Agnes remembers to give him his medication; they got carried away in that confusion, but he's not going to disturb him, he'll be hoping the pain doesn't return during the night. He covers him over properly and went to his room, but John is holding a secret from Agnes and the people in his household, while he was out earlier today he got the news that another nan was badly beaten; only this time it's not fatal, this other man he was told was the other one who took part in the beating of Denis. While he was away he tries to get in touch with as many of the men and tell them this vendetta has to stop, and the police will want to talk to them on Monday. But the police is not going to gather any creditable information from them; they stick together with their story, and the police! Well! They were never any good at this sort of thing. But they took it out on these two men because they're not from the district; the one that is dead he's said to be from the parish of Wilmoth Bay, the other one! No one knows where n he's from. Their motto is they cannot allow a man or men to come from an outer district and be beaten up in one of their own. John probably won't tell Agnes at all; he fears if he tells her she's going to start worrying that he might get involved. But he's involved; he takes them on as workers and they come under his jurisdiction; and to a man they are loyal to him. But for now he'll put all that out of his mind and concentrate on his daughter departure tomorrow.

Sunday morning is overcast, it looks as though it's going to rain; when the sun goes behind the clouds it casts a dark shadow; not exactly a good day to travel. Everyone is up bright and early making ready for Ammi journey to the airport, John makes sure the car is ready to move when they're ready. They got about two hours to burn, Florence and Maggie are ready, while Ammi went to her mother's grave for one last visit to bid her farewell. When she returns they still have a little time in hands; But John wants to go now, he would like to leave a bit early so he doesn't have to rush. Ok folks; load up; let's give ourselves ample time he said it's a long drive, remember? Well Ammi stuff is already in the vehicle, Maggie already taken up her seat but Ammi is in the house saying goodbye to Agnes and her little sister. Come along now Ammi call Florence; you don't want the plane to leave you. Now they're all loaded and ready to roll, Agnes didn't come to the car; she was overcome with emotions; she just waves goodbye from the window. As John was reversing out into the road Ammi ask him to stop, why? Do you forget something? he asks, no Dad;

but please stop, he stops with the tail sticking out into the main road. She hops out and steps back into the yard, she just stood there looking around. Well she's just having her fill of the surroundings she grew up in; she might never see it again. Come along Ammi said her Dad; it will be here when you return, she walks back and off they went. There wasn't much conversation on this long journey, everyone was in a samba mood, Florence attempt to make small talk but didn't get much response, the hundred and forty miles journey is going to seem like four hundred. They stop off at a restaurant for no particular reason; certainly they're not hungry, more to cool the tyres, he's trying to make sure they don't have a blow out on this long journey. that would be a disaster. But Florence and Maggie did eat something; the other two didn't touch a thing, but John is putting a brave face on the situation; he didn't eat; he couldn't; his heart is full of grief. He told Donald in conversation some time back that he knows he'll never see his daughter again, he must have had some kind of a premonition, he's trying to hold back the tears but at some stage before that plane takes off the tears will fall. The remainder of the journey was less hazardous; they're now on probably the best drivable stretch of road in the country, John can burns some tyres now knowing he's not going falls into any craters.

Are you alright John ask Florence since he was so quiet, he answers yes but sound a little unsure, she continues to talk to him without much of a response, but she knows he's suffering and she's trying to get him to talk and keep his mind off Ammi departure, but right now she's not making a good job of it. They make good time reaching the airport with plenty of time in hand, he unloads the suitcase, and they'll wait for him there while he went to park the vehicle. On return they make their way to reservations and check-in, now they've got about two hours before the plane takes off; but for John it will seem like minutes. They settle down to wait for the call, Maggie went browsing; it's the first time she has ever been to an airport; and she's fascinated with the things on sale, the others were out in the reservation area trying to make small talk. No sooner the passengers were told to making their way to the departure lounge, the passengers got up and began to bid farewell to their love ones. John holds his daughter's hands and attempting to give her advice, but he has done that already, for him at this moment he's in a state of confusion; he would love to say don't go but he knows that would be futile. But there's nothing odd about his behaviour; he's a parent who cares deeply about his children and now he's losing his favourite child to England and there's nothing he can do about it. You have to let her go now John said Florence, and then the tears begin to fall; not only from father but from daughter too; as she makes her way towards the gate she exclaim; oh Dad! I'll write as soon as I get there. As she was passing through the gate she waving to Maggie come back in a hurry; she just manages to get a glimpse of her sister disappearing in the yonder, bye Sis. Be sure to write as soon as you reach; and I'm sorry I wasn't there to say goodbye properly, I'm so sorry Sis, but Ammi is gone through and that's the last they'll see of her. It will be probable another hour before the plane is in the air, but one thing for sure; John isn't leaving until the plane is airborne. There wasn't any delay and the flight takes off on time, they watch from the balcony as the plane takes to the sky and disappears in the blue yonder. The mood is still samba but the tears have ceased, the journey back won't be any better than the one to the airport. For John there's now a huge void in the family household that will never be filled, no, not as far as John the father is concern. At home Maggie tells Rupert she didn't say goodbye to her properly; I was too busy looking at all the nice things in the shops; and now I feel so disappointed. But Rupert is a tough young man; while his sister is ruing her action he's rather melancholy about the whole situation, he'll be hoping that one day he too will be going to England. Agnes will be missing her greatly; she was her helper when she's got too much to do, but she also knows that they have taken the right course of action and get her off to England. As for Florence, even though she's much older and now married; but Ammi was her soul mate, and now she's gone she (Florence) is left with two elder women; can she have a relationship with them as she had with Ammi; only time will tell.

However that Sunday evening John's got a visitor, it's Pastor Green, he calls to find out if Ammi got away without any hitch, John draws him the whole picture, brother Thomas! Sister Ammi was sent from the good Lord, we'll be missing her every day that goes by, we'll always remember her in our prayers he said, thank you Pastor; she was the shining light around here. But it seems we're going to lose all the young people; they're all to England, I lost my daughter because of the state this country is in, the Government should be a shame of themselves, the young men and women who should be the future of the country have to leave to foreign land to make a life for themselves. It's a sad state of affair when one has to leave one own country to seek their fortune in another country, soon there'll be only old folks leave here he said. Then that would be not only a sorrowful affair but a disastrous for our country said the Pastor, but I believe people will soon stop leaving; as soon as the novelty wears off. But by the time the novelty wears off as you suggest Pastor, many of the district will have no one left. Take our own little district for instance; most of the landowners are gone and the purchasers are nowhere to be seen, they just buy up these land and leave it lying there, before long it will be covered in bush; the place is like a ghost town. The church has lost some of its members too said John, yes said the Pastor and he went on to name four more of his brethren's who are planning to immigrate. My congregation will be down to less than half, and that's not good for the Church; we should do something Brother Thomas. But what can we do? Right now Pastor there's nothing we or anyone can do; not even the Government, the anxiety and the desire to know England is out weight anything here to stop people leaving. But we can pray Brother Thomas; we can pray, isn't that what we do when we want the good Lord to help us? Every day every night we should send up our prayers to the Lord for help, and we certainly will Pastor he said. For Brother Thomas! If he could change the course of time so his daughter could be here he would, but for now whatever the result of their prayers Ammi has already left the country. Before the Pastor leaves he'll pray with Brother Thomas; he'll ask the Lord to keep watch over servant Sister Ammi; to guide and protect her; and to give comfort to Brother Thomas in his hours of grief.

21: The Flight

The flight is going to be an ordeal for Ammi; she was shaking even before she entered the plane, she would probably be better off taken the ship even though it's a twenty-one day journey. One thing for sure; to endure this nine hours plus flight; she's going find it sheer hell. Her seating position was by the window; and that's the worst place to be when you're afraid of heights; right now her nerve is jangling it's almost audible. The stewardesses are ready with instructions about parachutes; but for Ammi there's no point; she's shaking like a leaf, the girl needs help; but at this moment no one took notice. However she's not the only one who is got the phobia; her fellow passenger sitting next to her is far from been comfortable. She's not listing to the stewardess instruction either; she is trying feebly to make small talk with Ammi; she's obviously to try and disperse the fear but to no avail; she can hardly get the words out. However Ammi is not interested in anything the passenger has to say, she's up in the air and she doesn't like it; she should be on dry land. She can see her whole life flashing in front of her; think about the plane falling out of the sky and kill everyone. Her mind it seems is unable to get away from the thought of a tragedy; and if she lives through this ordeal; before this plane landed at Heathrow airport she'll die a thousand deaths. This nervous fellow passenger gives up trying to talk to her; she's making her even more nervous, this's her first time on a plane too and Ammi's actions are having a bad effect on her; she's going to ask the stewardess when one comes along to transfer her to another seat. But she's not going to checks to find a stewardess, no; she's too nervous to move; to walk about in a plane high up in the sky she hasn't got the nerves to do that, well! She thinks it's dangerous, so she stays put waiting until a stewardess walks by. By now the flight long clears the Island, they're over open sea, Ammi had no idea of anything that is happening; her eyes are firmly closed. The passenger is anxiously looking around for a stewardess, she can see them in the distant but she's not going to hail them and she's certainly not going to walk towards them either. Well! it's been gossiped back in the Island and some people might have held to it; that if you walk along in the plane flying in the air there's a chance you might fall through; and it seems this passenger bears that in mind. But one must remember that these people the ones from way down in the country are near-primitive people; so their fearful behaviour regarding a plane shouldn't be too surprising; they have to be given time to get themselves acclimatise to the modern world.

The captain made the announcement about the flight and wishes everyone a pleasant flight, but Ammi good as freaks out when she heard the duration of the flight; she begins to shed tears, she doesn't think she's able to endure that length of time up here. By now she has done the unthinkable; she wet herself and the tears begin to flow even more, well she knows not what to do; and she couldn't do anything; her nerves are jangling; parts of her body are out of sequence with the rest. But she and her fellow passenger soon reacted in a similar manner; except she (Ammi) made a louder outburst when the plane hit an air pocket; she must have seen her own funeral right before her very eyes. The stewardess is coming around to serve drinks and whatever else the passengers needed, now is the chance for her fellow passenger to ask for a move. She explains in the feeblest way as to why she would like another seat; the stewardess will comply but after she's finished serving drinks. All this time Ammi us sitting in the wet; one thing for sure' she'll be praying to the good Lord to see her through this ordeal. The stewardess returns sometime later; now miss, why do you want to move she asked, well it was difficult for the poor girl; maybe she didn't want to tell the stewardess she didn't want to sit next to this nervous passenger; and that she's nervous herself. However she manages to get her message across; and stewardess Lacy seems to be one of those humane and sympathetic people and agrees to move her. But firstly she notice Ammi was looking a little off-peak; the look on her face was frightful; she tried to talk with her while the other passenger were sitting there on the outside. Well! The stewardess wanted to ask the uncomfortable passenger if she'd heard or notice anything odd about her Ammi, but she got no response; that passenger was far too afraid to care about Ammi, her fellow passenger. Well! The stewardess moves this passenger to another location; taking her hand luggage with her and gets her settled. She then returns to Ammi, she could see that she was praying, quietly of course, this stewardess was very considerate; she stands and waits until Ammi opens her eyes. Are you alright dear she enquires, Ammi shakes her head but tells the stewardess nothing about her being wet; may she's ashamed or too nervous to talk.

But it didn't long for stewardess Lacy to realise her predicament; she'd seen it all before, then she had a thought about the instructions of the parachute; she thinks she didn't take in any of it, well there's no point talking to her about that now she thought.

Would you like something to drink she asked, Ammi shakes her head again but says nothing, by now everyone it seems is having something to eat, drink or both. I'll be right back said stewardess Lacy, and off she went. In about five minutes she returned with a hot cup of cocoa and biscuits, come on now you must drink something; here's a lovely cup of cocoa and some biscuits she said, she didn't shake her head this time but she made no attempt to take the cup of cocoa and biscuits. What's your name dear she asked; she speaks at last, Ammi she said, they had been flying for over three hours now and that's the first time she had spoken. Hi Ammi I'm Lacy, anything you need just ask me; and don't be frightened. But while talking Lacy reaches for the radio and shows her how to use it, but she won't be able to; her hands are not going to react to mind command, Lacy will have to do it for her; she's hoping that will help to settle her nerves. But Lacy has to leave her and return to her other duties. Have the biscuits Ammi; dinnertime I'll fix you something nice ok dear she said calmly and tried to reassure her before walking away. She didn't touch the biscuits but she has a few sips of the cocoa. Well she has calmed down somewhat; enough to try to use the tissue to mopped where she's sitting, but she's not going to move; she's got no intention of doing so. Whatever else is going on in her mind all she's hoping for is to set foot on dry land, up here in the sky is not where she wants to be. It's dinner time and people are enjoying the tasty meal, true to her word Lacy fetch her a tray with dinner, here you are Ammi; eat something darling; you'll feel better. Thank you she said, but suddenly she begins to cry, come on now Ammi dear; what's the matter; are you feeling ill? She shakes her head looking towards the tray of food before her. Now Ammi if you don't tell me I can't help you said Lacy sternly, Ammi beckoned to her to come closer, she didn't sit in the empty seat left by the other passenger, no; she moved closer and leans over to her. Ammi put her hand over her mouth and whispers; I wet myself she said with tears in her eyes. But this air hostess not only sympathetic but tactful too, oh I'm so sorry; but that's nothing to cry about dear, it happened me more than once, don't worry; it happens to the best of us she said. That seems to let her feels somewhat less ashamed; if the stewardess has done it then it's not too bad. After you eat something I'll take you somewhere to get change said Lacy; but please don't worry dear. That seems to have done the trick a little; she began to pick at the food, the stewardess leaves.

Sitting in the wet must be quite uncomfortable; but with no one noticing or that could imagine her situation she tries to eat something; but she's got no appetite; she's still a nervous wreck. Right now she's thinking;

if she had known what's like up here she would have left home, the thoughts of what is and what might have been keeps coming. She could be wondering what has happened to the passenger who was sitting next to her; maybe she's fallen out of the plane, of course her mind was elsewhere when the stewardess moved her to another seat, ridiculous thought like those kept roving in her mind. But she recollects her thought and tells herself how silly she's been to be thinking that way, whatever she has prayed for it appears her prayer has been answered. Well it's sleeping time and the light is turned off which makes her a little less nervous. Lacy returns on the scene; she's ready to have her cleans up, she removed her tray and take it back to the kitchen. On return she speaks to her in a whisper; come along Ammi and take your handbag with you, she nervously rose from her seat for the first time with eyes bulging. Lucy tries as always to let her feels at ease; and off they went. Of course she's got no clothes to change into; but Lacy borrowed a dress and a pair of nickers from one of her colleague who is about the same size as Ammi; and they made some arrangement for Ammi to change back into her own clothes when she collects her suite case back at Heathrow; so she can return the stewardess clothes. Well she was fearful to leaves her seat to walk in the plane and she's fearful to walk back, but with Lacy's assurance she scrambled back. But Lacy has seen it all before; she didn't put her back at the window, no; she move her to another seat away from the window. These planes were never full with passengers whenever leaving the Island; so there were always plenty of empty seats available. Lacy gives her an extra pillow and turned her light off, sleep tight Ammi; and I'll see you later, thank you Lacy she said only this time she says it with little less emotion. But whether she was asleep or pretending to; nevertheless there was no more action from her until breakfast was served in the morning. This time another hostess is serving breakfast, what would you like ask the hostess nice and kindly like, a soft drink thank you, anything else she asks, nothing more thank you said Ammi and the hostess went on her merry way. She opens her can of Pepsi Cola and sips from it; but she's not going to drink from it anymore, no, she's going back to sleep and hoping that when she wakes up the plane will have landed. Some hours later there was an announcement that they're over the Irish Sea; of course that means nothing to Ammi she just continues to closed her eyes pretending to be asleep. An hour or so later the passengers were told to fasten their seat belt, Lacy remember her nervous passenger and was back on the scene to help her harness herself in. We'll be landing soon Ammi and when we touch down remain in your seat; I'll come and get you; ok dear? Ok and thank you she said. But the worst was yet to come for this terrify passenger, the plane begins its descent and Ammi's life flashes in front of her eyes once more, she grabs hold of the seat rest and breaks out in cold sweat. She couldn't understand what was happening; maybe she thought the plane was falling from the sky. But whatever her thoughts she keeps them to herself; everyone else is minding their own business and no doubt there are other passengers on board suffering the same ordeal. The plane has landed and taxying along; the poor girl must wondering what is happening; maybe she thought the plane was going to take off back into the sky. But soon the plane comes to a stop; and Ammi is alive but still terrified; her eyes were telling her feelings. The announcement comes to unforeseen your seat belt; which means its time to go. Bot Ammi is not going to move; not only because Lacy told her not to; but she couldn't move even if she wanted to; she's still terrified. But no one else is moving either; no; they're waiting for orders, they don't want to do anything that they shouldn't like getting up and collecting their belonging or walking along the passage, these country pumpkins think they might be breaking the rules. Realising the situation the Captain made a second announcement, unfasten your seat belts and take your belongings with you and get off the plane, and thanks for flying British Airways. Now it's a stampede; even the ones who were terrified seem to gather their wits and now in a great hurry to get their feet on dry land; the land of the mother country. But for Ammi who is still seated waiting for Lacy must have many thoughts going through her mind, she might be pinching herself to make sure she's alive. Please Lord she prays don't let me travel in another plane again. The last passenger is off the plane except for Ammi, she's about to nods off when Lacy comes by carrying a paper bag, the content is Ammi dress and under ware. Come along Ammi she said; get your thing together we're getting off, she got up gingerly and collects her hand luggage then they set off to collect her suitcase.

Accompany by lacy she collects her suitcase; now Lacy takes her to the ladies room to change off in her own clothes and return the ones she's wearing. By now she gathers her faculty and behaving normally, she couldn't thank Lacy enough for taking care of her all through her ordeal. But knowing how nervous she was on the plane Lacy wants to make sure she knows where to go to meet her folks. Who's coming to meet you she asks, my two cousins she said, but I'm not sure where to meet them she, ok! Don't worry; come with me said Lacy, and she took her to where she supposed to be. She places her in an advantageous position where she can see everyone and her cousin could see her when they arrive. Now it's time for Lacy to depart, Ammi dear I must dash; I must meet up with my crew,

Ammi moves closer, thank you for everything Lacy and I hope one day we'll meet again, so do I said Lacy, but write your address where you're staying in London. Ammi dictates the address where's she's staying while Lacy writes it down, one day when we're here if I've got the time I'll look you up said Lucy; oh! I would like that very much Lacy, she said, I would love to see you again. They then embraced, take care now said Lacy as she departs, and Ammi was still waving even though Lacy wasn't noticing. But sometime in the future they both will probably get the biggest shock of their young lives; there's something between these two women which they neither knew of. Now that Lacy is gone and she's on her own; she is feeling awfully lonesome; she's hoping and wishing her two cousins arrive soon. There're hundreds of people moving about; but they're all strangers, she must have thought she's on another planet. To see so many people in the same place at the same time must seem miraculous to her; considering the most people she had ever seen at any one time is in her little church. But where they're all going she asks herself are they all travellers? She stood watch and wait. But there's nothing else she can do; or there's nothing else she knows she can do like asked renovation to make an announcement for her cousins to find her. however long it takes her cousin to collect her she isn't going anywhere, she doesn't know what time it is; she hasn't got a watch and there are no clocks on walls to be seen anywhere; outside it's quite dark, and it seems as though she's been waiting for forever. It's a long time since Lacy leaves her there; can they forgot she's coming today; if that be the case what happens now; what do I do, or what am I supposed to do, who do I ask and what do I ask them; the questions keep coming.

The time for more worrying is now; she notices the constant leaving of people while fresh ones keep coming in and still there's no sign of her cousins. Her legs are tired so she seated herself on her suitcase on the ground still alert to any signs of them if and when they turn up. The times passes and she's still waiting, what if they never turn up she asks herself, is not like she's a few miles from home where she could walk however long it takes, here she's among a multitude of white people; all strangers and speaking different languages and minding their own business. But the language is not different; it's English; only it's a refined type English compare to her broader type of pathwa English. They don't bother about someone like me; and why should they? They don't know me and vice-versa, but they seem fairly happy with themselves coming and going. But for me; I have nowhere to go unless Daphne and Hillary come and get me. She begins to dosed off sitting on her suitcase; jetlag is now getting the better of her; and considering she hasn't slept through the entire flight she could be sleeping standing up. But every time she opens her eyes she's been thinking all sort; I shouldn't have left home; and I should have listened to my father. Her mind was working overtime when she heard voices calling out her name, and even though she's jet lag and could barely keep her eyes open she recognised the voices immediately; those were that of her cousins. She stood up in a hurry, over here she shouts repeatedly waving her hands, and the girls spotted her and hurried towards her. Where were you she kept repeating with tears in her eyes, but the girls didn't bother to explain they just get hold of her and all three women embraced crying; the cousins kept saying I'm so sorry.

After their long embraced and managed to look each other in the eyes, we must go now said Daphne; we'll tell you what happened on the way. Hillary got hold of the suitcase while she and Daphne walk hand in hand through the crowd towards the hired car. The driver was Milton a man from Jamila; the same country as themselves, one of the few immigrants here who's got a vehicle. He's one of those who came here on the first ship to sailed taking immigrants here; the Wind rush, a nice man but one wouldn't want him around more than necessary, he's got an attitude and at time can be overbearing; Ammi was told later. This is our cousin Ammi Daphne said to Milton as they approached the vehicle, but he's more concern about the police who is coming towards them, we better hurry he said; there's a copper coming; we got to move, they just quickly put the one suitcase in the booth and get away fast. Hi Ammi he said, sorry about that but if that copper had caught up with me he's going to give me a ticket; and I can't afford a fine right now. Anyway did you have a good flight? But by then Ammi was fast asleep. T The poor girl must be awfully tired said Hillary; we're not going to get anything out of her, not for tonight; maybe tomorrow. It's a shame she's not awake to take in the scenery said Milton, there'll be plenty of time for that said Hillary, but there wasn't much talking on the way home; with Ammi a sleep Milton just concentrate on his driving while the two cousins enjoyed the ride. They're home; sixty-three Grange Road, and it was a hard job to wake her; however they managed to get her up and out of the car, this is where you're going live said Daphne, but Ammi is unsteady on her feet and appears couldn't to couldn't care less about the surroundings; all she wants to do now is to get into a bed. Come on said Hillary; let get her inside before she falls over, Milton collect the suitcase and they went inside, but he's not stopping though; as soon as they pay him his money he'll be off. They paid him; he says goodbye and leaves. Daphne and

Hillary share this double room and now with the arrival of Ammi it will room the three cousins. Ammi sits in the one single settee in the room, the cousins are looking forward to a conversation with her; but that was never going to happen; as soon as her bum hits the cushion she was sound asleep. I never know the girl snores said Hillary; hear the bungies she's dropping, an adage for snoring back home. Daphne takes a blanket and spread over her, the problem now said Daphne; we are not going to get any sleep; not with Ammi dropping those bungies. Well it was rather late and the room is cold, the old paraffin lamp is not heating up the room properly, the warmest place to be now is under the covers, Ammi is not feeling the cold right now; she's too sound asleep.

22: Meeting of The Cousins

It's Monday morning and Ammi begins to feel the cold; in this weather the chair is no place to keep warm so she climbs into the bed with her cousins, something they usually do back home. In a family with girls of similar ages; when they visit and stop overnight it not unusual to find four or five young women sleeping in the same bed; and if the bed isn't big enough they'll take to the floor. I'm freezing she said; put me in the middle, they let her in, are you going back to sleep ask Hillary, oh no she said; I'm now wide awake. Thank God for that said Hillary, what do you mean by that she asks, we didn't get much sleep last night; you were snoring so loud it could wake the dead. don't talk so silly she said; I never snore, really said Daphne mockingly, it's a pity we didn't have a tape recorder to recorder; you would hear what you sound like; it's like you're fighting for breath. Seriously though; do I really snore? Are you saying you don't know that you snore, asks Hillary, come to think of it; I heard one cannot tell if one snores; someone has to tell one said Hillary. You didn't hear that said Ammi; you just make it up, ok! I take your word for it she said; I snore, now tell me about England. We want to hear about home first and what's happening out there said Daphne; and how is my father? That question Ammi was dreading being asked; she wishes she didn't have to explain to Daphne that her father was beaten up; and badly too. Well before I answer that; I have a letter from Dad for you, I have no idea what's in it but what I can tell you is that Uncle Denis was beaten up and is now staying at our house. Dad took him there to look after him; he had already seen the Doctor; but Dad had arranged for the Doctor to come to the house on Monday to see him again. Hearing that Daphne who was under the covers sits up in bed, why the hell was he beaten up? And who beats him up she asks frightfully. I have no idea; neither does Dad or the police, they're still carrying out investigations, and Dad is making his own enquiries too. Well what kind of condition he's in she ask, but there's no need hiding the truth from you; I think you need to know said Ammi, he was badly beaten; very badly, and his condition is quite serious. But you could say he was lucky; Dad… Daphne interrupts, are you saying he was lucky to be beaten up? You didn't allow me to finish said Ammi, what I was going to tell you is that he was lucky Dad went to look for him. He wants to talk with him about something important, Dad went to his home and he wasn't there; so he went to his plantation; and there he found him lying under the cluster of runner beans, Dad managed to get him the car and take to the Doctor.

After hearing all that Daphne has become somewhat aggrieved; she begins to shed tears; and Hillary's comments; maybe he got into a fight over one of his dice game didn't make her grief any less. you remember it happened before when uncle John had to intervene, you remembered the brown man whose name I can't remember; lost his arm playing dice she said, I remembers it well said Ammi; he was lucky to be alive too, but Daphne knows all that they're saying is true; but it's her father and she didn't really want to hear all that. So Uncle John is taking him to see the Doctor on tomorrow she asks, no! The Doctor is coming to see him, Dad doesn't want to move him; he's in constant pain. Well read the letter Ammi bring said Hillary; all you need to know might be in there, what about this letter Ammi she asks, where's it, in the suitcase; you'll have to wait until I unpack. The bed is too warm and she gets up into the cold room. Get it now said Daphne; can't you just let me rest for a while she asked, no said Daphne; go and unpack; I'm anxious to see what's in that letter. Take it easy said Ammi; there's nothing that you can do; so don't go beaten up yourself; cry if you must it's normal; whatever needs to be done Dad will do it; he will take care of him. I must write a letter to thanks uncle John for taking care of Dad she said, now you been silly said Ammi; Dad been taking care of uncle Denis from the day he was born; did you ever feel the need at any time to tell him thank? Of course not; they're brothers for God sake. Uncle John doesn't need your thanks said Hillary; I don't know how you suddenly come by that idea. Alright! Alright! Get off my case the both of you said Daphne; it was just a thought, and a bad one too said Hillary.

They settle down to talk about other things, so what else is happening home ask Hillary, oh! I'm sorry to hear about the death of Miss Mildred she said, and I too said Daphne; you said in your letter it was only a short illness, yes! It's seemed she's been carrying the illness for some time but she kept it to herself. By the time we found out about it she was too far gone; she died soon after. But I have to take a share of the blame said Ammi; I was too wrapped up in looking after sick people and didn't notice my mother wasn't well. But it's just like you though Ammi; always want to help people said Hillary; and who's helping you? But I'm sorry to hear about Miss Mildred; she was a very nice person. There a few people died since you two leave home apart from my mother. But there's one good thing happening too, the Government send carers to look after the sick people in the district. Then what about those you said in your letter you were taking care of ask Hillary, the carers took over that role; and they're doing the best they can. How would you know that, asks Hillary. Well! The Member of Parliament give me the job to supervise them for two months and report back to him, what was the pay like ask Daphne, it was only a temporary job and a one-off payment. I was first asked to introduced the carers to them as some of them didn't take kindly to strangers; hence the supervisor's job. Then how is old Mrs. brown; I always wanted to send her something; but I keep forgetting, well you don't have to bother anymore, about a month before I leave she died. Oh! The poor dear; her husband died some four years before we left, said Daphne, and she wasn't well herself. Poor Mrs. Brown; she was so kind; she was always giving me one penny to buy bulla cake. Well a few years after Mr. Brown died she took ill and became bedridden, her only daughter up and leave her, she went away and never to be seen again, she was the one caring for her mother; she must have got fed up; she just up and leave the poor sick woman alone. Only the good people died early said Daphne; she was a good person. So what else is happening back there ask Daphne, well Dad become a Christian and got baptised, what? Exclaim Hillary surprisingly; Uncle John got baptised; he was the last person in the family I expect to get religion, he rules everyone in the district and most of them are afraid of him. Well he's now a Christian and a sincere one too said Ammi, and you will be please to know that I'm also a Christian too; and I got baptised last week, just before I leave. There's no surprised there said Daphne; you wanted to testify from you were about twelve years old, and if I remember rightly the Pastor wanted to baptise you from that age; but Uncle John wouldn't let you. That's not exactly true; dad wouldn't mind even though he wasn't a Christian then; but Miss Aggie had objections; she said I was far too young to be baptised; and that's why I didn't. So now you're a fully-fledged Christian what you intend to do now try and convert us too? I didn't say that; but it wouldn't be such a bad idea; would it? she asked. But tell me; are you going to church? No! Not since we been here; well why not asked Ammi; we couldn't be bothered said Hillary bluntly. Speak for yourself said Daphne; I would've gone if I could find a church.

So what you're saying; there're no churches here in England? Even you don't believe that said Ammi; we'll find a church and we'll go; all three of us. There's no church here for us to attend, said Hillary, that can't be true said Ammi, there're churches everywhere, and you should be a shame of yourselves that from all this time you been here neither of you bothers to go to church. Especially you Daff; you always attend church back home; how is it that you change? We couldn't find any Pentecostal church said Hillary, and then what about other churches; you could have gone to any other church. Like what church you're referring to ask Hillary, well this is England isn't it? There must be many churches of England about and other churches too like the Presbyterian or Anglican; and even though I never worship at any one of these churches; if there's no Pentecostal church about I would gladly worship at any one of these denominations. I don't want to go to any of those churches said Daphne; I've grown up going to the Pentecostal church and if I want to visit a church that's the church I'm looking for she said. The bibles talk of rendering your heart; you're not going for the people, no; you're going to worship the Lord said Ammi. Whichever church you attend God is there; and you can worship him there too. Well I don't think I would feel comfortable at any one of those other churches said Daphne, but like me you never been to any of those other churches said Ammi; so you have no idea of how you would feel being there; you might be surprised and like it, as I said before; as soon as I got settle we're going church hunting; I won't allow you to weirdos to carry on living like heathens. But I'm surprise said Ammi who seem fully recover from her jet lag, and considering her ordeal getting here. I thought coming here that my two cousins would be fully indoctrinated in a church; any church; just as when they were home; instead I find two atheists, what happened Daphne; you usually like going to church. Nothing happens; as we told you; there's no Pentecostal church here she said, well I must tell you; I'm aghast said Ammi. Then what about me Angel of mercy asked Hillary; Have you got any opinion about me; I seem to remember how difficult it was to get you going to Sunday school said Ammi; there's an old saying, a leopard never changes its spots; so I'm a leopard now am I she asked. From we were little you were always to righteous for my liking, you only just arrived here and you can't wait to convert us; don't bother to try it out on me; keep your preaching away from me.

Daphne had enough of the church debate; she wanted to see the letter her Uncle sent her, will you get out of the bed Ammi and starts to unpack; I want to see the letter she said, Ammi was willing to oblige, she gets the letter out and handed it to her. Daphne keeps looking at it as though she's afraid to open it, I've got a funny feeling about this letter she said, what do you on about ask Ammi, you ask for it now you don't want to open it; here! Let me do it; and she handed to her. What could be in it that you're fearful about asked Ammi while she's opening the envelope, well nothing else in it except paper see she said, and I'll read it for you; But she was surprised when she reads the letter, Daphne is not going be please when she hear the content of this letter, it's all about her father; Uncle Denis. Ammi remembered her Dad gave her the letter before her Uncle Denis was beaten up, however she's got to hear it. I'll skip the greetings bits she said, the money you're sending to your father there's a chance he's gambling it all away, you need to check with him about this said the letter, and it went on to state further the contents. She was shocked to hear to say the least; she trusted him that's why she sent her hard earns cash home for him to save it for her. She's hoping one day soon she would return home knowing she's got some money saved there. But according to this letter she might not have a dime, how could Dad do that to me? But you can't say for sure that is the case said Hillary, Uncle John thinks he's gambling my money away; and if he thinks so I know it's so she said. Uncle Denis is a gambler; but the money he gambles might be his and not your money said Hillary. How could you think that, didn't you hear what uncle John said in the letter asked Daphne. What do you think I should do she ask the others. I don't rightly know said Hillary; write and ask Uncle John perhaps and ask him to check it out, and that is probably the only thing you can do said Ammi. It's not hard to believe this can happen; it just hard to believe that your own father would squander the little money you sent him to save she said. But I do remember Mom telling him during her sickness that he would gamble the last shirt on his back. Naturally you're not going to send any more money for him save said Hillary, of course not said Daphne, and anyway right now I don't think he's in any fit state even to think for himself said Ammi. I'll write to Uncle John and ask him to try and find out about the money; I still can't believe Dad would squander my little savings away she said disappointingly. stop beaten up yourself girl said Hillary; it's out of your control; I know it's hard to take but sit tight and do the only thing you can do; what's that asked Daphne; wait until you hear from Uncle John. It's now well past twelve o'clock; they decided to get out of bed and make breakfast; I'm going to make you a proper English breakfast said Hillary, egg and bacon with lusting of beans, and make it quick said Ammi; I'm starving. Then she begins to tell them of her ordeal on the flight, and if it wasn't for one stewardess name Lucy Parker she has no idea how she would manage. Lucy Parker; did you said Lucy Parker Hillary asked repeatedly, yes said Ammi; she even borrows clothes from another stewardess to lent to me. But why asked Daphne; you won't laugh if I tell you? Of course not she said; some people are just not good at flying. But she was hesitant to talk about it; she blushes. Come on Ammi; don't keep us hanging said Hillary, did you wet yourself? Ammi looks at her in amazement, how did you know? she asks, I didn't; I just guess. But come to think of it; if you have to change your clothes on a flight the most likely reason would be it got wet said Hillary, yes said Daphne; but drinks could spill on it; yes said Hillary; but the amount of drinks on your tray wouldn't cause that amount of damage for you to change clothes she said. So you wet yourself? Hillary asked flippantly; she begins to laugh quietly while Daphne couldn't help herself but laugh out loud, you really pee yourself she asked. You said you wouldn't laugh said Ammi; well it's rather funny to hear that you pee up yourself since there're toilets on the plane, said Daphne. So what happened? You couldn't get to the toilet? Well you might as well know, I was frozen in my seat; I couldn't move; and I'll never fly on another plane again, that's my first and last time.

So I take it you'll never return home? asked Hillary, because if you decided to return home one day you can't walk and you can't drive; but maybe you can swim. Very funny said Ammi, so what happens to the dress she asked well! When the plane landed she took me to collect my suitcase and we went to the toilet and changed, she was really kind. This Lucy Parker is she about my height and quite fair with sweaty nose asks Hillary, she fits that description; but I don't know about the sweaty nose said Ammi. Why? Do you know her? Well we have a cousin named Lucy Parker and there can't be two people with the same name in our little Island said Hillary. Do you know about her too Daphne ask Ammi, yes, but if she's the person in question she's not really Hillary and my cousin, no, she's your cousin by your mother side; her father is a white man, hence her long hair and straight sweaty nose. But how come you two knew of her and I don't? When we were about fourteen and you were about nine she and her mother visit Miss Mildred a couple of times, in fact if she's the same person she's your first cousin. But I don't know my mother's sister; I never even heard her talk about having a sister, but if all that you said is true what happened is really a coincidence; she even asked me for my address where I'm staying. Maybe she knew all along said Ammi, she should be of the same age as me said Hillary, well that's another thing you have to write home about; you should ask Uncle John about it; he will know said Daphne. I can't get over it said Ammi, she looks after me like a sister, but if she knew why didn't she say; why the cloak and dagger? Come to think of it she went out of her way to get me dry clothing's. I'll look you up whenever I'm in London she said, so I think she knew who I was all along? If so how asked Hillary; she must have seen your name and checked where you're from said Daphne. That makes sense she said, I have a feeling you'll get a visit from her someday she said; I hope so; I really hope so said Ammi.

Well her English breakfast is ready and they sat down to eat, I'm so hungry I don't care about the taste; but after she had eaten she expresses her taste for it, I'm looking forward to another helping tomorrow; it was very tasty. Still sitting at the table Ammi wants to know what she can expect once she started to look for work. Well you better prepare yourself for some rough times said Daphne, the white people don't like black people, when we came here it took us over a month to find this dead-end job we're in; and the fact that we haven't got a profession makes it doubly hard. But you might fare better said Hillary, you're a dressmaker. However it doesn't makes no difference whether you have a profession or not; as long as you're black they won't want to employ you, said Hillary. You remember when we were at school; all that teaching about the mother country was so fascinating; we all wanted to go to this mother country, we never considered the people might be hostile. Now we're here and bear in mind that they asked us to come; they want us to do the work they haven't got the manpower for or don't want to do, but now we are here they treat us like we're nobody, they're so hateful and racist at time you want to kill some of these bastards. They don't even want to rent us room; some immigrants had to sleep on the street for how; long God's only knows, we were lucky to get this accommodation said Hillary. But this landlord is a decent man said Daphne; I don't know why but he treats us like how a person should be treated; he and his wife; and you couldn't find two nicer people. We told him about you coming; and would like you to stop with us; and he agrees straight off, all he would like at some point is to see you. Isn't that tells you anything ask Ammi, you shouldn't judge everyone to be the same, there're good and bad people in this world and I'm sure the good outnumbers the bad; thank God. All we're saying is for you to always be on your guard, your little miss goodie attitude won't cut any ice here said Hillary, hate is out there; and these people have no qualms telling you so. You can't be thin skined out there, there's a lot you're going to have to take on the chin and grin and bear it.

Hearing all that dire report about the people here didn't dampen Ammi's spirit, if anything it makes her more resolute. Yes; she's going to arm herself with the words of God as her guide and protection, she believes she's ready and prepare for any eventuality. She wants to have a look outside; arriving here yesterday she didn't see anything of the surroundings, she was far too sleepy. She puts on her shoes and makes for the outdoor, wait up said Hillary I'm coming with you. They're not going anywhere; Ammi just wanted to stand on England own soil and have a good look around. I'm in England she said; talking to her cousin, all my dreams are here now until I decided to return home. When will that be? asks Hillary, there're people here right now would like to return; unfortunately they can't make the fare; because they can't find work to put some money together. We can only hope that things will work out good, for the best. But the words return home comes lightly; many of those who are here got no intention of returning home however the hardship, however the discrimination and however the bigotry of the white people; they're going to make here their home, Ammi and her cousins will no doubt find that out too. Moreover; apart from those whom their parents sent them here most of the others have nothing home to return to. Well she'll have seen enough, they return indoors; she wants to know why the smoke is coming from the building; she thinks those houses were factories, even though she's never seen a factory before. Of course the cousins would explain the reason for the smoke, they're all houses and they all have what is known as a fireplace; they burn coal to keep the house warm, thus the black smoke coming through what is known as the chimney. We don't have such facilities so we used a paraffin lamp said Daphne, anyway don't bother yourself about those things now, soon you'll understand about everything that is puzzling you now. What are your plans for me tomorrow ask Ammi, well it's you and me tomorrow and for the rest of the week said Daphne, Hillary is going to work and she'll take next week off while I return to work, so what are we going to do tomorrow, she ask again. What would you like to do ask Daphne, well! I would like to see Oxford Street she said; I heard so much about it I would dearly like to see it. Is it a long way from here she asked, I don't think so; but we never been there either said Daphne, we been promising ourselves to check it out one day but we never get around to it.

Tell me; how long you guys are here now ask Ammi, I know what you're going to say said Hillary; but we never feel the urge to go there. Anyway for someone who supposed to be a Christian you're surely interested in matters of the world, said Daphne. What do you mean asked Ammi; are you insinuating that I'm pretending to be a Christian? I'm insinuating nothing she said; I just make a statement. Well! She was somewhat disappointed with Daphne assertion; she believes in herself and is faithful to the cause. I never said you weren't a Christian; how could I; I don't know how much of a Christian you are, what I said? Just call it a slip of the tongue. Don't worry said Hillary; little Miss Goody Goody here will soon have forgotten all that Christian malarkey. Referring to Hillary she said; you speak like a heathen; you always were wanton growing up; I was hoping now that you're in England you would be a changed person. She'll never change said Daphne, she's always being that sinful person awful person she always was. You're going to hell girl said Daphne; you and me both said Hillary, and they burst into laughter. Anyway back to taking a look at Oxford Street said Ammi; been a Christian doesn't mean you can't visit nice places seen nice things and wear nice clothes, no, as long as you don't become possessed by those thing material things then you're alright in the sight of God. You know that for sure asked Hillary; yes! And when I go to church I don't render my garments even though I always want to look good. Ok! We'll check out Oxford Street one day in the week; but tomorrow we're going to Labour Exchange; we're going get you enrolled for a job; and the sooner the better said Daphne. Labour Exchange; what's that, she asked; that's where you go and tell the authority you're new in the country and is ready to work; and after a certain time if you don't get a job they'll provide you with money to live on. But only until you find work she said, so this dear cousin is where you're learning curb begins. The three young women relax together to enjoy a lazy Sunday and gossip about many things. Did you have a boyfriend home Ammi asked Hillary, no, I'm a Christian and you know Christians don't have boyfriends they have husbands. Then I suppose you'll be looking for a husband soon asks Hillary, and no; I won't be looking for any husband or bot friend either. But if I have to have a husband sometime in the future; and if that is what the good Lord wants of me; then I will meet a husband, but I'm certainly not thinking of boyfriend. You just wait until nature calls little Miss righteous; you are going to wish you have a man by your side said Hillary flippantly.

Ignores her Ammi; she's man-crazy said Daphne, I can't help it if men find me attractive said Hillary; you're blowing your own trumpet now said Ammi; and that's doesn't become you; self praises as they say are no recommendation she said. One more thing; when you think that men find you attractive they only want to use you; and when a woman allows herself to be used and becomes common soon no man will want to talk to her. You're not even back on the shelf you're nowhere at all she said. Well! For one who never had a man friend I don't know how the hell you know so much about the subject said Hillary; and I'm not common as you're insinuating thank you; and you never know of me running around with every Dick, Tom and Harry. I never say you were common at all said Ammi; I was just making the point that one should be very careful about ones self. The night is getting old; the other two can stay up as long as they want but Hillary is going to work tomorrow so she's going to hit the sack, she went to the bathroom; on return she bid good night and went to bed. The old black and white television which Ammi find fascinating is still on, and even through the conversation rages on their eyes were on the television. Of course there's nothing like it back home; radio was their only good listening, she recalled, when they always listen to the radio in the early morning before they were off to school; they always love listening to the programme from overseas; especially the country and western songs from Nashville Tennessee. We used to love it said Daphne; and you know what; we never know how good those days were, no said Ammi, and we never know we would end up in a cold country either where we have to light a lamp to keep warm. One never knows what the future holds for one she said. Well Ammi landed yesterday but she still hasn't unpacked, so while Hillary is asleep she begins to unpack with Daphne in attendance; of course there some nice mangoes and other goodies in her luggage for them; It was late but for Daphne the aroma of the bees box mango was too taunting to resist; so she ate two before she goes to bed.

Admiring some of Ammi's dresses Daphne ask, did you made these dresses yourself? Oh yes said Ammi; do you like them? They're beautiful dresses said Daphne, it shouldn't take you long to find a job if you can make dresses like these, I wish I learn to do something like this. How long did it take you to learn the trade she ask, well! About four years; but I had a good teacher who becomes more like a friend and eventually becomes a part of the family. I don't understand said Daphne; what do you mean she become a part of your family, well! She's a wealthy person and her husband died some years ago, they didn't have any children and she hasn't any family of her own; so she adapted herself into the family. But she later found a man and got married, he's a Member of Parliament and a very nice man, and he and Dad are the best of friends too. At their wedding I was their maid of honour, well it's a long story but I can tell you she's a wonderful person. It's well past midnight and they decided to go to bed; tomorrow Ammi will face a new challenge; she'll be out in the unknown armed with only what she had heard. The girl from the bush will be facing people she never had thought she would meet. In fact she never had any dealing with a white person before; this expected encounter she's hoping doesn't turn into an ordeal, they said good night and went to bed. Monday morning was cold; very cold, Hillary was up early to light the smelly paraffin lamp and then went back to bed, when she gets up again to prepare for work the room should be just about warm but smelly. She was up an hour or so later and the room is not exactly warm but the chill is taken off, enough for her to get dressed for work. She didn't want to wake the others but Ammi was awake to tell her to have a good day, and you too said Hillary; and see you later, she departs and Ammi gets her head down once more back under the covers.

23: The Labour Exchange

Today will be Ammi first experience of trying to get a job; but first she must enrol at the labour exchange. This exercise is always a strange one for immigrants and sometimes can be darn right daunting. But not necessarily because of the authority; or because of the immigrants are not used to such exercise, no; mostly because of the discrimination and bigotry. So today will be the beginning of her young life trying to make it on her own; and as broad-minded and thrust full she is; her naivety about the attitude about the people she will be dealing with might be her waterloo. She will have to learn tolerance and probably turn the other cheek according to her religion; the only question is how long will her tolerance allow her to turn the other cheek? This young woman who depends on her God for guidance; her faith and tolerance will be pushed to the very limit. Her resolve will be tested like never before; and if she didn't come prepared for the trials and tribulations that are awaiting her; then she'll be in big trouble. Daphne take a look at the clock, wake up sleepy head it's time you get up she said while stretching her limbs, but there was no respond from Ammi. She pulls the covers off her, come on she said shaking her; we've got things to do. Ammi raised her head lazily from under the blanket; what time is it she asked, time you got up said Daphne; you're going to sign on today; remember? We talked about it last night; so we did she said; I could sleep the whole day long she said while taking her time to get out of the bed. Looking up at the clock she exclaimed; I wonder what time it is in Jamila now she asked, why you want to know that ask Daphne, I was dreaming I was there she said. Well there's a five hours time difference between countries; so work it out she said Daphne, well from my reckoning they will be still sleeping she said. She gets out of the bed; but with the old paraffin lamp ran dry the room's not very warm. She's tempted to jump back in the bed, however with no paraffin oil in the house it was too cold to sit and have breakfast; they just have a cup of cocoa. Then they horridly get dress and set off carrying the paraffin oil tin, on their way back after they had concluded their business they will buy some paraffin oil. They're standing at the bus stop when Daphne exclaim; oh sugar! I forgot to tell you to bring your passport she said; we have to go back and get it. But she didn't forget to tell; she (Daphne) did tell her last night to put her passport in her handbag in case she forgets it in the morning. No need to go back home said Ammi; I've got it, thank goodness for that said Daphne; I didn't want to walk all the way back. The bus arrives and they boarded; they went upstairs where Ammi could get a better view of the surroundings while heading toward their destination. Is there anything I should know before I face whoever I'm going to face Ammi asked, not really said Daphne; just be yourself and speaks the truth. It's not an interrogation just details about yourself; you've just arrived in the country just tell them what they ask. As if I would lie said Ammi, speak the truth and speak ever, remember that little poem? Yes I remember said Daphne and little Miss goodie, goodie wouldn't lies, very funny said Ammi. Arriving at the labour exchange the place was jam pack; the queues stretched so far back that some people were standing outside. This's going to be a long day said Daphne who was standing in the queue with her cousin to give her moral support. Ammi herself never stand in a queue before; all this is new for her; in fact she never seen so many people in one place before; not where she's from; not even at her gospel prayer meeting The queues are moving but slowly and people are getting impatience; there're an awful lots of noise and some people seem to be arguing as to why they didn't get their giro. What's this giro asked Ammi, it's a form of payment she said, as I told you last night; when you signed on and looking for work until you find a job they'll pay your rent and give enough money to live on until you find the job you're looking for. You mean they give you money for doing nothing she asked, only until you find a job said Daphne; that's the way the system works; and I don't know much more.

There were only a few black people compared to the number of white people; and some of the white people standing in the queues are darn right unfriendly; the wat they look at you; it's more like hostile. There was one black guy standing in the queue adjacent to us; he seemed a little agitated, Why are you looking at me like that he asked a white fellow, stop it; I don't like it he said in a loud voice, some people turn and stares at him; maybe they're wondering what this black bastard is going on about. Then in the other queue standing this white guy with his stare fixes firmly on this black guy, why you keep looking at me the black guy asked again angrily. I don't like your face said the white guy; I felt like kicked the shit out of you he said. The black guy tried to ignore him, but by now a lot of the people were paying attention to them. Now the white guy was fully focused on the black guy; he just kept glaring at him, this was quite strange; there're other black guys there; but this white guy chooses this one black guy to pick on. Well this was a black guy I mean a really black;

just the way some white people are whiter than normal. Well the white guy couldn't contain his stare, no; he walks right up to the black guy and kicked him in the shin and spot on him. But this white guy bit off much more than he could chew, the black guy punched him in the mouth and knocked him to the ground, he stood on his throat and probably would have killed him if some of the black people didn't run to the white guy's rescue. But they didn't do it to save the white guy life, no; they do it to prevent the black guy from committed murder. By now it was pandemonium, the place was in confusion; the white people wanted blood; a black guy beaten up by one of theirs; I'm not having it said one white guy who was previously arguing with the people on the other side of the counter about his giro. He then advanced towards the black guy in a menacing way, but by then the black people were even more angry and ready for a fight. There were shouts of let's get the black bastard, but before any further action the police arrived and things got even more heated. Ammi must have thought she came all the way from the Caribbean to get caught up in a race riot. The white guy was still lying on the concrete bleeding severely, somebody should help him said Ammi, you mean somebody like you said Daphne; don't be silly she said; let him bleed. A white guy overheard her comments and began to pick on her, but unexpected to her surprise another white guy came to her rescue, leave her alone this white guy said, however he was a bigger guy than the one that was picking on her. The guy lay off and walked away, thank you said Daphne to the white guy, that's ok he said.

By now the two police arrested the black guy without asking any question about the incident, meanwhile the white guy was lying on the concrete as though he's the innocent one. But the black people would have none of it; at this point law and order mean zilch to them. They're not going to stand and watch one of theirs taken away wrongfully; and remembering what they heard about the police when they get a black man in their jail; they beat the hell out of them; there's no way they are going to let the police walked off with this guy without a fight. They're outnumbered by far but so what they would have to arrest us all, said one black man. The black people surrounded the police; they handcuff the black guy and wanted to take him to the police vehicle, but the action of the black people prevented them from doing so. At this time the ambulance had arrived; the people are asked to move so that the paramedics can see to the beaten white guy lying on the concrete. However the action of the police didn't pay off; one of the staff in the form of a woman emerged from behind the counter and confront the police. She came to the aid of the black guy, you shouldn't be arresting this man she said; he's done nothing more than defended himself. Pointing to the white guy being attending to by the medics. He's the one you should be arresting she said; he's been nothing but trouble from he entered the building. Of course the police didn't like that; a white person coming to the aid of a black man. By now other white people have come to the rescue of this black guy, well the police had no option than to release him; and a loud cheer had erupted from the few white people who were in support of this black guy. However one of the police the smaller of the two wasn't satisfied; he's been hell-bent in making an arrest; he began to interrogate the black guy who was beginning to get very angry. Well he's a six-footer black man with a muscular build; from his actions it could be he's been in a fight before and didn't care too much about the police. I'm not telling you a f***ing thing he said; if you're going to arrest me then go ahead. But what the policeman was trying to do is to goad him into doing something rash like strike him; and he would probably succeed. But one black man intervenes and calms him down. Meanwhile with all that was going on his partner had walked away and stood by the door; it seems as though he didn't want any part of his partner behaviour. This policeman walked away reluctant; he was bursting with anger and couldn't contain himself; he was heard saying; those dirty stinking black bastard. By then the ambulance had taken away the injured man and the two policemen leave too; this bad policeman withdrew disgracefully; unable in his disgraceful attempt to arrest an innocent man.

Now people were talking to each other about the incident; and there was an uneasy calm hanging over the place, it seems some white folks were behaving as though they wanted to start a riot. But even though the black folks were outnumbered by more than ten to one they have no fear of fighting if that's what these white folks wanted. It's not a myth that folks from this Island (Jamila) are noted for their fighting qualities; and some of these black men seem as though they would like a punch up too. They may be ignorant to the rules of law in this country but they're not going to let that bother them; they will stand up to any physical attempt directed against them; and don't underestimate the women either. Well the time has gone due to the incident; the exchange is about to close; most of who are here have to return tomorrow. Daphne and Ammi set off back home; they'll think on what had happened here today, she has seen at first-hand the hate and bigotry of some white people toward black folks; and hate like she had never seen before. Well where she comes from there's no discrimination; of course she's among her own kind, people with mostly black skins if she had no knowledge of what she will be up against then; she most certainly know now. The time is gone four-thirty and is the rush hour to get home; but they didn't have any problem getting on the bus as they boarded it at the thermal. But by the time it reaches a few stop people were fighting to get on; something else she learnt today; that whenever she gets a job she'll have to run the gauntlet just like these people. They're dying to get home to get something to eat; it over seven five since they last have a cup of cocoa. But they had to stop on their walk home to fill the can with paraffin oil; they won't want to be sitting in a cold room when they got home. It's a good walk from the bus stop to their home; and they were quite tired when they reach indoors, but Hillary was home before them and she prepared dinner; it's nearly ready. I could eat a horse said Ammi as she slumped herself in the one single settee, well I didn't cook a horse said Hillary; I cook chicken she said facetiously; very funny said Ammi. Then she asked; whatever you're cooking isn't it ready yet? It is now she said, take your seat at the table, honestly hilly; her pet name I can't move from here I'm far too tired; put it on a tray for me. What your last servant died of ask Hillary, but she fixed her dinner on the tray and took it to her. Meanwhile Daphne who is not complaining of been tired is helping Hillary in the kitchen; they get their meal and take their place at the table. Now they begin to tell Hillary about their day at the labour exchange and how they nearly got caught up into what could easily turn into a race riot. So you get nothing done at all today ask Hillary in an uncompromising manner, how could we asked Daphne; It seems as though you don't believe a single word we've said she comment. It was pandemonium at that place; and let me tell you I tried not to show it because of Ammi; but I was beginning to get more than a little frightened. I'm not like you who always seem to want to get into a fight; you seem to forget you're a woman, that brawl today I don't want to get caught up in it if I can avoid it. Anyway believe what you want; that's our story and that's the truth; right Ammi? of course she said. Anyway I never go around purring for a fight said Hillary; the incident you're referring to I didn't go picking on that woman and you knows it; she came at me and I only defend myself against this nasty white woman she said. In this country one has to stand up for ones self otherwise one gets trampled on, you're beginning to sound like a philosopher said Daphne; all I'm saying a woman should behave like the gender she is. But Ammi was oblivious to most of the conversation; she couldn't even finish her dinner; she was fast asleep with the tray almost capsized in her lap. The poor dear said Daphne; she's exhausted from all that carry on today. They didn't wake her; Hillary removed the tray while Daphne put a blanket over her, tomorrow they'll try again to get her sign on and hope it won't be another day like today.

Tuesday morning the weather is as cold as the day before; Hillary got up and is getting ready for work, the other two are comfortable under the covers; they won't be getting up until a little later. But Daphne is awake; she wants to talk to Hillary about the lamp; would you light the lamp please Hillary before you leave she asked. But the lamp is already lit; only the room is not warm as yet; it'll take some time. She would like the room to be warm before she and Ammi got out of bed. Hillary is running a little behind time; what do you want to talk to me about she asked, make it snappy I'm running late. Oh! Don't bother I'll talk to you about it later she said. Hillary is about to walk through the door; you two have a good day now and don't start any more fight at the labour exchange she said flippantly. Go to work and closed the door behind you said Daphne as she pulled the blanket back over her head. It approaching eight o'clock and Daphne is up; Ammi is awake but still under the covers, come along now Ammi you know we have to go back to the labour exchange and we shouldn't be late getting there she said. The room is warm enough so she can get out of bed without shivering. They had something to eat and are now ready for the journey to the labour exchange. The busses should be running almost empty this time of day; so there shouldn't be any trouble getting on; so they should be there in good time. At the labour exchange they recognised some of those who were there yesterday; and the queue is not as long; but only because they're early. But is the same old same old; people are complaining that they didn't receive their giro last week, one young man was sitting on the counter even though the staff was dealing with someone else next to him. He was still talking to himself in a loud voice about his giro when a tall man appears from behind the door and told him to get himself off the desk, he didn't argue he slowly got off it and stand aside. Ammi was next in the queue with her cousin behind her; but only to give her moral support. Have you got your pass-port asks Daphne, what a time to be asking said Ammi; yes I have it. When it was her turn she didn't sit down; she should; but not used to the system she's waiting to be call; and she did. Whose next asked the staff; and Ammi walked forward and sat down, your name asked the staff in a melancholy manner, my name is Amanda Thomas Mom; and this is my first time here. The staff looked at her knowing she's an immigrant, have you got your papers she asked; oh yes she said while reaching into her hand nag for her pass-port. The staff scrutinised the document and written down what she required, she then looked at the employment sheet of paper in front of her, what job you are looking for Miss Thomas she asked, dressmaking job Mom. The staff raised her head from looking at the paper and looked at her as though she was frightened. A dressmaking job she asked, yes Mom I'm a dressmaker she said. Well she (the staff) didn't ask any further questions; it sounded as though she made a sighing groan and cast her attention back to the job sheet. There was a few minutes of silence while she scanned what could be a work sheet. Then she handed Ammi a piece of paper with details on it, using her pen to pointed out to her that her next signing on date was next week, Tuesday. But she also pointed out to her that she could come to the office any day of the week to check if there's were any job available. Thank you Mom said Ammi; as she got up and walked away; she then collected her cousin and went.

How did you got on asked Daphne on their way home, well she was surprised when I told her that I was a dressmaker said Ammi. Well you can't really blame her; I don't know of any tradesperson, men or woman, who're here as immigrants; we're all labourers said Daphne. Ammi told her everything of the encounter, there wasn't anything unpleasant or difficult about it she said; and the woman was alright too; she said my next signing on date is next Tuesday at eleven o'clock. But I can always pop in any day of the week to check if there's any job going. Well you seem to have done alright girl said Daphne. But what have you got planned for me tomorrow she asked; I would still like to go to Oxford Street; can we? We can, said Daphne; but bear in mind that I've never been there before either said Daphne. All the time you've been here and you've never been to Oxford Street asked Ammi; I can't believe it, she said surprisingly; how could you lived here all this time and never been to Oxford Street? I don't see why you're surprised; we told you that already. Well I think we should go tomorrow said Ammi. Ok! We'll go, said Daphne; I wouldn't want you to start having nightmares about it, she said sarcastically. They were home before Hillary and Daphne got busy preparing dinner while Ammi settled down to a spot of bible reading. Not much longer after Hillary arrives; and Hillary being Hillary she can't help being sarcastic with her comments, the rebels are home I see; did you caused any more affray today she asked flippantly. You know Hilly; one day the joke is going to be on you said Daphne with a serious face, keep your shirt on said Hillary; the trouble with you Jamilan is that you have no sense of humour, I wonder where you're from asks Daphne. So Ammi! How did today went she asked; did you manage to sign on the dole? Oh yes! I signed on alright; but what do you mean the dole, so Daff didn't tell you? Well when you signed on it's not only for work but you'll be getting pay too; and that is called the dole money, but don't worry; you'll soon begin to get the hang of things. They chatted all the way through dinner until it's time for bed; but it's only Hillary; the others are up watching television; and ever since Ammi arrived here she's fascinated by the old black and white screen; and of course being a country girl and a Christian she had never been to the cinema ever; even though the only cinema house in her parish is not to far away in the town. It approaching midnight and the room is getting cold as the paraffin lamp is turned off, the screen is showing the test card. I'm cold said Daphne; I'm going to bed and you should do the same too; don't forget your plan to plunder Oxford Street tomorrow. What do you mean plunder; I'm not going steal or buy anything; I'm only going to browse, and with that said they turned off the television and went to bed.

24: Oxford Street

Wednesday was the same as any other day except it began to snow; something of which Ammi had never seen before, she heard all about now she's going to experience it. Hillary got up and getting ready for work; when she pull the curtain and see the snow; she woke up Ammi to come see. She reluctantly got out of the bed as she was curious about what Hillary wanted to show her. What is it she asks as she was getting out of the bed, and then she saw the snow. But instead of feeling unhappy about it her face lit up with a huge smile. Good heavens; snow she exclaimed looking through the window in her nightie. It looks so beautiful she said; She stood there for a while admiring the snow kept falling while Hillary gets ready for work, I'm leaving now she said; you have a good day now. But by the way what has Daff got planned for you today she asked, oh didn't we tell you; we're going to Oxford Street she said, it's my idea. I would like to see the west end and Oxford Street; so we're going to have a tour. What kind of a Christian person are you anyway asked Hillary facetiously, she likes to tease her. Oxford Street and the west end is for people of the world; people like me; you're a person of the church what do you want with Oxford Street?. Don't be dwarf said Ammi; What do you think we're going there for; I just want to see the place she said; I've been heard so much about it. But Hillary didn't tarry; she didn't want to be running late, well watch yourself and tell me all about it later she said as she went through the door. Ammi was still standing by the window when Hillary leave, why are you standing by the window asked Daphne as she pushed her head up from under the blanket; I'm admiring the snow she said gleefully, snow! It snowing asked Daphne surprisingly. Why don't you come and see asked Ammi, what for; I see snow before; I'm going back to bed; anyway it's too early to gets up she said. Wanting to get a feel of the snow Ammi puts her boots and coat on and went outside in the garden, but she wasn't long out there she rushes back in; took off her heavy clothing and went back to bed.

It's now ten o'clock and they're just getting out of bed, however by twelve o'clock they were ready to leave the house for the west end. Outside is bright and cold but there isn't much snow on the ground; they make their way to the bus stop. I must tell you said Daphne; neither I nor

Hillary ever been to Oxford Street before; how many times are you going to tell me that Daff; are you nervous? No; it's because of the transport; I know the eighteen buses take us to Paddington green; and from there I have no idea what other bus to take to Oxford Street, but we'll ask. They got on the bus to Paddington Green and from there they foot it to the Edgware road; not knowing that they could actually walk it to Oxford Street even though it's long walks. they began to as directions. Ammi was feeling the cold; her winter coat was a bit flimsy but she's determined to see Oxford Street. Then there was a man coming towards them smiling; why was he smiling; they had no idea; but they are going to ask him for direction. Excused me said Daphne almost blocking the man's path, could you tell me what bus goes to Oxford Street? Hello my little darlings he said grinning like a Cheshire cat, how nice to meet you he said as though he knew them from some wear. Still smiling he asked as though he was curious, so you want to go to Oxford Street? Yes said Daphne, You don't need a bus my darlings; it's a crisp day; why don't you foot it he asked gleefully. This fellow is a braggart; thought Daphne; trendily dress and the way he walks is as though his shoes mustn't get dirty, however he seems quite friendly. But it seems a little strange to them that a white man who they never seen before was behaving as though they were old friends. Why don't you walk with me my darlings I'm heading in that direction, Ok! Thank you; we'll walk along said Daphne. Come along darling she whispered to Ammi mimicking this man; Ammi nudges her with her elbow as to say be quiet.

They set off walking behind this boastful fellow, he seem to have a stylish of walk the girls observed; but keep their thought to themselves, he turns to them; are you darlings going to shopped? Oh no said Ammi; we going to look around, how nice he said; a day of leisure. They arrived at Marble Arch, this is where I say goodbye my darlings; Oxford Street is straight ahead he said pointing in the direction. Thank you very much they said; he turns to them with a huge grin on his face; have a good day now my darlings; and he turns and walked away. Thank you again said Daphne as she made a remark to Ammi about the way he walks. But they were grateful to him though; now they know that they can walk from Paddington Green to Oxford Street even though it's a fair distance. They're now in Oxford Street and even though it cold Ammi seem to forget about the weather; she's been attracted by the fashion in the window; she never seen fashion displayed in shop window like this before; she's seen it in magazines back home but that's all; she feels as though she could go on browsing for hours. The shoes were most fascinating; I'll get a pair as soon as I can afford it she said. My week salary couldn't pay for a pair of any of these shoes said Daphne, but she wasn't in awe of the fashion as her cousin who seems to find herself in another world; one which she seems overcome by. The evening begins to get dark and colder; it's time for them to return home. But Ammi wants to browse some more, Daphne grabbed her by the hand; come along; we're going; I'm cold and hungry; we can come again another day. They agreed it's time to go but they're not in the mood to walk all the way back to Paddington green; now they have to ask again what number bus to take to where they want to go, but they were quick to get the right direction. On the way home the discussion is about the dresses and shoes, and so many people walking about; what are they all doing asked Ammi, I suppose the same as we were, window shopping said Daphne; except they might have bought something and we don't she said.

Hillary was home when they return and she's seen to the cooking, as they walked in Ammi exclaimed; something smells good; never mind that said Hillary; look at the time; I thought you two got lost. But Ammi was feeling quite chuff, lost! How could we got lost, if you not sure about where you're going you only have to ask someone. It's not as easy as that; but I'm glad you feel so confident about your travels since you haven't been anywhere yet she said Hillary sarcastically. But don't worry; you'll soon think differently. So tell me about your day she asked as they dine, and that was the cue for Ammi to begin an illustration of the descriptions of the dresses and shoes; her eyes lit up when she talks about it. We'll have to plan another day for the three of us will go again she said, I would love to look at those shoes again. I'm not going tp walk about again in this cold said Daphne; when the weather gets warmer then we'll go. When might that be asked Ammi, when the winter is over she said, and when will the winter be over? Ammi asked, the end of February; I think that's the beginning of spring. I can't believe you're going to let a little cold weather stop us from going back to the West End said Ammi, don't worry said Hillary; you'll soon change your tune; if you think this is all there is to the winter; girl you just wait. Hearing the way Ammi talked about the clothing's Hillary asked her; I suppose you lost your faith? What are you talking about she asked hastily, I mean that you have back slide, a term they used when someone lost their faith in the Lord and stop going to church. Why do you say that asked Ammi, well it seems you're into fashion now and wanting fancy clothes. You're planning to buy high heels and fancy dresses she said, Christians are not supposed to dress up in fancy things. Firstly I'm not planning to buy any of those fancy dresses or shoes as you put it; I just admired the style; as a dressmaker one day I probably will be as to make clothes of those styles and… Daphne intervenes. Well you did say you would love to but a pair of those shoes; was that a jest? Ok! What are you two saying; Christians are not supposed to wear good clothes too? Well I must tell you; the bible didn't say so; so long as one doesn't indulge into material things one is not doing wrong in the sight of the lord. Render your heart and not your garment; that's in the bible too; and from you returned all that you talk about is the fashionable dresses and shoes said Hillary. You better be careful; the good Lord won't like it she said flippantly. if you're going to make jokes like that I'm going to bed said Ammi; one doesn't make idle jokes when referring to the Lord; you need to get down on your knees and ask forgiveness, and for your information I haven't lost my faith in the Lord. That will never happen; and I want to thank you for reminding me that I must at all time be on my guard; I'll ask the good Lord to forgive me for my action today. But Hillary is not finished as yet; she must have another dig, just you wait until the next time; you'll sin again, what's in the blood always in the blood; and fancy clothes is in your blood she said comically. There was no response from Ammi; but Daphne thought enough is enough and told Hillary in no uncertain term to shut up. I'll pray for you said Ammi as she's getting ready for bed, however she's not going under the covers before she read her bible; her usual attitude from back home. Then she'll kneel and pray; and she'll ask the Lord to have mercy on her vile cousin. No one was in the mood to watch television tonight; the discussion has taken up all the time, so they said good night and went to be. Oh! What have you two got plan for tomorrow asks Hillary before she pulls the covers over her, there was no reply from Daphne, what have you got planned for me tomorrow, Ammi asks. Go to sleep, said Daphne, tomorrow we'll think of something, and that was the last word.

25: The Plan that Never Happened

Before Ammi arrived in the country her cousins had informed the landlord of her coming, they had to ask his permission if she can live with them until she can find her feet. Well it's very difficult to find accommodation; and even if she gets a room she wouldn't be able to pay for it on her own. The majority of white people are not letting rooms to black folks; and there're only a handful of black people own houses. But this landlord, Mr. Owens is one in a million; the very best, they were in luck when they got a room at his place to rent; the nicest couple you'll ever likely to know. When they told him about Ammi coming to stay with them other land Lard would have objections and even if the answer was yes they would increase the rent immediately, but not Mr. Owens; no; he agrees for the women to live together. However Ammi is here nearly a week now and they haven't yet introduced her to the Owens, so come this afternoon Daphne will take her to meet them. Having no specific plans for today they decided to go walkabout, they dress for the purpose as the weather is quite cold. But while they were ambling aimlessly about Ammi had a thought, why don't we go check out some churches she said; we got nothing else to do. Why not said Daphne; but where do we look? Come on now said Ammi; churches shouldn't be hard to find; or we could ask someone. But they were standing only a stone throw away from a Church of England when they asked the first person who comes along; an elderly gentleman he was glad to show them the Church. But the women weren't observant; if they had they raised their head toward the skyline they would have seen the steeple. They walked toward the building and read the posters on the notice board outside. It read the time and order of service and other future programmes, they made note of it. Daphne wasn't too keen on the prospect of them coming to this church, you're not thinking of coming to this Church are you Ammi she asked, not only me but the three of us she said, If there are no other churches we'll worship here. But you know nothing about the Church of England; you're a Pentecostal member, well if there is no Pentecostal Church here until we find one why not worship at the Church that we can find? A Church is a place of worship; the Lord name is mention call; and the bible said; wherever the name of the Lord is called he's there to bless and do good said Ammi. But let's walk around to see if there're any other Churches around. It was getting close to three o'clock and the evening was getting colder; but they continued their walk until they see another Church in the distant. They walked towards it; and it turns out to be the Anglican Church. They went in the big open space at the front to read the advertisement on the board, and then they wondered inside for a quick glance. I've never been inside one of these Churches before said Ammi, neither do us said Daphne. Looking at the huge chandeliers and other gadgets Daphne comment; they must have carried out ritual here; I don't like it here. But Ammi didn't like it either; however she didn't make any comment regarding what she was thinking; if they had a question to ask about this Church they couldn't; there was no one around. I hope you're not considering coming to this Church said Daphne, oh come on; don't be an alarmist; different denominations worship in different ways. Did you see the candles; they burned candles too she said. But it probably might seems like a ritual; but that's their way of worship said Ammi, how do you know all that ask Daphne since you never been to any of these Churches.

Well do you remember Mr. and Mrs. Robinson she asked, of course said Daphne; I remembered them; what about them? They behave as though they were better than everyone else; never did like those two; and if I remember they were crazy about you said Hillary, maybe it's could because they never had any children. Well they were Roman Catholic members; always wanted me to go to church with them said Ammi, I would but Dad wouldn't let me; he never believed in that Church; he said they burned candles and worship the Virgin Mary; and this Church is of similar faith. However it wouldn't do any harm to come and see the way they do things; after all it's a church and since people worship there I'm sure the Lord is there too. Well you would be on your own; I wouldn't be coming said Daphne. The evening closing in fast and it's time to return home, they didn't set out to look for Churches but they found two; and now Ammi has to decide which of the two they're going to come Sunday. They're in walking distance of home so they horridly back; they have an appointment with their Land-Lord, Hillary was at home and do the dinner; but she's not happy. I can't believe you two are home and I have to come home from work and cook dinner she said, I'm not your housemaid she said. Ammi apologised, I'm so sorry Hilly' you shouldn't have to come home and cook; we should do it, but Daphne acted as though she couldn't care less. You shouldn't moan about cooking dinner before Ammi arrived here I did most of the cooking and I didn't complain; so if you come home and don't want to cook; don't cook she said in a displeasing manner. I don't know why you're getting hot under the collar; I wasn't complaining said Hillary; I only suggested that since you two are home you could do dinner. if I was at home and you were at work then I would do dinner; if I remember; that is the arrangement. But we weren't home we were out all day she said, Ammi is new here and would like to see something of the area she's living in; so we went walkabout. What would we be doing sitting indoors looking at the four walls, she comments angrily. However Ammi observed some hostilities between the cousins; but mostly on Daphne's path, she's beginning to think that there's some kind of animosity between them; but they're trying their utmost to disguise it. Hilly apologised for her comment but Daff seems not want to accept her apology; she feels the need to reprimand her (Hillary) and reminded her of the days when she always does most of the cooking, she's behaving as though she's got an axe to grind.

Standing over the dining table arranging the plates Ammi asked, tell me; is there anything going on between you two? I detected some hostilities here; why is that? There was no response from either of them, she then asked again; and when there was still no response; she was left in no doubt that all is not well between them. She stops handling the utensils and sat on the side of the settee facing them. Well three people living together medium size bedroom; they're always closed to each other; we shouldn't have envy and animosity among us; and this is what it seems like here. Looking directly at Hillary she asked; Hilly! What's going on? She (Hillary) attempted to say something then pauses, she seems a little reluctant to talk about it. But then she speaks, looking at Daphne with a vicious steer, Well I tell you she said; madam there is got the idea that I stole her man; a man who never say boo to her, how would you know said Ammi, how would you know? Well I know she said. Is that true Daff asked Ammi, I don't know who the hell you think you are; you only just arrived here and you're acting like some kind of a mother Teresa; Ammi apologised; I just don't think family should be holding malice. Well I'll tell you the whole ridiculous episode said Hillary, I went out with this man a couple of times but only to the pub, the pub? What is the pub asked Ammi, what we call rum bar back home said Hillary, Ammi was aghast, back home women wouldn't be seen dead in a rum bar; it's not allowed, girl! You have a lot to learn, you should remember we're not home now. Here men and women go to their local, what's local asked Ammi, another name for their pub she said, people drink relax and have a good time there. It's seems I've got a lot to learn she said, you most certainly have said Hillary. Did you go to this pub too Daff she asked who was sitting on the bed fiddling with her nighty; but it's not yet bedtime. Of course not, she replied angrily; only because he didn't ask you to comment Hillary, and that remark gives Daphne the cue to have a rant. Hilly she said; you have that bad habit of wanting the man that other people have, you remember back home you know Dan and me were friends and you still went with him. You know Daff you're a hypocrite; you didn't want Dan, no; only when you see he became interested in me; why don't you speak the truth? You and Dan Ammi asked Hillary; how is it I didn't know what was going on? Well you were too taken up with your Church; you hardly ever be with us said Hillary. Is Hilly telling the truth Daphne asked Ammi, I don't know who the bloody hell you think you are interrogating me said Daphne; believe what you want to believe she said angrily. Again Ammi was aghast; she put her hands at her mouth at the sound of Daphne using the words bloody hell, Daff! What's come over you; why you getting so angry? We're family; we should be able to sort out our differences without been angry and holding a grudge. I'm not angry; but you're questioning me as though I was the guilty one here she said. I never thought you were guilty of anything at all Daff, I only asked you if what Hilly said was true; and if you think that was accusing you of anything then I'm sorry.

But Hillary couldn't hold on to her silence any longer, the thing about you Daphne you're only a pretender; I never tell you before; you and me always be together; we know everything about each other and I know that at twenty-seven you're still a virgin. So all this talk about me stole your man it's just pretence. There was a an uneasy hush from Daphne; as though she wanted to erupt but probably thinking what Hillary said it true she remained quiet. There's no shame in been a virgin said Ammi; I believed in finding the right man; the man whom I'm going to settle down with for the rest of my life. Ok little Miss perfect; we all know you're a virgin said Hillary; you never even talk to a boy of your age or otherwise. You stay well clear of anyone in trousers. Anyway you say you're a Christian; and no one expects you to go looking for a boyfriend. If you want to insult me you go right ahead; you're making a good job of it said Ammi. Yes I'm a Christian; I give my heart to the Lord because I want to live a Christian life; and no, I don't have a boyfriend on my mind. Is the bible tell you to live as a eunuch asked Hillary; be celibate for the rest of your young life; Go back and read your bible; in the good book the Lord said go out and multiply; and I think that mean having children. Daphne who was feeling somewhat thoughtful of what Hillary said about her being a virgin speaks. The bible also said one should marry before having children; you seem want to run around with every man who said boo to you. Hillary burst out laughing; no man ever said boo to me. If they did, I would tell them where to go, and anyway I'm unmarried and I'm not pregnant. Ammi who wanted to be solemn couldn't keep a straight face either, why would a man said boo to a woman she asked with a smile; and what does it mean? But before Daphne had time to explain Ammi the peacemaker stood up; look at us she said; behaving like children; quarrelling among ourselves. We're family; we've grown up together and we shouldn't be bitchy to each other; if we… there's a pause as Hillary find something in what Ammi said for her to joke about. Christian shouldn't swear she said with a dry face; your God is hearing you, what are you talking about, asks Ammi, you just swore; you just used the word bitch. Daphne with her hands over her face smiles; knowing her cousin just been her normal self; having a dig at Ammi. There's a big difference between the word bitch and bitchy said Ammi; and you know it, but you just can't help yourself been the joker. But let me tell you why we weren't here today since that's why we're having this conversation; no, argument she said. We went for a stroll just to have a look around the neighbourhood as Daff said; we then have the idea that since we're walking about we might as well look for Churches in the process. We found Churches alright; one of those Churches we're going there on Sunday she said. We you said; who's we asked Hillary, we means we three; and don't you try to say you're not going said Ammi. But Hillary is adamant, how are you going to get me there; drag me? But Ammi knows she's all talk; when the time comes she'll be there. We shouldn't have to explain ourselves like children said Daphne, Hilly always like to have things her own way; what's good for her should be always good for us; that's her motto. Let's not start that again said Ammi; Daphne you must stop picking at every little thing she said; sometimes it's better to see and blind hear and deaf. Suddenly Daphne seemed to be reformed. I've had enough of this conversation; conversation? It wasn't a conversation; you were quarrelling said Ammi. Anyway all this talk about men had gone on long enough said Daphne; is anybody hungry she asked; I'm starving and I'm going to warm up the dinner. We were supposed to eat a long time ago, I'll come and help you said Hillary, they're back on friendly terms again. See to the table Ammi she said as she went with Daphne into the kitchen. Standing over the dining table Ammi clasped her hands together and look up to the ceiling in reverence to God; thanking him that the family have put aside their differences and once again harmony reigns. We shouldn't be having dinner this late; it's not good for the digestion said Daphne, and this was the evening when we were supposed to go and see Mr. Owens, remember? We'll have to do it tomorrow, Ammi is here for nearly a week now and it's only right and proper that he knows. We'll go and see him tomorrow said Daphne; and we mustn't be complacent and give him cause to think less of us, he's a good man and we should do what is right to remain in his good book. Well! All is quiet on the western front once again; the girls are in harmony with each other and long it remains so.

26: The Landlord

Thursday was cold and damp as the day before, while Hillary has gone to work the other two women are in no hurry to get out of bed, under the blanket is nice and warm. But they were forced out of bed and not for the first time by the smell of the old paraffin heather, it begins to smell which means it runs out of oil and there's no spare supply in the oil can; and if they want to keep the room warm someone had to go and buy paraffin oil. They got out of bed as they must; the smell is unbearable. Daphne hurriedly gets some clothes on and leave for the shop with paraffin can in hand. The shop is not too far away and she makes haste to there and back, back indoors Ammi opens the window to help rid the room of the smell. But it is very cold so she puts some extra clothes on while keeping herself busy trying to keep warm. It wasn't long before Daphne return; now they can power up the old paraffin heather, of course it takes a while to warm up the room. But in the meantime they can clean themselves up and make themselves presentable to meet The Owens, but first they had to have breakfast. Ever since Ammi arrived here she fell in love with the bacon; and this morning she's going to have a hearty helping of English breakfast; bacon and egg accompanied with beans; a couple a slice of toast and her usual cocoa tea. You're a hearty eater Ammi; you know that comments Daphne, I only eat what my stomach can hold she said, and anyway you wouldn't want me to meet this Mr. Owens on an empty stomach would you? Empty stomach exclaimed Daphne; how can you talk about empty stomach after eating all that food? Are you sure you'll be able to walk up the stairs, she asked. She pulls her plate back when Ammi reaches for the last piece of bacon on the plate, don't be greedy she said, Ammi smiled mischievously; let me have it since you don't want it, Daphne looked at her; I don't want you to get ill so I'm eating it. Breakfast is over and it's time for them to make a move, now Ammi be on your best behaviour when we meet these people; and try to make a good impression. You telling me that asked Ammi, have you ever known me to behave anything other than proper? Well no said Daphne but I just thought I should mention it. Ammi grabbed a scarf to put around her neck, you're not going outside said Daphne; you're only going upstairs; you don't need a scarf; why don't you put your coat while you're at it joke Daphne. I just wanted to look presentable she said, presentable asked Daphne sarcastically; Mr. Owens is a married man with his wife; I don't think he's looking a woman; and the last time I look you were a black woman; and he's a white man she said with a giggle. Don't be silly; let's go if we're going said Ammi seriously; I don't like where this conversation is going.

However as a habit whenever she (Ammi) sets out to do anything she usually prayed to the Lord for help and guidance; so she kneeled by the bed pulled Daphne down beside her and delivered her supplication to the Lord, then they set off to meet this nice Mr. Owens. Ammi was circumspect walking up the stairs; she was almost on tiptoe. This is a quiet house even with two rooms of tenants, and the Owens are quiet people; they walked quietly and spoken quietly; one hardly knows when they're in. They treat their tenant with a degree of respect and the tenants treated them in likewise manner. It was approaching midday; Daphne gently tapped on the door, who is it asked Mr. Owens, its Daphne Mr. Owens, come in Daphne he said, she open the door and walked in with Ammi behind her. Good day Mrs. Owens she said as she stands ready to introduced Ammi. This is Ammi Mr. Owen; the cousin we talked about, he was sitting in his comfortable armchair in front of the television with Mrs. Owens adjacent to him. He stood up and extended his hand, hello Ammi; I've heard a lot about you; it's good to see you. Daphne thought how nice of him to say that; but she didn't recall telling him a lot about Ammi; but it's good for him to say so nevertheless. Good morning Sir she said; it's good to be here, I hope you'll like it here Ammi; have you ever travel abroad before? No Sir; this is my first time. Observing the girls still standing Mrs. Owens commented; let the girls sit down before you started to interrogate them Don, the girls smiled amusingly. Oh! I'm so sorry ladies he said; have a seat, but Don who was in high spirit love the chance to have a conversation and wanted to know about where in Jamila Ammi and the others are from. But Ammi was surprised when Mr. Owens began to tell her about Jamila; the country she born and grow up in; but know nothing about it. The north coast is one of the most beautiful places in the world he said. But he was talking to them thinking that they knew of these places with some of the most beautiful beaches. Ammi was feeling somewhat ignorant to the fact that this white English man knew so much about her country and she knows nothing about it. But she's not one for pretence; she considered pretence as a lie and a sin. I never been to any of those places Sir; I don't even know much about St. Manor the parish I'm from she said. How about you Daphne? I supposed you have been all over the Island; oh no Sis; I'm just like Ammi; never have any cause to go touring the Island. Listening quietly Mrs. Owens commented, so you been all over the country; ha, ha, ha, stop showing off and get the girls a drink. Oh forgive me again ladies; what would you like to drink, how about a drop of the old white rum he asked flippantly, he didn't for one minute believe the girls would drink white rum. I like a drop of the Captain Morgan myself he said with a great big grin and mischievous intent. oh no Sir; we don't drink anything with alcohol said Daphne, in fact Ammi here is a Christian; and her religion forbids drinking anything with alcohol; but we'll take some soft drink Sir. So you go to the Pentecostal Church right Ammi he asked, another surprise for Ammi; how would he knows without she tell him she considered quietly. But then she remembers he said he been all over the Island, and if he knows the Island well then he knows the people habit too. Have you ever been to the Church Sir she asked, no! But I was living in that lovely country for over twelve years and I would like to live there again he said. My best friend Mosely's wife was a Pentecostal member; we were thick as thieves we were; where he goes I go; unfortunately he was shot; and that's when I decided to return to England. A darn shame; I lost a good friend in old Moose, so you see ladies I know all about the clap hands and hallelujah praise the lord.

But I don't think you're going to find any of that Church here; at least I haven't seen any; again Mrs. Owens observed her husband not-stop talking. Donald gives the girls a chance to say something she said, take a breather, Ammi smiles, but Mr. Owens is in one of his talking moods. So where are you going to worship Ammi he asked; have you find a Church yet? No Sir; we're looking around but so far we have only come across the Church of England and Anglican, but we'll continue to look around she said. Well good luck to you; hope you'll find your kind of Church, I know you people are lively worshipers; you like to sing clap hands; you don't get that in these Churches. But we can worship at any Church Sir said Ammi, God is everywhere, so until we find a Pentecostal church we're going to the Church-of-England. Well young lady you must be one in a million; the Pentecostal member I knew would never go to any of the main Churches, because they're too dull. We'll go Sir because it's a way of life for us to go to Church on a Sunday said Daphne. Anyway I believe it won't be long before there're Pentecostal Churches here if there's none yet she said, soon there'll be Ministers among some of the immigrants that are coming. Do you go to church Sir asked Ammi, he hesitates, he never been close to any Church before or after the day were Married said Mrs. Owens; I don't know what he's afraid of she said. Then I take it you're a Church goer Mom asked Ammi, oh yes; I'm a catholic and I wish he would come to Church with me sometime. But he never answered Ammi question; no need, his wife answered it for him. I'll get you something to drink, two cokes coming up he said gleefully. The girls could have died from thirst from the time you should have gotten them the drink said Mrs. Owens. But this Land Lord is a very sociable man; whom as he said his best friend was a black man, he's comfortable talking with these black girls. He returns with the drinks, now then Daphne; you want to know if it's alright for you tree ladies to live together, yes Sir she said, well you know I'll have to increase the rent, yes Sir; I expect that would be the case. But I'm not going to until Ammi get herself a job he said, you're going to get a job Ammi don't you, he asked facetiously even though the girls can't see the joke, oh yes Sir; I just hope I get one soon she said.

Thinking about the bulk of immigrant coming here they're mostly labourers he commented; assuming Ammi was one of the unskilled workers. It's not easy to find a job when you're a labourer he said. But Ammi retort; I'm not a laboured Sir; I'm a dressmaker. Well good for you Ammi; that's what this country needs; more people like you he said. Well as soon as you have settled in a job I'll increase the rent; but don't worry; it will only be by five pounds he said with a smile. Daphne gasped; it's almost more than what she and Hillary earn together. Five pounds Sir she asked, you think it should be more he asked mischievously. But this white man like his little joke, a practical joker you might say. With his wife looking at the television and an ear in the conversation she speak, Donald stopped pulling the girls leg she said casually, I'm only kidding girls; only kidding he said, don't worry; as soon as Ammi get herself a job come and tell me. Daphne who was shocked by her landlord's five-pound rent rise calmed down now she realised he was jesting, thank you sir she said; we'll do just that.

Now that is settled the girls wanted to leave but doesn't know how to say good night; they don't want to appear ungrateful to Mr. Owens, and he wants to talk some more. Do you know anyone here other than Daphne and Hillary he asked Ammi, no Sir; I know a few people from home that is here but I have no idea of their whereabouts she said. But Daphne is getting sleepy; she's nodding off; but it's only pretence; she's hoping he'll see that they wanted to leave. Well he didn't seem to notice but Mrs. Owens did, Donald can't you see Daphne is sleeping, say good night and let them go she said. He stood up, good night ladies; and it was good to meet you Ammi, good night Sir; and thank you; and good night Mrs. Owens; it's good to meet you mom she said, good night girls said Mrs. Owens calling from the comfort of her armchair. Standing at the door Mr. Owens turns on the passage light and watch them go; it as though he was longing for someone to talk to, even though these two young people could be his daughter in age. They would certainly make good parents; unfortunately they're not blessed with children. Looking at the clock it's gone five, you realised we've spent the whole day with Mr. and Mrs. Owens said Daphne; Hillary is not going to be please for us to be home and not cook again; and she would be right to do so, well yes; but how could we just walk away from the Owens; that wouldn't be manners, and that Mr. Owens! Boy he can talk; doesn't he love to talk said Ammi. But a nice man nevertheless she said. You're not going to meet another white man like him said Daphne; most white people here just don't like black folks. Maybe it's because he travelled and lived amongst black people said Ammi, could be said Daphne; I wish there were more like him.

On returning to their room Hilly was already home, Hillary wasn't about to say anything but Ammi pre-amp her thought. Now Hillary! Before you say anything let me explain she said, explain about what asked Hillary, about why we didn't cook dinner. But why do you want to explain; you were upstairs with Mr. Owens didn't you, she asked. Well yes; but I thought it's unfair for you to come home and cook dinner while we are home, you have a right to be angry she said. Forget about it said Hillary; just tell me how much Mr. Owens increased the rent by, he didn't said Daphne; he'll increase it he said when Ammi gets herself a job, and how much will he increase it by then she asked, I don't really know; we'll just have to wait and see. After some long talking the evening is running late; looking at the clock it's approaching ten, this's the second night in a row we're going to eat this late said Daphne; it seems to be becoming a habit. Don't blame me said Hillary; I don't know what you were discussing with Mr. Owens all day, By the way; as a matter of interest; what time did you went to see him she asked, about mid-day said Ammi, and you been talking all this time? What were you talking about she asked; putting the country to rights, I suppose. Well Mr. Owens is a good talker said Ammi; he likes a conversation; he knew so much more about our country than us; what do you mean so much more than us; we know nothing about the country we were born. Did you know he was once living there; Ammi asked Hillary, no! But I'm not surprised. It could be his fore-parents were slave owners she said; and come to think of it; it could be that our fore-parent was owned by his ancestor. Thanks for the history lesson in slavery said Daphne, it's late but I'm going to have something to eat, they all sat and dine. We can't go to bed straight after we eat said Daphne we'll give ourselves colic; we'll have to sit up for some time for the food to digest said Daphne, what are you baby ask Hillary, talking about digestion; well I'm going to the bath room and straight to bed when I return said Hillary; anyway I'm the only one going to work tomorrow she said, you two can stay up for as long a you want, and off she went. True to her words; as she return from the bath room she didn't hesitate she went straight in bed, good night she said as she wrapped herself in, I don't want to know what you two are doing tomorrow was her last words as she pull the blanket over her head.

27: The Search for Work

It's Thursday morning and Hillary leaves for work while the others were still under the covers, but before they went to bed last night they decided to go job hunting today. Daphne explained that another way of getting a job other than relying on the labour exchange is to walk around looking for it. These jobs are advertised on notice boards outside of factories and other places, you look for what you can do; you then walk into the personnel office and ask about it, and if you're lucky and they like your face you might get an interview. This morning they have cereal for breakfast even though Ammi would like bacon and eggs; you shouldn't have a heavy breakfast every morning; you should give your stomach a rest. Nonsense said Ammi; my stomach doesn't need any rest; I haven't eaten enough for it to need a rest; you just didn't want to do breakfast this morning. Well they have their plans for the day; they're going to the biggest industrial compound in the country. The day very clear and bright but it's bitterly cold, they wrapped up the best winter gears and set off. They make their way to the bus stop; this time of day the bus will be running near empty; Ammi likes that; she can ride upstairs and admires the scenery. It wasn't long before the Trolley bus arrived, they boarded going in the opposite direction of the labour exchange; Ammi will experience some new scenery. The place they're going probably have the most factories in the country; something Ammi had never seen before. They had to change to another bus though that put them directly in the vicinity of the estate; and then they can walk around. Looking around Ammi was marvelled at the steam of pollution coming from the buildings, she has no idea what to make of it; Daphne who is here for over two years didn't know what to make of it either. But there's no surprise there, these are country girls who are just trying to get acclimatized to the outside world. They looked on many notice boards but there was nothing about dressmakers. But Daphne saw a job she thinks she could do; it would be good if she could get a better job than the one I'm in she said. She went in the personnel office accompanied by Ammi to ask about the job; they were glad to get in out of the cold even though they know it wouldn't be for long. Entering the office they could see two people; one was working away at the typewriter, the other one just sat there looking at them entering the office. They stand in the small waiting room for a short while mainly to allow their body to get a little warm. She (Daphne) approach the small window and tap on it, there was no response, she taps on the window again but still there was no response, she knew they not only hear the tapping on the window but they saw them as well. Well! She didn't tap on the window again immediately; no, she stood back and waits a while.

But as she decided to try again the man slides the window open, can I help you he said chewing what could be gum. I would like to apply for this job if it's still available Sir, it was a packing job, I'm sorry he said that job is gone. Well! Whether the job is gone or not she had no way of knowing; but one thing for sure; by their actions these two are definitely not appreciative of black people. Well it clouded over but still bitterly cold; they been walking about now for quite a while looking on notice boards without any success; it's about time they start to make their way back home. They caught the bus to Hamsden where they have to change for the eighteen which would take them home. But standing at the stop was this black fellow; not too handsome but not hideous either, they could see he was secretly looking them over. As new arrivals in the country it good to meet people you have something in common with; even if it's only the colour; so long as they're from the Caribbean. It was approaching the rush hour and there were several white people at the bus stop; but this black guy was one of two black people there. He slowly walked s towards them, hello ladies he said with a grin, I'm glad you two stop here; I was beginning to feel lonely. Daphne thought it's a good job Hilly wasn't here; she would tell him where to go. But Ammi said hello to him and nothing more; Daphne looked at him with disdain but said nothing either, of course Ammi had no experience of men and their chat-up line. But she was like civil to this man even though Daphne was hostile, well she couldn't it do any harm talking to him. My name is Derick and I'm from Jamila he said, and that was the cue for Ammi to get talking. Well he must have noticed something interesting about him otherwise she wouldn't be having a conversation with him; or a black person from Jamila she might feel she can talk with him. Unfortunately the bus has arrived and the conversation comes to an abrupt end, they pushed their way on to the bus but he was separated from them by the crowded on the bus. He reaches his stop before them, on getting off he waved goodbye and Ammi did the same; however Daphne totally ignored him. Two stops later the girls alighted; we didn't even ask that man his name said Ammi, why would you want to know his name she asked, you fancy him or something, Don't be so silly said Ammi; it's just good to meet someone who is from the same country as ours. Anyway you were talking to him too; did you fancy him asked Ammi, I didn't talk to him at all said Daphne sarcastically; I couldn't even if I wanted to she said, you were deep in conversation with him. I talked to him because he seems pleasant enough she said.

Some excuse said Daphne; if I say jump off the bus are you going to jump she asked, No; but I can't see the relevance said Ammi, the relevance is; because you find it necessary or interesting to talk to him you think I should talk to him too. Did I say that? When did I say that she asked; what came over you Daff; it's so unlike you to be snobbish; I sometimes expect that sort of behaviour from Hilly but not from you. We're out together and we stick together; that man wasn't been rude; no, in fact he was quite civil; I couldn't very well walk away; it would be rude and ill-mannered, she said. How kind of you said Daphne; I must remember your considerate nature; or maybe it's your Christian principles at work here. Well I just can't see any reason to be rude. They reached home and the banter is over, they're going to rustle up dinner before Hillary gets home and she's due shortly, there mustn't be any argument about they being home and didn't prepare dinner. Sometime later there was a slam at the front door; Hillary had arrived; I told that girl not to slam that door said Daphne; one day Mr. Owens will have words with her. How do you know its Hilly asked Ammi, she's the only one who slams the door; She walks in; and it's later than her usual time, why are you keep slamming the front door ask Daphne; there's no reason for you to slam the door. If you mean this one time, have you ever considered that I didn't mean to slam it; it just happens? The door just gets away from me, and then it always getting away from you said Daphne. Listening to the two of them going on about the front door Ammi intervene, how is it you're so late tonight she asked; couldn't you get on the bus? Oh no; that's not it, I was asked to do an hour's overtime; and I would probably ask to work on Saturday too but the boiler's broken down. Anyway when are we going to eat she asked; is dinner ready yet? Soon said Daphne who was is in the kitchen dishing out. Someone set the table she said, but the other two didn't want to sit at the table tonight; they rather sat where they can see the television. Hillary went into the kitchen to give a hand, put mine on the tray she said; and Ammi would like here's on a tray too s. Why don't we just throw out the table since no one wants to use said Daphne; it's only taken up space. Stop being cantankerous Misses said Hillary; come and sit down and have your dinner. She makes herself comfortable by herself on the table; the other two take their seat in front of the television with their dinner.

So what did you do today Ammi; Hillary asked while eating, we went job hunting she said, and did you get a job she asked, no; but I think we should go out again tomorrow. Where did you take her Daff; she asked, we went to Kings Park but there wasn't any job advertised for dressmakers she said, there was a packing job I went after; but they said it was gone. But I reckon I wouldn't get the job even if was available she said. Like the time when after the canning factory for a job; this man actually told us to clear off; he didn't even want to talk to us; you remember Hilly asked Daphne. Ammi was shocked to hear that, really she asked surprisingly, she actually told you that, she did said Daphne. But Hillary curses him disgracefully; using some of the foulest language you wouldn't want to hear; but even though he deserved it a woman shouldn't be using those nasty words; back home she would be arrested. And the man! I don't think he understood a single word Hilly was saying; he knew you were angry; very angry; that's all. But Hillary was unrepentant, I should have slapped him in the face she said; dirty white man telling us he doesn't want us there; who the hell he thinks he is? I hate these people. Well you did went to him for a job; he didn't come to you; you're the one who intruded on his privacy said Ammi facetiously. You can joke about it; but wait until you go for a job and they tell you they don't you there because you're black; then I see how you like it said Hillary. Nevertheless your behaviour did have me baffled; almost to the point of been shame said Daphne; I didn't know you could use such foul language, and that's not the behaviour of a lady, Ammi smile but said nothing. Lady! Don't come it with me; I'm no bloody lady; neither or you; don't come to me with any moralistic argument; how can you exercised morals living amongst these dirty racist bastards. Your land Lord is white and he seems quite clear to me said Ammi sarcastically, and I met him and discovered he and his wife are very nice people. Anyway you would be wrong to tar every white person with the same brush; people are different; some are good and some are bad; that is the way of the world she said. But Hillary had no remorse regarding her action towards that man; and even though it was well over a year ago she's still seething about it. You know what said Daphne; you shouldn't be living under this dirty white man's roof if that's the way you feel about all white people; would you like me to move out she asked, no! I didn't say that; all I'm saying you should choose your words a little more carefully.

Observing where this argument was going Ammi call a halt to the proceedings, she notice how easy it is for those two to have an argument; it won't be long before they are having an all-out war. Come on now; you two must stop this she said, every little words from either of you seem to cause an argument, when are you going to start behaving like family? If you hate each other then you shouldn't be living together; it's not healthy to be sleeping in the same bed and each one carrying a grudge. Frankly you should be a shame of yourselves; I thought you had settled your differences a few days ago, but it seems that was a pretence. There was a long hush with them only steering at the television, Hillary got up and began to collect up the plates while mumbling something, if you have something to say why you don't say it said Daphne. Hillary replied angrily, I'll tell you what I'm saying; you're carrying a grudge because you believed I take away your imaginary fellow; and you're never going to get over it; so I better look for accommodation elsewhere. I certainly don't want you to move away on my account said Daphne; but sometimes you have a way to say the most hurtful things, and what do you mean by imaginary fellow, she asked. I told you once before and I will tell you again said Hillary; I had no idea that you fancy the man; I never even seen you and him talk; but as I said before it's all in your head; and there's a word for women like you, but Daphne didn't response. Ammi was uncomfortable with their behaviour; she asked, tell me something; before I arrived here is this the way you two always behaved? And if that be the case how come you're still living together? It's bad; it's very bad, something art to be done about it, you should decide right now who go and who stays if you can't patch up your differences. There were moments of calm, well what you are going to do she asked; someone speak up. I don't hate her; why should I asked Hillary, but it's obvious she's hates me; she's carrying the hateful feeling that I stole the man she loved. But I said before and I will repeat myself again; I have no idea that she and this man were anything; even so; we only went out to the pub twice, we met there as arranged and parted company there after a few drinks. Did this man know you had a crush on him Daff; asked Ammi, I don't know; how could he? I couldn't get the chance to talk to him. You can stop right there said Hillary; I know what you're about to insinuate, if you...; but before she could add anything further Ammi interrupts. You mean you never talk with him? And yet you're accusing Hilly of stealing him away; what kind of madness is that? I think you owed her an apology she said.

But Hillary doesn't want an apology; she would like things to go back to the way they were and live together as one happy family. Daff! You have change said Hillary; you never used to keep malice nor bear grudges; now you're behaving completely out of character, but if you don't want us to share accommodation I will move out she said; and I will go with a clean mind and a pure heart. Now the mood has changed, Daphne appear as though she was going to shed tears, realising that what Hillary was saying was the truth; she was probably feeling somewhat a shame. I don't want you to move out on my account she said, we're not going to fall out over some man, and with her eyes flaming red she nearly apologised, we're family and we shouldn't allow some man to come between us. But Hillary was ready to forgive and forget; she stood up and went over to her sitting on the bed and sat beside her, they cried and embraced. I'm so sorry to let you think there was something going on between this man and me I'm so sorry she said. Ammi couldn't hold back the tears either; she went and joined them, but her tears were tears of joy; joy to see her two waring cousins be friends again; and hoping that will be the end of their feud. We won't talk about this ever again said Ammi; and they all agreed. It's quite late and normally Hillary who is going to working would be sleeping by now. I must have a cup of cocoa said Daphne; anyone would like a cup, oh no said Hillary; I'm going to bed, and off she went while the other two went to the kitchen. But before she pulled the blanket over her head she asked, so what are you two up to tomorrow? Ammi replied; we're supposed to be going to the labour exchange; today is when the woman told me to come back said Ammi. Are you sure asked Daphne; It should be next week Friday; you should only sign on once a week, let's go check on the card said Ammi, and she was right; it's this Friday. Well good luck to you; I hope they find you a job, good night she said; then she covered her head with the blanket. For now it's all quiet on the western front, peace reign within the family once more but for how long; this argument will never go away.

28: Signing On

Friday was freezing cold; it will snow during the course of the day according to the weather forecast, and if you're not working you wouldn't want to get out of bed. But Ammi is singing on today at eleven o'clock and for the third time she'll be going there and she doesn't want to be late. They got out of bed quite late but make haste with whatever they're doing so as to get away in time, Daphne reminded Ammi to take her particulars with her in case the people there wanted to see them again. Outside is bright; but the snow begins to fall, however while Daphne was complaining about the weather Ammi was relishing the challenge of walking in the snow. They set off to the bus stop about five minutes' walk away, they were alone at the stop which is not unusual for this time of day as the rush hour had passed, however they have to wait a long time for the bus to arrive. The old trolley bus was never a transport one can rely on; when it's not late it's broken down. After about fifteen or so minutes it had arrived but because of its lateness it was jam-packed; nevertheless they managed to get standing room. At Paddington Green the snowfall was heavier than where they'd come from; and even though it was up to their ankles Ammi wasn't complaining; her cousin wasn't happy about it though. It's a short walk to their destination and they make good time, nevertheless the place was jam pack as usual, the queues had stretched all the way back to the door. I thought we would get here on time comment Ammi looking at the queues; we're on time said Daphne; it's just gone ten forty-five; and your appointment is eleven o'clock, we'll be here all day said Ammi. Well we should get out of bed sooner said Daphne; so let it be a lesson for your next visit. The queues are moving but slowly; Daphne is standing in the queue with her cousin to keep her company. The day is running late; Daphne looked at her watch again; look at the time she said, it's twenty to one; it looks as though you're not going to get seen to today, oh well said Ammi; we can't do anything about it. But whatever happened over the other side of the counter the queues began moving; but faster, Daphne commented that more staff might have to turn up. At last it was Ammi's time to be seen; she took the seat at the desk and waited while her cousin went and sat back waiting for her, almost immediately a staff arrived with papers in hand. Amanda Thomas she inquired while perusing through the papers, yes I'm Amanda Thomas, and this woman was a different person from the one she saw the last time.

The woman sat down but didn't say anything for more than a couple of minutes, she kept looking at the documents, she then looked at her (Ammi) and looked at the paper again. What is your profession Miss Thomas she asked, of course she is looking at it in the documents she was reading; but perhaps she couldn't believe a black immigrant could be a dressmaker. She was quick to reply; I'm a dressmaker Miss, with her head still down in the documents she made a low groaning noise as though she was in pain or doubtful of what she was hearing. Talking while looking at the papers she commented, you have an interview on Monday Miss Thomas, then she paused as though she was having a second thought, and there's a giro here for you too. Of course Ammi had never seen a giro before; she'd heard people there arguing about it but never seen one. She remained quiet while she (the staff) continued to write; and after a few minutes she presented her with all the necessary papers. Then she rose to her feet and walked away with not so much as by your leave. Realising that she's finished with her Ammi got up and walked away, she then walked towards Daphne who was sitting over yonder. Is everything alright she asked; I don't rightly know she said; the woman said I've got an interview on Monday but she didn't say where; and I was also given a giro, a giro exclaimed Daphne in surprised, speaking in a low voice she asked; how could you get a giro; you only signed on three days ago, of course I have no idea; so why asked me she comment. So where do I take this paper to get the giro money she asked, pointing to the window, that's where to go to collect the giro. They got up and walked over towards the window; there was a small queue of about four people, but soon she collected the giro and off they went. Having left the building and began to make their way home Daphne still couldn't understand how is it she could get a giro; after all she is in the country less than a week; she's still mulling over it. How could you get a giro; if I didn't see it I wouldn't believe it, and three pounds she comments, I don't understand. We have to wait over two weeks to get one of those things, referring to the giro; and you come along and get one in what? She paused to think, four days? Some people got all the luck she said. How and where do I cash it ask Ammi, at any post office said Daphne, and where you have to go for this interview she asked. The woman didn't say and I haven't looked at the paperwork as yet. Let's have a look said Daphne, looking at the paper and realised the job is around here; somewhere in the same vicinity. This place should be around here somewhere she said, do you know where asked Ammi, no; but the address is Dorsey's Clothing Elan Road north-west eight, and we're in north-west eight she said.

We have to ask someone but not today; it's getting dark and I'm cold and hungry said Daphne. Well they need to find Dorsey's Clothing before Monday; so that when Ammi set off for her interview she wanted to know directly where to go so as not to be late. Then when are we coming back to find it asked Ammi, tomorrow; we'll come back tomorrow said Daphne; and if Hilly is not working she's probably come along too. It was a somewhat a quiet journey home; mainly because Ammi fell asleep on the bus, Daphne allowed her to sleep and only wake her when they were close to where they supposed to alight. When she woke she apologised, I'm so sorry I dozed off she said; I didn't realised I was so tired, but Daphne was complimentary, don't worry; there's no cure for sleep she said; you're not used to be out in the cold so long. The evening is getting colder and they hurriedly make their way home, Hillary was home and seeing to dinner, Hilly! I'm cold, tired, and hungry; what have you got for us to eat asked Ammi, come and make a cup of tea and make a cup for Daff too, that will warm you up until dinner is ready. But tea for them doesn't mean tea in a sense of the word, no; they don't drink; tea is a word they used loosely back home, they drink cocoa, chocolate or herbal tea; but the local referred to everything as tea; Dinner won't be long; it will be ready in a jiffy said Hillary, a jiffy? What's a jiffy asked Ammi, a local slang I picked up meaning soon or quick; oh! Well I hope dinner will be on the table in a jiffy said Ammi with a smile. Unfortunately the old paraffin lamp is giving off the foulest of smell and no heat; Daphne is doing her best to get it to work but to no avail. Hillary walked in with the dinner and complained about the smell; how long are we going to inhale this stench for she asked while put the dinner on the table. We'll have to get a new lamp tomorrow said Daphne, but can we afford one though asked Hillary, the three of us will chip in said Daphne, what do you mean the three of us ask Hillary; Ammi just got here remember?. I remember alright said Daphne; but she's got money she said as she gives up on the lamp and is putting some extra clothes on to keep warm. I've got a giro from the labour exchange said Ammi sitting at the table in her winter coat, you get a giro? But how asked Hillary; you only signed on three days ago. That's what I would like to know too comment Daphne; maybe she should take back. Wait a minute now; nobody is taking anything back said Daphne, if she was given a giro; and in this case she did; then they gave it to her on merit. Government doesn't give away money to anyone unless they are due it, she said. What merit asks Hillary, when you became an authority on Government affairs. I'm only saying we need that money to make up to but a proper lamp. I agree said Ammi.

But now Ammi wanted to know for sure if the giro was given to her on merit or it's a blunder by the authority; according to her religion she shouldn't accept anything unless it was rightly her's. So you think I should return this giro she asked, if I was given to me in error then we should take it back. But Daphne wants to hear no more talk of taking it back; how much is this giro she asked; three pounds said Daphne. That's a couple a pounds less than what I earned this week including my overtime said Hillary; some of that can help towards buying a paraffin lamp, that's what I was thinking, said Daphne. Well after all is said and done Ammi was glad she could help towards something, she handed the giro to Hillary, if this can help to pay for the lamp then put it toward it she said. But Daphne intervenes quickly, I thought you would to send something out of it to Uncle John she asked, I will when I start working; there's no hurry she said. The argument seemed to br settled; a part of the giro is going towards buying the lamp; for tonight they'll wrapped up the best they can to keep warm. You are lucky person Ammi Thomas said Hillary, you're not even in the country a full week and yet you collected money; your man must be on the job she said with mischievous intent. What are you talking about asked Ammi, which man on what job? But she was slow to pick up on Hillary's quip, did you pray and asked anyone for help last night she asked; I remember you did, Well it seem as though your prayer is answered; your man cone through and delivered. Now Ammi catches on, you want to be careful she said; one doesn't make mockery using the name of the Lord. You know Hilly; you were always a vile person and is time you changed, and let me tell you; it blasphemous to use the name of God in vain, you should always remember that. Daphne wasn't happy either with the sort of joke; we know you must have your little joke Hilly; but don't you think you should choose your topic more carefully she asked. Oh come on now said Hillary I'm I the only sinner here; Daff you start behaves like little Miss Goody, goody here, all I said was her man is on the job; what's blasphemous about that she asked with a serious composure. What is a joke to you is death to others said Ammi sternly, the bible said that too asked Hillary, no; but someone said it long ago. Anyway come Sunday we are going to church she said; you need prayer girl; someone has to pray for you. Who are we that are going to church she asked; I didn't remember making any promise or arrangement to go to church; oh no! Not me she said. But Ammi knows she's only gassing; on Sunday they'll all be going to church all three of them. Just out of interest which church are you considering going to she asked, the nearest one here to us; the Church of England said Ammi. What! She exclaimed, alarmingly; but none of us ever been to a Church of England; and as far as I hear they worship differently from a Pentecostal church, no; I won't go there she said; and neither should you. But Ammi wasn't deterred; you're talking like someone held a grievance against certain churches she said, a church is a place people go to worship God regardless of their religion, the name and words of the Lord is spoken there, wherever my name is called; I'll be there to bless and to do good; sayeth the bible. The thing about these Christians they just can't help wanting to preach to people all the time; they just can't help themselves said Hillary. But don't bother to preach to me; I'm not ready to take the plunge yet; in fact that's not for me; I'm only young and got a lot of living to do. Ignore her said Daphne, she just likes to sound off; and behaving as though she's tough. Ammi smiled and quote a Christian saying, the viler the sinner the richer the blood, I supposed the vile sinner is me, she comments. Well! I may be a sinner but certainly not vile. It's nearly midnight and time for bed; and Ammi will do what she usually does come bedtime; she kneeled to pray, Daphne usually joined her; but Hillary only occasionally does; however tonight she was the first to kneel beside her (Ammi), She's a pussy cat really; she just likes to appear tough.

29: Pathfinding

Saturday morning no one wanted to get up; under the blanket is warm and cosy but the room is very cold; there's no heat at all; however the sooner they got up and get a move on the sooner they'll sort out their heating problem. Ammi reminded the others that they have to go check out the whereabouts is Elan Road the place where Dorsey's Clothing locates. So they decided to kill three birds with one stone, they'll go seek out Dorsey's Clothing first thing and then go shopping for a paraffin lamp while doing the usual shopping at the same time, so with all that chores to do they got out of bed and make ready to move; once again there's no breakfast this morning; it's far too cold; a cup of cocoa will suffice. Firstly they're going to find Dorsey's Clothing; it cold outside but it's better than inhaling that foul smell indoors; and with all three together it was a good feeling to get on the bus when it arrived, the warmth inside was feeling rather nice. Arriving at Paddington Green they made their way up to Edgware Road and then they'll ask their way from there. But this place wasn't hard to find; in fact they walked right by it a couple of times when they were going to the labour exchange. It's an easy place to get to comment Daphne; you don't have to change busses. Thank God for that said Ammi; if I get the job here I don't want to run the gauntlet twice every morning getting on the bus. What time is your appointment asked Hillary, Ammi paused for a reply, you know I didn't even check she said; I was only thinking of where about of the place. Oh well! No big deal said Hillary, the most important thing is that you know where to come on Monday; you can check out the time on return. What do you mean you? Aren't you coming with me asked Ammi, well yes; but now it seems I might have to change my plan, I take the week off work to be with you while Daff return to work, but if you get this job on Monday you might start working on Tuesday; I've nothing to do with my time for the rest of the week, but you don't bother about it she said; I'll think of something. Now that one of the chores is complete they set off back to their local shopping in Hamsden. On arrival there they first check out where to buy the paraffin lamp, they only just arrived before the post office closed though; and Ammi cashed in her giro; and now they can go looking to buy a lamp.

They got a wide choice of paraffin lamps, with it being the main source of heating for ordinary people there are lots of different kinds available. They'll buy the best one can afford with the help of some of Ammi's giro, and there's no need to buy oil there's full can indoors. But it's a clumsy item and they would struggle to get it home using public transport, so they asked the shopkeeper to look after it for them while they went and do their usual shopping. Well everything has gone to plan; all they need now is to get back home, they collect the paraffin lamp and got one of the local minicab to take them home. They're lived not a million miles away from where they are now; so the fare is the minimum. They were glad to get back home to power up their new lamp to warm up the room; but it will take some time so until then they'll keep their coat on, in the meantime Daphne is making cocoa for everyone. Ammi was not only cold but tired, she cuddled up in the settee while waiting for the cocoa; but by the time cocoa was ready she nodded off. Being out in the cold for so long has taken its toll on her; Hillary took a blanket and put over her. About an hour or so later the room was well warm; warm enough for them to take off their winter gear. I'm going to see to dinner said Daphne as she headed for the kitchen; Hillary had nothing to do other than sit back and watch the old black and white television. There was nothing interesting on the box to watch so she turned it off and while Ammi was still asleep she went and join Daphne in the kitchen to help with dinner. The time is approaching six o'clock and while they're in the kitchen Ammi awakens, oh look she said, it's snowing again, but it seems no one heard her, so she went into the kitchen to join them too. It snowing heavily she said, why so surprised asked Hillary; we're in the heart of winter, and anyway we're finished outside for today thank God. But it's a beautiful sight though said Ammi, well I wouldn't want to be out there if I can help it said Daphne, and thank God we managed to get a good heater, and you won't be saying it's beautiful when it frozen solid and you're out there walking. It's doesn't matter how long I'm in this country I'll never get used to this cold she said. Dinner is ready to be brought in, go and set the table Ammi said Hillary and take out the drinks, what drinks she asked; orange or ginger beer, anyone will do she said; and so it was done. At the table they have a lot to talk about, Ammi recalled the man they met at the bus stop on their way home from Kings Park; but neither she nor Daphne could remember his name. You know Ammi; I think you fancy that man said Daphne; you seem quite willing to talk to him, don't you start that again said Ammi, what? Asked Hillary; little miss prim and proper here see a man she fancy? Is he a Christian like yourself she asked mockingly. Don't be silly said Ammi; we were just talking; and anyway you were in the conversation too Daff. Anyway he wasn't saying anything untoward or behaved as though he wanted to chats us up; but you were behaving as though you want to argue with him; and what for? Only you know. Well I didn't like him she said; you didn't notice but his eyes were up and down all over us. I can't say I did notice; and I think you just make that up said Ammi, you didn't notice because you were too deep in conversation with him said Daphne. Don't exaggerate said Ammi; it's good to meet people from our neck of the wood whom you can communicate with and reminisced about home; don't you think so Hilly? I share your compliment she said, these white people you can't talk with them as you would with someone from home, but Daphne couldn't believe that Hillary is agreeing with Ammi about something, jokingly or not she's always in opposition of her.

I never thought I live to see the day, well, well, well she said and paused as though she's waiting for someone to ask her what she's on about, and she didn't have to wait long. What are you talking about asked Hillary, you agreeing with Ammi she said, well wonders never cease she said with a hint of earnest. Well I know little Miss righteous here is never going to stand around to be chatted up by any man; at least not yet; maybe when she's back slide she said facetiously. Backslide Ammi asked; she looked at her with sympathetic eyes, I just know you would come out with something silly like that, you just can't help having your little joke, let's talk about church; you remember we are going tomorrow she asked. I'm not going said Hillary promptly; I can't; I'm having a visitor, what visitor asked Daphne anxiously; how could you be having a visitor without telling us. Well I'm telling you now haven't I? Well who is this man she asked, does it have to be a man? she asks Hillary, no; then who is it Daphne asked insistently. It seems she had the thought that this visitor is the man she has a crush on; a Mr. Dickenson; a man they all knew from home. This gentleman was a highly respected person back home and was a friend of Ammi's father John Thomas; a much older man than these girls. He's in his mid-forties while they're in their late twenties. However some women like older men and Daphne seem to be one of those women. As her suspicion gets the better f her; so is her action; she's demanding to know who this man is; but Hillary is not telling. Calm yourself Daff; why are you getting yourself work up over nothing asked Ammi, Hilly is old enough to have her own friends, whether it's man or a woman, my only criticism is; we're all living together; it's only right and proper that if you're inviting someone to our room you should inform us beforehand, you should show us some respect in that regards. I'll be blunt and you're not going to like what I'm about to say, it's would be really presumptuous of you to bring in a stranger to our room without telling us, this I would say to Daff if it was she who is thinking of doing what you're about to do. Daff! You too must stop thinking that way, it seems as though whenever hilly talk about a man any man;; you deem to believe she's talking about the man you said you have a crush on. You have to get away from that position; it's not doing you any good at all; and to be frank; you're accusing hilly of something she's not guilty of. But Hillary had become accustomed to Daphne's accusations; she's not going to be drawn in another of her suspicious argument. For your information I'll tell you she said; I was only joking, but Mr. Dickenson heard that Ammi is here and wanted to come and see her today; but… Ammi interrupt; Mr. Dickenson from home she asked pleasantly; I would love to see him; when is he coming she asked. He's not; I told him we were going to church, I should have told you from Wednesday but I forgot. So you see Daff there's no man coming to visit me; not even the man you love she said facetiously. Ammi didn't want to say anything; but she feels she must, Daff! You should be a shame of yourself; I don't know what's happening to you; but you have changed your behaviour, are you seriously telling me that you love a man who never even talk to intimately? Nevertheless you're willing to make a fool of yourself over him? That's not the Daff I know and grew up with. But she didn't have anything to say; it appears she's full of remorse; she hangs her head in shame and went to the bathroom. But even Hillary was concern about her, do you think she'll be alright Ammi she asked, I don't know; but I'm concern about her. She was a bit long in coming back so Hillary decided to go and check on her, while she was gone Ammi began to change in her nighty; but she's not going to bed as yet; when everything is quiet down it doesn't matter how late she's going to write home. Hillary had gone to check on Daphne for some time now and Ammi was concern how quiet the place was; so she decided to go check on them.

She went to the bathroom but the door was closed, she taps on the door but didn't call out any names, there was no response so she tapped again a little louder. Is that you Ammi asked Hillary, open the door Hilly she said, the door is open and Ammi walked in. The toilet seat was closed and Daphne was sitting on it, she was crying and whispering something to herself; looking at the wall on the other side of the bathroom. Hillary looked at Ammi and shook her head; maybe to say she can't get anything out of her, now Ammi was really concerned. Daff! You alright she asked, but she didn't respond, I can't get a single word out of her said Hillary; what must we do she comment; as of now they're thinking the worse; is their cousin going funny in the head. But Daphne is fine; nothing the matter with her; if anything it's just plain and simple shame, shame of her ridiculous and stupid attitude; she'll have to come to her senses and fast otherwise she'll be making herself a laughing stock. Ammi and Hillary were conferring standing by the door, I know you're talking about me; but I'm not mad nor ever going to she said, so you can talk let me hear. Hillary move quickly to her; drops to her knees and embraced her, are you alright Daff she kept saying, you give us one hell of a fright. Ammi sat on the side of the bath, why did you do this Daff she asked; do you know how much we worried about you? You could give us a heart attack. Still sitting on the toilet seat and probably feeling much a shame of herself; I'm so sorry; can you forgive Hilly; I know I made a fool of myself and accused you wrongfully; please forgive me. Oh stop apologising said Hillary, everyone is entitled to make a fool of themselves now and then, she hugged her again to reassure her that everything is fine between them. Looking on Ammi was very impressed with Hillary's action, knowing the way Daphne behaved towards her; some other person would probably never speak to her again. But Hillary showed good attitude and love for her cousin; and forgive her for her shocking behaviour. Come along Daff; it's quite late; let's get to bed said Hillary with her hand on her shoulder, she rose to her feet; still with watery eyes, I could do with a cup of chocolate she said, I'll go and put the kettle on said Ammi as she made her way to the kitchen. It's quite late but they sat almost in silence and have their cuppa, Ammi broke the silence, I plan was to write a letter or two tonight but I feel the sleep's coming on she said, I'll have to do it another time. You're here just over a week now and you haven't written back home as yet asked Hillary, talk about neglect; that should be one of the first things you do, I can imagine Uncle John being restless for not hearing from you. You're so right Hilly she said; I think I got carried away for just been here, I know I shouldn't neglect them; that's the last thing I intend to do. Right after Church tomorrow I'll get down and write them all. All of them asked Hillary, how many people you intend to write to? Well! I don't remember if I did tell you about Miss Florence; she's the one who taught me dressmaking; she's like a family and I must write to her; and Maggie too; she'll be dying to hear from me. They had their cocoa and chocolate and it's time for bed, remember everyone we mustn't sleep too late in the morning; remember we're going to Church she said. But do you know what time their service start asked Hillary, oh yes; the first service begins at eleven o'clock; we should be there for ten forty-five she said, get there early and have a look around. Ok said Daphne; see you all in the morning. She's sleeping on the left side of the five-foot bed; she walked around to that side. Ammi kneels to pray but she didn't bother calling the others this time; probably because it was nearly two o'clock. After prayer she stood up and bid the others good night; and may the good Lord bless us all she said, then she went to bed.

30: A Visit to The Church of England

It's Sunday morning and the winter was in full swing, the snow is heavy on the ground and it's very cold, Daphne got up early and light the paraffin lamp and went back to bed, whenever they decided to budge the room should be quite warm. The clock is right next to Ammi and she kept watching it; she doesn't want to be late for church. They'll get out of bed round about eight o'clock, getting tidy will take some time, as there's only one bath for the tenants; and they'll have to take turns to have their wash, and as usual; on Sunday morning they like to settle down to a hearty breakfast. It'll be some time for them to leave, Daphne turned off the paraffin lamp; she would like to turn it down low and leave it on; so that when they return the room would be still warm, but she dare not; these lamps have a history of catching fire sometimes. At the front door they met Mr. Owens coming in, he's being out to get the paper, good morning ladies he said with his usual glee, the girls returned the compliment. Without asking about where they're going he comments, so you find a church to visit it seems he asked, oh yes Sir; the Church of England said Ammi as they paused at the door. Well I hope you'll like it there he said, have a good day now, I hope so Sir said Ammi; then they went through the door. The church is only a short walk away but because of snow on the ground it will take much longer. Going to this church none of them knew what to expect; it will be a new experience for them, however Ammi is looking forward to it; and even though it's not her ideal choice of place to worship; she's open-minded about going there. Reaching the church there weren't many people about; even though when they were looking around earlier in the week there was an abundance of people here, it could be the effect of the cold weather. They walked up toward the door passing the notice board, Daphne paused to have a quick read of it; but the others didn't, Ammi had already made note of the time initially; so there was no need for her to stop to read the notice board again. They couldn't tell if there were many people in church; not from where they were this church is so much bigger than the one they were accustomed to. So with the people looking at them in full glare as to say; what the hell are you doing here; they made their way up stair where they will have a Panoramic view of everything one and everything. According to Ammi's watch service should start in about five minutes. The people coming in but no one was coming upstairs; there's no need to; this church is big enough to hold hundreds of people and there were only a few seated somewhere near to the podium. They look up to see partly because of the others who are there kept looking up; they that coming in have no idea of what or who they were looking at. But when they reach somewhere in the middle of the Church where they could see upstairs they paused to have a look. Some looked and moved on; but this one woman stand and glared; it seems as though she wants to make sure she'll able to give a good account of what she was looking at; three black women. The time she spent looking she must be thinking it's the presumptuous thing she ever saw; how dare these people come here, she walked slowly to join the others. Hillary made some derogatory comments; but Ammi reminded her to remember where she is. We felt like we were aliens just fallen from the sky and landed in the wrong place. But Hillary finds it difficult to contain herself, have These dirty white people have never seen black people before?, she asked; and she didn't whisper. However there's no one white person upstairs sitting to hear; they're all downstairs. But Ammi was quick to reprimand her again; Hilly! Remember where you are; that tongue of yours one day is going to get you into serious trouble, calmed yourself; looks can never hurt you she said. But however much she talked; the others the other two were feeling uncomfortable been there. But Ammi wasn't feeling averse to the way they were feeling, no; but she's in the house of God and she's going to behave in likewise manner. She's looking forward to is to see the measure of service and how different if any it is from the one she's used to. Suddenly there was a bell ringing and the sound of singing; and the voices of children. The few people stood when the Minister emerged in his milk-white robe with a touch of blue up at the shoulder; he was looking all majestic. Ammi didn't believe he had seen them. He hasn't got on his podium as yet. Hillary made a quip; when he sees us he might ask us to leave, is as though she knew something that the others didn't, don't be so dramatical said Ammi; for what purpose would he do that? People don't get turn away from churches she said; that's unheard of.

The Minister reached his place on the podium and people sat down, now he saw them; and by doing so he was distracted; is as though he didn't know whether to look at his programme or look at them in the balcony. However he began the service and every so often he glanced up at them. They only have to sit and listen; they couldn't follow the service; they didn't pick up a programme on their way in; they only realised that when they saw the people all with programmes. Well it was a strange service; so different from the one they accustom to; they don't know what to make of it; the one hour service seemed more like four hours; tedious, boring and without meaning. Hillary has begun her analysis; no, her criticism, before the Minister concluded the service she wanted to leave; but Ammi persuaded her no to. However it wasn't long after the Minister ended the service and make his way behind the children towards the front of the church outside. They make their way down from balcony and try to mingle with the few people there by walking among them on their way out. Then they observed the Minister stood next to the notice board greeting the people as they emerged from the church, Ammi thought it was a good gesture. She turned to the others and asked; shall we go and greet the Minister? What for asked Hillary, Daphne looked at her and then comment, when in Rome; we'll go and do what the others do she said; and Ammi was in Harmony with her. However! By then they were the centre of attraction; but the area became alive compared to when they first arrived; and even those people who were passing by were noticing them. They make their way to the Minister who seems pleasing to see them; he's smiling broadly. Ammi is got a good feeling; it's good to be she's thinking, the Minister was pleased to see them. Oh how wrong could they be; her good feeling will soon become one of despair. Not speaking the truth about the service Daphne was the first of the three to shake his hands. In doing so she was feeling rather good, nice service Minister she said. Still smiling broadly he reached for her Ammi's hands; and with a hearty shake he told them in no uncertain term, ladies! It's good to see you; but please don't come back he said with a deceiving grim on his face. The other two were right behind and heard fully what the Minister said; so do other people who were close by.

By now Hillary is seething with rage; and been the quick-tempered person she is, she advanced menacingly towards the Minister, not exactly a lover of white people and certainly no respect for this dirty white man; as she would have said. What did you say she asked with furious intention? But Ammi was quick to act, before the Minister have a chance to respond she drag her away. Ammi knew she would abuse the Minister verbally and he would deserve it; but to drag her away seem the right thing to do at the time. However while Ammi pulled Hillary away Daphne had a quiet word with him, you don't want us to come to your church she asked; and with several people looking on; and with the smile gone from his face he comments in the nicest manner, you don't have to come here Miss; there're many more churches around. Daphne got the message loud and clear and she's not going to argue with the minister; she's only wanted to clarify what she thought she heard. You should be a shame of yourself she said; posing to be a messenger of God, she turns and walked away. But the Minister wasn't bothered; he stood there with the smile return to his face; and with no remorse at all for his action, he continues with his greeting. Of course most of who were there appear to approve of his action; and looking around they were probably the only black people there in the vicinity; they felt like they were in the lion's den. There was no one there that would speak up on their behalf however sympathetic they might be feeling; it might be a case of don't rock the boat. They didn't wait around; the many eyes that were on them and with the feeling that they not wanted around there they discretely walked away. Well they came, they saw but they didn't conquer; but they witness from first-hand the deceptive action and racist attitude of someone who supposed to be a man of God. They now knew it was folly to come to this church; on the other hand seeing is believing; if they didn't come they wouldn't be in a position to talk of what they had experienced. They're all furious from the experience though; more so Hillary, looking at Ammi with anger in her eyes she commented, you shouldn't have pulled me back; I was going to slap him in his face, angry talk of course. You wouldn't slap a man of God in the face would you; asked Daphne mockingly, a man of God;? What man of God she asked sarcastically, the man is the Devil; no wonder his sermon was so dull. I couldn't understand any part of it; and no wonder this huge church only got a few people in it. You can't say that said Ammi; it's only the first time we being there; and the last said Daphne; that goes without saying said Hillary. But Hillary probably should have been born a man; her whole action is that of the opposite sex; she's got a violent temper and could get out of control at times. We should go back there when it's dark and rip all the paper of the notice board she said, you mean vandalised the place asked Ammi, have you got no shame? Are you going mad hilly? Why don't you start behaving like a decent young woman? Did you hear that Daff; she wants to go and vandalise the church, I didn't say that said Hillary; only the notice board, it's part of the church too said Ammi, but why would you want to do that in the first place, we're all angry too; but we don't let our anger get the better of us; control yourself woman. I don't know whom you think you are; some kind of mother Teresa? Daphne giggled; Mother Teresa doesn't preach she said looking all innocently. What are you saying Daff; you're agreeing with madam here that I'm always preaching? Oh no! I'm only saying, Ammi interrupts, well I'll tell you; someone has to talk to her to start acting like a lady; and if it means I have to preach then so be it.

The Minister behave abominably; no doubt about that; but that doesn't give you the right for wanting to vandalise the church, certainly not she said. He supposed to be a man of God; but not everyone who said Lord, Lord will enter the kingdom of heaven, a quote from the good book she said; some are deceivers; lying to themselves and others; but someday their sins shall find them out. However all Hillary wanted to do is to get home out of the cold; no nice words from the bible or anywhere else are going let her feel any better. Walking home was a bit difficult; the snow had frozen and the road becomes slippery. Without the proper shoes they will be slipping and sliding, however they'll be home in a few minutes. They reached home and everyone tried to do something; and with the room freezing cold the first thing Daphne settled down to do was to power up the paraffin lamp while Hillary put the kettle on, no one was taking off their coat until the room warmed up. They sat around drinking gups of cocoa; the room will soon warm up; the new lamp is working adequately; they will soon be able to remove their coats and then they can sit back relax and reflects on today's event. However Hillary found it necessary to start blaming Ammi for their experience. I didn't want to attend this church today or another day she said; but you force me to by preaching your mambo jumbo to me; and look what happened. We all could end up in jail; or they could gang up on us and do us something nasty. I'm hoping that will teach you not to be too liberal-minded. What do you mean end up in jail; why would we end up in jail asked Ammi, there's nothing the matter with the church; just the Minister; and even though the people didn't make us feel welcome either; they didn't do us anything. You with your more than righteous attitude; one day it's going to lead you to somewhere or to something you regretted said Hillary. I suppose if he had slapped you on the left cheek you would have turned the other one, and I know; don't tell me; that's in the bible too she said. But Ammi is unrepented; she can take all that her cousin thrown at her without any feeling of hostility. I thought it was the right thing to do at the time; I still think it's the right thing to do; but not with that Minister preaching there. So all we have to do now is come Sunday we'll go looking for another church; we'll find one that will accept us black folks; there has to be one she said.

If you're glutton for punishment I'm not said Hillary, can't you understand that these nasty white people hated us; why are you trying to make out like they're good people she asked, white people are the devil; and they hate black people; that is so from the beginning of time; and it will always be so; the Leopards cannot change their spots. You know

Hilly; you led me to believe that you're ignorant said Daphne, if you hate these people as much as you say why don't you return home; they would certainly be out of their way, there's no one holding you here and moreover you chose to come here. I didn't know anything about white people before; I never had any dealings with a white person until I came here she said. Fair point said Daphne; that's a sensible enough excuse; but you're here nearly three years now and feeling the way you felt you shouldn't remain here. let me reminds you; you're living under the roof of one of those dirty white men, and we should be thankful to him for helping us out when we couldn't get a room. We're tenants but; look at the way he treats us; not as tenants; but as people living together. I can't argue against what she said; but he's only one, and I'm sure there're many others like him said Ammi; that's why you should choose your words more carefully. Alright! You two can get off my case now; I get the message; don't say anything derogatively about these nice white people; the wrong they do us doesn't matter she said; ok! Let's eat. That's the most humane thing you said from we returned said Daphne; I'm with you on that she said Ammi sarcastically. Daphne got up to make her way to kitchen, anyone want dinner on the table? I have to ask because it seems as though we're not using the table anymore; we preferred to sit in front of the television or on the bed. I'll come with you said Ammi; I want mine on a tray; and me too said Hillary, that table had to go; it's only taking up space said Daphne. It was the night of Z-Cars and Ammi had no intention of missing any of it, she along Hillary hastily get their food on the tray and settled down in front of the old black and white. Daphne! Well she was more at ease around the dining table; but she's got more than one eye on the television too. It had been an eventful day; a day that will stick in their memory for years to come, but time is a great healer; and one day they'll look back on this day and wonder about it as a passing phase in their lives.

31: Writing home

It over a week since Ammi had landed on these shores, her Parents had expected her to white home the day she landed, They'll be worried sick for not hear anything from her. Her father John Thomas must be having sleepless nights; and young Maggie must be making trips to the post office to check if there's any letter for her from her sister. Mrs. Florence Hollins now Mrs. Faster must be tearing her hair out; she really wants to hear what this England is all about, and of course that's where her farmer in-laws the slave owners are from, but she never been there. But they'll all get letters; only Ammi hasn't got around to writing as yet. However tonight the night she's is begining her letter writing. The others are watching television but she won't be distracted; but tonight she's won't be distracted; she's feeling too guilty for not writing home. However she won't be writing to everyone tonight; she can't; but she'll certainly make a start. You should be writing to Uncle Denis too Daphne; said Ammi, in fact from I gave you that letter Dad sent; you should reply immediately to find out how is Uncle Denis doing; and come to think of it you never bothered at all. She got up from the television and sat at the table, you want to know the honest truth; I've completely forgotten about it she said, with all the goings-on here it completely slips my mind; now I'm feeling awful, and I know it will appear as though I don't care; but that would be so far from the truth. Well you shouldn't feel too bad; I'm in the same boat said Ammi; and you're right about the goings-on; meeting up with you two I seem to forget about home, and I need to do better; I must do better; one day I'll be returning home. Are you sure about that asked Hillary who's got one ear on the television and the other ear in their conversation? You're right about events overrides your memory about home; since you arrived here you appear to be right in your element. You're not going back home; you're here for the long hall she said with some certainty. You can keep thinking that said Ammi; but you don't know my mind; I must return home one day and soon; I don't intend to leave my families for good. Oh yes? The longest liver will see the most said Hillary; I might not be here but somebody will tell me, you're not going back home, no; you'll bury here she said. We'll see said Ammi; there's an old saying; what's coming you don't have to go to meet it; no; it will come to you, what's that supposed to mean asked Hillary, I would like to know too said Daphne, work it out for yourselves; I've got no time to explain she said. In other words you can't explain your own parable; fine philosopher you are.

Are you going to write your letters; or; or you going to sat there looking at the writing pad asked Hillary, Ammi chuckled; I'm going to write. Are you going to mention in your letter to Uncle John about our experience at the church of England asked Daphne, oh no; said Ammi; I don't want him to worry; and if mention anything like that I know exactly what he's going to telling me to do; to pack my suitcase and return home, oh no; what he doesn't know won't bother him, I think you're right said Daphne; there's no need for them to know that. Daphne settled down to write to her Dad; but she paused and fiddling with the pen, now I'm about to write this letter I begin to feel anxious about Dad she said, I wonder if his condition has improved, there's no way of knowing other than when we write and they reply, said Ammi. If the letters take five days to reach home; I suppose it takes the same five days to return isn't it asked Ammi, I supposed so said Daphne. But you could send a telegram if you are very anxious to hear; it cost much more than letter said Hillary, but that's what you should do if you think the matter is quite urgent she said. The letter will have to do say Daphne; me knowing quicker about his condition is not going to change the way he is. That's a terrible thing to say said Ammi; it sounds as though you're not too bothered about the way your Dad might be feeling. I'm sure she didn't mean it the way; it probably just came out badly said Hillary; she just doesn't know how to choose her words. You telling me that asked Daphne anxiously, you're the worst person I know for choosing the wrong words, only when I'm angry said Hillary; if that be the case you're always angry said Ammi with giggles. Ammi has completed the letter to her father, I'm tired she said; that will be it for tonight, tomorrow I'll sit down and write some more. Daphne was still writing; but when Ammi have a glance at her letter she only writes a few lines, is that all you manage to write all this time she asked. Daphne looks up at her, I really don't know what to write, and could you help me, Daff! He's your father; you should be able to tell him thing and ask him thing; why do you find it so difficult? Ask him how is he feeling; he had a beating that nearly cost him his life; remember she asked. You don't have to ask him how it happens; I don't think he would want you anyway, but you could ask him if the Doctor is looking after him.

But she was never one for writing letters; when she sent monies home to her father she just scratches a few lines and registered the cash and sent it off. But Daphne is not going to converse with her father; not even in a letter; Caribbean children are not in the habit of talking with their parents. That is not something the parents entertain, no; their motto is; children should be seen but not heard; how illiterate can those parents be, is almost as though they want the children to grow up in ignorance. Their parents never brought up to be communicative; and they do the same to their children. So there's no wonder this grown woman of twenty-nine years old have difficulties finding words to write to her father. With Ammi it's so much different; even though she was never a talkative young woman she and her father had a good rapport, they could talk to each other. Tell me what to write she asked; have you ever write to Uncle Dennis before asked Ammi, Well yes; but I didn't have to ask him about anything. Give it here said Ammi, and she took over, she puts her own words to make up the letter, for her it's not too difficult; the man is her Uncle. Would you like to read it she asked, do I have to she asked, good heavens woman; it's your father; read what I write, it's your Uncle she asked, so what's the problem. Problem? It's not a problem with me; it's a problem with you, here it is said Ammi putting it down on the table, read it if you wish. Well she read it; at least she said she did, and there was nothing to said or do about it other than to put it into an envelope and sealed it. During this letter writing Hillary was asleep, still reeling from her experience to the Church of England; she couldn't hold up any longer to hear the discussion between her two cousins regarding writing home. Well! It late, Ammi shook Hillary, wake up sleepy head; let's go something hot to drink, she groaned and lazily and raised herself up from the bed, it doesn't take two people to make a cup of cocoa she said unwillingly, Of course not; but it stopped you sleeping; and if I let you sleep too much now you're not going to sleep tonight said Ammi, if you let me sleep too much? What the hell; Did you hear that Daff she asked. well it seems she wants to take care of you said Daphne, you mean she wants me to go and make cocoa for us all instead of her, It's only a ploy and nothing else, call yourself a Christian; you're full a deception lady she said. I'll come with you to the kitchen but I'm not doing anything. But all three went to the kitchen and see to what could be supper. At the table Hillary had a question, tell me Ammi; why don't you like to cook, who said I don't she asked, well from you arrived here you eat and drink but you never prepare anything she said, or maybe you can't cook. Daphne interrupts, can you cook Ammi she asked, not you too she comments, of course I can cook, only what Hilly said is true, you never cook from you arrived here. Well a woman should be able to cook said Hillary, when you find a man, no; if you find a man and if you unable to cook he might walk away from you find a woman who can satisfy his stomach said Hillary, there's an adage, and the way to a man heart is through his stomach. Somehow I know you would bring some man in this conversation said Ammi, if you're man crazy I'm not, can we talk about something else please. These Christians can't stand the truth she said, what truth? You just want to talk about men; you seem to get your kicks out of it said Ammi, all I was asking is when you're going to start doing some cooking around here? You heard what they said; the proof of the pudding is in the tasting, until you cook something we can't tell if you can cook she said. As much as I don't want to agrees with her Ammi; she's right said Daphne, it seems as though the two of you are ganging up on me, ok; I got the message; whatever happens tomorrow I'll do the cooking she said, and if the two of you both can restrain yourself from reprimand me about my cooking or lack of it; I think we should drink our cocoa. Good idea said Hillary; I'll look forward to dinner tomorrow; they had their drinks and went to bed.

32: The Interview

Monday the weather is still quite foul, Daphne was up early to prepare for work, the other two were still tucked up under the covers, and they can sleep an extra couple of hours. Good luck with the interview said Daphne as she was about to depart from the room, thanks Daff she said in a muffled tone coming from under the blanker. She has powered up the lamp before she left; so when these two budge, the room will be warm. It's approaching nine o'clock Hillary observed, she's under the blanket but she's not sleeping just a bit hesitant to get up, however with the room warm it's easier for them to get out of the bed. Come on Ammi it's that time now said Hillary lazily, that time for what asked Ammi as she pulled the blanket further over her head, time to get up she said; do you forget what you have to do today? But there was no response from Ammi, Hillary pulled the covers off her, come on; get up; we have to shake a leg, shake a leg? Where do you get this kind of talk she grumbled lazily as she got up and sat upon the bed, street talk; you'll soon pick them up too. It won't take them long to get ready. Let's have a proper breakfast; when we leave here we know not when we'll eat again said Hillary, why not make a couple a cheese sandwich to take with us asked Ammi, a good idea said Hillary. The clock is ticking and they're going to make sure they give themselves ample time to get there. Check that you have everything Ammi, everything like what she asked, well like your passport; they might want to see it she said, but I'm only going about a job; not to take a plane she comments. Ammi! You're not backing in Jamila now; you're in England; here these people want to make sure you are who you said you are; pack your passport and let's get a move on she said kindly but with some authority. They set off to the bus stop but the snow was heavy under food; which makes walking somewhat difficult, and up till now they haven't got proper winter boots. They were alone at the bus stop when this black man with a white woman came along; they knew he was from Jamila just by looking at him. Hello ladies he said smiling; but the white woman had a somewhat sombre face, hello said Ammi, are you enjoying the cold he asked, Daphne who hates to see black men with white women thought; what stupid question; how could anyone enjoy this bloody cold weather, she wasn't amused. You're from Jamila and so do I he said, he must be a joker this one Hillary thought, asked a question and answered it

"

himself, how did you know asked Ammi, oh; I can tell he said. But for the time they were talking he never introduce the woman; and she never said a single word. Well neither did Hillary; she practically turned her back on the man, you could say she's choosy to who she talks to. Well they were still there when the bus arrived a good ten minutes later, by then Ammi told him about her interview and he told her he's looking for a job too. If you're still going to this interview you better get on the bus said Hillary sarcastically, well she behaved as though she was angry, maybe it's the sight of a black man with a white woman. But Ammi with her usual gracious attitude; feel she should behave the way of a Christian; she said goodbye to this couple and boarded the bus, the man wave goodbye to her. There were only a few people on the bus, but they went upstairs; the view is better. You seem to talk to every Dick, Tom and harry; you must be desperate to talk to people like them said Hillary. You know Hilly; you're behaving just like Daff; the other day at a bus stop the same thing happen; she behaved exactly the way you behaved today, maybe the two of you had some kind of arrangement to behave in likewise manner; well I don't think it's nice she said. Well good for you; I'm not out looking for a man; I'm here to accompany you to your interview she said almost angrily. Hilly; are you going be angry all the days of your life? I thought it was only white people you're mad with; but no; you're angry with everyone. Even this black man who was just trying to be nice, that dear girl it's not a good attitude. You shouldn't be preaching to me she said; you should be concentrating on your interview, not what man I should talk to because you talked to them, the man saw two black women and thought he had a chance to chatted them up; even though he's with his white woman, in this cold weather I don't want to talk to any man. Ammi laughed out loud; what the cold weather got to do with anything, I think you just have a mean streak said. By now the bus is pulling in to its last stop, they embarked and were making their way to their destination. They made good time, arriving at the factory gate Ammi looked at her watch; it's just gone ten fifty, she's got time in hand. They pushed the gate and walked through, there was only one man in sight; and he is walking towards them not looking any too friendly.

Can I help you he asks; holding a couple of small articles in his hands, I hope so said Ammi; I'm here for an interview, are you sure it's here he asked in an unpleasant kind a way; interview for what he continued, I'm here about a job said Ammi reaching in her handbag for the paper that was given to her. But Hillary been here for nearly three years had a little experience about situations like this, and she didn't like the man approach, she also realised by looking at him that he's not the person they're here to see; she asked; are you the personal? But whatever his answer would be there was no time, a woman walked towards them and said hello, are you here about a job she asked in a friendly tone. Yes Mom said Ammi; I was sent from the labour exchange. If appearance counts for anything this woman is one of the good people, come with me she said as she turned and walked towards the office. It's still not eleven o'clock as yet; but there is no one to be seen working, they could see the machines but they all lay silent. They are wondering where the workers are; they couldn't all gone for lunch. Entered the office the woman shown them to the chairs, have a seat she said as she's about to go through another door. I'll be right back she said pleasantly, thank you mom said Ammi who was now feeling much more comfortable than when they were confronted by the man outside. The girls were whispering things to each other while their eyes roving the office, there's nothing interesting to see just an office with a table and chairs. The woman return with a man, as they walked towards them it's as though the man saw someone he knew but hasn't seen for a long time. Hello ladies he said reaching across the table to shake their hands and with the woman standing next to him he asked; are you both come about jobs he asked still smiling, No Sir; just me said Ammi. they now both seated; and with the woman looking at the papers she asked; who's the dressmaker, I am mom said Ammi, can I see your papers she asked with her hands stretch halfway across the table. Ammi reaches into her bag and produced the single sheet of paper. She didn't spend any time reading it; she was back to the ones she was already looking at. She said something to the man next to her in secret, have you got your passport Miss Thomas, Hillary looked at Ammi and smile as to say; I did tell you they might want to see your passport. Yes Mom she said as she reaches for it, she scanned through it kind of quickly and handed it to the man, and he also looked through it and handed it back to Ammi. So you both are from Jamila he asked, yes Sir said Hillary, and where you were living he asked, we're from the St. Manor Sir she said, St. Manor? I know it well he said; and looking as though he was pleased with himself for telling us he knows our Parish. But before there was any response from the girls the woman intervened, oh! Ladies this is Mr. Dorsey and I'm Mrs. Dorsey, he once lived in your country; he might even return she jested. He looked at her in a kind of loving fashion but said nothing. Ammi thought; is this coincident; since she been here this is the second white person she's come across who live in Jamila.

How long were you living there for Sir asked Hillary, Oh! Off and on for about ten years, and then he couldn't stop talking about the places he been all over the Island; he seems to love talking about it just like Mr. Owens. Darling gives the girls a break said Mrs. Dorsey; you don't want to be late now do you she comments; it seems as though he has appointment elsewhere. He looked at his watch and slowly rose to his feet, goodbye Miss Thomas and you too pointing to Hillary, I'm Hillary Sir, well bye now he said. Mrs. Dorsey got up and went after him; I'll be back shortly ladies she said as she followed him through the door. However what Mr. Dorsey doesn't know as he never gives them a chance to said much; is that they knew nothing about their country other than what they read, they never leave their little District to go anywhere; they are referred to as country bumpkins. While they were away the girls had a chance to talk, and for the first time Hillary saw two white people whom she seem to like, he's a very nice man she whispered, Ammi couldn't believe her ears, but he's white she whispered, so; she asked, however Ammi didn't stretch the point. Because of the friendliness of the Dorsey's she feels she's got a good chance of landing the job; and so do Hillary. I've got a good feeling you're going to get this job she said, well I hope so, I really hope so she said. The door pushed open and Mrs. Dorsey returned, she didn't say anything; she just take a chair, where were we she asked, oh yes! Miss Thomas as you can see we're not working; the workforce is out on strike since last week, they'll be back but I don't know when, but let see what you can do. Who do you work for before she asked, no one Mom; after I learned to make dresses I sewed from home for the local people Mom, so you never work for a company? No Mom. She was sitting hunch back in the chair; now she's sitting upright; but she didn't say anything for a while except turning the paper. She's got up and calls Ammi over to the window; and looking out on the shop floor she asked, have you ever work one of those machines before? I can't say for sure Mom looking at them from here, but my foot machine looks similar to that Mom. But these are electric machine Miss Thomas; you ever used an electric machine before? No Mom; but it's shouldn't be much different from my foot machine Mom, it's only the electric Mom. She didn't respond to what Ammi said, come and sit down Miss Thomas she said, reaching into one of the draws she fetched out a magazine, take a look at those design; have you ever seen anything like them, oh yes Mom, I was thought looking at dresses like these. After a lengthy interview she took out what looked like a huge ledger, Miss Thomas she said; I'm going to commit myself to something I never thought I would have done, I'm going to take a chance on you and I'm hoping you won't let me down, thank you Mom; I'll do my very best.

Somehow I know you will Miss Thomas; and she continues to write in the ledger. I will tell you about the rules we work by Miss Thomas; but until the workforce returns you won't be coming back, so we will write to you and let you know when, and if you don't turn up when we say you should, then we'll give it to someone else. How do you feel about that Miss Thomas? It sounds alright Mom; I'll be here. Then good she said rising to her feet, then she looks at Hillary who was sitting there observing, and what can you do Hillary, she remembers her name from the time she (Hillary) told her husband, nothing Mom I'm just a handy person. Are you working now she asked, yes Mom; but I'm looking for another job, anything to get away from that one she said. Well I'm feeling generous today she said with a smile, we'll write to you if and when a job become available she said, oh thank you Mom; that would be good, they got up shook hands and said goodbye.

Walking away from the office towards the exit the man was present again, of course there was no need to speak to him, but by the way he looked at them one could tell he didn't want them there. On their way home they have time to reflect on what they just been through, it was a good day all round even for Hillary who wasn't there for a job. But Ammi wanted to know why the workforce is out on strike; what it's all about? Why they aren't working, she was told by Mrs. Dorsey the workforce was out but she didn't say why. But Hillary explained the best she can; people take industrial action for better wages or better working condition, other words for this industrial action is strike; or down tools; a word from the street you might say. So what's going to happen now while they're not working, well! The convenor or whoever is heard of the union will negotiate with the Dorsey's for whatever they are striking about, well it goes something like that anyway she said. But don't worry; you'll pick things up as you go along, well I hope they'll return to work soon; I can't wait to get started said Ammi. They were home before Daphne and dinner have to be provided; this is a good time for Ammi to show her cooking skill in the kitchen. Who's going to cook dinner asked Hillary, but it's just for her to hear Ammi's reply, I know what you are trying to do said Ammi; to remind me about cooking as I promised; well there's no need; I'm going to provide dinner. Who me? asked Hillary, I wasn't thinking anything of the sort, ya; right said Ammi sarcastically. Well after a cup of cocoa Ammi headed for the kitchen and begins the cooking, Hillary settled down in front of the television. Hilly could you bring me the oil please, of course the cupboard is in one corner of the bedroom, but there was no response, Ammi went in to see; but only to find her dozed off in front the television. She didn't wake her; she gathered whatever she needed from the cupboard and went back into the kitchen. No sooner Daphne arrived, why is this girl sleeping this time of the evening she asked loudly; Ammi heard but didn't respond, she went into the kitchen, and seeing Ammi cooking she asked flippantly; what are you doing? I'm cooking dinner; can't you see? But if you don't want to eat what I cook it's alright just the same she said slyly. Don't you worry; I can't wait to taste your cooking; so hurry it up she said.

But Ammi can cook really; living with her Mother-in-law she bound to pick up some of her cooking skill; and one thing about those old Jamilian's they can cook. Being here for a short time living freely; she didn't get the chance to show what she can do in the kitchen until now. She didn't ask for help as the others do, she set the table and brings in the dinner, Daphne was watching the television while Hillary was still asleep. Wake up that sleeping beauty said Ammi; dinner is ready, come on; wake up; only when someone just got pregnant they sleep the way you do she said while shaking her. She woke and stretches before she got off the bed; come along before whatever Ammi cook got cold she said; a hint that her cooking might be a waste of time. They settled down to eat; well! Said Ammi, well what asked Hillary, well what the food taste like she asked, it's a bad habit to interrupt someone when they're eating she said; I'll tell you when I'm finished, Daphne laughed at her comical remarks; but Ammi asked another question. Oh! Another thing Hilly; are you pregnant she asked, What the hell are you talking about she asked, well Daff said only when someone is in their early pregnancy they sleep so much, so are you pregnant? But there was no yes or no response; allow me to eat my dinner in peace; and don't ask silly questions. But come to think of it; I should be living with a man instead of living with two women who are still innocent of men she said wittingly. You know what; it's something to be proud of said Ammi, a woman shouldn't allow herself to become common; soon the men are going stay well clear of her, are you talking from experience asked Hillary, no! But that's common sense; isn't it? What you think about that Daff she asked, but she didn't respond, Daff! Is she right she asked Hillary; but still there's no response from her, can't you see; Daff is a shame to admit she's virgin said Hillary, then supposes she and I are in the same boat said Ammi; and I'm sure that is nothing to be a shame of. But you know what Hilly; I can see we're a different kind of people; reputation means nothing to you now; but I hope one day you won't live to regret your action. Anyway how did you enjoyed the dinner she asked; wanting to end that kind of conversation. Ammi we know you can cook; we were only pulling your leg said Hillary hastily as though she doesn't want to talk about it. So you enjoyed my cooking she asked again smiling, what you want; a medal she asked; the meal was good; you must do it more often. But what Daphne wants to know is; did she get the job, no one bothered to tell me about the job she remarks, oh Daff; I'm sorry; with all the talk about men I got side track, Hillary smiles, well what happen she asked furiously; did you get the job? Well yes and no she said looking at Hillary while fiddling with a spoon.

She was deliberately lingering with her report as she noticed Daphne was getting over-anxious to know, but it was just a prank. What do you mean yes and no? Hilly what does she mean she asked anxiously, calm down Daff, can't you see she is just mucking about. Well I'll tell you, if you would please said Daphne, Ammi smiles broadly; but she gets a kind of angry glare from her. On paper we got the job; but the firm is out on strike; and until they return we haven't got a job, what do you mean we she asked curiously, well I was promised a job too, but you didn't go for a job she remarked, well no; but you see Daff; she was with me during the interview; and it seems Mrs. Dorsey liked her face. So she promises her a job if she would like to work there said Ammi, and no one was going to tell me she said, don't be silly; we were only playing a prank on you. But here's the thing said Ammi who's feeling a little mischievous. Hilly met some white people she like and she doesn't think they're neither smell or dirty, she couldn't take her eyes off this Mr. Dorsey even though his wife was sitting right there. You're not speaking the truth said Daphne surprisingly, don't forget you're a Christian. Tell her hilly said Ammi, there's nothing to tell; they are just two nice people; he… Ammi interrupted; and that Mr. Dorsey has a nice smile; your words not mind, well isn't he white dirty and smelly; or you change your mind; what happened asked Daphne sarcastically. Don't go on about it she said; well I'll tell you Hilly; from now on whatever you said about these dirty white people we should take it with a pinch of salt, you're so right Daff said Ammi. Think what you want she said; I just hope they return to work soon so I'll know about the job. So what kind of a job you been offered asked Daphne; thinking that if Hillary gets this job she'll leave in the job she's so wanting to leave. You know; she didn't say said Hillary; but it's a clothing factory so it should be light work; I hope. Some people had all the luck comment Daphne, maybe had I gone with you today it would me who get the offer, well I'll tell you said Hillary; it seems if we hang around this one long enough (meaning Ammi) good fortune will come our way. As much as I appreciate your compliment; I certainly not warrant that claim, whatever you get or didn't get it's under your own steam; nothing to do with me. But saying that; it seems as though you two have no thrust or confidence in yourselves; your own ability, you can't go about always hoping for the best; no; you must put some belief and determination in it too. Hillary wants to be sarcastic as usual, I'm going to the bathroom before she starts preaching to us again, and I too said Daphne smiling. It's coming up to ten o'clock, Ammi clear the table and turn to her bible, when they return she try to engage them for a while in bible reading, of course they've got their own bible; every black person from that country will always have their king James version. Another eventful day mainly for Ammi ended, what is going to happen tomorrow they haven't planned it yet.

33: Looking for A Place To Worship

Tuesday wasn't so much a cold day, it had rained fairly heavy overnight and washed most of the snow away, Daphne had gone to work and the other two just about getting up, what are we going to do today Ammi now that you have got a job pending asked Hillary, I don't know said Ammi; I should be asking you, well we can go browsing around the shops she said, I know said Ammi; we'll go looking for a church, but where asked Hillary, what do you mean where? We get on a bus and go anywhere. Ok! We'll do that said Hillary; and it's not so cold today; so we can go into town and ask around. God idea said Ammi; we'll have breakfast and then go. So they leave out close to eleven o'clock, they have decided to take the old trolley bus going in the opposite direction toward where they went the day before. In a whole the day turns out to be quite nice considering its winter, Ammi is feeling quite high spirited and talkative. We're not coming back today until we've found a Church she said, one that we won't get turn away from, and how are you going to know that asked Hillary, Ok! One that we hope they won't chuck us out of. Their transport arrives and they went upstairs, any black person we come across we'll ask them said Ammi; they'll know the kind of Church we're looking for. You did say any Church would do until you find a Pentecostal Church asked Hillary, yes! And I still stand by that. It could be that if we visit another Church-of-England they would welcome us there, it's possible she said, but you would have to go first and then tell me what it's like, I'm not prepared to run the gauntlet again said Hillary. you see Hilly; people are not the same everywhere, look at those people we encountered yesterday; they seem to be nice civil human beings, I think the world is like that wherever you go; some are good and some are not so good. But while they were chatting away two passengers come upstairs, they were two black men, the bus is nearly empty but they choose to take the seats directly behind them. One of them was quite conspicuous; you couldn't help looking at him; he's got this very huge nose which completely spoils his features, the other fellow was quite nice really; but short. Big nose was aching to talk to them, they could almost feel his presence piercing their back. But he chooses to talk to his friend instead. I bet these two beautiful ladies are from Jamila he said a bit loud behind their backs, I don't think so said the little fellow, but the conversation designed for the women ears; but they're not going to respond. Excuse me ladies said big nose; I'm I right that you're from Jamila? Ammi was thinking of not responding at all to him; but then she remembers what she said to Hillary just before they got on the bus, oh yes she said; we're from there. Told you Dave; I knew it he said as though he has just hit the jackpot. Where in Jamila you're from Miss the little one asked politely, St. Manor said Ammi, But Hillary doesn't like the conversation one little bit; she wouldn't mind if they would clear off.

Nevertheless she asked them in an abrupt manner in their own country broken English, patwah to the natives do you know of any Pentecostal church here? Big nose thought that was the cue for him to speak; he's about to say something, there's… I'm talking to your friend said Hillary abruptly; and stop big nose dead in his tracks, Ammi looked at her with one of those looks as to say; how unkind but said nothing. There is a Church in Hamsden Mom; but I have no idea what Church it is, in Hamden she asked as though she wasn't sure of what the little fellow said. Yes Mom; and I saw a few black people going there. Ammi thought immediately that this must be a Pentecostal Church. Does this bus go pass there she asked, no mom; but I can show you where to get off; and you can walk it from there he said. Thank you very much she said, but by then it seems big nose become coy to say anything; so just to be polite Ammi asked, are the both of you from the same place? Still big nose said nothing, but the little fellow replies; no Mom, but we've been good friends for a long time. Hillary notice how polite the little fellow is; referring to them as Mom, it seems she doesn't mind chatting to him, but not with big nose; he's too ugly in her opinion. But some people from that country are like that, if you're ugly or have any DE formative features they will avoid you like the plague, Hillary is one of those people. Could you tell us where to get off she asked the little fellow, sure Miss he said. When you got off cross over the road; walk pass the clock and go straight up the high road; looking on the right side of the road you'll soon see the Church; you can't miss it Mom. But By then big nose was sitting quietly, the man who was so impetuous has lost his zest. But Ammi always the civil one; as they (the men) were getting off she thank him directly. Now Hillary was feeling a bit concern as to why the little fellow kept on addressing her mom, Ammi! Do I look old? Ammi look at her, what kind of fool question is that she asked, do I look old she asked again, why? Do you feel old she asked, well that little fellow kept addressing me Mom; and looking at him he looks older than me.

I really can't believe that you let that bothered you said Ammi; maybe he was just being polite; unlike big nose who you insulted; the poor man feel so small; Hilly! Why do you do a thing like that; I could never do such a thing. The poor fellow said nothing more; not even when they were getting off, you didn't have to be so rude and abrupt all the time; it's not becoming. That man should wear a face mask; his nose is too big; how does he go around with a nose like that I do not know she said. Hilly! Sometimes your attitude leave me speechless, that's what that poor fellow born with; he didn't give it to himself; what do you want him to do; cut it off? Take a stock of yourself woman; you're nothing special yourself. We're nothing special; the image we're is because of our parents. Damn you Ammi Thomas; you always seem to have some kind of moralistic argument for everything; are you going to spend your entire life trying to be prim and proper? Well no; but I'll always try to be the best person as I can, and you know what? It does no harm to be polite to others; no harm at all; and sometimes it gets you what you desire which otherwise wouldn't. I know where being civil and politeness can get you most of the time, people take liberties; they overstep the mark; I don't want to be civil and nice she said. What you mean you don't want to be civil and nice to some people; you mean you'll civil and polite to the ones you like, well I suppose that's understandable said Ammi. Now they have arrived at their stop, they got off and proceed just as the little fellow directed, they didn't have to look far; the Church was right in their sight. The little fellow said he didn't know what kind of church it is; but a few black people go there, well he must be either blind or can't read, which wouldn't be a surprise; maybe over a third of the immigrants arrived here can't read ay all. In big bold letters displayed over the door high up; it says Methodist Church; and on the noticeboard there are several captions displaying the name too. Reading the notice board all the information's they needed if they were to visit were all there. We're coming back on Sunday Hilly she said, maybe said Hillary, no maybe about it hilly; on Sunday the three of us are coming she said, she didn't reply just sort of groan. Well Hillary is not exactly the church-going type; even from home when she was a teenager, she would be sent but most time never wen. But now been older her attitude toward church could be changing; and with three of them living together it might not be too hard to get her to church. Ammi is got all the information she requites regarding the time of service, Sunday morning along with Daphne and hopefully Hillary they will be coming back here. Now they'll make their way back home in time to prepare dinner before Daphne got home. But Ammi was in for a big surprise; but a pleasant one. While they were walking back to the bus stop she come face to face with an old acquaintance, a Mr. Dickenson; a man who was highly respected in the community back home. A private landowner he owned a fair size farm with many lives stocks, someone like him would have people working for him on the farm. It's hard to understand why he sold up and come here, but he's not alone in that regards; there're a few others like him. He never got married; even though there were many women around who would love to be Mrs. Dickenson, I supposed he's got his reason.

Bless my eyes; is this Ammi Thomas he asked gleefully as he advances towards her. I heard you were here and I was coming to see you last Sunday he said; but I heard you were going to church. Ammi wasn't sure how to greet one of her father's friends; she struggled a bit for words. It's good to see you Sir she said, yes! I heard you were coming; but Hilly told us after we had already made plans to go to church. Well how long have you been here he asked, just over a week Sir, well I won't ask you how you like the place; you haven't seen any of it yet. Have you start looking for work as yet he asked, Oh yes; I've been interviewed for a job and they seem willing to take me on; but the workers are out on strike she said. that was very quick; what type of job did you go after he asked, but before Ammi replies he corrected himself, oh I forgot; you were learning dressmaker before I leave home didn't you? Yes Sir; and now I am qualified, then you shouldn't have too much trouble getting a job. Then he turns to Hillary, how could you forget to tell Ammi I was coming he asked, how did I forget? I just forgot she said in an abrupt manner, Ammi noticed instantly the way she spoke to him and she didn't exactly like it, back home she wouldn't be in a position to talk to him at all. But she suspected something is going on between them, like some sort of friendship. She remembers Daphne words and even though no names were mentioned; this is the man she has fallen for. He didn't respond to Hillary comments; instead he asked; so what you girls are up to now, we're going home; yes Sir said Ammi; we're going to get the bus, no need; come with me; I'll take you home. Of course Hillary knew he's got a car; and Daphne too, it's obvious Hilly been in it once or twice even though she didn't exactly said so, but I suppose she would want to keep that a secret between she and him. Ammi was quite pleased to be riding home in a car; the only time she had been in a vehicle was when Florence got married last year, and meeting Mr. Dickenson she's feeling somewhat safe and secure, well! Being in the presence of an older man gives her a feeling of safety. Well how is your father Ammi he asked, have you written to him as yet? Yes Sir; but I haven't got a reply as yet, Hillary chuckled, and you only wrote to him on Sunday she said; I don't even think the letter leave the country as yet. Well whenever you write again please send him my regards, a very good man your father Ammi; and the people of Danville lucky to have him, help me too when I couldn't get anyone to work for me, I won't forget Sir; I'll tell him she said. They reached home but sat in the car at the gate, would you like to come in Sir asked Ammi, I would love to Ammi but I must go and get my friend Jude; he's waiting for me. Well why don't you have dinner with us on Sunday asked Hillary, are you inviting me he asked, we are inviting you, oh yes Sir; please come said Ammi. Ok! I love to have dinner with you ladies, and Ammi you can tell me all about home; what's happening since I leave. Dinner said Hillary is three o'clock, three o'clock it is then he said, and they emerged from the car and he went on his ways. Ammi was rather chuffed to meet him; she knows he was a good upstanding man in the district; now she'll probably look to him as father figure. But she's got a few questions for Hillary; and she wants to ask them before Daphne comes home.

They're changing their clothes and while doing so Ammi asked, so how long you and Mr. Dickenson been seeing each other? Who the hell said we're seeing each other she asked, don't you go spreading rumours now. Good heavens! Calm down girl; what came over you? You did said you and him been to the pub didn't you, she asked, yes! But we're not going out as you seem to think, but was only asking. Well I'll tell you, he would like us to be an item but I don't want to, I don't like him in that way; he's too old, we're just a friend. He would like more but it never going to happen, so there; and I hope you're satisfied now. You know Hilly; I'll say it again; I have no idea what happening to you nowadays; you're so thin skin; you seem to take everything personally and seem to want an argument, I do hope you're no guilty about something you're not telling us. What's that supposed to mean she asked, I've got nothing to feel guilty about she said angrily. I say what I mean and stand by it, and one more thing, my conscience is clear. Hilly! Stop talking; let's go to the kitchen; we're going to do dinner, and that was that, the peacemaker has spoken, she might have agreed to disagree but kept it to herself. Daphne had arrived later than usual, she's been working overtime, hi everyone she said as she dropped her bag and run to the bathroom, on return she settled in front of the television to watch one of her favourite show emergency ward ten, she might be considering becoming a nurse. How long am I going to wait before I get my dinner, she jested, not long now Daff said Ammi; then mumbled something to Hillary but out of distant of Daphne's ears. What are we having asked Daphne with her eyes glued to the soap opera, don't be so impatience; you'll see what it is when you get it said Ammi. Everyone dinner is on a tray, they will want to watch the old tele too. Ammi handed her the tray, this food takes so long coming; my stomach could develop wind she said facetiously, it shouldn't take two people so long to cook a little food she jest, there's an old saying, many hands make light work; you too should remember that said Ammi. Eat your food; it's not a good habit to talk while you're eating, yes Mom; I will obey Mom joke Daphne. But she (Daphne) noticed that with all the talking there were no words at all from Hillary, she thought it was most unlike her, she's the talkative one; and with all the sarcasm she kept quiet. They should have a lot to talk about though; and they will, the encounter with the two fellows today Ammi can't wait to tell Daphne about it, and Hillary doesn't mind talking about it either; but when it's about Mr. Dickenson she is not too eager to talk about it, in fact she rather not talk about it at all. So what happened today asked Daphne; did you find a Church? We found a Church all right; a Methodist church; thanks to two black men we met on the bus; right hilly she asked as she wanted her to take part in the conversation, right she said; but you can go on and tell the tale. So what's the matter with you asked Daphne; can't you tell the tales too, you been quiet from the time I walked in; it's as though you're not here; is there something wrong? Why there must be anything wrong she asked, one doesn't have to be a chatterbox all the time does one? Really comments Daphne, yes really said Hillary. All right; all right said Ammi are you two going to kick off again, I thought we call a truce last week; and everything seemed to be going so well. We're not quarrelling I just not in the talking mood said Hillary, so you not in the talking mood; well how much talking it takes to tell Daff that we met Mr. Dickenson today; he drove us home and he's coming to dinner on Sunday she said.

Well I didn't want to mention it because I know its sore point to talk about in front of Daff; so to prevent an argument I rather not talk about it. last Sunday he was supposed to be coming to see Ammi; but we were going to church; and when I told you; remember what happen she asked, yes said Ammi; but we did agree to bury the hatchet too remember; she asked. What do you mean we asked Daphne; you weren't involved; we just tell you about it, a figure of speech daff said Ammi. Well the way I see it; we're family living together; and if there's a situation in the family we all should try and sort it said Ammi, all for one and one for all; I can't remember where I hear that she said. But Daphne suddenly got religion, she feels she should show some civility, so what happened today hilly she asked; and leave nothing out, Hillary didn't hesitate; she began to relate. She was suddenly backed to her usual self. You were very unkind to that poor man though Hilly said Ammi; what happen asked Daphne. Well this fellow, well! He wasn't exactly handsome and… Hillary interrupted, he's ugly; you can say it, he's got a hooter that spread right across his face; he's ugly she said with some venom. But that doesn't give you the right to belittle the fellow said Ammi, Daff! She was rude, very rude, she let this poor fellow feel so embarrassed he said nothing until they got off the bus; I was feeling bad for him. Well he shouldn't be talking to me; I wouldn't want anybody see him talking to me she said, who the Devil you think you are asked Daphne; going about insulting people, one of these day you're going to meet your match; somebody is going to slap you across the face, they can try. Let me remind you in case you forgot; you're women; those are men talk said Ammi, let them try? So what are you going to do? Fight them like a man would? I said it once and I'll say it again; you need to take stock of yourself, and Daff you have got nothing to say; look at the way you behave toward the man at the bus stop the other day; you're six of one half and half a dozen of the other. So tell me about the Church said Daphne, well as I said; it's a Methodist Church in Marsden; and these two black fellows said a few black people go there, so we're going there on Sunday she said. After they had exhausted the discussion they decided it's time for bed, well peace reign once more; all is quiet on the western front; but for how long. It's always going to be so with these three carefree women, one is outgoing and worldly, one is a Christian and a true one too; and the other one is uncertain of what she wants to be; the phrase inbetweener would probably fit her character.

34: Attending the Methodist

This Sunday is a big day for Ammi, the thought of going to a Church where there are black people raised her enthusiasm sky high, the last words of her beloved father constantly ringing in her ears, don't abandon your faith; when you go to England find a Church to worship. This Godly young woman will live by those words and probably dies by them. Today the weather is kind, the snow is gone and the sun is out; not exactly warm but quite pleasant. They're about to leave but before they do Ammi invite them to join her in prayer, after prayer Hillary make sure the paraffin lamp is turned off and then they set off. I'm only going to see if any nice black men are there said Hillary with a serious expression, Ammi sigh, even on the Sabbath; the day the bible said to keep holy; you find it necessary to make joke about the Church, girl you're vile, never mind she said, the good Lord will soon show you the folly of your ways. But comical Hillary is not finished yet, I hope when we go to this Church they'll find you a preaching spot; I know you'll be good at it she said smiling. But it brings a smile to Daphne face too, she'll be good at it alright; she's just the sort to enter the Church even for the first time and they invite her to the rostrum she said. Not you too said Ammi, I hope you're not picking up her vile and careless attitude and make jokes about it. But with all that the banter doesn't bother her; she has became accustomed to Hillary's moods swings. She's like a pendulum; one day she's angry with the world; the next day she's cracking jokes about everyone and everything. They were the only three people at the bus stop; and when the bus arrived the driver was a black man; and according to Hillary he's Barbadian; she recognised his accent. It was a short bus ride; about five minutes; and as they were about got off this driver calls; excuse me ladies; he said it twice, what? Asked Hillary abruptly, her response might have put the driver off, are you sure this's where you want to get off he asked, they didn't respond; as they were getting off the conductor a white woman waved goodbye to them; they respond in a similar manner. The walk to the Church is a short one; and there aren't plenty people about; probably because it's too early; and working people having their well-earned lie in. They paused to look at the notice board for no apparent reason; they have already seen what they need to earlier in the week. They were encouraged to see other black people going in too, but it a good ten minutes before service commence and there're only a few people arrive. They didn't bother to look around as they did at the other Church last Sunday; if they did they would have seen their friend Mr. Dickenson. Daphne was a little surprise to see him; she knew back home he been to Church even though he wasn't a regular. But they never went to sat by him, no; they sat a long way from him, after service they'll join him. There are quite a few people coming in; and by ten o'clock the building was about half full; and to their surprised most of them were black. Well she's not a racist neither does Daphne; but they're so much more at ease here amongst their own colour people. Talking among themselves; Ammi in particular waiting in anticipation to see the preacher and hear this sermon, while comical Hillary spotted something she can jest about, a black woman wearing a badly fitted wig, but Ammi reprimanded her before her joke went too far, her answer to Ammi was; spoilsport!. Suddenly a door pushed open and everyone stood; they stood too, it was the emergence of the Preacher, a white man looking all elegant in his white robe. He makes his way to the pulpit; and when he has taken his place he beckons to his congregation to sit; and then went into his sermon. But he didn't preach; more like teach or tell a story, nevertheless it made good listening. However that's not exactly the kind of service they're accustomed to; and no doubt some of the other black people there too; but at least they could pray and listen to the word of God.

Before he leaves the pulpit he thanked everyone for coming, but people didn't leave immediately, no; there were lots of greetings and people trying to make new friends. Just about when everyone was about to leave he asked for their attention. Sisters and Brothers; can I have your attention please; and everyone stop and those who were facing the way out turned to attention. Hillary comments quietly; a white man calling black people Sisters and Brothers; he's putting it on, Ammi shushed her to keep quiet. Everyone is waiting for his announcement, on Sunday there'll be a new order of service he said, instead of ten o'clock we'll be starting at ten-thirty; so you'll have half an hour longer to have a good breakfast and get dress. Well! He states get dress deliberately, he noticed how well these people dress coming to church, something these white people don't do; they seem to attend church in their even in their working gears. But these black people! They're accustomed to their church in their Sunday best. He continues, and don't forget to tell your friends; and better yet; bring them along, thank you Brothers and Sisters and God bless. He then came among the congregation to greet the ones who were hanging around. Ammi noticed how the black people had warmed to him she comments, before long this church is going to be full of black people. Well they were also greeted by the Pastor, good to see you ladies; I hope you enjoyed the service he asked, we did Pastor said Ammi; she later tells her two cousins she wasn't sure what to call him Pastor or minister. Well I hope to see you again net Sunday he said, oh yes Pastor; we'll be here she said; her two cousins didn't utter a single word. There'll be an inquest; but that will keep until they get home, especially Hillary; she'll have a lot to say about this day and this Pastor. But the big surprise is awaiting outside, as they emerged from the church standing outside directly in front of the building was Mr. Dickenson, he saw them before they did him, hello ladies he said as they were unknowingly making their way straight towards him. Hello Mr. Dickenson said Ammi happily, she was pleased to see him but wasn't so sure about the others; if they did they weren't showing it. Were you in Church she asked, oh yes; I've been coming here for some time now he said, and you didn't say comment Hillary kind of angrily. It didn't cross my mind really he said; but when I saw you here the other day I knew you would be coming here to Church. Selfish man comment Hillary, we been looking a Church to go to since we been here but couldn't find one; other than the one we been to and the Minister told us to clear off. Ammi looked at her and smile; he didn't say that; he said in a nice way we shouldn't come back. The Minister really said that asked Mr. Dickenson, oh yes! Said Daphne; with a smile on his face. I can't say I surprise he said; you'll find some of the most racist people are people of the Church. Well they're not really Christians, no; they're doing a paid job. But don't change the subject said Hillary; why didn't tell us about this church, didn't you think Daff and I might want to go to Church too? Selfish man she comments. Well I must admit it never cross my mind; I must apologise.

Hillary I'm so sorry; but I didn't think; and as I said it didn't cross my mind, can you forgive me he asked, Ammi hearing this nice man almost on his knees for something he has no need to had arose her curiosity; remembering her attitude towards him the other day; just like today she talked to him without any respect at all, and that's wrong; this could only happen in England she thought. Then she had another brain wave, she wonder if she knew something bad about him so he has to accept her action. Calm down Hilly said Ammi; don't you ever forgot anything?. Suddenly Daphne who was standing there quietly listening; burst into action, obviously hurt by Hillary's attitude too. She usually forgets anything; her brain is like a sieve. But of course for Daphne the little green eyes monster is coming to the fore, this is the man she's got a crush on but who never paid her any attention; Hillary is the one he's got eyes for. Well the day is not exactly cold; all depend on how long one stand out in it, he didn't asked he ordered, ok ladies! Come with me and I'll take you home. Ammi was so please to hear that, come along you two she said; and they set off following him to the car park. But he's not just dropping them off, no; he's also stopping for dinner, he was imitated. However it's early for dinner; but he wants to have a chat with Ammi about home, he dearly would like to know what happening there since he leaves. The girls don't have to get busy start cooking, no; the dinner is partly cooked from the night before; so they can afford to sit around and reminisce with Mr. Dickenson. The conversation rages on well into the evening, and it's getting to that time to eat, soon dinner was on the table, and this evening with a guest present everyone dines at the table. I understand you're baptised Ammi said Mr. Dickenson, yes Sir; but how did you know? Suddenly he realised that he probably shouldn't have asked as Hillary gave him a furious glare, she could be the only one who told him. But she certainly didn't want that question to be asked in the presence of Daphne, but she owns up quickly, I told him; who else could tell him she asked with some anxiety. Trying to smooth things over he commented, well good for you Ammi; from you was going to school the signs was there, what they used to call you? Little Miss Florence Nightingale isn't it? he asked. Daphne caught and moved about on the chair uncomfortable, isn't that so Daphne he asked, why asked me she said, you seem to talk to everyone except me, am I a shadow she asked. Oh Daff he said; a name he'd never called her before as he'd never say anything to her before at all. I'm so sorry; I never thought, but please let's not fall out over that; we can't; we shouldn't; we're from the same district and I watch you ladies grow into fine young women, we're all friends here. Of course some of that comment was to flatter the women; and to avoid any unpleasantness he's hoping it works; and as an older person he feels he should clear the air. But what he didn't know is that she (Daphne) is got a crush on him and of course he never takes any notice of her. Well some women prefer older men; and Daphne is one of these women trying to be tactful he asked; Daphne have you got any hot pepper? I might have she said, Ammi joined in, I'll get it for you Sir, but Daphne was more than glad to fetch it, you sit down; I'll get it she said.

Well the rest of the evening has gone somewhat pleasant, the awkward moments have passed and Mr. Dickenson would like to return the favour. Ladies he said; the dinner was so wonderfully nice and I enjoy myself so much; I would like to return the compliment, would you like to have dinner at my place on Sunday? I'm cooking he said. Can you really cook though or you just rustle up something asked Hillary with a wry smile, say yes and then I'll surprise you he said. Ok! Yes; we will said Ammi, Ok! That settled; Sunday it is he said. Well it's running late and tomorrow is a working day; and he doesn't want to outstay his welcome, he rose to his feet, Ladies! Thank you for a most pleasant evening; but all good things must come to an end; it's time I take my leave of you he said with some glee. The women all stood, thanks for keeping our company Mr. Dickenson said Ammi, and we'll keep yours on Sunday said Daphne smiling. Hillary walked him to the door but she didn't return promptly, during the entire afternoon she was the less talkative, however with him gone there'll be the usual inquest on the evening proceedings. Hillary took a long time to return and Daphne is wondering why, Have you settled your differences with him now asked Daphne as Hillary return, what differences she asked? Oh come on now; we're not fools; anyone could see all isn't well between you two; even though he being the gentleman tried not to show it she said, and you think the same she Ammi she asked. Well you're asking me as though it's something Daff and me had discussed; and you know I wouldn't do that, but I notice the way you reacted to anything he said in a hostile manner; that led me to believe there's something wrong between you two. But Hilly; this is a fine man, I needn't reminded you who he was back home, I must tell you; since we met him the other day I feel kind of happy to be in his company. So what are you saying asked Hillary, just try to sort out whatever differences you have without causing any animosity; please she said? But Daphne isn't as angry when Mr. Dickenson's name is mention, she probably kicks the green eyes monster into touch and now that he talked to her, but one thing for sure she got a mighty crush on him.

But Hillary is about to make a confession, she feels she should clear the air and put everyone mind to rest, she know what Ammi said about Mr. Dickenson is true; and she certainly doesn't want any bad feelings with her cousins because of him. Well it's getting past their bedtime; Daphne is in the bed but she's not yet asleep, Ammi is watching the television; of course she's not working as yet; she'll be on her own from tomorrow. And Hillary? Well she's sitting the table and about to tell them what they're aching to hear. Daff are you asleep she asked, not yet she reply, and aren't you working tomorrow she asked, yes but I think you should hear this now; tomorrow I might change my mind, I'm all ears said Daphne. She went straight to the point, Raymond asked me to marry him and... she paused as Ammi asked who is Raymond, she hesitates; Raymond Dickenson she said; who did you think I'm talking about? Daphne jumped up from under the blanket and sat up straight with eyes bulging in amazement. Of course neither of them knew his name was Raymond; back home everyone addressed him as Mr. Dickenson. Raymond! so you call him Raymond she asked with some anxiety, yes; his first name's Raymond, and I call him Raymond and he call me Hillary; what's wrong about that she asked angrily. So what else happened; what else did you do; did you bring him here she asked with jealously, acting as though she's ready for an almighty quarrel. But her jealous comment not only anger Hillary but Ammi too. Daff! She said in a loud voice as she turns off the television, why don't you calm down and stop accusing hilly of things you don't know about, you're allowing your jealousy to be getting the better of you, you shouldn't be angry with Hilly; she's has done you nothing. As it so happens; the man fancied her and not you; that's not her fault, you told me some time ago to grow up; well why don't you grow up and stop acting like some love-struck spoilt child she asked looking straight at her.

But Ammi words weren't of much comfort to her; she's got the crush and she's got it bad, you don't understand she said, she doesn't love him she's just using him. That brings out the anger in Hillary; shut up you fool she said with so many wraths that the little table flipped one side. Used him for what; I haven't taken his money and certainly haven't taken him to bed, and if that's what you're thinking you can get that right out of your miserable mind, and another thing; this is the first time he ever been here, unless you bring him here yourself she said. There's no need for that Hilly said Ammi, I seem to remember we had this conversation more than before; and pledged to be civil to each other's, I can see you didn't mean it. However Ammi wants everything to be out in the open she asked, so what happened; he asked you to marry him; she inquires; not for her sake but for Daphne's. Well he asked me two times; on both occasions we were having a drink at the pub, the second time I told him never to ask me again. I couldn't marry a man so much more older than myself I told him, and he got angry and words said, and Daff that's the last time we went out together she said calmly, and if you don't believe me I don't give a... Ammi interrupt quickly as she was going to said something unsavoury. Hilly! Mind your language, come on now; let's go to bed; don't forget you're working tomorrow; and look at the time she commented. Let's end this argument and put it behind us as a bad experience, Daff just jealous that's all; but she'll get over it said Ammi. You think so asked Hillary, maybe she doesn't want to get over it; some women like to be that way, and you don't she asked as she puts her head under the blanket. They didn't get a whole lot of sleep, that night Hillary didn't sleep in the bed;

she settled in the settee, but in the morning they both leave together for work.

35: A Return to The Labour Exchange

This week Ammi is home alone, she has to sign on at the labour exchange, she assured her cousins she'll be able to find her way there and back; so after she had something to eat she set off to sign on. Since her interview at Dorsey's Clothing she heard nothing in regards to the job she'd been promised, when she goes to the exchange she'll have to tell them what has happened regarding the interview; here's the offer of the job but the workforce is out on strike. Getting on the bus for the first time it struck home that she's alone, she got there though without any difficulty at all, but as usual the queues are long and the place is noisy with people arguing about one thing or the other. She joins the queue to her signing on counter, it will take some time though; but heck; one thing she's got plenty of is time. Well it was a long wait; it's approaching nearly two o'clock and she's only halfway there, and her legs began to hurt; and with no one to talk to she's becoming bored. After about another hour she eventually reaches the counter; it's her time to be seen. She handed her card to the member of staff; she signed her on and told her to go over yonder where there was another member of staff waiting. She was reading from some documents when she got there. Miss Thomas she asked while making herself comfortable on the chair, yes mom; that's me; take a seat she said. There's a letter here about you, now let see she said while perusing the papers. But this staff was a jolly sort, she was chewing what could have been chewing gum and humming a tune at the same time. Miss Thomas I've seen you have had an interview but they were out on strike she said as though she was reading from the paper, yes said Ammi; and the job was promised to me. That's what written down here Miss Thomas; they're back at work now and you should go and see them tomorrow, the job is still on offer to you, isn't that good news Miss Thomas she said cheerfully as she chewed away. Very good news thank you, but what time should I go there she asked, she handed her a sheet of paper, it's all in there she said as she gathered up the rest of paper. Good luck Miss Thomas she said as she walked away. At that moment Ammi was feeling quite chuff, she makes her way to the labour exchange all by herself and gets the job she's been offered; she might have considered it progress. However she chooses not to read it until she gets home, she gathered her things and left, it's a better feeling going back home rather than when she was coming. On the way home she trys to gather her thoughts, isn't it ironic; whenever I'm out with the others there was always someone we met who wants to talk to us, by myself today I never met anyone of colour. When she reached home and looked at the clock; it won't be long before the others are home she thought, she was about to look at the paper she's been given at the labour exchange; but she thinks better of it, I can't let those two come home from work and dinner is not ready she thought, so she heads for the kitchen. Well there were leftovers from Sunday so she didn't have to start from scratch; dinner will be ready soon. Well it wasn't long before the others arrived, something smells good said Hillary as she inhales a whiff of the cooking, and good evening to you too said Ammi sarcastically from the kitchen. Are you alright Ammi asked Daphne, but she didn't respond, wash your hands and set the table she said; the dinner will be coming in now.

So what do you do today asked Hillary; did you spend all day indoors? No; today was my signing on day; but neither of you remembered. Good grief said Daphne; how did I forget; Hilly, why couldn't you remember she asked. Hillary didn't respond, Ammi I'm so awfully sorry she said, tomorrow I'll phone in sick and go with you she said. But I know why we forgot she said, after that argument we had last night we went to bed almost this morning; that why. But Ammi was strides ahead of them, there's no need to take time off she said; I've been to the labour exchange, all by my little old self she said. All by yourself asked Hillary surprisingly, why are you surprise; I have to go and you lot weren't here; so who did you expect to take me? Well done to you girl said Daphne; I'm proud of you, Hillary looked at her; a look to say who the hell is you to be proud of her. So what happened; did you get signed on she asked, of course; and it seems like the job is waiting for me; but did they said that asked Hillary with interest; Dorsey had offered her a job there too. Yes they did; and she reaches into her bag for the paper they gave her. They want to see me at ten o'clock tomorrow she said looking at the piece of paper, the strike must be over said Hillary. Well I better call in sick and go with you; they did offer me a job too, yes said Ammi and probably you should come along too. Or why don't you let Ammi ask them about you instead asked Daphne, if they still want you they will tell her to tell you, yes! That seems right enough she said, but can Ammi find her way there she asked. Well I find my way to the labour exchange; and this place is just around the corner from there, don't worry; I can find my way, and that was the discussion over regarding work. Well it's early and since there's nothing to do other than watches television; Ammi decided to write another letter to her folks back home; I know Miss Florence is dying to hear from me she said; I'll write here's first. She wrote to her father last week but there's no reply as yet; She's anxious to tell him things; things like the Church she been to and will be going every Sunday; and moreover she would love to hear from someone back home; mostly her father. *242*

36: Returning to Dorsey

It's Tuesday morning and the snow returns overnight and more is expected, the others have gone to work; Ammi gets herself together and prepares to leave, there's no way she's going to be late for this appointment. She sets off for the bus stop; a journey she is making regular since she's arrived here, and she's becoming accustomed to travel on the bus too. On the way all she could think of work and those machines; and she never used an electric machine before, she's hoping to get this job to work on one of these machines; even for the experience. She reaches Dorsey's Clothing factory earlier than she wanted to, the small gate was open but she couldn't see anyone about, however she entered through to the gate into the factory. She knows the workers are back; it's awfully noisy with machines going, she recall the last time she was here you could hear pin drop. She rapped on the office door; and almost immediately Mrs. Dorsey open it, Miss Thomas she said looking at her watch as to say you're early; Come in and sit over there she said, would you like a cup of tea she asked, yes thank you Mom she said. Well she (Ammi) is not a tea drinker but for the sake of cooperation she'll make an exception. No sooner she was back with another woman, Miss Thomas this is Miss Healey; your chargehand, she thought of what she said, your chargehand, what does she mean? But she tells herself if she gets the job all will be made clear. Good morning Miss Thomas she said while she was still standing up, good morning Miss Healey said Ammi. Mrs. Dawson produced couples of document for her to sign, after which she sat up in her chair with a ledger in her hand, it looks like the same one she had the last time she was here. Miss Thomas you'll be starting on Thursday, we expect to see you at eight o'clock, how do you feel about that she asked, just fine Mom; I'll here she said. She turns over some pages of her ledger; then she closed it, report to Miss Healey when you arrive she said as she stood up. Oh! Is your cousin working she asked, yes Mom; but she asked me to ask you if the job still open for her Mom? Tell her to come and see me she said. Well good luck Miss Thomas she said, see you on Thursday, thank you Mom said Ammi as she rose to her feet. Then she turns and asks; what shall we call you Miss Thomas she asked while opening her ledger again as though she was looking for a name, but Ammi thought she shouldn't be asking; she's got her full written down on the document given to her, then she thought again Mrs. Dorsey wanted to be formal. Please call me Ammi Mom; everyone does, then Ammi it is, see you on Thursday Ammi she said as they disappear through the door. Miss Healey who was doing nothing other than observing is about to leave too, bye Ammi she said, Bye Miss Healey; and she went through the door in a hurry as though she had forgotten something. On her way out Ammi realised she was beeing watched, but of course she expected it; they'll be peeling skins off her when she starts working she tells herself. Well it was good news all round; she got the job she wanted and her future employer wants her cousin Hillary to come and see them.

However she doesn't know what kind of job is on offer for her at this clothes factory; she's got no skills. She was anxious to get home to tell the others that she'll be starting work on Thursday. It's only three o'clock when she got the bus home; she's anxious for the others to come home; right now she's on cloud nine; the thought of a pay pocket keep ringing in her head. She then get cooking; preparing dinner until the others come home. Well dinner is prepared but she's not going to eat, no; she's waiting until the others come; so she's going to settled down to watch television. However she wasn't watching for long before her cousins come home, one of the characteristics about Ammi is that she can't stand being alone, growing up in a big family she's used to having people around her, being alone in the room even for a few hours gives her the creeps, so when the others arrive she was more relief. Come on she said; go wash your hands; dinner is ready; and it's on the table, she said it as though she's giving an order. Give us a chance to come in will you said Daphne, Hillary didn't say anything; she went to bathroom, returning quite quickly, she's anxious to hear if they still want her at Dorsey's. She took her seat at the table waiting anxiously for Ammi to tell her if there's any message for her from Mrs. Dorsey, but Ammi was talking about the weather and how cold it's getting, but right now she's got no interest in the weather neither does her cousins; they want to hear about the job she (Ammi) went after. But Ammi just playing a prank; she knows they're anxious to hear about her day; she's just hanging them out to dry for a while. Well are you going to tell us or not asked Hillary, what about she asked, she got a vicious look from Hillary as to say what the hell are you playing at, what about the job today she asked. Oh that! It's alright she said casually, Ammi! What are you playing at asked Daphne, do you get the job or not? She burst into laughter, but the others weren't amused, yep! I'll start working on Thursday she said casually as though she didn't care. Well show some zest as though you're pleased to get job said Hillary, Ammi smiles, course I'm pleased; how couldn't I not pleased? she asked, well you don't show it she said. I'm please for you said Daphne, The next thing we must remember now is to tell Mr. Owens that you got a job said Daphne; and hope he doesn't increase the rent by much she said. But maybe we shouldn't tell until I receive my first pay pocket, remember I'm only on trial, or better still we'll tell him when the two-week trial is; then I'll know for sure if they're keeping me on she said. No! Said Daphne we must tell him the moment you start working, you'll be going out each morning and coming back in the evening; you must be working if you're doing that; he probable notice; he'll then take it that you're working; he might then think that we're hiding it from him. Yes! You're wright said Hillary we'll tell him at the end of the week; we don't want any bad feeling between us and that nice man.

You change your tune said Ammi; he's a nice man now is he? What happened? Nothing happened; he was always a nice man. Hilly! Sometimes I think you're just full of wind; there's a word for people like you; windbag, you just gas off when the feelings take you said Ammi, but Hillary didn't respond she just smiles. So what did they said about me asked Hillary anxiously; do they still want me? Ammi ignores her and remaining quiet looking at her plate, she asked again; only this time she shouts but shouts so loud as though she's angry. Oh yes! They wanted you to come and see them before Thursday she said with a big smile. Then why were you holding out on me; don't you want me to get a job there she asked, don't be silly; I was just pulling your legs said Ammi, you see Daff; the joker doesn't know when her leg is been pull said Ammi. Hearing that bit of good news it was pleasantries all round, I should call in sick tomorrow she said and go and see them, no don't do that said Daphne; I'll tell them you took ill when I get in, thank you Daff she said.

Wednesday Hillary waste no time, as soon after she had something to eat accompanied by Ammi they set off to Dorsey's Clothing's, she's more than anxious about this job. Crossing her fingers and everything else hoping they'll take her on; and hope that whatever they give her to do will be better that of her present job. But to her surprise she's been given a good job, a very good job; better than she had expected. She was put in charge of the storeroom, this is where every piece of clothing comes in and is given out; a responsible occupation. She was over the moon about the position given to her; and come hell or high water she's going make a success of it. They wish they could get a job there for their cousin too; and get her away from that horrible job they been trying to get away from. But they couldn't very well ask for a job for her, no; not yet; they have to prove their worth first and that takes time. Things were progressing nicely in the right direction for them both, more so for Ammi; the management must have seen something in her they like; after the first week they offer her a training course, a course she gladly accepted. They'll be sent her to a dressmaking school to learn to read plans, as much as her work is good; she must be able to read the drawings; she'll be at this school for a month before returning to Dorsey's Clothing. Well as expected some of the workers take exception to them; for whatever reason they prefer if the two black women weren't working there, and even though they never said so; their actions speak louder than words. There was one who was outspoken; Mary; she couldn't hold back what's on her mind, I don't like foreigners she said; especially when they're black, Hillary who hate most white people wanted to confront her but think better of it, she doesn't want to do anything that would jeopardise the best job she ever had since she been here. But it hard to be working with people who you know dislike you mostly because of your colour, this woman made no bones about it; the hate within her is so strong that she tell them to their face what she thinks about them, it hurts; it hurt like hell. But the girls found favour in a worker called Lucy, she's a fairly beautiful woman about twenty-nine with long flowing jet black hair. It was on the third day; at lunchtime she went by Ammi's machine and introduced herself, hi Ammi she said; she probable heard it from the chargehand, I'm Lucy; are you and your friend going to lunch she asked. Ammi paused throat, thank you; I don't mind if I do she said; she extends her hand; hi Lucy; I'll get my bag. That offer by Lucy was to let these two black women know that not all white people are racist; and she would love to be their friend if they would have her. Well Ammi and Hillary never been to the canteen before; they usually bring pack lunch and ate by their machine the two days they're here. They would probably have gone to the canteen before; but because of the hostile nature of their workmates they think better of it and stop by their machine.

Entering the canteen with Lucy there were people in the queue waiting to be served; others were already having their lunch but suddenly everyone was looking at them, they're now the centre of attention. So what's new; they went to church and the reaction was the same, they better get used to it. Sits anywhere said Lucy; I'll get my dinner and join you presently. They open up their pack lunch trying to ignore the inquisitive eyes, but it easier said than done; when you know that some of those eyes if not all are eyes of hate; it's difficult to ignore them. Lucy returns to join them and begins to talk, but Lucy it seems is one of that especially good human being as they'll find out later. Looking at Hillary she asked; are they still looking at us asked Lucy, Now! Hillary can be at times a mighty feisty person and can be very offensive with her language, but hearing Lucy used of the word; us, she couldn't help cracks a laugh, oh yes! They're looking at us alright she said still laughing, Ammi smile; she was pleased to see Hillary's reaction. From that first day of having dinner at the canteen with Lucy; these three trumpet nave up a friendship, but Ammi will be leaving at the end of their first working week for training. Hillary will be without her cousin Ammi; but she's got a friend in Lucy and now they're always together. But as time went by it somewhat reasonable to say there was a good relationship with most of her works mates; except for nasty Mary who was not only a racist but a jealous person with a mean streak. She was a machinist who constantly ruining dresses, she had to be taken off the machine; but she wasn't sacked, no; she was offered the position of a sweeper; and she took it with the intention of applying for another job; the storekeeper; but was refused. Probable she was content in doing the sweeping up; but to see someone come along and doing the job she was denied of; especially when that person is a black immigrant; she couldn't contain her rage and anger. Friday lunchtime she went into the office and handed in her notice; and by doing so she makes it quite clear as to why she's leaving. Audible to those of who were passing going to lunch, talking to Mrs. Dorsey she commented; you can stuff your job you nigger lover she said among other things. She was told to leave quietly pr they would call the police. Well she leaves the office but not the shop floor, she approaches Hillary for a confrontation; however that didn't amount to anything; she was evicted from the premises forcefully by a very large gentleman. There was a thought that Mary would lay wait for them outside, so Lucy joins force with Ammi and Hillary just in case, however it seems Mary have licked her wounds and disappeared. That was Ammi last day at Dorsey's; on Monday she'll be off to Gladstone training school, but somehow she wasn't looking forward to it; she feels she has settled in nicely in her job after just over a week.

37: Gladstone Training School

Monday was another cold and damp day; Ammi left home early to make her way to Gladstone Training School; she knows where to go; she'd checked it out during the week. Arriving there she walked up to a small outhouse; she could see a man walking about; and he saw her to as she approaches; there was no need for her to say anything. Can I help you he asked standing boldly at the small window, yes said she said; I'm here to see Mrs. Gladstone, she's expecting me Sir. What for he asked kind of furiously, I will be attending her School Sir; and she's expecting me, and she's expecting you he asked as though he's doubting what she has said; yes Sir; she's expecting me. Waits here he said kind of angrily; I'll go and see if she wants see you; and off he went but slowly. When he was gone Ammi considers the attitude of this man, he was less than pleased to talk to her; but there's nothing strange about that, somehow she was almost expecting such reaction from the moment she saw the man she's going to deals with. He told her to wait there as though she was going to gate crash, she's getting very used to what is to expect with some of these white folks. Well it could be that he deliberately takes his time; he doesn't return for another twenty minutes or so; the poor girl was nearly frozen. Then out in the not too distant she could see the man coming, walking behind a woman; she has a feeling this could be the person in question. This woman is fairly tall; about five foot eight; but quite elegant with a tape measure over her neck. Miss Thomas she enquires looking straight at her, yes Mom that's me, she wasn't surprised to see it was a black person; it's obvious she had been been told by the Dorsey's the kind of person she's to be expect. The woman extended her to greet her; good morning Miss Thomas; would you come with me please she said politely, and off they went. She glances back and could see the gateman stood looking in her direction, Ammi with her thoughts wondering what's going through his mind. The woman took her inside one section of this huge building, she then leads her to an office, sit here Miss Thomas she said, and would you like a cup of tea? Yes thank you Mom; and she disappear into another room with glass door; she (Ammi) could see her making the tea. She returns shortly with tea and biscuits, here you are Miss Thomas; this should warm you up, Ammi thought how kind; she most have noticed the trembling in her voice. She makes herself comfortable, now then Miss

Thomas; she paused and stood up, I'm Mrs. Newman she said with extended hands to greet her for the second time. Welcome to Gladstone Training School, thank you Mom she said as they shook hands, but for some strange reason she was feeling somewhat relax talking to this strange person.

Well Ammi thought it was a good start; the word welcome means I don't hate you; it was a good feeling. Mrs. Newman didn't have any papers or documents to look at; no need; she's well verse by Dorsey on the person that was coming; and her conversation was direct and face to face. I'm going to teach you how to read a plan she said with an almost smile; and you're expected to be qualified at it within a month; and you will be Miss Thomas; is as though she was compelling her to. But Ammi didn't have anything to say to that; only in her thought, she's not asking me she's telling me; what if I can't? Maybe I'll get deported. We're all women here Miss Thomas so don't be coy about anything; if you have a question please ask it. What she was saying to Ammi tactfully; don't think because you're black you should hold back in asking questions; well that's what she thought, thank you Mom; I will. After further discussion she got up and went out onto the floor. A great big open area; all the students are visible but the place is quiet. She returned accompanied by another woman, Miss Thomas! This is Miss Murry; she's going look after you, Ammi stood up; good morning Mom she said; and they shook hands, they sat down; then she stood again, Miss Murry will see to you Miss Thomas and I'll see you later; then she leaves. Now then Miss Thomas how much plan reading have you done? None Mom at all mom; I made dress using the tape measure, she pull the draw and outcome a catalogue, take a look at this she said; is there anything there you never seen before she asked curiously, oh no Mom; I've seen them all before; only I never had cause to use them. After a while Miss Murry got up, come with me Miss Thomas; and they went out into the big open space; once again the eyes were on her. But Miss Murry did what she thought was the unthinkable; she took her around the class of about nine young women and introduced her to them all. What's your first name Miss Thomas one young woman asked, Amanda; but everyone calls me Ammi, I'm Catharine; but everyone calls me Cat; nice to meet you Ammi she said; and the same here said Ammi. Miss Murry taken her to a desk, this is where you'll work Ammi; she was shown more catalogue and drawing implements. Have a look at these Ammi; and get used to them; I'll be back to see you.

It's getting close to eleven o'clock and she's still sitting there in her coat looking at what's on the table, Then cat came by; she was please she did; it nice to talk to someone; and even though she knows she was been conspicuous she's feeling rather better because of the welcome she gets. Why don't you take your coat off and hangs it up she said, where Ammi asked, didn't anybody show you to the coat room? No! Not yet, ok! Come with me; I'll show you; and off they went. Well they didn't return immediately, no; Cat was versing her in the coat room of everything she needs to know. It's now lunchtime; Cat is taking her to the canteen; but she (Ammi) has her pack lunch so she returns to fetch it. At the canteen Cat brings her a cup of tea without asking her; well! She's not a tea drinker; but she'll have it through sheer curtesy; and on this occasion like in the office she'll have it with her sandwich. But during lunch another student came by; Cat she said; why do you keep Ammi all by yourself; but Cat ignores her, hi Ammi; I'm Francis; but you can call me Franc she said with the most broad grim, hi Fran; good to meet you; won't you sit down she asked, then she wonder why she said that? It just happen instinctively she tells herself. But it seems as though these two had history, Franc! You're too bloody nosey; everything you want to know; why can't you allow something to pass you by? But why keep Ammi all by yourself; I would like to know her too. Ammi sits and secretly smiling; I never know I would live to see the day when two people quarrelling over me. Ladies! Please don't quarrel over me; I'm not worth it; honestly?. Ammi you don't want to know this one said Lucy, everyone and everything I have she wants, we were friends and… Franc interrupts; I didn't take away your boyfriend; I told you that a thousand times; why you can't believe me. Ammi smile openly, I can't believe it she said, you better believe it said Franc, oh no! not you said Ammi; I've got the same thing going on with my two cousins indoors; what with women in this country that they always have to be arguing over men? She never lacks her own company; men or women; she seems to get her kicks out of cutting in said Lucy. The trouble with you Lucy girl you can't forget; whenever you hold something you never let's go said Fran. But the bell went; and it's time to return to their tables, I'll come and see you later said Fran; any time said Ammi.

But now Ammi is left in a peculiar position; she would love to have both girls as a friend and it's good to know that on her first day she made friends that are quarrelling over her even though she wasn't sure if it's good or bad. It's nearly four o'clock; everyone is clearing up their table, Miss Murry came by, how is it going Ammi? Is there anything you want to ask me? Can I think about it and ask you tomorrow Mom? Sure! And if there's anything you need to take home to study please do, thank you I will, see you in the morning Ammi, thank you Mom and you have a good evening. She looks at all the articles on the table and decided to take home one of the plans; tomorrow she's be well familiarised with it. At home the others wanted to know how was the day at training school, it was better than I thought she said; I made two friends and they quarrel over me, what did you do asked Daphne, well nothing; Lucy didn't introduce me to Franc and that was it; franc accused Lucy for keeping me to herself. Strange affair said Daphne; the first day at school and two people haggling over you; so what did you do, well nothing; but I told them I have the same situation indoors, you told them that asked Daphne frightfully; why would you go and tell them that? Well you and Hilly always arguing over men; well man she said; and I hope I hear no more of it. Hillary said nothing; maybe she thought Ammi was saying what needed to be said; but Daphne was none too pleased. So what about the school Ammi asked Hillary; do you think you'll like it there? Well! Today went pretty well; and if it continues in a similar fashion I could get to like it, anyway I'm there to learn not to have a good time; like or not. Tuesday! That's when her learning begins; Miss Murry was at her desk first thing to give her a task today and the remainder of the week. After a couple of weeks the teachers were very pleased with her work, I've heard a good report about you Ammi; keep up the good work said Mrs. Newman on one of her patrol; thank you Mom; I'll do my best. By now she and Lucy have what seems to be a close friendship, and when Ammi told her that she's a Christian and what it means she couldn't fully grasp it; why? Well! he would like to visit Ammi on a weekend and they would go to the West Indian blues dance, and how did she know about these blues dances. Well this is her story; she and her friends were passing this house one Saturday night and there was a party going on; and the music and people dancing, they stop and would like to go in; but the man at the door said no. I could see these people having a good time; and I wonder why they wouldn't let us in; it couldn't be because we were white, no; there were lots of white women in there, but we never leave immediately, no; we stop outside to enjoy the music. But when Ammi told her she had no idea about blues dance she asked, then where do you go to have fun, I go to church; and we sing and clap hands. Well it seems from what she heard and what she had in mind; if she heard tight Caribbean folks are supposed to be fun-loving people hence the music; and it seems she wanted to be a part of it. Sometime later after Ammi return to Dorsey's, Lucy would visit her and find the kind of person to rave with in Hillary.

38: Return to Dorsey's

After a month at Gladstone Training School Ammi returns to Dorsey's Clothing with a very good report, she was told by one of her workmates who was eavesdropping in a telephone conversation, firstly she asked Ammi; who is Mrs. Newman? She's the owner of the training school, why do you ask; only I heard your name mentioned. This young woman could learn so much more she heard; it seems she would like you to stop on longer. Are you sure you heard that asked Ammi, that's what I heard, well that's good of her to say that; but I wouldn't want to carry on any longer. Nothing has changed since she leaves; she was back on her usual machine. Two days later she was called to the office; Mrs. Dorsey wants to speak with her, she enters the office with no expectation, come in Ammi she said, Miss Healey was also present. You'll ask to join the union she Mrs. Dorsey. Well! Ammi is got no knowledge about joining a union apart from what her cousin Hillary told her; she had already joined up. You know what is the union Ammi? Oh yes mom, Hillary told me about it, but when I'm to join mom? At tea time today would you go and see Mr. Grey, do you know where he is? No Mom; doesn't worry; Miss Murry will show you, and after a short chat she went back to her machine. Soon after tea she went to the little office as she was told; Mr. Grey was there; he's visible from a long way off; there's large pane of glass one can see right in the little office. She taps on the door, come in the voice said, she entered, I was asked to come and see you Mr. Grey said Ammi; assuming that he's the person in question, but he ignores her; he was looking through some papers. Ammi thought he could be pretending because he doesn't want to talk with her, well he knows she's there; she didn't say anything further she just stood and wait. With his head still down in the paper he points Ammi to a chair, sit down he said; but Ammi remain standing, she thought what Hilly said was true; this man is an ill manner beast, but she's not going to wait any longer, I'll come back when you're less busy she said to herself, she opens the door to walk away. However she was wouldn't want to be there for any length of time, no; the little room stink; and with the place very hot the stench is somewhat unbearable; doesn't he smell it she asked herself. now he shows some response, Miss Thomas where are you going; you must sign up, what Ammi said is completely out of character; but she couldn't accept his attitude; she had to respond. She didn't go back in, no;

standing at the door she comments, I won't allow someone like you who area racist treat me like the way you do; you don't like someone like me and I don't like you either, she then walks away; she got his full attention; looking back she could see him looking at her.

She went back to her machine knowing fully well she would soon get a visit from Miss Healey or Mrs. Dorsey; but she was wrong; the day ended without any such visit, however she knows whether it tomorrow or the day after but she'll get a visit. At home she talks about it with the others, Hillary joke that she has become a hell raiser like her, don't you liken me unto you she said; that will never happen; only I couldn't allow that little man to treat me like dirt, and I didn't swear like you would, no; I just speak what's on my mind; I just couldn't tolerate his nasty attitude so I got out of there quickly she said. But I didn't swear to him said Hillary; believe it or not; I wonder why not comment Daphne; something seems to have changed, I can be civil too you know she said, I'm glad to hear it said Ammi. Back at work on Wednesday she was summons again to the office; she suspects it's about her confrontation with Mr. Grey. Come in Ammi said Mrs. Dorsey; and sitting at the table was this Mr. Grey. Good morning Miss Thomas he said, Ammi looked at not with anger but to think how this man boldly and innocent greets her as though nothing was wrong. She didn't respond, take a seat Ammi said Mrs. Dorsey; now then Ammi; I understand you walked away from joining the union; unfortunately it's one of the criteria if you want to work here. But mom I went to join and he totally ignored me; she stops short of calling him by his name; so I walked away. Is that right Mr. Grey? asks Mrs. Dorsey; No! That's not right at all; I was busy, but for the first time Ammi lost her cool, she knew this man treat her like a no-body; probable not because she's woman, no; but certainly because she's black. All lies Mom said Ammi; I suspect he doesn't like black people; my cousin Hillary had similar experience with this man, but let me tell you Sir; as a Christian I go to church and as Christian make it a point to be civil to everyone; and telling lies is not something we do not cherish, but you Sir; you're a lier. But the look on Mrs. Dorsey's face tells a story, she had no doubt in what Ammi was saying; and it seems she's got no love for the union and probable even worst for this Mr. Grey. However she asked; would you sign up now for the union Ammi? oh yes Mom; if I must; This Mr. Grey had the necessary document at hand, he didn't say much; just sat there looking as though he was angry. After all had been said and done the papers were signed, thank you Ammi; you can go now, thank you Mom. As she was exiting the door she turns to this Mr. Grey, Sir! You must learn to love yourself before you can love others, she turns and walks away. But later her in a conversation with Hillary about what she had said; she asked, but why did I say those things to that man Hilly; I suddenly took a leaf out of your book and be nasty to someone, I know I shouldn't have done what I did. Well! If you feel so bad about it why don't you go and apologise to this man; or you can't bring yourself to do that? No! I won't apologise; but I'll pray for forgiveness; my God who sees and understand everything will forgive me. Ammi! There's no reason to beat up yourself over this man; you did what I should have done; and whatever you said to him; good on you. As time lapsed Ammi has excel in her position; the company was putting more responsibilities on her, she was entrusted with the more expensive materials. Her position in the firm was becoming more important as the management recognised she had become trustworthy and responsible.

But there were some changes in her friendship between her and Lucy; they were still friends alright; but not a close friend as she's been with Hillary. When Lucy turned up at their home in Grange road it was on the invitation of Hillary; it's seems she has found a white person to whom she's got something in common with. On Saturday Lucy turns up at about eleven o'clock; and from the moment she arrives it was like a missing friend arrives for a reunion, and considering they had all week at work; they were bending each other's ears one couldn't get between them. When she was introduced to Daphne who was cooking it was just hello and backtalk quietly with Hillary. After dinner she expressed her love for West Indian food to the point where she would like to learn how to cook rice and Pease. I'm not a good cook she said; you must teach me how to cook these West Indian dishes. It getting close to ten o'clock and she wouldn't mind stopping over; she jokes about it; but Ammi also jokes that she can't, well If I can't stop over I must go now; don't want to miss the last train; If I did; then I would have to stop over she said. Butt was obvious she clearly wants to stop over; whatever she and Hillary were planning she would have to be here for them to carry it through. She gets her coat and her bag; time to go she said; she and Ammi embraced and she said good night to Daphne, Hillary walks her to the front door, but she didn't return immediately; it seems they were putting the finishing touch to their plan. When she did Daphne asked her what were they talking about all this time, I thought she hurrying to get the train, don't be so nosey she joke. Well they knew each other since the day Ammi introduced them at work; now they seem to build up the kind of friendship they thought Hillary wouldn't have with a white person. But Daphne finds it necessary to comment on the way they were bending each other ears. You seem to find a soul mate said Daphne; what nasty thing the two of you were cooking up she asked; we weren't cooking up anything nasty as you put it; and you shouldn't be so inquisitive. Ammi herself was wondering how is it that in such a short time she was away at training school these two have become so close, she thought she would be the close friend of Lucy; but it obvious she prefers the company of Hillary's. Whatever they had planned and it's obvious there's something. She's coming back next Saturday she said; she loves Daphne's cooking she said with a smile. That's not the reason she's coming back said Daphne sternly; why don't you tell us the real reason she's coming. Well put it this way she said; what you don't know won't hurt you. The other two are left in the dark wondering what their cousin is getting up to with her newly found friend. But up to a point Ammi was not too displeased, it good to see Hilly laugh and stop been miserable like she's been lately, knowing the way she used to speak hatefully of anyone white; it's even more odd the way she hits it off with Lucy. But she did speak well of the Dorsey's, Ammi thinks she might even like Mr. Dorsey in other ways; could it be she's hiding her true feeling and pretending it's hate?.

Talking about hate said Daphne; tomorrow we must tell Mr. Owens that you are now working Ammi, oh yes! But Daff; how does the hate word let you remember Mr. Owens, Hilly; you forgot the conversation we had last week about white people, you hate all white people including our Land Lord; remember? I said no such thing; I might say all white people are the same; but I would never say anything derogatory or nasty about this man; he and his wife are good people; the best, So you change your tune now that you find yourself a white friend, typical; it just typical of you said Daphne; you sprout your mouth off freely without thinking. Right then; tomorrow we'll go and see Mt. Owens; why we asked Hillary; it only take one person to tell him; then would you go asked Daphne, of course I will; don't see why not; I can talk to people and be civil too; right Ammi she asked sarcastically, of course you can; if you can bridle you anger said Ammi, like you did with the union man asked Hillary. Union man asked Daphne, what happen? Should I tell her or… alright; Ammi interrupted, I didn't take too kindly to his ill- manner and might have said something I now regret; things you wouldn't consider being bad perhaps. Well I say good on you; I met the man and he's a nasty piece of works; only he caught me on a good day. Well, well, well, little Miss righteous said something she now regrets, said Daphne, honestly Daff; I expect that comment from Hilly but nor from you, don't try and be who you aren't, I'm sorry Ammi; somethings are not to be laughed at, I'm so sorry.

39: Dinner Date

Sunday they have plenty to do; but not in the form of work, they'll be going to church and later they'll be going to Mr. Dickenson for dinner; and no one is looking forward to it more than Ammi, she looks upon him as a father figure and likes to be in his company. They set off to the bus stop; but the weather is quite foul; however they were in luck; they didn't have to wait too long for the bus. As they boarded they were greeted by a woman they made her acquaintance last Sunday, she remembers Ammi's name but not the others, she showed a little disappointment when Ammi couldn't remember hers, don't think too hard about it she said it will come to you later. They made their way to the church; but inside they parted company; Ammi was feeling a little guilty for not remembering her name. There're plenty of seats available; and they would like the seating's they had last Sunday; but unfortunately those seats are taken. While seating they looked around for Mr. Dickenson but he wasn't anywhere to be seen, maybe he's not coming today said Ammi, well it's early and service hasn't start as yet said Ammi; he might turn up later. But no sooner he arrived, Ammi waved to him; and he went and joined them. If your ears were burning we were talking about you, she said, all good things I hope he replies, we thought you weren't coming today said Daphne, I'm not late, am I? Oh no said Ammi; I was delay putting the finishing touch to our dinner he said, Ammi looked at Daphne and smile wryly. And how are you Hilly he asked as she wasn't saying anything while the others were chatting away. Well! She was quite receptive in her response; I'm fine she said; how are you? Oh! I'm quite well as you can see he said gleefully. Ammi was surprised to hear the pleasantries between them; she's hoping that Hillary is not playing one of her game to be unpleasant later. Ammi who was sitting in the middle nudged her with her elbow; she would like to tell her to remember where she is; but she just glares at her. However they settled down for the service, the Pastor went through his usual storytelling; but with meanings. Now black the people are plentiful in church; Pastor Moore congregation is growing by the week; but mostly by black people. But when Mr. Dickenson leaves his seat to joins the white man to do the collection they were surprised, well he didn't tell them that last week after service Reverend Moore had asked to perform that task; of which he accepted gladly. After the service and the reverend were greeting everyone; when he reaches them he was full of zest and enthusiasm, well that's something they notice with him from the first time they visited his Church, he's a happy soul; always full of life; and he loves to greet people that way.

Hello ladies; good to see you again he said smiling broadly, hello pastor they said; thank you for a good service said Hillary, Ammi looked at her and smile; as to say the flatterer, but she joins in the deception you might say, yes; it was a good service thank you Pastor. But in his zealous ways response; ladies! I'm Reverend Moore; but I didn't catch your names, Ammi thought; we been addressing him as Pastor; now we know he's a Reverend; of course they couldn't see the difference. Hillary was the first to extend her hand, I'm Hillary Reverend she said smiling broadly, and the others followed after. I hope to see you next week again ladies; and I would like to talk to you next Sunday before service; if you don't mind, oh no; we love to Reverend said Ammi, he walked away with the same pleasant smile he approached them with. Well they are not going to delay; as soon as Mr. Dickenson and his colleague finish count up the collection they'll leave with him to his home. They were sitting in Church waiting for him; it's too cold outside to be standing out there, soon he emerges from the back room, are you ready ladies he asked, we're ready said Ammi. They set off to the car, why didn't you tell us that you are one of the Nasser asked Ammi; I forget, but it's only last Sunday the Reverend asked me if I would like to it, but Ammi would like to ask him if he's going to be a fully-fledged member of this Church but she decided to hold that question until another time. They set off to his home in Oak Roar, it's not a long way away; they will be there in about five minutes or so. These are the kind of afternoon Ammi cherishes, going to Church and after Church she and her family gather for a relaxing time; and with an older adult like Mr. Dickenson among them she'll be feeling rather good. Indoors the ladies make themselves comfortable, now then ladies; look around and help yourselves to whatever you need or more to the point, whatever is there you need he said while arranging the table; well! Even though the women are there and would do it if he asked; but he invited them to dinner so he does it.

But then suddenly Daphne begins to displaying the kind of trait they had never seen before, she seems to come alive whenever Mr. Dickenson is around lately. We're here as your guests; shouldn't you be looking after us she asked, well ladies I'll tell you; I was hoping I would get some help putting dinner on the table he said talking from the kitchen. Well why didn't you ask? You only have to ask she said. Then would you like to come and give a hand Madam he asked, I might she said as she rose from the little settee and went to the kitchen. Hillary whispered in Ammi's ears; she's where she wants to be; right next to the man she's got a crush on; she can stop hating me now. Ammi nodded in agreement but said nothing, she for one is rather pleasing Daphne has come out of her shell and makes a move on the man she loves; and if he feels the same about her then they'll be together. The evening is going with a bang, Daphne brings the dinner in and help prepares everything, she was like the woman of the house, and her action from time to time brings a wry smile to Ammi's face. But Hillary was somewhat subdued, she might be thinking about when he asked her to marry him and she refused; not once but twice, however he seems not to let that bother him, probable it's the furthest thing from his mind. But he needs to clear the air; as an older person who watched these three young women grow up; he doesn't want to lose their respect; and he thought he's the one to bring matters to a head. At dinner they were all cheerful; a lot of topics are been discussed; Using his spoon to gently tap on his glass of Coca Cola; he calls the ladies to attention, I've got a little matter to clear up he said. Hillary looks at him in wonderment, maybe, she's thinks, he's going to ask her again to marry him in front of her cousins; and with hope that she might say yes, but she was so wrong; this man knows where and when he's not wanted.

I guess you might have heard I asked Hillary to marry me he commented, but no one responds; well if you didn't; I'm telling you now, I asked her for her hands in marriage but she turns me down twice. Well I'm not the man for her and she made it clear; and I respect her for that, even though she said I was too old. So Hilly don't feel bad about it; you have done the right thing; and I hope we can be friends always. Hillary looked at him in amazement; she didn't expect him to put it so bluntly, I didn't say that; did I said that she asked as though she had regrets. Well yes you did he said, but you shouldn't feel bad about it, I've learned a long time ago that it's a woman's prerogative to say no, and Hillary; believe it or no; I respect your honesty. But even though he clears the air Hillary was still looking somewhat gloomy, maybe the honesty of this man is too much for her to handle. But she perks up later when Daphne asks; which way to the bathroom Mr. Dickenson? Oh come on now he said; we're in England now; here people tend to be informal, we're all adults here; and be it may that I'm the old man here; but please call me Raymond; I love that name. Ok Raymond directs me to the bathroom, Hillary burst out laughing and Ammi cracks a smile too. The rest of the evening was fun, Raymond talk an awful lot about home, he seems to relish talking about

Mr. Thomas; Ammi's father, would you return home Ammi asked; you know Ammi; right now I would love to; but I can't he said, what would I return to; someone else owns the farm now, no! Ask me again in five years' time and I might give you a different answer.

While they talk Daphne begins to gather up the dishes to take back to the kitchen, which take the notice of the other two, Hillary mumbles something as Raymond went to kitchen after her; what are you mumbling about asked Ammi, don't you see; she can't wait to move in, Ammi didn't respond; she only smiles. He walks back in the room, I cook; and I do like cooking; but the part that I don't enjoy is the washing up after, so thank you Daphne; thank you very much he said loudly. She returns to the room, you don't have to thank me for doing the dishes Raymond; a single man have with three women for dinner; how could we walk away leaving you to do the washing up, no; that would be very unkind, nevertheless thank you just the same Daff he said. But Hillary the court jester picks up on every little thing; she whispers in Ammi's ears, he calls her Daff; whatever next she asked. However with all the going on Raymond come to realised that he might have a chance with Daphne; even though he was blown out by her cousin Hillary that doesn't mean he can't go courting the other one, and little does he know that with Daphne he only have to say the word. Well as all good things have to come to an end; it's time for them to make tracks home, tomorrow is another day and they all are going to work. Ok ladies get your coat and I'll get mine, wait a while till I warm up the car he said; it shouldn't take long. After about a few minutes he toots the horn; and they come and loaded up and off they went, As he was dropping them off Ammi comment, we thank you for a lovely evening Mr. Dickenson, Ammi! You forget so soon Ammi he asked; Raymond! And don't you forget it he said, they all smile, good night ladies he said as he closed the car door.

Before bedtime there'll be a discussion about tonight; especially about Daphne; so when are you going to visit him again Daff asked Hillary, what kind of question is that she asked; why make you think I'm going to visit him again. Oh come now; we have eyes; we can see, he only has to ask; and you would move in tomorrow. I don't know what gives you that impression but… Hillary interrupt, right Ammi she asked, well Daff; we know you like him; and you know what; I think he like you too she said. But she didn't stop there, and what about you Hilly; I notice your reaction when he talks about asking you to marry him; you were dumbstruck because you didn't think he would be so open about it. But he's honest and a respectable man; you should know that; we've grown up with him; and he didn't want you to think he's carrying any ill-feeling against you because you refused him; what decency; very few men would do that. Well I'm glad the air is clear and we can both get on with our lives said Hillary brashly. They're still talking about the evening when Daphne remember, guess what we didn't do she asked, what asked Ammi; we didn't go to see Mr. Owens she said. Good heavens said Ammi; we completely forgot, we don't have to lose any sleep over it said Hillary; you can go see him tomorrow after work, yes; I'll do that; and please don't let me forget.

Monday evening they were having dinner but no one was sitting at the table, dinner was eaten in front of the television; a habit nowadays; they are not going to miss out on the Z-Cars episode. Ammi raises her head up; aren't we forgetting something? She didn't have to said anything further, yes I know said Daphne; I must go and see Mr. Owens; I'm going now; I'll finish my dinner when I return, I'll come with you said Ammi; after all it's about me, they went immediately. It had gone seven-thirty and they were thinking it's too late to knock on his door, but they are halfway up the stair so there's no turning back now. They tap on his door, who's it he asked, Daphne Mr. Owens, come in Daphne he said loudly; they both entered, Mrs. Owens wasn't in the living room, good evening Sir she said, is Mrs. Owens well she asked, good evening ladies; oh yes; she's fine; she just having a lie down he said. They were still standing; sit down ladies take the load off he said; They be seated, so you get a job Ammi he asked with some delight, well he knows that's why they come to see him, yes Sir; I'm working, it's with a good firm I hope he asked; I think so Sir; they sent me to the training school to catch up on what I didn't know. What you didn't Ammi if you don't mind me asking; well I was no good at reading the plans; so they sent me to learn how. Well good for Ammi; I hope you'll make the best of such opportunity; I'm trying my best Sir. Now you want to know how much I'm going added to your rent, well ladies its one pound; I can't be fairer than that. Oh thank you Sir said Daphne; we can afford that, but obviously the young women have no knowledge of haggling; even though there's no reason to; this land-Lord is helping them out. So tell me about your job Ammi he asked, well he just want to talk really. Oh it's Dorsey's Clothing in Edgware Road Sir; and I quite like it there, well! It generally will be the case with your first job; sometime later you probably will be looking for another job; another job with more money; but it's good that you like the job you're doing; good on Ammi. Mrs. Owens walks in, hi Daphne, hi Ammi, now Donald; don't keep the girls up; they're working tomorrow. It's a welcome relief for the girls; not wanting to be unkind they're reluctance to say good night, but good old Mrs. Owens does it for them. They stood up; thank you Sir said Daphne; and they make for the door, thank you Mr. Owens and good night Mrs. Owens said Ammi, keep up the good work Ammi he said as they depart. Back at the room, Hillary can't wait to hear how much Mr. Owens has raised the rent, come on then tell me she said, he double the rent? No! It's a pound more said Ammi, a pound more? One pound more she asked surprisingly, that's one good white man she said, so you see said Ammi; there're good people in this world, regardless of their colour.

40: Easter At Church

By now Ammi is taking a more active part in the church, but the whole ethos of the Church has changed somewhat, from the quiet calm orderly way of worship that used to be the norm; this Church and probable like many others that has accommodate black people their style of worship has now changed; and all because of the emergence of immigrants. Their congregation has grown and keeps on growing, and their service has become livelier and a more cheerful audience. The songs are tuneful and lively and the Reverend has become a preacher instead of a storyteller. This lively energetic man is now enjoying a nearly pack Church week after week, and every Sunday there's always someone new attend. But an unexpected change was to come from Ammi too; this young dedicated Christian who had her feet well-rooted in the Pentecostal church; it didn't seem possible that she could change religion and conform to another denomination; even though they're not too dissimilar, she jests to her cousin that she wishes they would clap hands too. Well! You can't have everything; one day that might happen said her cousin. Easter Sunday would be the day that would change Ammi life for good; she was to meet in church the man who was to be her husband; but of course she doesn't know it yet. This Church has got an organ but hadn't been played for some time; it seems that as the attendant dwindled so whoever the organ player stop attending too. On that Sunday the Pastor as he has now become known to his flock; talks about the organ and he hopes one day soon they'll have an organ player. Well in the audience there was an organ player; he was a newcomer to the Church like many others, this man didn't have any qualm or fear to put himself forward to face an audience, he stood up; talking aloud from where he was sitting, Pastor he said; in the broad Jamila accent; one could wonder if the Pastor understand all that said. I can fill in for you until you find someone, pointing his finger directly at this man he asked, you play the organ Mr… not knowing his name he paused, Drake; Wilfred Drake Pastor; I could help you out if you wish. But it's obvious that this Mr. Drake's not only bold but eager to play also; he may be thinking that this is his chance to show off his talent. Well Sisters and Brothers; it seems as though we've got an organ player among us, the good Lord works in wondrous ways. Well Mr. Drake would you like to come and talk with me after the service he asked, sure thing Pastor;

I love to he said. Well the Pastor gets into his newly found form of preaching; almost like the type one would likely to be hearing if one was back in the Caribbean, and his congregation seem to like it. When one zealous woman calmly shouts amen; the entire congregation turned and steered at her, if she could became invisible she would, that might be the first and last time they'll hear that from her. It was a great Easter Sunday; after the service the people would gather together in and out of the church making new acquaintances; it was wonderful. Meanwhile that day In the Pastor's chamber Mr. Drake was having an audience with him, they planned to meet sometime next Saturday for him to have a trial on the organ; and if he was capable enough then he would certainly be the organ player.

The Pastor was satisfied with Mr. Drake's playing; in fact he was amazed that Mr. Drake played so well. Where did you learn to play the organ like that Mr. Drake he asked, A black immigrant from the Caribbean comes here to work; how could he play so well; who would have thought him. Be assured that for even a Pastor; those thoughts will be going through his mind. Well they were all supposed to be illiterate, so the Pastor can be forgiven for his reaction when among his newly found flock of immigrants there's one who plays the organ and plays it well. Mr. Drake was feeling rather please with himself too; the fact the Pastor not only like his way of playing but seems to like him too. I was taught by my mother he said proudly, and where does your mother lives asked the Pastor, my Mother is dead Pastor he said, that must have raised some odd thoughts in the Pastor's mind, she died when I was a teenager, and she's from Jamila where I'm from. Well the name Jamila has opens up a further conversation, I heard about that country he said; I would like to go there one day, oh; it's a beautiful country Mr. drake; someone like you Pastor with money would love it there, oh! I'm a poor man Mr. Drake; but one never know he said; the Lord works in mysterious ways; one day if it pleases him I might be on a plane to your country. Hillary mourns, why didn't he had this conversation in his dressing room instead of from the pulpit; but then again she thinks it shows openness; and the Pastor can have a good rapport with the congregation, yes;; I think it's good. This Sunday the Church was almost full, as words got around more and more people are coming, but there're plenty of white people too; at first when these black immigrants began coming most of the white people ceased from attending. But something must have happened; they're coming back; and be it may that some of them could be new faces. Today the pastor Moore was double please, in fact he was excited, and having a packed

Church and an organ player could be something he never thought would happen.

Looking all elegant in his white robe he begins the service, it was a lively audience as is expected; the hymn singing was joyous and melodious; and with their new organ player it was a good evening all round. Mr. Drake has now become the centre of attraction for some of the women; not least of all Ammi, she couldn't take her eyes off him. After service the usual greeting of everyone went on for some time, people are not only making new acquaintances they're making long term friends too, some of these new friendships will probably last a lifetime. But Mr. Drake himself had had an eye on Ammi from the very first time ; so when the greetings started after the service he made his way straight for her. Conversation wasn't difficult between them even with the other two women present; in fact on that Sunday along with Mr. Dickenson the friendship was forged, and the gang of four has now become a gang of five. They dally in the Church long after service ended; and when they did break up the happy union it was well past five o'clock. Mr. Drake went his own ways and Raymond took the ladies home in his car; but he didn't stop even though Daphne would like him to. Well, indoors they're going to gossip; there are lots to talk over; especially Ammi newly found lover according to Hillary. So when are you going to tell this man you fancy him she asked; why do you think I fancy him? she asked; I happen to think he played the organ very well, and so say all of us; but we didn't have our eyes fixed firmly on him; but you did, said Daphne; anyway! Not because you're a Christian it's not a shame for you to fall in love with someone, and how would you that she asked, a friendly jibe at the expense of their cousin who they think fall in love with the organ plater. But he's a nice man said Hillary; and if you didn't fancy him I would make a move on him; that bring smiles to their face, but what if he doesn't want you asked Daphne; you can't make a man love you if he doesn't; he'll just use you and walk away. Well you got to have confidence in yourself said Hillary; and there're ways to let a man love you even if he's reluctant to. Listen to the expert said Ammi, anyway that's foolish talk; not the kind of conversation I want to hear she said, why asked Hillary. It's against your Christian principles? Well I'm going to she said; I'm going to invite him for dinner; I would like to see this relation blossom; it's about time you have a man friend she said. Anyway I'm not too comfortable living with two ageing adults who are still virgins; something ought to be done about it. Ammi exclaimed in a loud voice; what the devil is wrong with you; can't you keep your mind out of the gutter? I had enough of this conversation; you might say something worst, let's do dinner she said as she headed for the kitchen. I'll give you a hand said Daphne, let this vile person sit by herself and ponders her thought.

But Hillary knows just how to get these two going and somehow she enjoys doing it; she's the joker in the pack. But she doesn't like her own company; no; she likes to be with the cousins, she went into the kitchen to join them. What are you saying about me; go on and tell me; I can take it, you my dear cousin? You have raised your importance far too high, and with your one-track mind that shouldn't be she Ammi. I take it that is putting me in my place in a nice kind of way mother Mary she said facetiously. Well say what you like you two; you can't help the way you are; and so do it; and come to think of it; I'm the only one out in the cold here, Daphne you get your man and Ammi seem certain to hook the organ player; not bad going at all for the both of you. God help us said Ammi; even in the kitchen, Hilly! There must be something else we could talk about; but nothing comes to mind right now; so please set the table. Daphne was attending to the salad, you're the Christian here she said; you should pray for her; you must see that the girl need a prayer. That I'll do said Ammi; however we'll all pray together; we'll make it a priority after dinner; or better yet; every night before bedtime we'll pray together. I'm not ready for that sort of a life as yet; I'll pray when I'm good and ready; not because you two said so, gash! She said; a person can't make a little joke without around here without you two threaten her with prayer; I think that would mean I've done something really nasty. You never give up do you Hilly; why don't you go and set the table as I asked said Ammi. if one can't have a laugh one may as well be dead, I'm going to set the table; thank you she said. At dinner the conversation was a different topic, Ammi is still waiting for a reply from her Dad and so does Daphne; up till now there's no news about Daphne's father condition, and Ammi who had written to both her father and her friend Florence is anxious to hear from them. It's over two weeks since; and she's been wondering if there's anything wrong. It's Saturday morning and as no one was working they were late getting up, it's about ten o'clock and the postman arrives; they know; there's the sound of the letter flop and letters falling through. Anxious to know if there's any letter for them but no one wants to get up, go see if there's any letter Daff said Ammi with her head under the covers, why don't you go; I'm still asleep she said. You're talking to me; how could you are asleep; there was no response from Daphne, hilly, Hilly she calls; but she's not responding either; she obviously not sleeping but no doubt pretending to.

Well Ammi realise it's up to her; the other two have no intention of getting up, she got out of bed and went to check if there's any letter for them; and there was. There were lots of mails and among them were three letters for them; one for Daphne and two for Ammi, but she's not going to try and read them, no;; the room is too cold, so she powers up the paraffin lamp and went back to bed. Is there any letter asked Daphne lazily from under the blanket, yes! You got a letter said Ammi, hand it here she said pushing her hand out from under the blanket, it's on the table said Ammi; you have to get up and get it; she groans, have you light the lamp she asked Ammi, yes; the lamp is lit; it's there anything else you want? No thank you dear; when it warm I'll get up; and she dived further under the blanket. Well Hillary didn't expect any letter; she hasn't written to anyone home for quite some time. What time is it she asked; but no one answered; she had to see for herself, good heavens; look at the time she exclaimed, Ammi asked; what time is it, time we got up she said; and she got out of the bed. The room is warm so she stretches herself and walked towards the other side of the room, oh look; letters she said attempting to look; is any there for me? No! There aren't said Ammi as she too rose from under the covers. Give it here she said while sitting on the bed, Hillary handed them over, she gives one to Daphne who was now sitting up in bed. While Ammi was reading hers with full attention to the content; Hillary notice Daphne was a bit glum; she's not reading, Daff! What wrong she asked, Ammi look at her before she could answer, Daff! She said looking at her sympathetically; she suspects immediately that her father might have passed away. Daff! Is he? Yes! He's gone she said; Uncle John said he was buried over two weeks ago; he died long before we wrote the letters. Oh Daff! I'm so sorry said Ammi, Hillary went to her side of the bed and cuddled her; Daff! I'm so sorry she said; then all three embraced in a huddle. What do I do now she asked, what can you do; except write to Uncle John and thank him for all he has done, said Hillary. Do you think I should send him some money she asked, don't you even think about it; Dad won't thank you that; but do what Daff said; write and tell him thanks. With Daphne's bereavement Ammi forget about her letters; she'll read them later; all their attention now is directed on Daphne; trying to comfort her, they're quite aggrieved; what started out as a wonderful Easter day turns out to be quite sorrowful. Later that evening on his return to church Raymond calls to pick them up, he was given the sad news, he knew Dennis not as a friend; but as John's brother, now he'll mourn with Daphne and the girls for their lost. There won't be going to church this evening; and with Raymond have his sight set on Daphne; he will stop and give her as much comfort as he can. They were up until late before Raymond decided to leave, if there's anything I can do please don't hesitate; let me know he said as he was leaving, thanks Raymond said Daphne. The following morning Daphne was the first to get out of bed; she lights the lamp but she didn't return to bed, no; she makes herself busy seeing to breakfast. But when the others were still hugging the blanket she went and pulls it off, get out of bed you lot she said; it's still Easter and we have thing to do, Ammi got up lazily; Daff you all right, of course I am; why don't you come and sit down said Ammi; I'll finish up what you're doing after I have a wash. I'm all right I tell you; I can't go on mourning forever; Dad is dead and bury; it's over; he's gone; I must get on with my life; and to be honest I can't, I feel any deep sense of sorrow. But even though the others weren't too surprised to hear that they had expected her to show a little more remorse. Well unlike Ammi; she and her father never had that deep father and daughter relationship even though she's the only child.

41: Lucy Revisited

After the Easter it was back to work and colleagues were talking about how they spent the holiday. But Ammi has got quite concerned about the relation between Hillary and Lucy, they always in each other's ears all the time; and the other white folks must have noticed too; the closeness between these two; to Ammi it was a little unnerving; whatever they find to talk about they're always at it. On Saturday they usually go shopping; all three of them; but this Saturday Hillary wasn't coming; she had to stay home waiting for Lucy. What are they up to asked Daphne, I have no idea said Ammi; but I hope that whatever it is she won't regret it. But while they're out shopping they ran into Mr. Drake; the organ player, well on a Saturday here at Hamsden the local shopping centre; the immigrant come out in force; but not everyone is out shopping; no; some is just out for a wander around. They didn't stand around they went for coffee, well none of them are boozers; these two women never even seen the inside of a pub. Ammi was really pleased to see Mr. Drake again; that's the first time she's talking to him since Easter Sunday. Coffee had lasted for some time; and with the weather quite cold outside it was good to sit there and talk about everything. Well Mr. Drake appears to be a shy man when it comes to woo the opposite sex; and Ammi doesn't know whether she's going or coming, well she's got no experience of dealing with a man romantically either. So Daphne does what Hillary said she was going do at Church on Sunday; invites him to dinner. But he didn't respond to the invite; instead he asked; are you inviting me, Miss Thomas? And that was the first direct approach he made to her since they met, oh yes she said; if you want to, oh I want to alright he said; I would love to have dinner with you. However from that moment Daphne was almost invisible; they chatted away at the table and by all accounts, they had eyes only for each other. Ammi now seems to be consumed by the feelings of love; she seems to have forgotten why they were here, don't forget we have to do shopping said Daphne when she notices the time; but she's got to repeats herself for her to hear; considering they are sitting at the same table. Oh Daff we should've done the shopping by now she said, Daphne just smile and said; yes we should. They walked out the coffee bar, and as Mr. Drake had nowhere special to go he walked around with them doing their shopping, we'll see you in Church tomorrow Mr. Drake said Daphne as she walked away to give them a bit of space to said goodbye. But they won't be kissing or even holding hands, no Sir; not this young woman; she lives by her Christian principles; if their encounter led to marriage then that's when intimacy will take place; they said goodbye and make their way to the bus stop. But today is their lucky day for meeting their friends, there was a toot of car horn but they take no notice; the toot was coming from the other side of the road, it was Mr. Dickenson. Well he didn't toot again he went and turn around and pull up at the bus stop, needless to say they were glad to see him; in this cold weather a car ride is like manner from heaven. He didn't stop when he dropped them off, why don't you come by for dinner asked Daphne, she already invited Mr. Drake; but he's for Ammi; and since she has her eyes fixed on him (Mr. Dickenson) she would like to extend the invitation to him to; and she might be thinking the more the merrier. I love to have dinner with you ladies; what time is dinner he asked; of course he had no knowledge that Mr. Drake will be there too. Round about three o'clock she said; and don't be late, Ammi smiles looking at her. Well! By now he should be picking up the signals Ammi thinks to herself; and realising that he's got a very good chance with her. Will there be a favourable outcome for either of these women? We'll have to wait and see.

Their day is running late; they were out shopping later than expected; all because of the meeting up with Mr. Drake, however when they enter the room Lucy was there to greet them. We thought you were lost; we were just thinking of sending out the search party she jokes. Oh we met an old friend said Daphne and had coffee with him, who is this man asked Hillary; anyone we know? Yes said Ammi; it was Mr. Drake, Hillary stood up looking at Ammi as if she had committed a crime. You had coffee with him? What else did you had with him she asked insinuatingly? But Ammi had no answer to that question. We had coffee together and now you have no need to ask him to dinner tomorrow; we had already invited him said Daphne. However there was no mention of Raymond coming too. While all the talking continues Hillary was looking in the mirror and straightening her herself; Ammi notice a small suitcase in the corner; she know it's not belonging to any of them; so it must be Lucy's. Are you going any way Hilly she asked, no! Why do you asked? No reason said Ammi, when Hillary didn't say Ammi asked again, well are you going out? We're going to a party she said in a low voice, you mean you're going to a dance said Daphne disapprovingly. So yes! We're going to a dance; what wrong with that she asked. But you never go to any of these dances before she said, well! There's a first time for everything; and anyway I never had anyone to go with. Looking at Lucy Ammi asked; have you ever been to one of this dance before? No! But I passed and heard the music; I told you remember? And boy does it sound good she said with some glee. Hilly you have change; said Daphne, you not the same person we leave home together, going to dance and stay out late at night; I do hope you know what you're doing, she seems concerned for her cousin. Now Ammi realised why at work these two were always in such close rapport; she also realised why she couldn't be Lucy's best friend; she's not her type. The time is nearly ten o'clock and they're ready to leave, aren't you going to tell us not to wait up asked Daphne, oh yes! Don't wait up she said smiling, and off they went. Well now that the party girls are away and the other two had time to think Ammi asked, shouldn't we start preparing Sunday dinner from now; if we leave it until tomorrow we'll be rush off our feet, Daphne agrees; so they set to work doing some of the preparation for tomorrow's dinner. Sunday was clod as usual but Ammi and Daphne is looking forward to dinner after Church; in a word they're in love even though they're coy about it. Well they are new to romance; for both of them this is their first encounter with men in that regards. When they got out of bed it was only Hillary alone and she was sleeping in the settee; still fully clothed, Lucy might have decided to go home after the dance they thought, not knowing what to think they didn't disturb her. They carry on with what they're supposed to do and get ready for Church; Hillary won't be coming with them today.

The Church was pack to the rafter; Ammi comments; isn't it wonderful to see black and white people sitting together and worshipping together, you see Daff; that's the power of God's love. After service the usual greeting; with everyone behaving as though they all have something in common; this always went on for some time. They set off back home with their two dinner guests, Mr. Drake and Mr. Dickenson, in the long run these two men will end up being the best of friends. Arriving back at home Hillary was up and about and finish preparing dinner, is she feeling somewhat guilty for going to dance last night and wasn't able to go to Church with the others? If that was the case she certainly wasn't going to show it. When her cousins walked in with the two men she wasn't surprised; but she was only expecting Mr. Drake. Hi Hillary said Raymond, hi Raymond she said but not too enthusiastically, hello Mr. Drake; how was the service she enquired, oh! It was good; why wasn't there he asked, she was thinking of telling a lie; but with Ammi and Daphne present she thinks better of it, I went to a party last night; and I was too tired when I come home. I didn't know you were a party girl

Hillary said Raymond, I'm not; and that was the first time she said. But Ammi is more than anxious to know what had happened to Lucy, so what you done with Lucy she asked, Hillary looked at her as though she didn't want to say, Ammi; I'm going to tell you but please don't go on about it she said, Daphne stop what she was doing and give Hillary her full attention in anticipation of hearing some bad news; she couldn't wait she asked what happened. Well she was dancing with this guy the whole time and… Daphne interrupted, and what were you doing she asked, do you want to hear or not Hillary snaps, keep quiet Daff said Ammi. Their two house guests sat quietly listening; they couldn't do otherwise in this one room; they too are interested to know what had happened. Go on Hilly said Ammi, well she told me she was going; and she'll see me on Monday, and she took her bag and went. That's it asked Daphne, well do you want me to paint you a picture she asked, you mean she left with this black guy asked Daphne who seem to want the full details about Hillary's night out. Yes! She leaves with him, but did I said it was a black fellow? Well no! But only black men go to those blues dance; Hillary knows she's right she didn't respond. Well I thought we went out together we would be coming back together; but she didn't seem bothered about leaving me, the two men smile suggestively but said nothing.

Well! Let that be a lesson to you said Ammi; take time to know someone before you latched on to them as a friend. Wise words Ammi said Raymond; we all should remember that, Hillary looks at him as to say; I hope you're not referring to me. Mr. Drake asked; do you and this friend work together? All three of us work for the same company said Ammi; and she's a nice person really, well this nice friend won't be in at work come tomorrow he said, and what are you talking about asked Hillary, I know what you're thinking but I don't think Lucy is that kind of person. Mr. Drake take a deep breath, if she's in at work tomorrow I'll have you all at my place for dinner on Saturday. But Hillary replies kind of smartly, you don't have to make a bet for that, if you want to invite us to your place for dinner just go ahead and invite us. Well! Ammi heard enough of and decided it's time they eat, anyone for tea, coffee or chocolate she asked, both men wanted coffee; I'll get it said Daphne; and off she went, the other two get to work preparing the dinner. Now dinner is served but the table is not big enough for everyone; so Hillary take here's on a tray and sat in the settee, well the way the situation is she's the odd one out; the two men at the table are wooing the two women sitting there. The evening is going quite well; and with the meeting of people from the same country it's always a good time to talk about home. Are you considering returning home at some point Mr. Drake asked Daphne, a regular question among immigrants, yes I would like to return sometime in the future he said, but Raymond is getting weary of referring to him as Mr. Drake, Mr. Drake! My name is Mr. Dickenson; but I don't go tell anyone to call me that; no; I like to be informal; so people call me by my first name; Raymond; and all my friends call me ray; not that I have many friends here, I love that name he said. So Mr. Drake! What should we call you; we're not going to keep calling you Mr. Drake, oh no! He said facetiously. Well! Mr. Drake was please about Mr. Dickenson comments; I'm so glad you bring that up Ray; I was getting weary of it myself, my name is Wilfred; but please call me Wilf; and I love that name, they all laugh as Wilf take a leaf out of Ray's book. Always for a laugh Hillary shout from the settee; pass me the pepper Wilf she said all serious looking, with pleasure madam he said as he handed it to her, everyone smile.

Well as time went by these five people have become a little group by themselves, they were taking it turns to have dinner at each other's home; the clan was forged. By now the relationship between Ammi and Wilf has developed into romance; and he would like to ask her for her hand in marriage but he doesn't know how to. A bold man Wilf when dealing with the public; as will later explain; but when it's about the opposite sex he's a lost soul; the man is coy to pop the question. He talks to his good friend Ray about it and asked his advice, but he didn't think Ray's advice was a good one, no, so he approached Hillary, and knowing how deeply Ammi feels about him she laid it all out for him. In her usual brash manner she asked, are you a man or a mouse; get some backbone man she said; go and ask the woman; you might get a surprise she said abruptly. So you think she'll say yes he asked timidly, do you think I'm a mind reader? How the hell should I know what she'll say; the man is got no spine she mumbled. But Wilf didn't hear that, what you say he asked, Wilfred! I hope she says no if you ever get around asking her, if you're going to be a wimp now; what the hell you're going to be if she marries you. Well I only come to ask your advice Hillary; not for you to tell me what a wimp I am, thanks anyway he said; I'll leave now you in peace. I'm sorry Wilf; but you just caught me at a bad time, now listen! She's ready for that question; you should ask her the next time you meet, thank you Hillary; I will. However! While he's contemplating proposing; Daphne and Raymond is planning to move in together. They had no time for an engagement or a big wedding. Nearly two months after the day they moved in together they got married in a quick ceremony at the local registrar office. Daphne eventually gets her man; a man nearly twice her age; but she doesn't care about that; to her age is just a number.

By now Wilf and Ammi are engaged, but they don't want a registrar office wedding; no; they want a proper Church wedding, with all the trimmings. She wrote to her father and told him of the man she's going married, he was somewhat please when he learned that he plays the Church organ, to him he must be a God-fearing man if he plays the church organ. He was especially pleased when he learned that Mr. Dickenson his old friend is going to walk her down the aisle, if it wouldn't be he himself she couldn't have a better person to the honours. They're now making plans for the wedding, one night Ammi after returned from Wilf, Hillary began to ask questions. Well it wasn't so much a question just Hillary been wanton like always. Did you make the man happy she asked, what are you on about asked Ammi? looking directly at her she asked, are you still a virgin. I won't respond to your sinful and one-track mind thinking, but remember this, and even though I know you're going to tell me I'm no expert on the subject of infidelity; and you would be right, but I believe a man will have more respect for a woman if you save yourself until you're married. I supposed that means you're still a virgin she said in her usual beguiling manner. Oh! Go to bed you vile woman said Ammi humorously. Well on the fifteen of August a bright and beautiful day; they got married in a beautiful ceremony at their Methodist Church. Nearly a year earlier Ray had bought a three-bedroom house, and that's where the reception will take place. Well Ammi look upon him as a father figure and he likes that; and somehow it seems as though he would like his old friend Mr. Thomas to know he's keeping an eye on his daughter. At the reception there were letters from home to be read at the reception before the cutting of the cake, a letter from the bride's father, sister Maggie and her friend Florence now Mrs. Faster, she was proud to receive those tributes from home; and so was her guests; they clapped and cheered enthusiastically. But there will be no honeymoon for the newlyweds, no; they'll enjoy Sunday; but back to work on Monday. Well they couldn't afford a honeymoon anyway; however for these people it's just not their style to go away on honeymoon if they were even back in their country of origin. The little group remain together; the bond is even closer; they'll never split up; at least that's what they think; and with two of the women now married; the group is enjoying life to the full. But now the joke is now on Hillary; at dinner one Sundays afternoon she had to tolerate a lot of friendly jibes. On this particular Sunday afternoon everyone was in high spirit, Wilf remember a bet he had with them regarding Lucy, well she wasn't at the wedding and there wasn't anything said about her ever since that one time. Tell me Ammi darling said Wilf, they all smile respectfully; he never addressed her or anyone else darling before. Tell me! What happed to Lucy he asked, why didn't you invited her to the wedding? I couldn't she said, what do you mean you couldn't he asked, she means she couldn't because she doesn't work there anymore said Ammi. What happen asked Raymond, all we know she was taking too much time off and they sacked her she said? Well now; that's not why I asked about her; you remember the bet we had and… Ya, ya, ya Hillary interrupted, I remember; so what; she didn't come to work that whole week; what do you want a medal? Oh no; no need for that he said; just make me a cup of chocolate, what your last servant died of masa? (a word used back home meaning man) Let your wife do it, and then there was laughter.

Well for these people life seem bright for the future, on a visit to Hillary who's is now living by herself; Ammi thinks she should have one of those moral conversations with her. Married life is something to be cherished she said to Hillary who seems determined to remain single; there were many soothers but there were no wedding bells. Are you going grow old be a spinster all your life she asked, don't bother about me she said; I'm not rushing into any marriage. Rushing in with whom Ammi asked with intent; I haven't seen you with anyone. Listen hilly! You're in your thirties and not getting any younger; when you begin to get lines in your face few men if any are going to admire you then; now is when you should try and find that right person. Honestly Ammi; are you always going to preach and give advice? You want to climb down off your soapbox sometime, she said a bit annoyingly. I know you're angry said Ammi; but I don't want you to throw your life away; Daphne, settle down and get married so as myself; you seem determined to act like a teenager without no consideration about your future. Settle down she mumbled disdainfully, neither of you ever seen the inside of a man underpants until the day you married; so don't talk nonsense. You talked about it as though it was a disgrace to keep oneself pure until the day they find a man to marry; the bible said so you know she commented. Well that was the end of the conversation; Wilf who is now own himself a car call for his wife; that including Hillary; they're going for dinner at Raymond. What were you women gossiping about he asked smiling merrily, women talk dear said Ammi, you wouldn't want to know said Ammi, dear, darling; whatever next Hillary mumbled, she rolled her eyes and look up to the roof of the car; as to say mind your own business. Your wife was on her soapbox as usual she said; when you are going to tell her not to preach always she said with her usual brashness. Seriously though said Wilf; it's time you get yourself a man; we're concern about you. Comedians, that's all we need she said; a comedian, the wife's a preacher and the husband a comedian; God help us she said sarcastically. Well Wilf never got to know what their gossip was all about; not that he did really wanted to know.

42: Wilf The Man

By now Wilf's reputation had spread far and wide, not only for his organ playing; but outside church he's noted for playing the piano too; but mostly he was now fame for officiating at weddings, and with more and more immigrants arriving there were plenty of wedding to officiate. His reputation spread far and wide; not only among the local blacks but all over London among the black community; the man is like a celebrity. He's got his own style of officiating, his turn of phrase was comical; and among those who have no prior knowledge of the Queens English. He was admired; and with that he strived in his endeavour. Most of these weddings if no not all were to avoid the tax man; there were weddings almost every week. Ammi was very proud of her husband, in letters to her father she spoke highly of him, in reply her father talked about the picture of the wedding took pride of place in the home. They would go everywhere together; these people didn't hold hands but one could see the love between them. The family was stronger because of the togetherness of these two; and Raymond plays his part too. Ammi would confide in him like a father and the bond between him and Wilf grew stronger. There was more to celebrate with the arrival of Maggie; to her it was like from home to home, the group was still enjoying a wonderful time; and being the younger amongst them they cherish and take care of her. A week after arriving in England, a fairly educated young woman it didn't took her long to land an office job, of course she's been living with her dear sister Ammi and her husband; and Hillary is living there too. However the house they are living in is not belonging to Waif, no; it's belonging to the Owens; but he's in charge of it now. During his constant visit to Ammi when they were courting he was introduced to this nice Owens; and from then on they had developed a friendship. But living in London all these years after returning from Jamila had taken its toll; and now the couple had enough of city life and wants to return to their roots back in the country. However they would like to keep their house; well! It's their only source of income apart from their small pension; and not wanted to put it in the hands of an agent he entrusted it to Wilf in a care takers capacity, he'll handle it as he sees fit. The couple who are now in their twilight years unfortunately are without children; and there's never been any talk of close relative or otherwise. Wilf had accepted the offer gladly; this is a chance for him to better himself, well! The arrangement means he'll have a room in the house rent free while he took care of it. It was a gentleman's agreement; an account would be set up for Wilf to bank the rent, an amicable arrangement which over the years had never been broken.

With the population of black immigrant increasing the thoughts of many who had the desire to return home had been dashed, and as they begin to produce a second-generation it begins to feel like home from home. But Maggie has started to cause concern though, she's is taken up going to blues dances, and as the older sister Ammi feel responsible for her wellbeing, and moreover her father expects her to watch over her little Sister. From their upbringing they would be in Church on Sundays, but no; she has taken up with some newly found friends who seem to live for Saturday night. However there's nothing Ammi could do other than talk to her as a big sister in her usual bible-persuading manner; but Maggie is not a child; a woman of thirty-two is old enough to decide for herself what she wants to do with her life. However the family was still close and Ammi is not going to give up talking to her. The family began to produce first-generation children; Daphne was the first to give birth to a nine-pound baby boy; which makes Raymond a very happy man. Approaching sixty years of age he had thought he would never have an heir, at the christening he was beaming with joy and delight; he thanked his wife for giving him his son, this little bundle of joy has brightened up my life, he said. Now there were two houses in the family not too far apart; and needless to say they were becoming more overcrowded as new family arrived. Every chance Maggie had she would be at her cousin's Daphne to spoilt baby Richard, probable coming from a large family she misses that attachment. However in all her letter to her father Ammi never let on about her sister behaviour; the last thing she wants is for her father to worry, that secret will remain here in England. But for Maggie! Well she hardly ever wrote; her letters were far and few between; at times big Sister had to remind her to write home.

Well over the years a number of relatives had arrived from the Caribbean; from first cousin to distant families, and the forerunners who was supposed to return after five years took roots here with no intention of returning any time soon. People back home take it as a good omen for they themselves to immigrate too. But for the Drake's clan things were about to change dramatically with the arrival of one of Ammi's younger brother; Ben. When they met him at the airport all needed was a trumpet to proclaim his arrival, of course Wilf never met him before; but he heard much about him from his wife. Well he's the one she probably talked about mostly; even though when she was younger she and Sister Maggie were awfully closed. Well! From the moment they met at the airport these two men; one in his prime the other a dashing young man just turn twenty; they were inseparable. Wilf who was a very popular man; but was never one for socialising outside of the Church, well he had a good time when presiding at weddings. But suddenly this calm church-going organ playing man now seems to have a change of direction. He had never been to a dance of any kind since hem arriving in this country; but now with the arrival of Ben he began to go to blues dance. His wife turns blind eyes at first; anything that involved Ben it would be alright with her; and anyway she's hoping that as a married man the novelty would wear off sometime soon. But that' not going to happen, with great dancing and plenty of women that mixture is intoxicating. Ben was a good dancer and since arrived in this country he had his own following; well he was a brilliant dancer and Wilf with his reputation of public speaking that had preceded him these two guys had their own fan club. At first though Wilf couldn't dance; well he couldn't dance very well; but he's got the beat so it didn't take him long to be a decent dance. Of course Wilf usually got up to more than dancing; but whatever else he got up to her indoors would never know; and his loyal brother-in-law would always cover for him, honour among thieves you might say. By now Wilf and Ben are a duo by themselves; where ever there's one the other is not far away.

But with all that merriment Wilf was always wanted to do something constructive; things like business; but funds were lacking. However; not only funds were lacking but brains too. He hadn't got the brain for business, this man could be earning money from officiating at these weddings; and most Saturday's he would be the Master of ceremony at some weddings; and it's all for free. He didn't realise he could and should be charging a fee; to him he just loved to be the showman. He was turning his hand to other things though; but the outcome was never good, the management skill was never his forte. Now Wilf would like to have children but his wife can't conceive, however she was relaxed about the idea even though Wilf was restless about it, by now his best friend Raymond's son is getting to be a big lad, oh how would he love to have a child like that of his own. But as the years rolled by he was to do something unexpected, something that would cause unrest in the whole family.

43: Ben Gets Married

Wilf was over the moon when Ben decided to get marry, as far as he's concern this will be a special occasion, the cost of this wedding will be easy on Ben's pocket, not that things are cheaper, no; but because of the support of the family, he won't have to push too deep into his or her own pocket. When Ben introduced his future bride to the family some didn't approved, well the attitude as in many of families; no women are good enough for their brothers, some would show their impediment by snubbing that person; or even would tell her openly they are not good enough for their family, and in Ben's case his wife to be, Beatrice has encountered her fair share of his family ignorance. But that didn't affect their relationship; with the support of dear sister Ammi and Wilf his sidekick their plan to get married is moving nicely ahead. Preparations were all in place, and with such big family and most eager to help; even the ones who didn't approve; and bringing it all together was a doddle. By now immigrants could afford to buy cars and there were plenty of them, well! By now some of these immigrants renounced their country too and became British citizens; even though they're entitled to dual citizenship. Some rather cut their ties with the country of their birth, why? Only they know. It was a beautiful summer's day with not a cloud in the sky; one could see for miles and miles, a big day for the family and a great day to get married. Well Sir! A couple of things to know about the people from that country is; they love to dress up and they love to celebrate, and with Ben's wedding they couldn't wait to show off their styles and let their hair down. Of course that will come later which they're all looking forward to; even more than the wedding itself. At the Church in Marsden everything is ready for them, the master of ceremony will be Wilf himself; but he's also the organ player, he'll be smiling all over his face when playing here comes the bride. Pastor Moore will do the honour by conduction the ceremony; he had done this so many times before,

On this joyous occasion the line of cars was lengthy, in Marsden it took a couple of policemen to direct the traffic, probably they themselves never seen anything like it before. Of course for some of the guests it's a chance to show off their car too, well imagine these people never owned a vehicle before; a bicycle yes; but never a car; something they wanted all their lives but couldn't afford it. Owning one means the world to them; so why not show it off. The guest list was long; But it wasn't confined to the black immigrants only, no; there were many whites too; be it may that they were all women; and of course many of them were wives too; yes; wives of black immigrants. The ceremony went well as expected, Wilf made this day a special occasion to show off his public speaking ability; not that he needed to but hey; he's going do it anyway. But there was one thing the people who knew the families well would notice, none of Wilf's blood family was there; just as before when he got married they choose to stay away. However if it affected Wilf in any way he's not showing it, in fact he publicly announced that his wife's family is the only one he's got, and true to his words; over the coming years he never bothered about his own or showed any sign that he wanted to. Except for his younger sister who seems to hold a special affection for him; but nevertheless disliked his wife. Ben's bride was a beautiful woman, well a natural beautiful black woman; and with long flowing jet black hair there's a trait of Indian features. she was of normal stature with a heavenly smile; but on this her wedding day she was looking especially beautiful. The tributes from home were readied by Ammi, she's not a speaker at all but the tribute was from her father and it's about Ben; she isn't going to let anyone read it. The proceeding ended with the expected knees up in the big hall behind a pub this went on until one o'clock in the morning; the allotted time for any such rave-up.

With everyone going home happily some had to be carried; suffering from mostly the effect of white rum; well there's an awful of the stuff here in England too; mostly by coming through custom. The happy couple returned to their honeymoon suite; their double bedroom; but they wouldn't be alone for long, no; Wilf, Ammi and other members of the immediate family were there to congratulate and gossip about the wedding, there's more than a good chance this lot won't be at work tomorrow. There's another occasion that will take place there and then; one that every bride look forward to; the opening of the present, but as there's no present list they would expect all different kinds of gifts, from blanket to china and other popular stuff; and some of these gifts would be given to members of the family. It was well after midnight on Sunday when the party breaks up, some won't be going to work in the morning. For the newlyweds; well! They're taking Monday off; there's plenty to do in their one bedroom. But a few months later there was to be more good news; not long after Ben and Beatrice got married it was revealed that she was pregnant. Not that they didn't expect it to happen; but not so soon.

However they were celebrating even before the child was born. Well he will be the first of the Thomas's true line; and Sister Ammi seems more anxious for the birth than the parent. She's not waiting for Ben to write home to tell old man Thomas; no; she's ding the writing. Of course! As for as Ben is concern his dear Sister can do no wrong. Oh how happy old man Thomas will be; in his reply to Ammi he quoted; there's a place prepared for a picture of my grandson when it's born; well they knew it's a boy; the Doctor said so. However even though Ben is now a married man with his wife expected; he was still living a carefree life; he and buddy Brother-in-law for them it's business as usual; Saturday night was always dance night. One Monday the family had a fright; well! Beatrice was still working; seven months pregnant and she's still working; well there's nothing strange or unusual about that; but probably she should stop working by now on account of she carrying a very huge belly. Well the worst has happened, it's winter and a bad one; the snow was so deep it was up to the knee; everyone is hoping for rain; but the forecast suggested there's no rain expected. Well the snow lingered for over two hold week and frozen solid; and this makes walking treacherous. Going to work one morning Ben hold Beatrice's hands as she was finding it difficult to walk; but the unexpected happened. She slid on the icy road and even though Ben held her hands her entire body was lifted off the road and she fell flat on her back. She was in agony; now neither of them could go to work that morning; they returned home. Nut no one of experience was home to deals with a pregnant woman who's in pain. When Wilf and Ammi were home from work and hear what had happened they were alarm; they're thinking she might lose the baby. Well they did what is the right thing; they took her to the hospital; the driving was treacherous as the walking but they get her there. After the Doctor's diagnosis he told then it was a close shave; but the baby is ok.

But that didn't make it any easier for Ammi; she shed little tears; however Beatrice wouldn't be returning to work; no; not until after baby was born. Beatrice gave birth a few weeks early to a healthy baby boy and for the family, joy was complete. Ammi was over the moon to say the least; anyone would have thought she was the one who'd given birth; but such is how she feels about her Brother, Ben. If this child is spoilt it won't be because of the mother comment a church sister; it will be because of Sister Drake. But she and Beatrice had a special bond too; when some of the family didn't welcome her with open arms; both Ammi and Wilf stood Full Square behind her. As a sister-in-law she would help her in every way she could, and the fact that she can't have children of her own; helping cared for her nephew might have given her some fulfilment. When the child was to be named it had become a mystery, well! There were many of names given; but only four people knew what this baby boy was going to be named. These four people kept it a secret; the name was sent in a letter all the way from Jamila, his grandfather had chosen a name and it won't be revealed until the day of the christening. On Sunday in a packed church the family gathered, young Thomas will be christened today, Families are anxiously waiting to hear what name this little fellow is been given. Pastor Moore took him in his hands and sprinkled the water over his head; then repeated the secret words; I blessed baby Harold Devlin Thomas in the name of the father, the son and the holy spirit, at which time those who were interested to know his name; now they know. As time goes by young Harold was growing up a fine young man; being the firstborn in the family he was paid a lot of attention; but none more than his Aunty Ammi, she would buy him things and care for him in every way; of course with the full approval of his mother. The family knew she would like to adopt young Harold; but she would ask, well how could she tell a mother she would like to adopt her firstborn, no; not Ammi; a woman of principle and of Godly compassion; she's never going to do that. But as the year's rolls by the family had increased, other members were having babies too; some out of wedlock and most were having mix race children. But a scandal was to rock the family; a scandal that would concern Wilf; and of which Ben knew all too well about; a scandal that if it was to end up in court he could be named as an accomplice.

44: Wilf's Indiscretion

In one hot summer of sixties, a woman going by the name of Doreen turns up at the doorstep of Ammi with a child, at first she thought it was someone asking for charity; as it not unusual for that to happen. This Doreen a black woman from the Caribbean but from another Island, a brazen woman who lacks principle in every shape or form. Mrs. Drake she asked, there was no hesitance in Ammi's reply, yes! I am Mrs. Drake she said waiting for the next question. But there was none, well she noticed there was a baby in the basket; and anticipates she was going to begs her for money, but no! She put the basket down on the doorstep. This is Wilf's child; you can have him; I don't want him she said. Well she thought she wasn't hearing well; she asked, what did you say? I'm giving you your husband baby Mom; I can't care for him, needless to say Ammi was dumbstruck. But while she stood there in awe; this Doreen put the only thing she had in hands in the basket; the baby bottle; and then calmly walked away. Well Ammi didn't know to say or do; of course she would like a child of her own; but she certainly didn't want it this way. Stand looking at the woman walked away leaving her child Ammi didn't know what to do or say; well she's not the barbarous bitchy type of a person who would chase after this woman and probably put up a fight, no; she's the God-fearing Christian who would pray rather than quarrel. But thinking of what this woman said; true or not she was shaking with anger; he must have had some involvement with her in some ways. At that moment she couldn't think straight; the rage in her is clouding her mind, for a moment there she lost all thought of decency; should I leave the baby there and call the police she asked herself. But the baby was crying and been Saturday quite a few people passing by and noticing the basket with the baby. Should take the child in to feed it; and then what? Well! She thought she heard an inner voice telling her; after feeding the child should kneel and pray. She did what the inner voice told her to do; she kneels and pray; at the same time the baby ceased crying, she got up from her knees and took the baby out from the basket held it up for a good look; well she wants to see if there's any resemblance; and there was.

looking at the child there was no doubt who was the father of this child, it's like looking at a younger version of her husband, she must talk to someone; she's just arise from her knees but she's cherishing bad thought, well Beatrice was there but was oblivious to anything happening. Bee; As she calls her; could you come here a while? she promptly opened her door and went. What wrong Miss Ammi she asked; take a look in that basket she said with trembling voice, the child was making baby sounds; the kind of sound babies make whenever they're comfortable. A baby said Beatrice as she bent down and look in the basket, who does it belong to mom she asked, then suddenly she paused, and she wasn't saying anything for a while; she couldn't for a while, she recognised the features on the child; but she's not going to say. What do you think Ammi asked, well! She still not going to say; instead she asks; where did it come from Miss Ammi? A woman leaves it here not so long ago. But who is it belongs to she asked apprehensively, well Bea; can't you see she asked furiously. Up till then neither woman dear to mentioned or even suggested who this child belong to, but how could they? And even though the woman said the child was for her husband; and looking at the child she doesn't need blood test to know who is the father of this child. Recognised the fact but dear to said it Beatrice asked, so what are you going to do Miss Ammi; a question asked with intent, but there's no answer to that question as of now; there're too many ill thoughts going around in her head. She's fuming with rage but tries not to show it, the kind of rage she had never experienced before, as a Christian she prides herself on calmness and control thought, but this situation is going to test her resolve and her Christian faith to the very limit. She then got a thought, when the Devil enters into your life and tries to ruin it; it's only one thing to do; go and ask the Lord for help. Well she has already prayed; but she thought she'd do well to pray again. Bea! Keep an eye on the child for me; I'll be in my room; and off she went. There she prays; asking the good Lord for guidance in this her time of tribulation; and to forgive her for the bad thought she had in mind. Shortly after Ben arrives; all bright eyed and bushy tailed; hollo Bea he said gleefully as he moves forward to hugs her, she shuns him, get away from me she said angrily. Well! Ben hasn't done nothing wrong; well nothing he knows of; but she knows if this child belongs to Wilf; and it's evidently clear it is; then he knew about it. What's wrong dear he asked still trying to embrace her, she gives him one of those enviously look; get away from me she said looking at him from head to toes. Now she herself is fuming with anger, probable thinking the same thing could happen in their relationship too. Where is Mr. Drake she asked, I have no idea dear he replies, don't you dear me; you snake she said with such venom. What is it? what have I done he asked innocently, what have you done? What have you done she repeated viciously. Take a look in the basket she said; the child was now asleep, what am I looking for he asked as he bent down to look in the basket, then suddenly he spotted the child.

With eyes pulping he stood back up to attention; he looks as though he has just seen a ghost, looking subdued and probably can't think of anything to say; he decided on the only route of action, I'm just popping into the toilet he said as he tries to move away. Don't you move you rat, what are you going to tell your Sister? She's not only going to kill Mr. Drake; she'll probable to kill you too. Ben! How could you? she asked in a calm and tender voice; almost as though she was crying. What she was asking her husband is how he could knowingly let that happened and not informed his Sister. But she'll probably never learn or understand the adage; honour among thieves. Ben knew of his Brother-in-law's indiscretion; but he was never going to grass on him, but he did discuss it with him; as to what he's going to do when his Sister finds out? As she bound to. But one thing he didn't expect is to come home and find the baby there. Pointing to the room; your sister is in there she said; you better think of something to tell her, Ben smile ruefully, me? It's not my child; she took off one of her slippers and hurled it at, laugh? You dear to laugh; I hate you men, she said with venomous anger, who's laughing? I'm not laughing he responds quickly. While sitting on the stairs Ammi emerges from the room, she's been praying for some time, she walks by Ben without saying a single word. Picking up the basket with the baby she proceeded back into the room accompanied by Bea, they closed the door leaving Ben still sitting on the stairs. He's in trouble; big trouble; at this moment he's a very confused man; his Sister not speaking to him and his wife probable stop speaking to him too; now what am I to do he thought; the fireworks that are imminent will most certainly involve him too. Not knowing what to do he got up from the stairs and went through the door, he'll wander around aimlessly probably thinking of what to say to his Sister. It's getting late; he gathers his thought and returns home; except when he tries to enter he couldn't; the night latch was on, he was locked out; he tries ringing the bell; but to no avail. Well he didn't try to do anything else; now he knows the score; he's been locked out and when Wilf comes; if he comes; he'll certainly be locked out too. However he knows it won't be for long; probably just for the night till they calm down. But there're questions to be answered; and they're not going to get answered if they're locked out permanently. Ben went and spent the night by his cousin James, why are you staying here Ben he asked; You must have done something wrong asked Beverly; James's wife. I haven't done anything he said, she just got the hump and chucks me out. Without looking at him she gave out one of that funny sound; likely story she said; and leaves it at that.

Sunday morning a bright and sunny day; but for him it might as well be bleak, should I make you breakfast, asks Beverly; no thanks Bev he said; I'm going home now. Are you sure you have a home there anymore She jokes not knowing the seriousness of the situation. knowing the situation at home he comments; you know what Bev; you might have to put me up again tonight; get away with you she said, go on home to your wife, and off he went. It's a short walk home; this time the night lack was off, he enters expected to find Wilf there; but no; it appears he didn't come home last night, or he might have done; but wouldn't be able to enter. Come in here Ben said Ammi; even though he knew this meeting with his Sister was going to be a rough encounter; nevertheless he was somewhat pleased. He would rather her do to him whatever she will and get over this dreadful situation. But Ben is got his head in the cloud; this situation hasn't even started yet; until Will turns up and faces the music this household never going to be at peace again. He enters into the room kind of cowardly, closed the door Ben she said, there was a short hush before Ammi speak. Calmly speaking in a low voice she asked; did you know about Wilf's baby? He paused for thought; probably searching for an answer. Well he's not in a habit to lie to his Sister and he feels he shouldn't start now. Yes Sis; as he calls her, but let me explain, she wasn't surprised; she knows how close they are; it would be impossible for him not knowing. Well he explained the best he could; mostly to clear his own name, I did warn him Sis; I told him from the woman was pregnant to come clean and tell you; and you think that would make it any better Ben she asked. No Sis but…, but what she interrupts angrily; losing her cool for a while, but remarkable Ben set out to defend Wilf. You should go easy on Wilf Sis; it's wasn't his fault; she wouldn't leave him alone, he had a bit too much to drink one night and she took advantage of him. Ammi didn't respond to Ben's excuse, no; she went and calls Beatrice. Come with me I want you to hear this she said, and they walk back to the room. The baby was crying, Ammi picks him up and tries to hush him, but Beatrice noticed how caring and tenderly she was with the child she begins to have a thought; a thought that the expected crisis might not happen. Now she'd completely forgotten as to why she brings Beatrice in the room; the baby has taken up all her attention. Seeing what was happening Beatrice didn't bother to remind her that she was brought in here for a reason. Well! Up till now if there's going to be a crisis in the family only four people knew of it, for now it's been restricted to just the one household; however the culprit hasn't been seen for nearly two days. Well! He didn't come home last night; he must have known about this woman delivered his son to his wife; and not wanting to face the music he stays away. But this Wilf is not a brave man; in fact; with all his bravadoes in public speaking he's really a coward, his wife rules the roost in whatever the situation; the man is a pussy cat really; or probable one could say he's an obedient husband. It could be the situation that he finds himself in was a deliberate act regardless of what his brother-in-law said. The man is desperate for a child; one that his wife is incapable of giving him, and even though he knew people are going to think the very worse of him; they are going to think of him as this despicable and audacious man; he also knows most will be hating him. However he takes a chance hoping that when the wife finishes abusing him in whatever way; they'll still remain a married couple. It's nearly two days since the woman leaving the baby on the doorstep; and still Wilf hadn't returned home, of course the reason for his absence was clear. However Ben knew of his whereabouts, he's not at the woman's with whom he had this baby, no; the baby was a one night stand; and as Ben said he was drunk. He's at his good friend Raymond, he'll harbour him; but being a man of principle and the considered guardian of his old friend Thomas's daughter; he'll be hoping the situation resolves quickly. He no doubt will be castigating Wilf; but urging him to go home and face the music.

Because of the delivery of the little infant, Ammi couldn't go to work, and ironically she wasn't showing too much reluctance to care for this child. Well! On this day Will chose not to go to work either; his mind must be in a desperate place right now. He decided to go home with the intention that he'll be alone with his wife; if she's going to beat him up; no one will see. He approach his front door but didn't enter; he didn't even try the door; instead he rang the bell. Ammi didn't rush to open; she pulled the curtain to see who it was, seeing it was her husband she didn't rush to the door, she took her time carrying the baby. She didn't look at him, neither did she speak to him, she made her way to the sitting room with him following behind nervously. Well! He didn't sit; no; he stands by the door looking all guilty waiting for her to blast him. Well! This man who knows of his guilt; knows he deserves some kind of punishment and is waiting for it. There was a long period of hush; it appears as though she's letting him stew before she attacks him; or will she? But the silence was becoming unbearable; he stood there with tears running down his cheeks; like a little child who knows he's done something wrong and waiting to be told off. Suddenly there was a break in the silence, why are you standing there she asked calmly, you live here; why don't you sit? He sat feeling most uncomfortable. How is it she's been so calm after all that's happened; he questions his inner thought? Then she asked; why you don't pick up your child; you should get to know him she said calmly. He didn't know what to do; he doesn't think he should hold the child; it might wrongfully show his delight in the situation, he was a man on tenterhooks; not knowing whether to sink or swim. He's expected to have his clothes thrown out and given his marching orders; instead she's treating him as though she appreciates what he had done. Is she planning something detrimental for him but biding her time? He knew he deserved to be castigated, ridiculed or even had chairs thrown at him; but the calmness is unbearable. With apprehension he picked the child up; visible shaking he was; she then confronts him; looking at him with the kind of looks he never witnessed at any time of their many years of marriage; suddenly there was vengeance in her eyes. Now you can take it back to his mother and you should stay there with her, you have given up the right to live here anymore. Knowing that he's not in a position to say anything; anything at in his defence, and as the obedient husband he usually is; he walked out the door towards his car carrying the child. Don't forget the basket she said standing at the front door, the back to take the basket was like walking towards a furnace, not only was it humiliating but darn right shameful also. By all account this marriage is now over he tells himself, and he has no intention of shacking up with this woman, what happened that produced this child was a one night of madness that will never happen again.

So where does he go from here?. He could see his own future disappearing right before his eyes; and what does he says to the family when they get wind of it; how can he look them in the eyes? The questions were coming thick and fast. She didn't slam the door behind her, no; she calmly closed it and walked back to the living room, probable she's now planning the destruction of her husband. Aware that Wilf was there and is now gone; Beatrice knocks on the door, Well she and Ben didn't go o work either; he certainly wasn't going to leave his Sister alone in her time of distress; and so is Beatrice; but they kept a low profile. Miss Ammi are you alright she asked, come in Bea she responded. She was tiding up places that don't need tiding up. What are you going to do Mom she asked respectfully, I want you to help me pack some things she said calmly, he's gone back to his baby's mother; he'll be needing his clothes. Beatrice looked at her with her mouth wide open, she was aghast at what she said, are you sure Mom? Yes! I sent him back with the baby. But Miss Ammi don't you think you should talk to him first Mom and let him tell you how it happened? There's nothing to ask Bea; he went out and have a child with a woman because I couldn't give him one, it's no coincident; it was a deliberate act. How could it forgive him; I couldn't look him in the eyes, no Bea; we're finish, he got the son he wanted and I hope he'll be unhappy for the rest of his life. For someone else Bea wouldn't be surprised to hear such fury, most women would probably kill him; and he would probably deserve it; but not Miss Ammi. Well! She was always the calm one; the one that gives advice; but now to see her in calm and calculating anger; it's a side of her no one ever seen before. Bea is mighty concerned, but what kind of advice could she give her; and if she even think of something the rage she's in at present she probable turn her out of the room. But how could she stood by and do nothing, her Sister Maggie who now has a boyfriend is away with him over the weekend, she probably wouldn't know what to say to her either. She continues to pack his things, Miss Ammi! Remember you're a Christian she said; Please Mom; don't do anything foolish; give him a chance to explain. She didn't respond to that suggestion; instead she asked; where's Ben, he's in the room Mom, why isn't he gone to work she asked, Bea didn't have any answers. But ever since the baby secret been out Ben kept low; keeping out of his Sister's way, he's feeling rather ashamed and disgusted with himself. He now realised he shouldn't allow his Sister to find out about the baby this way; he thinks he should let her be aware of the situation. Do you want to talk with him Mom she asked, yes; would you get him for me Bea? She returns with him in his pyjama wearing his housecoat.

Do you want to talk to me Sis he asked humbly, sit down Ben she said calmly, you haven't done anything; stop looking guilty, or did you? Honestly Sis! As I told you before; he had some rum punch; we all did; Wilf must have had one too many and got drunk. He went upstairs to sleep it off and I believed that's where she took advantage of him, that's all I know Sis; honestly. However she hadn't been seen around the dance scene for a while; until a couple a months later she turns up pregnant and told Wilf that the baby was his and…she interrupt, and he gladly accepted. He's so desperate for a child that he would accept it whether it's his or not she said furiously. However it doesn't need a blood test to say who the child belongs to, the woman didn't lied she said; the world can see it's his child, and Ben; yes Sis; I don't blame you. I blame him; he's a grown man; he should be able to take care of himself, so you can stop tiptoeing about the house. Is she conveniently forgotten that dear Brother Ben is a grown man too? Only that he's younger. I'm so very sorry Sis; I wish it didn't happen, can I get you anything Miss Ammi; a cup of tea; Bea asked sympathetically, oh no thank you Bea; I'll be going upstairs soon she said. Well the only other person outside of this household who knew of the situation is Raymond; and that's where Wilf is with his baby, he'll (Raymond) be feeling rather concerned about these two people, Wilf is his dear friend; and Ammi! Even though is in her forties he still feels concern for her, he will do his uttermost best and try to resolve this situation, he feels it's his obligation to try. But the secret was bound to leak, this sort of situation couldn't be kept under wraps for long; it's now out in the public domain. Ammi resume working; but she was going to work as though nothing untoward happened, Thursday evening straight after work Daphne makes her way to see her cousin; they discussed the situation but what they have decided only they knew. That night it was quite late when Raymond came to visit her; like some members of the family he's anxious to see if the situation can resolve and these two get back together again. But others aren't too keen, in their eyes he's done the unthinkable and there's shouldn't be any way back for him. But there were mediators too; many of them; especially amongst the Christians who didn't believe in divorce; but they believe in suffering and forgiveness, if you been slapped once; turn the other cheek, and with that belief they would communicate with Sister Ammi and reminded her of what the good book said; forgive and forget; among other quotes, they would pray with her and try to talk her into reuniting with her husband. Others even though they go to Church every Sunday they didn't believe the same thing; they want vengeance; and they're the ones who advocate that Brother Drake as he usually referred to even though he wasn't baptised, to be cast out of the church.

It was getting close to Easter and everyone was getting prepared for the celebration, It was a beautiful early spring day, the tulips were popping out everywhere, this day Mr. Dickenson and his wife Daphne went to see Ammi; they want to have a serious talk with her, they cannot stand idly by and see these two good people separate because of one mistake; be it may a big on. Well! They talked and they talked; while Beatrice provided dinner as she often did in more peaceful times, dinner was on a tray and eaten in the living room. But they exhausted the conversation and there's nothing more to talk about; all they can do now is to wait to see if their intervention will bear fruit. However there's the obvious tension between them, so to get them talking won't be so easy. Ammi is grieving deeply; she can't believe her marriage have come to this, for better or for worst that was the pledge they gave to each other, they seen better times; now they're in the worst of time. Could she or should she make concessions and bite her pride and stick with him through this worst of time? Questions only she can answer and soon. Well as for Wilf? He's suffering; he's suffering badly; well! He loves his wife dearly and he wishes he could turn the clock back, now he's like an outcast, members of the Church and others turn away from him, well! To them he's done the unthinkable and they'll never forgive him. But there're those who he could depend on too; those who would like to see them back together again. He's still living at Raymond's with the child; but had to leave him with carer during the day for him to go to work, and in the evening Daphne would help out by picking the child up. He's making the best of a bad situation; and thankfully he's got a couple of loyal friends, but there are surprise lies ahead. By now Wilf stops going to Church; even though a few would like him back the majority wouldn't. Nevertheless on a bright sunny day one Sunday evening he turns up at church, To some it was a surprise; they didn't think he would show his face there again. But he's there for a reason and his reason is deception; he believes if he gets converted and confessed his sins that might help to get his wife back; well the man is trying something; there's an old saying; nothing can beat a try; only a failure. Well! He confessed his sins to God and the Pastor; and after a month or so he's considering baptism. By now he and his wife were passing amorous glances at each other's, probable his confession has work wonders. But there're those who were sceptical about his action, they didn't believe it was a true confession, no; in fact they believed it was only a ploy to get back with his wife, and they could be right. On the morning of a bright June's day Ammi turns up at Mr. Dickenson's home, well it would be too early for a visitor to call as they were still in bed; but not this one; she at one time holding a key to the front door.

Ironically it was Wilf who answered the door, she steps passes him as though he wasn't there; she went upstairs and taps on her cousin's bedroom door, who is it a voice asked, it's me she said, well she didn't have to say her name Daphne knew her voice, and she promptly opens the door. Raymond was still in bed but aware of her enters the room, bur Daphne was more than a little curious to see her there this early. What's wrong she asked holding her hands, is anything wrong she repeated, by then Raymond got out of bed and puts on his robe, quickly he presented her with an upright chair, come on he said; sits here, the tears begin to run down her cheeks. However they know why she was there; and the fact that she's there under the same roof as Wilf could be a good omen. But

Daphne has done something drastic; maybe it's on impulse, ever since he opened the door for her; Wilf was left standing at the bottom of the stairs, he's obviously hoping at some stage of she been there she'll say something to him. Well his waiting could be at an end, Daphne open the door and call out loud; Wilf! Come up here now and talk to your wife she said with some authority. Her action might even take Raymond by surprised, but Wilf was there in a flash, he walks in and; well he in peaceful times he's got the most mischievous smile. She looked at him; he looked at her and they both smiled but said nothing. But the doorbell rings again, who the devil is that question Daphne, I'll go see, it was Hillary, what do you want here so early she asked, but Hillary being Hillary she just walks past her. Where's everybody she asked in her usual brash manner, where do you think Daphne asked sarcastically, in their bed; you know what time t is? Hillary mumbles something, by then Ammi heard her voice and called; I'm up here hilly. What she is doing here she grumbled as she was climbing the stairs with Daphne behind her. Well! The fireworks were about to start, what brings you here this time of the morning asked Raymond, but she got no time for that question, she went and greets Wilf. Standing in front of him she's a tod taller, looking directly at him she asked, have you two make it up yet, no one answered; but they were more than glad the question was asked. She mumbled something, what are you saying Hilly asked Daphne, I'll tell you what I'm saying, and these two idiots are going to let a little thing like having a baby with another woman ruin their lives. looking at Ammi she comment, how long since you're married, no; don't bother to tell me, you remember I told you that you neither you nor madam there haven't any experience about men, well even though you're married you still haven't got any experience about men she said in her usual brash and Hillary like manner. So the man made mistake; no; maybe it's not a mistake; or may the woman forced herself on him; look at him she said with her usual impudence; he's a red-blooded man, you'll never know as you were always the good one. Daphne glared at her as to say; what about me, but you'll be surprised what we women can do to get a man in bed; at times the poor man got no chance of getting away.

I thank you Hillary for the lesson in infidelity; but how is it going to help these two asked Raymond, but he knew what Hillary was trying to do; but for a few minutes there she's just playing Devil's advocate.

But Hillary is not waiting for their input; she's directly to the point, take your husband and... she paused, take the child and grow him as though you give birth to him, you always want a child; now you get one; even though it wasn't the way you want to get it. You remember one of our favourite bible quote she asked looking her, no! What that asked Ammi calmly, the Lord moves in mysterious ways, you shouldn't forget; you're the Christian here; or are you? Ammi looks at her but says nothing. Until now Wilf hadn't said a single word, well! He would like to say something but he doesn't know where to start or probably afraid of what she might say. But suddenly Ammi speaks, where's the baby she asked, probable the sweetest few words Wilf ever hear in his entire life, with trembling voice he spoke; he's downstairs still asleep he said, well go and see to him she said; he shouldn't be sleeping this long. Then her mood changes, no; let me go she said; and off she went hastily. Well she didn't return immediately; maybe she has decided to accept the child and is trying to bond with him. Well! Hillary's outlandish way of giving advice must have gotten to her; she calls; Wilf would you come down here please, and he was down in a jiffy; Hillary jokes; that's the fastest she's ever seen a man move. They closed the room door and they were in there for some time, well a long time, the rest of the party make sure they're not disturbed, they have a lot of talking to do. Later that evening they emerged with baby and whatever else they need, they said goodbye to the others and headed to the car. But before the car move off Ammi went back inside; she embraced her two cousins, she then turns to Mr. Dickenson, thank you Sir; she always give him full respect, we'll try, she shook his hands and leave. From that moment on Wilf has been an avid follower of the religion, as time heals their wounds he was asked to play the organ again, he's back in the fold where he thinks he belongs, even though not everyone welcomes him with open arms. But once again sometime later her faith was tested.

45: Ammi Brings Maggie Home

Throughout the discord in her marriage Ammi she never at any time reveal it to her father and the others were forbidden to so either, he's the last person she wanted to know; he's an old man now and she would want him to worry unduly. Things are not quite back to normality as yet, but Ammi is very displeased with Sister Maggie, well! these days she hardly ever around, nevertheless she knew about what was happing in her marriage; she knew what she was going through, but her support was never there. One Sunday evening Ammi decided to go visit her; taking little Harold who is nearly a year and a half old with her, Hillary decided to come too. Well Maggie moved out some two years ago to live on her own; but mostly because she wants her fellow to come and go as she please, as a Christian principle sister Ammi wouldn't allow that carry on while she is living under their roof; she couldn't stand the restriction so she moved away. They turned up at her address and rang the bell; but no one came; they rang again and this time a man came to the door, a black man; who do you want he asked in a gruff voice, I want to see Maggie said Ammi with the baby in her hands; she took him out of his pram. What's your name he asked, never mind her name; she's her Sister said Hillary abruptly, well Hillary is not one to stand on ceremony; where's she; she asked. Wait there he said, I'll see if she's up, while he's gone Hillary comment, feisty ugly black man, and what would Maggie be doing in bed this time of the day she comment to Ammi, but Ammi is thinking about the way Hillary spoke to the man. He returned, in the broad Jamila broken English; she said to come; it's that room there, pointing in the direction of the back. Hillary looked as though she wanted to spit at him, I hate these ugly black men she said screwing up her face as though she smelled something nasty. Ammi smile at her; Hilly! Do you like anyone at all? Tell me which of God's creatures you really like she asked sincerely. But there was no time for an answer; they were making their way toward the door the man shown them. Hillary knock on the door and a faint voice said; come in; she pushed the door; but there was a high smell; she pulled back and said something to Ammi; she was concern about the baby inhaling such foul smell. Ammi put the baby in the pram and leave him in the hallway; then they went in leaving the door wide open; so as to make sure they can see the baby. Maggie was wrapped up under the sheet and was burning up with fever.

Looking around it was hard to believe she's living in a filthy place like this, she moved away from a nice clean house to live in this; Ammi couldn't understand why. Hillary pulled the sheet off her; Maggie you're burning up; how long you're like this? But she didn't respond. Well! Ammi didn't want to know anything; whether it's why, how, when or where, in a hurry she gets her suitcase and pack her few things in it; they want to get her away quickly from this squat. While Hillary was helping her to get some clothes on; there wasn't much to say as the stench of the place was so strong. Now they're ready but how are they going to get her to her Sister's place, well! They removed her from the room and seated her on her suitcase in the passage; then Hillary went to the phone box to call Raymond, she should call Wilf but Raymond was much closer. Not long before she returns to the house Raymond arrives, he's as concerned as them about another of John Thomas's daughters. There was no time to explain; they loaded up and went; straight to Ammi's place some four miles away. Hillary was furious with her for leaving her Sister's home to live in such dump. But Ammi was so much more sympathetic toward her sister; she now realised why she wasn't there to support her in her time of need. She won't be mad with, no; if it's mean taking time off work to care for her Sister; then so be it. Well Ammi being Ammi she took the week off work to care for her Sister; but Wilf was behaving rather oddly; maybe he's not approved of his Sister-in-law moves back in. However in recent days he's been acting rather funny. Well! Maggie was surprised to see her sister with a baby; but there's nothing else to do but tell her the whole story. Now hearing what her Sister tells her and what she had gone through; she broke down in tears; Sis I'm so sorry not to be here to help; she was very apologetic. Of course big Sister told her not to worry; its water under the bridge; but warns her that if she ever writes home she must never make mention of this matter. Well Maggie got better but she's got no job to go to; she lost her job because of her absentee; now she's out looking for a job. However it didn't take her long to get one. But now living with the family once again; big Sister will set her down and talk to her about her behaviour; she'll tell her she can't return to the way she usually live; and if she wants to live there thing must change. Well there's an old saying that a leopard can never change its spots; it could be it depends on how one looks at the leopard; well this one for certain does change her spots. Without too much encouragement from her Sister, Maggie began to follow to the Church; well that's not unusual for her; she was brought up in the Church. Now Ammi was feeling her old self again; her little Sister is back at church like when they were home. But better things lie ahead; Maggie has put her bad past behind her and got baptised; of course she's got the full support of her Sister. But better was to come for newly baptised Maggie; yes; she has found a man in the Church; a man that everyone says is a true Christian. It was a short romance; they married a few months later to the joy of the whole family. Everything within the family appears to be going well; apart from Wilf; however once again things were to be turned upside down; the worst news was to come.

46: John Thomas Dies

By now there're first and second generations of young black Britons, the population of Caribbean's has spread far and wide, there's an ever increasing population of mixed-race ethnics mostly of Caribbean descent. The days of the Teddy Boys is well and truly gone, one is most likely to meet a black man on the street any time of the night. People are reasonably comfortable; more and more Caribbean families are sending for their families and love ones; people are well settled here; some doesn't consider themselves immigrants anymore, no; they get themselves British citizenship and hold a British passport, they not exactly turning their backs on their country of birth, no; but they have no intention of living there again. Like the Thomas's many of the people in this huge family have married and produced children. Well! Let say everyone was doing their bit to increase the population of the country. Some families were living in different parts of the country, but that didn't make any difference to the amount of time the family spent together, come the weekend it was always a pleasure; especially for the children for families to loaded up and go visit their cousins; it's a good time for the family; except for Wilf. But bad news was lurking around the corner; news that would throw the whole family into mourning. On a wet Wednesday evening on the return from work the news was delivered; it was about eight-thirty; the doorbell rings; the tenant in the front room answered the door; but the caller wasn't for her; it was for Mrs. Drake. The tenant knocked at Ammi's door to tell there's a man at the door who wants to speak with her. If Wilf was home she would probably have asked him to attend; but these days he's hardly ever home. Not expecting anyone she slowly make her way to the door; she could see a figure standing at the door; the tenant leaves the door open which she shouldn't. She didn't know who this man was; she'd never seen him before; what the devil does he want with me she asked herself. As she approaches the man he asked; Mrs. Drake? Yes she said; I'm Mrs. Drake. The man presented her a paper to sign; would you sign here Mrs. Drake he said giving her a Biro. But before she signs she asks; what I'm I signing for? It's a telegram Mrs. Drake; but she couldn't sign; she fell to her knees calling for Maggie; Dad is dead Dad is dead she kept repeating. Maggie rushed to the door to find her Sister crying sitting in the passage and the man trying to comfort her. What have you done to my Sister asked

Maggie; at this point the poor man seems to be getting nervous. I haven't done anything he said; I only give her the paper to sign; what is it asked Maggie; it's a telegram said the man. But Maggie couldn't have heard Ammi said their father is dead; otherwise she wouldn't ask the man what he has done to her Sister. What's wrong she asked trying to embrace her; Dad is dead she kept repeating; but how do you know Sis? The telegram; it's the telegram she said. With the man still standing there Maggie signs the paper and took the telegram; she's in a hurry to read it; and exactly as Ammi thought; their father is dead. Now Maggie begins to cry too; but the man didn't walk away, no; seeing the two women crying he asked what the matter; well Ammi couldn't tell him but Maggie thank him for asking and tell him that their father is dead; the nice man sympathised with them but he has to leave.

When the news circulates among the family they were shaken to the core. Well he wasn't ill as far as the children are concerned, according to Florence the adapted member of family and the one who look in on him since the death of his wife in her letter she talks about him returned from his lifelong friend Leroy and complained for his stomach, it was about eight o'clock in the evening so he went and lay down in the spare room, as she didn't want to disturb him she went home. Early the next morning she returned to found him dead. However she and others suspect foul play; but it's never going to be proven. The family here are in distress; this is news they never expected; well John Thomas was a very strong man; as children they thought he was indestructible; and even though they're now adults it still knocked the stuffing's out of them. Now the rush is on to get home; and even though there's nothing they can do for him now; they will all book emergency flights to get there in a hurry. Well at this moment of bereavement Ammi is inconsolable, this woman now in her early seventies has taken it badly, she's the oldest of the family here but as the others know she was her father's favourite, she adores him. But it was also noticeable that Wilf never shown the kind of interest as a son-in-law should when the news arrived, well their relationship has once again taken a turn for the worse, a situation which will become clear later Within a week some of the family were home, others will follow later, and others from different part of the world, like Canada and America will be hurrying to get there too. But not all of whom is in a rush to get home are John Thomas descendant; no; some of them are close relatives; but they hold this man in great esteem. Arriving home Ben was well aware of his Sister's grief; she has taken it more badly than most, he wonders how she will act when she sees the actual body; he will keep a watchful eye on her. The family there was already making preparation; however the preparation didn't exactly coincide with the childrens'; however the differences will be sorted out later. People are still arriving from abroad; some of these people haven't seen each other since the day they leave the country. But this's no time for reunion, no; the order of the day is for mourning; the loss of this wonderful man will cast much more than a ripple throughout the district and beyond.

There will be lots of people milling about in the big yard; some were mourning; others were talking about John Thomas the man; plenty have tales to tell about what he had done for them. For the families abroad this wasn't a joyous homecoming; but their Uncle Derrick tries to comfort them; pointed out that if it wasn't today it would be another day; but they would have to return for what was the inevitable. John has seen many years; he was nearly eighty; Most people here hardly live pass sixty; they have a short life span mostly because of bad care and lack of medical treatment when taken ill. For Ammi this was another bad event in her life, her faith his being tested to the full; seen her father lying there she was legless with grief; Ben and one of the Sisters had was to support her; Ammi has taken her father's death very badly. In a situation like this especially when family is coming from abroad; and when the family is of the Thomas; a very important person in these parts; the turning out is going to be huge. Here people don't have to be families or friends to attend one's funeral, that's a tradition that handed down through generations, they'll come from all around; near or far; they'll sing all night as long as there're is food and rum; and that would be the situation for nine nights. There's plenty of goodwill and condolences for the family too; some of the greetings could be a little over the top, however they mean well; but it just because some of the Thomas's have left the country for so long and even though most of them return for short holiday; they never encountered some of these people they grew up with, but some of the niceties will have to keep until after the funeral. However there was a little complication from the offset; their Uncle Derrick had made some arrangement that weren't acceptable to the children. Now when these now adults were youngsters they grew with Pastor Green; a man who they admired highly but now retired, he was more to them than a Pastor to them and moreover he and their father were good friends. He had no objection coming out of retirement to conduct the ceremony; in fact nothing would give him more satisfaction than to say goodbye to his old friend than to perform the ceremony; and the children would like him to. But now that their uncle Derrick had made prior arrangements; they can't abandon all he had done, they'll change some things around somewhat; but they won't compromise on the pastor green conduct the ceremony. Uncle Derick was somewhat dissatisfied; however they didn't too concern about good old Uncle Derick too much; this is how they wanted it and that's how it's going to be. Nevertheless! After some consultation with Pastor Green; he advised them that they should compromise; he'll do the first half of the ceremony and Pastor Michael do the other half, and that was the final arrangement. John Thomas was to be bury on the coming Wednesday, six days after his death; the family is not keeping him longer than necessary. Tuesday it rained quite heavily; there was concern that tomorrow would be like today. But it seems the Gods are smiling on John Thomas; Wednesday was the most beautiful day; the sun was shining with a gentle breeze; Pastor Green commented; it's a good day for a funeral. At the church the crowd gathered; some are waiting to see the families. Pastor Green went into his sermon of which he speaks highly about his onetime brethren's and friend Brother Thomas. From then on it was a very lengthy affair; some of the eight children speak warmly about their father; others were too shy to speak. A great number of people gave their tributes; some long and some were short; some were good and some were not so good; but they were all from the heart. But the tribute that causes a stir was from Mr. Faster; his friend and one-time Member of Parliament; he makes them laugh and he make them cries; I haven't got enough time to speak about Mr. Thomas he said; when the good Lord made him he thrown away the mould; there wasn't a dry eye in the church; it was a tribute fit for a king. As for Ammi; she was supported to the pulpit by Brother Ben and Sister Maggie; she's shaking with grief; but with tears in her eyes she said her farewell to her beloved father.

The body was taken back to the house and buried at one corner of the land alongside his beloved wife Agnes; here there is no cemetery; everyone is buried on their land. They were still mourning him the following day and will continues to mourn for some time to come. Is as though they're feeling helpless now that he's gone; for a short time there the family seems at a lost; until Ben steps in and taks charge. The older Brother Sexton to whom they thought would be the spine of the family now that the old man is gone was less than effective to handle the situation. However! Before they return to England they managed to come to term with their lost and sorted matters out. But as the old saying goes; time is a great healer, as one week drawn to a closed and the new one begins; some were facing up to the hard fact that the old man is gone; they'll have to get on with their lives without him. Some members of the family will probably go on mourning for some time to come; but they'll have to come to grip with the situation; they have to; life doesn't stop because one person is dear; however essential that person was. Over the following weeks as the grief subsided; the family had time to reunite with the other half of the family who lived in other countries. They now have time to made arrangement for them to meet again sometime in the near future under happier circumstances. Now it's time for them to return to their chosen country, all loose ends are tied up; and with all the children living abroad they have to made arrangements with someone to take care of the graves and the family home. It was sad for them to leave; but their duties are back in foreign countries; so they said farewell one last time to the old man before they set off to the airport. But not everyone left at the same time, no; some were still here when others were home abroad; there were those who booked to stay longer than just coming to a funeral; they were those who haven't return to the country for years; so to kill two birds with one stone; they will be staying for some time longer. Returning to their chosen countries; they'll be leaving the last line of the older relative; four Sisters and one uncle; they were saddened to see them leave; especially dear Aunty Doris; the younger of the Sisters. Will they ever see them alive again? Only time will tell; but one thing for sure; with the demise of their Brother; for them life won't be the same again.

47: The Flight Back

It was a quiet flight back for the family, reflecting on what had happened Ammi asked what we are going to do now, what do you mean asked Maggie, with tears in her eyes she asked, who are we going to write to now with our problems? But we never did said Maggie; we never one time told him about our problem; because we; no; because you didn't want to upset him, Ammi didn't respond. But a few minutes later she comments; who are we going to look forward to seeing if we ever return home? Oh! Come on Sis said Ben, the old man is gone; we must now learn to live without him; and Sis! You're not going back home; I know it and you know it. Don't be too sure she said with tears in her eyes, anyway you could continue write to your dear friend Florence and our aunties; and don't forget Uncle Derick. I suppose you're right; but what would I be saying to them she asked; all they need is money; and when you send them a few pounds they never think to. As for Florence her sight is very bad, I noticed when I gave her the present I brought for her she couldn't read it; she pretends to; but I know she couldn't. These two were sitting together on the flight back; and that was a good job too; because Ammi broke down in tears again and again had to be consoled. But she was also saddened by the fact that her husband had shown little or no interest in her father's demised; and so is the family, in fact the relationship between him and the family will never be the same again. However the relationship between him and the families had never been the same since he went and have a child with another woman that his wife is now caring for.

On Return to England

On their return to England, the relationship between them had taken a turn for the worse; it appears she finds it difficult to forgive for the lack of interest and support during her dear father's death; and he appears not to give a damn. The friendship between him and Ben have diminished somewhat; he's not too happy with his behaviour towards his Sister; but it seems he's not too hard on him. But to show no in interest in his wife's father's death; he (Ben) took exception to that. But they still seem to able to communicate somewhat; But probably they hold some kind of dark secret for each other and wish not to have a disagreement; again the words honour among thieves come to mind. in fact Ben was his rock and he stood by him many a time, whenever there was a falling out in their relationship; and there were many; he would call on Ben to spent time with them; and once Ben is there dinner would be on the table; and for a short time there'll be some sort of harmony; until Wilf commits another of his indiscretion. As a matter of fact they hardly ever talk at all unless ben is around; he would say something to have words passed between them. But Wilf is not too particular about the relationship at present; he's using it for his own particular benefit; something Ben will soon discover. But it was a sad and peculiar affair to see two people who at the start of their young lives were so much in love and supportive of each other's; and to see them now in total disarray; pretending to be a married couple; the phrase keeping up appearances comes to mind, the only thing for sure exist between the now is hate. She tried to put a brave face on the situation and pretend everything is rosy in the garden, but Wilf! Well he didn't care what anyone thinks; not even Ben; he thinks he had found a new route for his life; and his Christian wife is no part of it.

Well his son Ferdy was now a grown man, she raised him from birth; from the day his mother leave him on her doorstep, he calls her mom and she loves him like a son. The father! Well his attention to the boy was less than a father, he hardly ever home to play the part in his life; he was far too busy elsewhere, doing what? Well! His ambition is getting the better of him; and as time goes by he was turning his attention to many things; and over the years these ventures were many; however none turns out to be successful. But Ammi with her Christian belief turned a blind eye; well she lost interest; she didn't want to know about anything; anything at all that he would get up to. However! He cherished the thought that she wasn't; Well! Either good enough or incapable of being involved in his many ventures. Or on the other hand, he might be thinking it's none of her business. This man who had little or no education suddenly believed he's bound for higher things, but dishonesty will never prevail. Ammi had become alone; her husband is only in name, well! They were using the same front door but only to come and go; they're not really wife and husband anymore. But thanks to her many Church sisters and friends who always rally around her and always encouraged her to be of good courage. However within the family Brother Ben and his children were always there for her too; she was encouraged not to sit at home and stare at the four walls; go out whenever she can, so most weekends she and Ben would head off to the country to visit relatives; something she enjoyed. She had gradually got over her husband it seems; her appearance was looking so much rosier; and sister Ammi was laughing again, but there was sorrow to come later.

Bun himself had now been divorced for some time and living close by big Sister Ammi; and from time to time he would drop by for dinner. On occasion Wilf would be home for dinner; but most time he had to cook it himself. But Ben can't stand to see his Sister suffers anymore; a man who doesn't stand on ceremony; he told him in no uncertain that his attitude stinks; and he should stop coming back; his going and coming is making his Sister ill. But even at that point Ammi doesn't want know that Wilf suffers in any way; she would tolerate his goings and comings even though he's not communicating with her. Deep down this woman still loves her husband; but she's trying desperately not to shows it. Well! If some of her friends know the truth they would certainly criticise her, how could you still love a man like that after all he's done they would ask. But whatever Ben said to him he never respond or retaliates; whether it's a ploy or out of respect his attitude is never to retaliate. In one of their talk which they have from time to time; Ben asked his Sister; Sis! How long are you going to stand for it; you're losing your self-respect at the hand of Wilf; your friends are beginning to think there's something the matter with you. I know you're talking about divorce Ben; and maybe it's something I should consider; but it could be he might be needing some kind of help. Help Sis! How could you say that? The man treats you like dirt Sis; and he doesn't give a damn. She looks at him surprisingly; Ben! Did you swear? Of course in all their years she never heard him sworn. I'm sorry Sis; it just pops out; but you can't continue letting him treat you this way; if the old man knew you were treated this way he would turn in his grave. Well that comment about the old man seems to register home; whatever Ben said afterword there was no response from her; she put dinner on the table for Ben and went upstairs. Maybe she's gone to reflect on their conversation or to pray. But Ben saw something to which he's concern about; Her Christian sister on occasion loosed her temper and would behave totally out of character; she would throw things at him with such fury and even threatens to strike him. Ben is thinking that one day she might completely lose it and does something serious. However! Whatever she does to him he would just smile and walks away; walks back to where ever he got up to whatever he got up to.

Over the years it was clear that Sister had lost her faith; maybe not totally but some, if and when Wilf return home she would go to work on him with abuse; some of the language is not fit to be coming from the mouth of a Christian; at times Ben who always mostly present had to calm her down. But whenever her fury erupts Wilf hurriedly disappeared without saying a single thing. However once again Wilf could be acting diplomatically, it appears nothing would please him more than his wife goes mental; went off her head and one day soon she's admitted to the nuthouse. This one-time good man has turned out to be a coward and a nasty piece of worn; she was the spine of their existence. He hardly ever had money for himself as he was mostly out of work; but she handled whatever little money they had and handled it carefully. But ben likes to be flashy, you'll never see him at anything outside without his suit and tie; and of course without any money in his pocket, he wants to be someone out of the ordinary but hasn't got the brains to accomplish such an ambition. However he's never going to stop trying and he's one of these people who cannot see when they're wasting their time.

48: The Action of Wilf

Well! At this point in time the pioneers are pensioners, most with nothing to do, others find work outside their specialised field; bot not particularly for the money; no; but for to give themselves something to do. Wilf a man in mid seventy wanted to do something that would keep him in the public eye; but now the people who once admired and loved him have abandoned him. The opportunist who would do almost anything to achieve his ambition is becoming desperate; the man who tried his hands at but every time have come unstuck, things like setting a business with other people's money, but probably because of his underhand tactics the business crumbled. Now he has turned his sight on bigger things; he wanted to be a politician, often he would dressed up in his very best; armed himself with briefcase and mobile phone and headed for parliament, the word is; he's got an audience with a politician there, in what capacity? Only he knows. Well the thing is; here's a man who seems to admire the thing other people do; and would like to be like them, except there's one difference; they have got the schooling and they have got the brains; this man hasn't; he's an imposter. But even at his age he could still acquire some sort of education; he could go to night school; many people do; even those who been to college and now retired; and with nothing to do some get themselves back to school for further education. But Wilf hasn't got time; he a man in a hurry; but the man knows nothing about politic other than what he heard or picked up from those he listened to. The fact that he's a good speaker; not an intellectual one; he might have thought that was all he need to be a politician. But as sure as the night come before the day he is on a hiding to nothing; for him the only way is down. During this time his sight was failing; and failing fast; his driving was becoming tedious and dangerous; and of course he loves driving; it makes him look more respectable sitting at the wheel of his big car. Nevertheless from time to time he had narrow escape regarding having an accident. Well his political ambition didn't amount to anything and didn't last long; he'd thrown in the towel and embarked on something else.

However when his political venture didn't pay off; he returns to the Church; but he wants to be a preacher; and with that he and his wife seem to reconciled somewhat, an action which pleased some of Ammi's family and a few of her church Sisters. But others weren't so gullible; they saw him for what he was, they believe a leopard could never changes its spots; this man is a pretender and imposter; there's no sincerity in him returning to the Church. But Ammi was pleased that her husband had returned to the fold, she knows there'll be whispers; but she won't let that bothers her, she'll doing her utmost best trying to make things possible for him and her to be a couple again. Ben wasn't too comfortable about the situation; but anything that would make his sister happy he's all for it. It was a period of calm before the storm, the family was in a good place right now, even though Wilf wasn't going any places apart from Church with his wife; and no doubt it was noticed by everyone; but Ammi was able to live with it. In fact; she knew Wilf was up to his old tricks again but she turned a blind eye, again. In a way he might be called a lovable rogue, with his always calm exterior and an infectious smile; and a somewhat a gift of the gab; it worked well for him. By now he acquired a piano and decided to be a musician, and he played it well too, but he has his sight set on some of the church Sisters to act as a choir; and some joined him willing. Well sir! Soon he and his choir were having short sessions at various churches in the evenings, except he was having no audience; nobody comes to hear him, the whole thing wasn't up to much to attract anyone. He soon began to pick on his wife's family for not helping him to succeed. By now the family has grown rather large, the Thomas is up to third generations, but the relationship between these new generations are not as it was with their parent; families occasionally meet; only when there's function within the family; and after that they'll probably never meet again until there's another function; and Wilf would never get their support. Wilf's son Ferdinand has left home; well he's a grown man now and an ambitious lad; feels he shouldn't be living under his father's roof; he went to Europe and make a life for himself there, he got married but produced grandchildren, and he was to figured greatly in his stepmother's death as will be explained later. But the older families are still rather close, some in London and others in the country, but however far it make no difference; they would often pay visits; and some of these visits included stopping over; some time for days. However Wilf took little or no interest in the family; and when his latest venture fails he's looking for something else to turn to. Well the man is possessed; he's not giving up; no Sis; if he dies he's going to die trying. He's a man on the move; always talking about having some kind of a project that he's either doing or setting up. But here is a man who can't completely sever his ties with the Church; he was soon back on the church path once again; only this time he was a preacher. Well he get himself a church which he shared with another preacher; it was a good arrangement; one used it in the morning and the other in the evening.

But there was to be one big disappointment, Pastor Drake has no one to preach to, not ever to his love-struck wife, she won't abandon her brethren and her church for her husband's church; probable she feels she owes a legion or gratitude to both Brethren's and the Methodist church. Here's a man who knew all the angles; he knows the bible well; nevertheless not even the people who used to be his choir bother to go to his church. But what he most certainly lost sight of is something in his bible; the good Lord see all thing and knows all thing, one can't fool the good lord; one only fool one's self. His wife to whom he paid no attention whatsoever was still hoping for him to succeed in his endeavour; even to the disapproval of the family. She was asked by one of her Brethren's; why are you not at your husband church, she replied; God is not mack, a quote from the bible. But it's not only the Christian side of Sister Ammi is at work here, no; she still loves him and for all the concern she'll be in love with him till the day she dies. However there is sympathy in some quarters for her; even though that sympathy comes very hard, they know that this woman knew no other man intimately; he was and is her first and only love; and most certainly will be her last. One would have thought he would go out of his way to loyal to the Thomas family. They're the only family he knew from he been to this country; his own blood relatives didn't want to know him at all; they've been carrying on some sort of a feud from back home. The only one he had some kind of a relationship with was his Sister Enid, the woman who hates the ground his wife walks on; and she would on occasion visited the home. But she been a Christian and observed the Ten Commandments won't allow herself to cherish the thought of hate even though she knew the woman hates her. But Mr. Drake was still holding on to his church Sundays after Sundays hoping that one day someone or people would turn up for him to preach to. But all hopes were dashed, what he's hoping for was never going to happen; one Sunday evening he locked up the building and handed over the key. But rest ashore if he had a congregation he would preach to them in the way in which they like, well! It wouldn't be sincere of course; the man is an impostor; but by God he knew the words.

Over the years ahead his many ventures all fail; and still living with his wife but very unhappy, well! He doesn't want to be there, but have the steel or the nerves to break away. Of course she still cares for him even though she knows he couldn't care less about her; well! She's the old fashion type; they married for better or for worse; till death us do part; she holds that oath sincerely. But now his behaviour is so brazen is as though he wanted to make a statement, a man at the age of about seventy-seven behaving in a likewise manner; a man aspired to be someone he's not; every day he would clad himself in one of his many suits with nowhere special to go; of course he's making the impression of an important person. But he was still a healthy man and quite nimble; and since he doesn't have the following he had once upon a time he went away, well! HE disappears; no one within the family had any idea of his whereabouts. But wherever he's gone to; it's a sure thing he'll be back, well! His prize car is still in the Gurage. He been away wasn't any concern to the family, no; their concern was about their Sister, she's not a spring chicken anymore nor her blood Brother and sister; and now living alone she was showing signs they didn't like. So Ben was spending lots more time with her than ever; and even though her Church Sisters often visited it appears it couldn't make up for the absence of her husband, she's being lonely even though she's never alone. She now devoted herself more to the church even at the ripe old age of seventy-eight; and she's trying to be even more active than ever wanting to do more. She's now without a husband and not for the first time; and not knowing if he's dead or alive she was urged by the family again to consider a divorce, but holding on to her Cristian principles she wouldn't; and the family knew why; they knew that deep down she believed that one day he would return. But she's gradually getting used to live life without him, be it my, with the help of her family and brethren's, she would occasionally smile and with Ben always around to take her wherever she wants to go it appears she's has gotten over him.

Ammi's Birthday

But the family was to do something to cheers her up; well! Ammi never ever celebrates her birthday; her birthday was always a secret; probable not even her husband knew her date of birth. Until one day Maggie was searching through some family papers and came across her birth certificate, she showed it to Ben and older Brother Sexton. Well! After some consideration they decided to throw her a surprise birthday, but knowing how long she kept her date of birth a secret Ben thought even though they're trying to cheer her up it might not be a good idea. However they agreed to go ahead with it anyway and hoping she would please and appreciate it. It was a well-kept secret, all the preparation was done at her house; and she also helped with the preparation; but with one little white lie she was told the party was for someone else; Geraldine, one of Ben's daughters. They could do that at her house; they have done it before; she was totally oblivious to the fact that it was for her own birthday. Today is Wednesdays; Ammi's birthday; but they usually out at prayer meeting; and that gave the family and a few guests time to wait for her at her home. It was the perfect arrangement, of course the brethren she's with at prayer meetings are in on the act. There's a routine after these meetings that the ones with cars would drive as many of the brethren's as their car could hold home, so this evening Sister Ammi will be the first to drops off. It was a cold winter evening; her house was in darkness as she leaves it, the driver waiting for to open the door and enter before he drove off, that's the usual way, of course he and the rest of the Brethren's aren't going anywhere. As she opens the front door and reaches for the switch for the passage Maggie beats her to it with the sound of happy birthday from the guests; and there was no doubt about it; she was surprised alright. She knows today is her birthday; but how on earth does anyone else know, her eyes were full of tears, well! She didn't deny it; but asked; how did you know? Don't worry Sis said Maggie with her arms around her, come and sit down. Soon her tears turn to joy, engulfed by a throng of well-wishers presenting her with birthday cards; something she never had in her entire life; for a moment there she was back to the old sister Ammi they always knew. There were calls for a speech; of course she's not a public speaker and with so many eyes looking on; even in her own home she blushes. But joined by Ben and Maggie she manages to thank everyone; her guests and her family; and a special thanks for Maggie to let the cat out of the bag, now everyone knows how old I am, and you what, I feel good about it she said, and they all cheer.

It was about ten o'clock, people were eating and drinking, soft drinks of course; these Christians are beyond drinking spirit, but amid all the gaiety who walks in through the door? Wilf. Now everyone stops what they were doing, and all eyes were on him; and these eyes were eyes of fury. But no one dares to ask him what is he doing here; after all this is his home. His onetime loyal brother-in-law and friend Ben was considering throwing him out; but he knew if he did that big sister Ammi wouldn't thank him for it and probable hates him too. At this point the party come to an end, everyone leaves except the family. Now the inquest begins and for the second time ben let loose, what the hell are you doing back here he asked, are you trying to kill our Sister? And there were lots more by other members of the family. But however much they asked or questioned, he remained silent, but then Wilf is like that, never was one for a quarrel or argument; not even when his wife is telling him off. However! Up till that point, Ammi never said a single word, it's sure as hell she doesn't like to see him crawl or subordinate; and to her she might not even care about where he had been; she was probably glad to see him return. Eventually he speaks; can I have a word with my wife now; he asked the family in his subdued manner, go ahead said Ben; we want to hear what you say to her, no! I'll ask her when you all are gone; I'll ask you all to leave no please; this's still my house he said. They all agreed to leave; and Ammi wants them to leave too, but as they were going through the door he calls out; Ben I would like you to stay, there was no hesitation on Ben's path; he stood by the door to close behind the others. Well! No doubt him like the others would like to hear Wilf explanation for his disappearance and what his intention regarding their Sister. The discussion begins; Wilf is not a smart man but he's not an idiot either, he first trying to get Ben on his side before he tackles his wife. Ben I know we can't be as we used to and probable you might even hate me, but been away has thought me a lot; a lot about the thing I done and shouldn't have done, and I hope you and the family can forgive me; and I'll do whatever I have to do to make it right given the chance. Ammi sat there in full attention asked, is this confession? If it is you can stop now, you can never be true to your words; tomorrow you'll do the same thing all over again; and she said it furiously. Ben went and consoled her calm down Sis; don't let him upset you. But under all that angry exterior beats a heart of love; a love that says I'm glad you're back. The talk went on all through the night, it almost daybreak and Ben is about to leave. Now look Wilf he said; I might as well tell you; you and me; we could never be the same again; no way; I've lost all respect for you that will never return; but you're my Sister husband; and she appears to want you back; I don't know why, and for her own sanity we will let things be; but have no doubt Wilf; we are watching you now. He wasn't only angry he was mad, now you can tell me to get out of your house he said furiously. Standing at the foot of the stairs looking all subdued he comments, Ben I would never tell you to leave; you know that; and I'll do what it takes to gain your respect again. Those words were music to Ammi's ears; she knows Ben is the one person he cares about; but she also knows that when Ben said something like a treat he means it.

Over the months ahead things have settled down somewhat in the Drake household, even though the relationship between him and the family is a little tedious. He's not going to church any more; but they are seen out together from time to time. But no many people thought this reunion would last; and they were right. Soon Wilf had embarked on another one of his projects, he's now decided to be a music teacher, starting from his own home he rented a place and turns it into a place where he can teach music. The man ambition knows no limit, there's a saying; a man should know his limitation; it a shame he doesn't know his; it's almost a certainty that this another of his project is bound to fail. He got a grant and acquired all the necessary musical equipment he needed to get started; now all his time was spent at his school, but misfortune was awaiting in more ways than one; well! After a few months things begin to go awry, the students he had expected didn't materialised; and the ones that give it a try, up and leave soon after. His partnership with Mrs. Clark is not paying off, the school is not paying its way through lack of students; and she's in it for the money; soon there was disagreement between them. But whatever happens, Wilf is not giving up, he probably feels this is his last chance to make it big; he got himself a new partner. Well this partner is someone who knows music; he could play and teach from notes; whereas Wilf is someone who can play more than one instrument, but he can only play by ear. Now the partner wanted to run the show; and that was never going to go down well with Wilf. However until they can attract music students and keep them; whatever they do will be in vain.

49: Ammi's Taken Ill

However! Meanwhile all this was going on Ammi was takem ill. One evening when Wilf returned home he finds her in bed running a high temperature, he didn't take her to the Doctor, no; he calls Ben; would you come and take your Sister to the Doctor? His car was out of commission anyway; and moreover he shouldn't be driving; and as I mentioned earlier; his eyesight isn't good. Ben didn't hesitate; he was on the scene promptly. But Ben didn't ask what the Doctor diagnoses; he just took her to collect the medication. Over the coming weeks she wasn't there was nothing the family consider seriously wrong with her; well! Whenever she was with the family she was always reasonable cheerful. But sometime later they come to realise that all that time she was carrying a serious illness. But as the weeks go by more and more she has to be taken to the hospital; either by Ben od their long time neighbour Brother Stanley. But the Doctors were slow to diagnose her condition, one Wednesday when Ben took her the hospital and after the Doctor had done their diagnosis he was summoned to see them; and there he was told she's got advance cancer. Ben a bloke with good communitive skill was strapped for words, however he managed to ask, advanced cancer Doctor? How could she have advance cancer all this time and no one knows about doc? Well Mr. Thomas we just discovered it said the Doctor. There's not much more Ben can say; he begins to run his own diagnosis through his head. How it is that she's been carrying such illness without no one even suspects. He remembers the last time they went to the country she was none too lively; he remembered how sluggish she was; she must have been carrying the disease all that time. Then he comes to the conclusion that she must have known about it herself but kept it a secret. Then he thinks again; Wilf! He must have known she was ill all this time but couldn't care less. Well! He wouldn't be able to tell what her sickness was; but for sure he knew she was ill but does nothing. Within a few days she was admitted to the hospital; probable they're going to try and treat it. Well for the short time she's in the hospital she seems to cheer up a little; there were many visitors; at times there were queues of people waiting to see her; one nurse comment; you're like a celebrity Mrs. Drake. She was sent home after a week and a half with medication. And she was glad to be home. By now she's never being alone; day and night there were people there to keep her company and cheers her up. Now Ben was like her guardian; he'll make sure the stuff she can eat is always there; well! She didn't like the ensure anymore; she had too much of it. However it was obvious that all is not well with her; Sister Dobbs her best friend rang Ben one evening; Ben she said; I don't like the way she's looking; you better come quickly; he was there in a flash. When he got there Wilf was there also; but there was no time to waste; he along with Wilf and Sister Dabbs he rushed her to the hospital. Well the Doctor treats her and sends her home; but she's now been given a date for admittance; and it's an early date; and the Doctor's words; Mr. Drake if there was a bed we would admit her right away. And that was the first time Wilf was present to anyone of her visit to the hospital. On the day before her appointment Wilf calls ben; don't forget you taking your Sister in tomorrow he said; Ben thought how odd; he who never shows any interest regarding his wife's illness suddenly showing concern. But Ben was somewhat pleased that at last he was showing a kind of interest; after all he's the one there with her during the night.

Sunday morning; the day she's admitted, they sat in the waiting room until the nurse came to tell her that there was a bed for her. With Wilf sitting in the waiting room chatting with someone; ben took her to her room and make her comfortable; she was sitting in a settee; see you tomorrow Sis; don't go anywhere now he said jokingly; but she did smile. Wilf was still there when he returns talking to his buddy. Go and say good night to your wife; I'm leaving now said Ben; well he took him here so he'll take him back home. But there's an uncomfortable atmosphere between them; ben would much rather not breathing the same air as him; unfortunately he can't do any better. On Monday the Doctors operate; but the operation didn't go well; when Ben went to see her he was told she's been taken back to the theatre. Well he hangs around but was told no one would be able to see her today; of course there were several other visitors; but no one could see her; and on this day there was no sight of Wilf. However the next day round about ten o'clock Ben calls by the hose; he's going to the hospital and he would like Wilf to come along too. I was about to call you to picks me up he said; they set off to the hospital; but there isn't much conversation between them; in fact these two once compatriots are now like strangers. Ben told one member of the family; I think I hate the man; and I hope he realised it. At the hospital there was an argument between them, Ben asked; did you sign the form of consent for the operation? I didn't he said; I have no idea about who signed it. At that moment Ben lost his rag; especially when he came to realise that he didn't even know what his wife is being operated on for. However Ben went to have a talk regarding the signing of the form; but the Doctor directs him to the appropriate person; she then told him the form was signed be Mrs. Drake herself; but it's not unusual; as long as the person is of sound mind and is an adult; then it's legitimate for that person to sign. But Ben was so hurt to know that Wilf never even bothered to know who signed his wife's form; he commented to the anaesthetist; it would show concern if her husband was with her in case she couldn't sign, wouldn't it? She nodded to him but said nothing. But worst was to come She's now having regular chemotherapy treatments but the onus was on Ben to see that she gets to and from hospital. Wilf! He shouldn't be driving; and not because of his license; but because of his eyes; nevertheless he drove to his makeshift music school so he could drive to visit his wife; but of course he wouldn't. But Ben still calls for him whenever he's going; not because he wants to, no; but because Ammi would like to see him there. However there was the constant row between them; his callous attitude evoked the anger of Ben; to see the way he's treating his sick wife; this is the result of fifty-plus years of marriage; the man can't wait to see his wife in the grave. It let Ben's blood boil; at times his conduct was ugly; very ugly indeed. But there's nothing more the Doctor can do for her; she's on barrow time; she was sent home under the care of the Macmillan nurse. But she was glad to be home; she might be thinking since she's going to die she rather die at home among families and friends who were always there for her. When Ben fetched her home it was clear she wouldn't be with them for long; all they can do for her now is to make her comfortable the best they can. By now young Ferdy was home again with his wife; and Ammi was glad to see him; well he's her son even though she never gave birth to him. But he took it upon himself to administer her medication, and she was pleased; well in some ways it was his duty; she's his mother; However it's was later believe that he wasn't giving her the medication at all, no; he was starving her of the treatment; an assumption that cannot be proven. But there was the notion among some that he would like Wilf and his blood mother to get together; so he was preventing any recovery by his step-mother, of course all this is conjecture, but where's there's smoke there's fire. The hateful Sister-in-law is now a regular visitor at the home, she'd eat and drink and even stop over at times; those of whom knew the situation wasn't too happy about it; but there was hardly anything they could do; the house belonging to her Brother and he wants her there.

By now there's near turmoil in the family; Ben thought the rest of the family wasn't doing enough to help; even though they were living in the country, he thought when they visit they could stop over to spend some time with her; it's always good to see how cheerful she is when the family is around. She's in severe pain and she won't be with us for long; but there was some joy on her face when Ben and the family were sitting at her bedside. But time was running out for Ammi; this wonderful thoughtful human being; one who cares for others more than she care for herself. One would have thought if there's a heaven Sister Ammi will be going there. One can believe she laid the foundation for herself by doing to others as she would have done to herself; she's lived by the good book; and the time has come when she must depart this world. Wednesday wasn't a good day for her; well! Depend on how one looks at it; she was dying; the breath was slowly leaving her body. Kneeling by her bedside Ben hold her hands with little or nothing to say; he was too full of grief; he just watched the last breath leave the body; Goodbye Sis and the good Lord be with you he said. But the evil Sister and Wilf were there too; pretending to be grieving, but it was quite clear their wishes weren't for her to live, no; they wanted to see the back of her and the sooner the better. But Wilf knew she was sick from the offset; and he probably knew it was cancer too and turned a blind eye. Amid the hate for his wife he might well be thinking; he doesn't have to cherish any thought of killing her himself, no; the cancer will do it for him. But there are those who believe he had his reason for wanting her dead; and that reason was a life insurance of which he's the benefactor. Now there was confusion within the family, Wilf and his son want a quick burial; a couple a days after her death; he doesn't wants to tarry. Now! Considering the families abroad who are coming to say their last farewell to their Sister; they're going to take some time getting here, but it seems he's got no intention of waiting for them. But his actions not only irate the family; but friends also. However when Ben heard there was an almighty rumpus; he wouldn't allow it to happen; which cause even more conflict between them. But the family from abroad did arrive in time for the funeral. But Ben had done something to which he regretted to this day; when he heard Wilf's intentions regarding the funeral he went directly to the home; he was going to have it out with him; unfortunately he wasn't there but young Ferdy was; and when he was stalling with the truth he sworn to young Ferdy; something he's not proud of until this day; even though there is bad blood between Ben and his father. The family from abroad have arrived and it was good to see them; now the family can begin to make arrangements with Wilf about how to proceed. As the family gathered; Nephews, nieces, Brothers, Sister and well-wishers who would like to say farewell; the families are looking forward to a good burial; sorrowful but good. But there was to be a lot of anger when the families realised that

Wilf wants them to have nothing to do with the eulogy and other arrangements; these were bad times. When Ben and two other members of the family turn up to compile the eulogy with Wilf; he told them it was done; how could you done it without any input from me and the family asked Ben, it's a short eulogy he said, then what did you personally puts in it asked Ben; well the answer he got leaves him shaking with rage. I couldn't suggest anything he said; I only knew Ammi since she came to England, there were moments of silence; they couldn't believe their ears; Ben shouts; what's the f… you're talking about; After fifty-plus years of marriage and you can't think of anything to say about your wife? Well he was so mad he used a few choice words which were quite unsavoury and unlike him. But the others could understand ben's action; they couldn't believe their ears either. Maggie comment; Wilf! You're really a stinker; you need a good hiding, you help sent her to her early grave; and now you know nothing to say about her; where was she living all these years she asked; with someone else? Well she was so mad the tears come flooding down; the man who she at one time had so much love respect and for has now shown his nasty side. But Ben rethink the situation and asked; out of curiosity; tell me Wilf; if you don't know anything about your wife to put in the eulogy; what the f… in it? Ben is at the point where he couldn't give a damn for his action. There was no reply from Wilf; so Maggie asked the same question, what's in the eulogy Wilf? I don't know he said; ferdy done it. When it was explained that Ben was written out of the programme; he was livid to the point of exploding; he charged out with the pledge that his feet would never cross this f***ing threshold ever again. But the others didn't follow after; they were pleading with him to change the programme, of which he has no intention; and their action irritated Ben, he thought they should follow him instead of on their knees to this nasty man. But for sure he wrote Ben out of the programme in fear that he would say things he didn't want the people to hear; he knew that if someone was going to say anything regarding his treatment towards her then it would be Ben.

50: Big Brother Sexton

While all this was going on, older Brother Sexton showed little or no interest about the what was happening; in fact when he was asked by one of the Brothers about what could he put in the eulogy; this younger Brother was appal of his reply, I can't add anything he said; I don't know her well enough. You're the oldest of the family and you know nothing about your Sister he asked; well big Brother; I'm a shame of you. This conversation was conducted in his home. When the news of that conversation got around the family was astonished; they could hardly believe it; they didn't want to believe it; this is the Brother everyone always looks up to. So why did he deny his Sister; was he a shame oh her? The family didn't think so; in better times the family had a good relationship visiting each other. Then why he denies his Sister; Well! He known of the treatment Ammi had received at the hand of her husband; he was made aware of the situation by Ben who was always there; but during the whole time of her illness he never did show too much of an interest; could it be Wilf means more to him than his own Sister? But the history of this man Sexton went back a long way; his help in before the start of immigration is quite admirable; the family looked up to him; they thought he was the man for all seasons. But the Brother has changed, coming to England the family was still a close-nit one; they all living in London and the harmony within the family was envious by outsiders; the Thomas was the family people from their district back home would write to ask about their own families. Sometime later sexton got marry; well he sent back home for his long time fiancée; a wonderful lady; the family was please when they got married. But they never remain in London for long after; they move to the country with half of the family follow after. But they made a good life for themselves; but wherever any of the Thomas's reside there was a tie that binds them all. However something happened; older Brother sexton is not the same person; the man has changed; he seem to have an envious streak about him; but that envy was always against his own family. Well! He seems always wants to compete; in his world he must have everything better than his family; it seems this Brother wouldn't want to see his family children prosper better than his. In fact when Ben and older Sister Betty who knew him well were sometime amazed about his attitude. Could this be the Brother they grew up with; the one time caring Brother who the entire family looked up to? It was hard to believe. But one is never going to know the true nature of a person unless one lives with one; and a family who scattered abroad; in different countries; they only meet on occasions when they can afford it; they're never going to know their family property; in the form of knowing what make them tick. But Ben and Brother Sexton was to have several disagreements in time to come.

The Church

It was a dreary Friday; not the kind of day one wants to be in a cemetery, but the crowd gathered; however it was noticeable that there was only one Hurst; it carried Wilf, his son, his son's wife and his evil sister Enid; needless to say there were whispers. With this vast crown and a big family like the Thomas; how is it that there's only one Hurst? But there it is; Wilf didn't give a damn about the family any more. But this never seemed to be noticed by the family until after the funeral when Ben puts it to them; he'll later explain. But the crowd gathered; the building a Church but only hired out these days for receptions; however that was where the ceremony was to be; and the crowd gathered. But to the disappointment of everyone it only a short ceremony; with among the two people paying tribute was older brother Sexton; it wasn't much of a tribute; but the irony is; he knows nothing of his Sister that would contribute to the eulogy; nevertheless he finds himself standing up in what is a makeshift church paying tribute, the hypocrisy of the man is overwhelming, he was told later by Ben that he had no love for his Sister; and he's traitor to the family. At the end of the short ceremony there was plenty of questions being asked; Ammi's church sisters knew Ben well; in fact he was one of their favourite people; they had expected him to give a good exaltation in the form of a tribute for his sister; but it didn't take them long to realise why; because of the bad relationship between them he could thrust him not to say something he didn't want the crown to hear; and of course there were many of Ammi's Church Brethren would like to pay their tributes too. But to say this is a grievous occasion is an understatement; not only were people mourning the dead; but the anger of some people in this huge crowd was evident. Some wanted to display their displeasure and confronted Wilf and told him what they thought of him; one, Sister Smith, couldn't withhold her anger and disappointment; well she like many would like to say farewell to their Brethren and never get the chance to. She confronted him and looking him in the eyes, you Sir she said; refused to call him by his name; you're going to hell; you will burn in hell for sure you wicked man she said with tears streaming down, Ben went and consoled her. But with all the anger that directed at him; Wilf is not saying anything; to him right now silent is golden, and of course there was no one here is going to give him any condolences; all they would like to give him is grief. But people would gather around Ben, Maggie and the ones they knew to share their grief. It was also noticeable that the only member of the family who was talking to Wilf was older Brother Sexton, his action caused many raised eyebrows, and many people thought this man must be a traitor; they give him a wide burp. The family themselves couldn't understand hi action; is Wilf hold some dark secrets for him? Or he didn't like his Sister, Ammi is not yet underground but the inquest has begun regarding Brother Sexton. Today is not a good day; Sister Ammi deserved better, she lived a good life a life which include helping others. But how unfortunate for her to meet the man who was to be her lifetime partner; a woman who knew no other man except the one she made her promise to; to love honour and obey; till death us do part. She lived by her principles and the Commandments of; a God-fearing person who does things one way and one way only; the right way. Then how is it she ended up with a husband who's a bastard; a man who not only lack knowledge; but lack the common decent principles of a human being.

The Burial

The journey to the cemetery was a painful one for the family; it was a long procession with plenty of cars, the one Hurst stood out like a beacon. At the grave the crowd gathered; and Pastor Moore who knew Ammi from that first Sunday she and her two cousins entered his church over fifty years ago. He was there to observe, oh how would he like to give a tribute to one of his faithful servants; but it wasn't to be; here at the graveside he looks on with renovation. The ceremony was conducted by the new Pastor, a sensitive man who realised the situation; giving his sermon he tried to bring everyone together; but people are far too angry and sensitive to the situation; they just wanted to see their dear friend and Brethren's laid to rest and then leave. It was particularly painful for the family; having no input the eulogy or took any part in the ceremony; it was quite difficult to watch Ammi buried without said farewell. The day was gloomy but for this family; this family whose population increase to four generations it was a sad time for them. However at the grave is not the place one voices their grievance, no; it would be disrespecting the dead; things will be said for sure; but there's a time and place for everything. One should remember the way Caribbean folks bury their dead; they usually got buried in what is a crusado; hymns that people would want to go on singing for a long time. But there was none of that here; and even though Wilf himself wanted to rise some sort of singing the people wasn't interested; they wanted to show their displeasure. To the family and many others it was good to see Wilf subdued with little or nothing to say; for a man of his onetime popularity and public speaking ability; a man who usually full of the gab; the shame that hangs over him as of now will be with him for the rest of his deceitful life. But somehow things could never pass off without a hitch; there's going be someone who decided to take the bull by the horn; someone with the conviction to say. this man shouldn't walk away today without someone tell him of his wicked ways and deception; someone who doesn't give a damn who he or she upsets so long as what needs to be said gets said. Of course, Sister Smith has said her piece already; but Mrs. Dobbs Ammi best friend is overcome with grief; Mrs. Dobbs a woman of similar yeast in age as Sister Ammi; old but still got some fight within her. As everyone was leaving the grave back to the church hall where the reception will be held; Mrs. Dobbs cut loose; I hope you're happy now that she's gone you wicked man; you never even have the decency to take care of Sister Ammi in her sickness; you want to see her dead quickly; what were you after Wilf? Her life insurance she asked, well I hope you don't get a red cent. Someone shouldn't tell the insurance company that you hasten on your wife's death to get the insurance. Wilf you can walk around in your suite looking all respectable; but that won't change who you are; a wicked and evil man; you'll spend your days in hell. He didn't have anything to say; even if he did he's not going to say anything in front of this pro Sister Ammi crowd. But with the crown looking on and whispering; this was an uncomfortable time for him, his son and the evil Sister.

The Reception

The Reception was supposed to be the high light of the funeral; plenty to eat and drink; and those who didn't get the chance to speak at the church would do so now, and if everything were as it should be; there would be plenty of well-wishers lining up to pays their tributes. But that didn't happen; people were to show their displeasure by totally ignored the reception; they went away about their business. The family themselves didn't attend either; no; they went away with those from abroad and held their own reception at one of Ben's son's home. Wilf was left in no doubt how people felt; and what will he do when that the dust has settled; well he probable go and hide out somewhere. Well he's got no friend in the people he usually hangs around with, like people from the Church and those who used to think he's someone special; the man burns his bridges and now he's a hated man in the community. The reception was a complete washout; a few people attend; but not who one might say were the important people.

Then what about Wilf's old friend Raymond one might ask, where was he when his good friend's daughter was suffering so many trials and tribulations? Well! He died some years earlier; he wasn't around to witness his friend's evil and deception. After a short illness, he died at the ripe old age of eighty-eight. But he outlived his much younger wife Daphne by many years; she died some years before and her body was taken back to Jamila; and was buried on her father's small plot of land; that was her desire; they leave only one who is now an architect. Hillary! Well her end wasn't so good; she never did marry; she lived alone for all her life; until she ended up in the home with more dementia; didn't a known a soul when the family went to see her. She was alive when her cousin died; but was unable to attend the funeral; heavens only know what she would say to Wilf if she was able to; she too dies soon after.

51: The Family

After all is said and done and the sister Ammi is put to rest, it's left to the family to heal its wounds, the action among some of them has left a sour taste in the mouth. Our family used to be one of unity; solid as a rock; when other families in disarray; not speaking to each other's; hold animosity; the Thomas family was solid as a rock; people hold high up in their esteem. So someone in the family has to do something and do it fast to prevent the family from tearing it's self apart. The main stumbling block is the friendship between Wilf and older brother Sexton, and even though Ben makes his feeling clear; this man is no longer apart of this family; never the less sexton and his immediate family was thick as thieves with him. The fact that they were never friend at any time makes it even stranger; when Ben confronted him regarding; he pointed out to Him (Ben) that he's a different person from him; he can't bear malice; and he can't see any reason as to why he should reframe from friendly with Wilf. On occasion when he's in London he would go see Wilf and make it a point to tell Ben about it, knowing that Ben rather no hear about his visit, one couldn't help wondering if his action didn't have some kind of meaning to it. But Bet told him in no uncertain term that he's traitor to the family; and as long as they live he could never forgive him. But there were other members of the family too who didn't see things Ben's way; these are members of the family who only believe in forgiveness; these are spineless people; lilied livered spineless people; people one never know existed within the family. if old man Thomas could know of their action and what is happening within the family he would turn over in his grave. The family is without moral principles; family loyalty means nothing to them; maybe it was so all along; Ben once commented to Sexton that if he was a member of some other families like the Mafia; they would take him somewhere discrete and shot him. Of course there was never this sort of situation before; a situation for members of the family to show their weaknesses, their strength and their loyalty; This once great family as for as unity and togetherness is concern has been blown away; and probable will never be the same again. But Ben himself has to shoulder some of the blame too; as he had accepted later, knowing of his Sister's mistreatment during her illness; he thought he should take the bull by the horn and took charge of caring for her. It would probably mean removing her from the matrimonial home; which would for sure create a confrontation between him and Wilf; and of course he probably had the law on his side; but at least it did would worth a try. Something he regretted up till this day, well! He knew in her last days even though she still loved her husband Ben could see that she didn't really trust him or his son Harold; there was a feeling that they were mistreating her at night and put a nice face on things during the day. However when Ben told the family of his suspicion they show little or no interest; especially big Brother Sexton; he practically accused Ben of trying to charged Wilf with things he's not guilty of; in other words he's saying Ben was lying. But as they never there as they should; well! They were there on occasion but not at the crucial time; it was all left to Ben. And Maggie dear Maggie; the Sister who Ammi take care in her time of distress; and look over her like a mother; well she's got better things to do rather than pay too much attention to her sick Sister; she was blasted by Ben in no uncertain term. But the story of Ammi's illness cannot be complete without bringing light the part dear Sister Barnes and her husband played; they were instrumental in helping her through her sickness.

When she was to go the hospital for whatever reason; if Ben who was working is going to be late; Brother Barnes and his wife were always there; not only to take her to the hospital but also to help care for her. Sister Barnes would take care of any chores in the home that needed to be done; and their friendship was to last to the very end. But Ben was to thank them; he expresses his gratitude to these two nice people; not that they want it or expected it, no; they just do what they did out of friendship and the goodness of their heart. Now a day Brother Barnes is not keeping much health and stop coming ou. Ben on occasion would pop in to see him; well! He's at that age when the body becomes weak and feeble; a realistic man; he commented to Ben, Ben he said; I'm looking toward my grave; I've been here long enough, Mrs. Barnes would comment; if Ammi was here she would pray for you for saying that. In this world; the good Lord made us all; but he knew all of us wasn't going to be good; there're going to be bastards; nasty people; people who can't and shouldn't be trusted. But we must be mindful also that among those dishonourable and even brutal people there're the good ones too; and we must be thankful that the good outnumbered the bad.

Well! As for Wilf; when the dust has settled he has almost become an outcast, his ambition to become someone important is now dash, his son and family has abandoned him; and with everyone giving him a wide margin; he drifts about aimlessly. This is a man dressed up every day in the old style with nowhere to go; probable trying to turn back the clock; he would from time to time turn up at various function without been invited; functions by people he used to know; and even though they didn't ask him to leave out of sympathy; he would be like a shadow there. One could say the man is got no principle; of course he's been talked about and not in a good manner. However that was in the early days of his wife demise; as he got older along with people he once knew; most have passed away; others reside themselves to their homes. Well! He hasn't been seen around anymore; what has become of him; no one cares to know. But there's an old Shakespeare; the evil that men do will follow them; he might now regretting his action and would like to turn the clock back; but another adage; oh what a tangled web we weave; he has done just that and now he's reaping the benefits of his evil web. His only son, Ferdy, has abandoned him for some unknown reason; and with his blood family not recognising him as part of their family; he's a man living without a purpose. Ben sees him from time to time; but he loathes the man so much he rather not been on the same street as him, as would many other people; he wouldn't cheer his misfortune if he should fall by the wayside; but he wouldn't have any remorse either.

Looking back on the relationship between these two men it goes beyond Brotherhood, they were Pease in a pod; where there's one the other is close by; their friendship was questionable in some quarters; the word jealousy comes to mind. But it was a healthy relationship; and one that was approved by Ammi. To see her favourite Brother and her husband in such a tight friendship must have brought good comfort to her. Looking back is not always a good thing to do; but it bring back memories; the good along with the bad; the good times like when Ben arrived in the country and before long he discovered that his Brother-in-law is the kind person he always wanted to attach to; and likewise him to Ben. He probably never had a happy growing up; it's not unusual for youngsters in Jamila to grows up knowing nothing but going to church; and it's a case of you have to go if you're living under your parents' roof. Work in the yard; work like making sure that firewood is there for cooking; and walking long distances for water; so with that there's little time left to enjoy one's childhood. So for Wilf and in some ways Ben too; they get the chance to break away; it's like turning loose two wild cats; the freedom of doing your own thing is now in your own hands. But for some people the confinement of their parent remains with them wherever they go; until someone comes along and breaks them out of their shell; and in Wilf's case; along came his Brother-in-law and introduced him to a bright new world out there; a world of music. He's now hooked; he's captured by the good times; blues dance and women and there's no going back. Those were wonderful times; times one likes to remember with fond memories; the bad times? One not particularly cares to remember any of it; there're very bad memories there that bring tears to the eyes. Whatever happens to change Wilf throughout all those times of happiness? It's hard to comprehend, the devil must have got hold of him and put a different man in his body; a nasty dishonest and callous person; one who to the people who once knew him; he has become unrecognisable; a real nasty piece of works. One shouldn't live on hate; but it will always be at the back of one's mind; and Ben will go to the grave with so much as hate; but remorse. However there's a lesson to be learnt here; try to know your family and what makes them tick; they're the closest and dearest; but at times when you think you know them you don't know them at all, there could be phrase; know your enemies but know your family better.

Thanks for reading my book; if you find something in it that reflects on your own life; I hope it won't be as bad and distressful as the way Amanda Drake's life turned out to be.

About Billy Dee Burnett

My inspiration for this book comes from the love of my family, a look into the life of a dear Sister and didn't like what I saw.

As an ex-civil servant I was always conscious of the people around me; I recon my inquisitiveness led me from time to time to delved into the life of others and observed from a vantage point their way of living.

It not being nosey; each one of us can learn from each other; and out of what we learn we can put that knowledge to a constructive use. We can all inspire each other in different ways.

www.ingramcontent.com/pod-product-compliance
Lightning Source LLC
Chambersburg PA
CBHW032046050726
47590CB00001B/151